international review of social history

Special Issue 28

Urban Slavery in the Age of Abolition

Edited by Karwan Fatah-Black

Published by the Press Syndicate of the University of Cambridge
The Pitt Building, Trumpington Street, Cambridge, CB2 1RP
1 Liberty Plaza, Floor 20, New York, NY 10006, USA
10 Stamford Road, Oakleigh, Melbourne 3166, Australia

A catalogue record for this book is available from the British Library

Library of Congress Cataloguing-in-Publication Data applied for

ISBN 9781108825757 (paperback)

Printed in the UK by Bell & Bain Ltd, Glasgow, UK.

CONTENTS

Urban Slavery in the Age of Abolition

Edited by
Karwan Fatah-Black

IRSH 65 (2020), pp. 1–14 doi:10.1017/S0020859020000085

Introduction: Urban Slavery in the Age of Abolition

Karwan Fatah-Black

Institute for History, Faculty of Humanities
Leiden University
Doelensteeg 16, 2311 VL Leiden, The Netherlands

E-mail: k.j.fatah@hum.leidenuniv.nl

Abstract: This Special Issue collects articles on urban slavery in the Atlantic world during the time when the institution of slavery was being abolished globally (c.1770s–c.1880s). At the time of abolition, most slaves were held on plantations, but this did not mean that the urban context of slavery was unimportant. In the cities of the Atlantic world, slavery was pervasive, and the cities themselves played an important role in the functioning of the slave system. This Special Issue seeks to examine urban slavery in its connection to the wider slave-based economy, and to address how slavery in the cities changed when abolition appeared on the political agenda in the Atlantic world. The articles in this issue find that urban communities went through great changes in the age of abolition and these changes proved crucial to determining the legacies of slavery and its abolition. Recovering the history of urban slavery in this area should come to inform the current mainstreaming of the memory of slavery around the Atlantic world. Attention to its history can provide new layers of understanding to the persistence of inequity and historical silencing today.

The institution of slavery permeated all aspects of social, cultural, and economic life in the early modern Atlantic world and has left a lasting legacy. The adverse effects of the slave trade and slavery in the Atlantic world and their association with anti-black racism have inspired the United Nations to declare 2015–2024 an International Decade for People of African Descent.[1] The history of slavery in the Atlantic world is determined by the trafficking of twelve million Africans to the Americas and their forced labour in plantation agriculture, as well as their resistance to this exploitation. Trade, agricultural labour, and resistance are central to understanding the transatlantic slave system that developed between Europe, Africa and the Americas. Given this context, the prevalence of an "agricultural myopia" in slavery studies comes as no surprise and few would argue that the emphasis on plantation slavery

1. "Resolution adopted by the General Assembly on 23 December 2013". Available at: https://www.un.org/en/ga/search/view_doc.asp?symbol=A/RES/68/237; last accessed January 2020.

has been misguided.[2] However, the importance of cities to the functioning of the Atlantic world, as nodal points in networks of trade, centres of power, places where enslaved people were held and employed and where racial hierarchies were forged, should not be overlooked.[3]

To date, the attention to slavery in the cities has often been limited to observations about the greater agency of city slaves.[4] This emphasis on urban slave agency in scholarship has a long history. The former slave and astute critic of American slavery Frederick Douglass had observed a key difference in the degree of freedom that urban slaves enjoyed compared to their counterparts on the plantations. Douglass wrote in his memoir that in the city "a slave is almost free". He also suggested a reason for this by arguing that "slavery dislikes a dense population".[5] In this same vein, Ira Berlin has emphasized slave independence in the urban context. His masterful *Many Thousands Gone* has inspired scholars for over a generation, even if the limits of his analysis of urban slavery are becoming apparent. In the book, urban slaves primarily appear to illustrate the contrast with their rural counterparts by showing themselves to be artisans and tradesmen and displaying independence, even when they survive as prostitutes.[6] More recent studies of the freedom that urban slaves occasionally enjoyed have begun to recognize more readily that urban life also involved public displays of racial hierarchy on city streets. Surely, bondsmen in cities had access to more opportunities and institutions that could protect them from their master's whims than their rural counterparts; but urban slaves were far from immune to the violence and cruelty that characterizes slavery around the world.

In her study of Bridgetown, the capital of Barbados, Marisa Fuentes reminds us of the violence of slavery in port towns. In the city, the strictures of slavery made "resistance to domestic violence a life and death decision".[7] The enslaved women of Bridgetown were "battered, beaten, executed and overtly sexualized".[8] Cities were sites of a "veritable terror" and served as stages where the slaveholding elite displayed its dominance through ritualized acts of disregard for enslaved life.[9] From Iberia, the Atlantic cities inherited the

2. Rosemary Brana-Shute, "The Manumission of Slaves in Suriname, 1760–1828" (Ph.D., University of Florida, 1985).

3. Mariana Dantas, "Urban Slavery", Atlantic History, *Oxford Bibliographies*, 28 April 2016.

4. Jorge Cañizares-Esguerra, Matt D. Childs, and James. Sidbury (eds), *The Black Urban Atlantic in the Age of the Slave Trade* (Philadelphia, PA, 2013).

5. Frederick Douglass, *My Bondage and My Freedom* (London, 1855), pp. 147–148.

6. Ira Berlin, *Many Thousands Gone: The First Two Centuries of Slavery in North America* (Cambridge, MA [etc.], 1998), pp. 54, 156–158, 207–208, 313.

7. Marisa J. Fuentes, *Dispossessed Lives: Enslaved Women, Violence, and the Archive* (Philadelphia, PA, 2016), p. 99.

8. Fuentes, *Dispossessed Lives*, p. 145.

9. Richard Price, "Violence and Hope in a Space of Death: Paramaribo", *Common Place*, 3:4 (2003). Available at: http://www.common-place.org/vol-03/no-04/paramaribo/; last accessed January 2020.

practice of segregating the execution of freedmen and slaves, emphasizing the difference between them. In many Atlantic cities the *pelourinho* (pillory) was a visible reminder of the consequences of transgressing the limits set by enslavement (Figure 1). Affirming the hierarchy did not only have a function in urban life but was part of the relation between town and country. If conflicts between overseers and slaves escalated on plantations, the masters could restore the subjugation of the enslaved by moving them to the city for punishment. This urban function could only be performed as long as cities were – at least in their daytime appearance – spaces of unchallenged white slaveholder power. The traditional emphasis by historians on slave agency in cities might have overlooked how important the affirmations of hierarchies in cities were for the survival of the system itself. The proposition of this Special Issue is to regard the interplay between urban and agricultural areas as communicating reservoirs of labourers and sources for slaveholder power and authority as well as their contestation. The more nuanced understanding of the possibilities and limits to slave agency in the city that has been developing in recent years, and an appreciation of the role of cities in the slave system as a whole, raises new questions about the period in which slavery was beginning to be abolished around the Atlantic world.

SECOND SLAVERY AND THE ATLANTIC CITIES

From the sixteenth to the nineteenth century, cities in the Atlantic world were primarily formed as a function of the trade and shipping between European markets, American plantations, and West African slave forts.[10] The economic function of these port cities shaped their occupational structure, and their near-universal reliance on slave labour. The mainstay of the occupational structure of Atlantic port towns was (as in any pre-modern society) composed of activities that were directly needed for the social reproduction of the town, rather than for industry or trade. As Wim Klooster demonstrates in the first contribution to this issue, slavery was integrated into every part of the occupational structure of these towns and slaves were a substantial part of the urban working population. These towns existed in relation to the trade lines, mines, and plantations in the hinterlands. Given the agricultural nature of the societies, the urbanization ratio was surprisingly high in the Atlantic colonies. It hovered around ten to twenty per cent in the Caribbean, which is a percentage that most of the rest of the world did not reach before the twentieth century.[11] The proportion of slaves to non-slaves in cities was always lower than it was in the plantation areas. Nevertheless, the proportion of slaves

10. Jacob M. Price, "Economic Function and Growth of American Port Towns in the Eighteenth Century", *Perspectives in American History*, 8 (1974), pp. 123–186.
11. Jan de Vries, *European Urbanization, 1500–1800* (London, 1984, reprint 2007), p. 6.

Figure 1. Public whipping of an enslaved man in present-day Campo de Santana in Rio de Janeiro. *"Punitions publiques sur la Place Ste. Anne" [Public punishments in Saint Anne Square], Johann Moritz Rugendas (1802–1858), 1835. Available at: http://objdigital.bn.br/acervo_digital/div_iconografia/icon94994/icon94994_185.jpg; last accessed January 2020.*

in the city could rise to over sixty per cent of the population in such emblematic plantation colonies as Saint-Domingue, Suriname, and Jamaica.[12]

By the late eighteenth century, the cities of the slave societies of the Atlantic world displayed common traits and comparable occupational structures. Much of the labour in the cities was done by enslaved women, without whom a city like Charlestown "would have ceased to function as a commercial centre for the cotton trade".[13] The different empires diverged somewhat when it came to building up administrative functions in their oversees towns, with the British being rather frugal, while the Spanish and French had a more

12. See Klooster, Table 1 in this issue.

13. Jeffery Glenn Strickland, Randall M. Miller, and Stanley Harrold, *Unequal Freedoms: Ethnicity, Race, and White Supremacy in Civil War Era Charleston*, Southern Dissent Series (Gainesville, FL, 2015), p. 284.

sizeable body of officials in their ports.[14] Landowners were largely absent from the Atlantic ports in the early period, with the exception of the larger ones, such as Charleston, Havana, Salvador, Recife, and Rio de Janeiro. Lack of land (and slave) owning elites in towns had been a sign of the frontier nature of most of these ports. This changed in the eighteenth century when capital started to accumulate in the colonies themselves and, on top of mercantile and administrative functions, the port cities of the Atlantic world became places where landowning elites congregated. This concentration of economic elites in the city was slightly offset by absentee ownership, with plantation owners residing in the French, Dutch, and British metropoles. Although absenteeism has garnered quite some attention from historians, the impact of this was minimal at most, and was even less important in the United States, Brazil, and the Spanish domains.[15] By the eighteenth century, urban slaves were engaged both in the maritime and mercantile activities of the town and in the households of the urban elites. Domestic and household work was quickly seconded by activities directly servicing trade and shipping. Being indispensable to the functioning of the cities made the abolition of their enslavement unimaginable to slaveholders.

By the late eighteenth century, slave owners clinging on to their slaves in town and country kindled fierce debates about the abolition of slavery in many societies in the Atlantic world. However, with the abolition of slavery in many of the formerly Spanish colonies, the temporary abolition in the French domains, and the end of the slave trade in the British empire, the beginning of the end of the institution arrived in the Atlantic world. Despite the beginnings of abolition, the importance of slavery to the Atlantic economies was far from diminishing. Transatlantic slave trading expanded after British abolition, as did slave-based plantation production. In the South Atlantic and on Cuba, the slave system was granted a new lease of life in the nineteenth century, and in the United States South, slavery entered a second phase of expansion and intensification that lasted until the Civil War.[16] Also in African societies, the nineteenth century "was more firmly rooted in slavery than ever before".[17] In Kingston, Jamaica, the ending of the slave trade seems to have had only a limited effect on the city. Trevor Burnard finds

14. Jacob M. Price, "Summation: The American Panorama of Atlantic Port Cities", in Franklin W. Knight and Peggy K. Liss (eds), *Atlantic Port Cities: Economy, Culture, and Society in the Atlantic World, 1650–1850* (Knoxville, TN, 1991).

15. Trevor Burnard, "Passengers Only: The Extent and Significance of Absenteeism in Eighteenth Century Jamaica", *Atlantic Studies*, 1:2 (2006), pp. 178–195. Available at: https://doi.org/10.1080/1478881042000278730; last accessed January 2020.

16. Dale W. Tomich (ed.), *Slavery and Historical Capitalism During the Nineteenth Century* (Lanham, MD, 2017).

17. Paul E. Lovejoy, *Transformations in Slavery: A History of Slavery in Africa*, 3rd edn, African Studies 117 (Cambridge [etc.], 2011), p. 244.

that the number of urban slaves increased after the trade was abolished.[18] The end of the slave trade shifted economic activities away from the plantations and towards servicing trade in the region – which was more of an urban activity. On the other side of the Atlantic, as Mariana Candido shows, the ending of the slave trade led to an increase in the number of urban slaves. In Benguela, the port through which the highest number of slaves passed into the Atlantic system, the end of slavery increased urban slaveholding as well as slavery in general.[19]

The nineteenth-century resurgence of slavery, sometimes characterized as the "second slavery", is strongly associated with the migration of slaves within slave societies. In plantation-rich Brazil, on Cuba, and in the United States South, train tracks were adopted early to facilitate the movement of people or goods between the port cities and the plantation areas.[20] Viola Müller notes that second slavery meant that a lot of enslaved labourers were moved from the city to the countryside – a move that has been noticed in many cities during this era.[21] In Brazil, the internal slave trade shifted the presence of slaves to the areas of the coffee boom, and the percentage of slaves in the urban population declined to fifteen per cent on the eve of abolition.[22] The forced migration to the newly expanding plantation areas coincided with a redirection in the routes of the transatlantic slave trade. The trade itself expanded despite British abolition and numbers of enslaved Africans in the Atlantic rose in this period. In the cities, the wars and revolutions had also increased the numbers of free non-whites in many colonies.

ABOLITION AND THE CITY

The new literature on urban slave and freedmen communities increasingly recognizes the role of familial ties, kinship, and the entrepreneurial role of women.[23] As Mariana Dantas and Douglas Libby argue in this issue, free

18. See the article by Trevor Burnard in this Special Issue.
19. See the article by Mariana Candido in this Special Issue.
20. Donnie D. Bellamy, "Macon, Georgia, 1823–1860: A Study in Urban Slavery", *Phylon (1960–)* 45:4 (1984), pp. 298–310. Available at: https://doi.org/10.2307/274910; last accessed January 2020.
21. Bellamy, "Macon, Georgia, 1823–1860"; Felix V. Matos Rodriguez, "'¿Quien Trabajara?': Domestic Workers, Urban Slaves, and the Abolition of Slavery in Puerto Rico", in Felix V. Matos Rodriguez and Linda C. Delgado (eds), *Puerto Rican Women's History: New Perspectives* (Armonk, NY, 1998), pp. 62–82.
22. Herbert S. Klein and Francisco Vidal Luna, *Slavery in Brazil* (Cambridge, 2009), pp. 75, 109.
23. Camilla Cowling, *Conceiving Freedom: Women of Color, Gender and the Abolition of Slavery in Havana and Rio de Janeiro* (Chapel Hill, NC, 2013); Kit Candlin and Cassandra Pybus, *Enterprising Women: Gender, Race, and Power in the Revolutionary Atlantic* (Athens, GA, 2015); Cynthia M. Kennedy, *Braided Relations, Entwined Lives: The Women of Charleston's Urban Slave Society* (Bloomington, IN, 2005).

black families naturalized the idea of black freedom and therefore played an important role in conceptualizing what life after slavery should look like. In the past, historians primarily recognized that urban societies, for all their complexity, had been places where there were clear limits to the power of slave owners over their slaves, even if this did not make slavery incompatible with urban life.[24] Atlantic cities provided an example of a future beyond slavery, and an example that politicians and administrators could view with optimism. Abolitionists on Puerto Rico tried to placate those who were apprehensive about abolition by arguing that urban slaves "have always seen public authority over the master's authority, respecting both".[25] As one of the leading powers in the Atlantic world, British abolition imbued others to take that same decision. Movements for abolition were very much an urban affair, both in Europe as well as in the Americas. In Rio de Janeiro and many other Brazilian cities, the abolitionist movement changed politics and public engagement. And the presence of these movements in the cities put pressure on the practice of slavery in these places.[26] The violent removal of abolitionists from slaveholding towns like Charleston were not uncommon in this era.[27] In Atlantic cities, former slaves were able to rise through the ranks and build meaningful lives for themselves, making the success of these urban communities an argument in the discussion about the feasibility of a complete abolition of slavery.

Attention to gender is changing the appreciation of the transformative processes that took place in the age of abolition. The status of the former slave is different from those who were freeborn, and both in the city and on the plantation the consequences of this distinction were gendered. The form in which the British legislators imagined to bridge slavery and post-slavery was through a typically urban institution of apprenticeship. Apprenticeship had a nice emancipatory ring to it, while leaving in place a role for the master. By imagining post-slavery as apprenticeship, the suggestion was made that the former slaver would be trained to become the master of a trade and through that the self-supporting director of his own future. The reality was very different. In its Atlantic agricultural context, apprenticeship meant nothing but a continuation of the same unskilled sugar cane cutting labour that the field slaves had performed before abolition. For women, apprenticeship proved a double-edged sword; not only did it mean a continuation of agricultural labour, in many cases their role in the workforce was reduced. While women made up a large share of field workers before abolition, they were denied a role as wage earners after it. Notwithstanding the continued marginalization that

24. Richard C. Wade, *Slavery in the Cities: The South, 1820–1860* (London [etc.], 1967), p. 4.
25. Rodriguez, "'¿Quien Trabajara?'", p. 68.
26. Camilla Cowling, *Conceiving Freedom: Women of Color, Gender, and the Abolition of Slavery in Havana and Rio de Janeiro* (Chapel Hill, NC, 2013), p. 43.
27. Strickland, Miller, and Harrold, *Unequal Freedoms*, p. 287.

also plagued them in the city, their ability to manage property and contribute to developing independent communities was greater there.[28]

Urban communities of former slaves were important in shaping post-slavery societies. The managing of slaves and former slaves in cities took one of two routes. In the cities themselves, there was a pattern in which distinctions were made between slave and former slave based on legal status. In other cases, we find the opposite. Legal status was deemed irrelevant and racial categories were strengthened, legally pushing black people, irrespective of their status, into the same neighbourhoods and excluding them from citizen rights. Abolition was accompanied everywhere by the promotion of respectability, Christianity, education, the nuclear family, and loyal citizenship. Slave women's respectability and public roles were pushed to the margins, while male labour became more transient and mobile. In the French Caribbean islands, a trek towards the urban estates followed the abolition of 1848. In the city, slaves were looking for legal redress and the protection of urban institutions.[29] In the Dutch Caribbean, the movement of slaves was restricted at the moment of abolition. The date of the actual abolition was chosen to fall in the middle of the rainy season, to further prevent movement between plantations and to the city and further restrictions were put in place to keep people from settling in town.[30] Still, if second slavery had been a move to the countryside, the abolition of slavery led to a move towards the cities where former slaves joined the communities of free people of colour that had developed from the eighteenth century onwards. These cities tried to deal with these free migrants by segregating them and developing a prison system that specifically targeted the former slaves. The United States abolished slavery "except as a punishment for crime" and after abolition the prison system flourished in former slave states, as it did in Jamaica and in other post-slavery societies.[31]

In some places, the rise of the community of free people of colour threatened the position of the urban slaves in the nineteenth century, in others no distinctions were made between the two categories, but were perceived as a single threat to urban society. As a response to that perceived threat, Brazilian urban governments began to restrict the economic activities of freedmen and slaves in the city, even raising taxes for freedmen who continued to

28. David Barry Gaspar and Darlene Clark Hine, *Beyond Bondage: Free Women of Color in the Americas* (Urbana, IL, 2004).
29. See the article by Marion Pluskota in this Special Issue.
30. Ellen Klinkers, *Op hoop van vrijheid. Van slavensamenleving naar Creoolse gemeenschap in Suriname, 1830–1880*, Bronnen voor de studie van Afro-Suriname 18 (Utrecht, 1997).
31. J. Thorsten Sellin, *Slavery and the Penal System* (New Orleans, LA, 2016), pp. 145–162; Diana Paton, *No Bond But the Law: Punishment, Race, and Gender in Jamaican State Formation, 1780–1870* (Durham, NC, 2004), pp. 192–195.

reside in the city of Salvador.[32] As Marion Pluskota shows in this issue, the mobility of slaves and former slaves was a prime concern around the Atlantic. When slavery returned to the French Caribbean, the authorities on the islands began to police the movements of slaves and created policies to keep them out of the cities. The growth of the slave population and their increased mobility created new fears of insurrection, and these fears were exacerbated by the traditions of newly arrived slaves to congregate in cities for annual festivals. In cities like Santo Amaro, in Bahia state, the slaves would meet in large numbers. Once they arrived from their separate plantations, they dispersed according to their African nation for religious celebrations that bordered on revolt.[33] In Rio de Janeiro, severe control was enacted to limit rebellions during these tumultuous periods. Enslaved craftsmen were often found at the head of the urban rebellions of slaves in Brazil.[34] Vagrancy laws were also introduced in the British Caribbean, and in Brazil, in 1832, both freed and enslaved Africans were to carry a passport at all times.[35]

Second slavery's pull to the agricultural production areas did not mean that slave labour in the city was no longer profitable. In Puerto Rico, the demand for domestic slaves was high and the relocation of slaves to the countryside threatened the status quo.[36] In the United States South, the value of educated and skilled urban slaves rose in the last decades before the Civil War.[37] As the *Richmond Inquirer* noted, "[a]s carpenters, as blacksmiths, as shoe-makers, as factory hands, they [slaves] are far more valuable than field laborers—indeed, intellectual expertness and manual dexterity are much more important elements in the price of a slave than physical strength and power of endurance".[38] Looking beyond the immediate dynamics of labour demand and supply, Richard Wade has noticed that the problem was control once the slaves were off the job. Life in the city, if they mingled with the other slaves and the rest of the population, made them "insolent" and therefore "worthless" to the owner.[39] Despite these pressures on urban slavery, even during the expansion of the cotton plantations in the US South, urban slavery in a city like Macon, located in the heart of the cotton boom, saw a continuation as a

32. Sidney Chalhoub, "The Precariousness of Freedom in a Slave Society (Brazil in the Nineteenth Century)", *International Review of Social History*, 56:3 (2011), pp. 405–439. Available at: https://doi.org/10.1017/S002085901100040X; last accessed January 2020.

33. João José Reis, "Batuque: African Drumming and Dance between Repression and Concession, Bahia, 1808–1855", *Bulletin of Latin American Research*, 24:2 (2005), pp. 201–214. Available at: https://doi.org/10.1111/j.0261-3050.2005.00132.x; last accessed January 2020.

34. Klein and Luna, *Slavery in Brazil*, p. 218.

35. Chalhoub, "Precariousness of Freedom in a Slave Society".

36. Rodriguez, "'¿Quien Trabajara?'".

37. Wade, *Slavery in the Cities*, p. 244.

38. Quoted in *Ibid.*

39. *Ibid.*, p. 245.

"viable economic and social institution".[40] Even if, as in the case of Macon, the percentage of slaves declined from 55.1 per cent in 1830 to 34.4 per cent in 1860, the real number of urban slaves increased from 1,452 to 2,829 in this period.[41] In the areas where slavery continued there was an uneasy balance with other supplies of labour. These areas appear to have been unattractive to free European migrants who had no wish to compete with slaves in the United States South. Industrialization did take place on a limited scale, but European free labourers did not move to the towns of the south.[42] If urban slavery declined in those years, as Hardesty shows for Boston in this issue, it was not because the labour demands in the city were diminishing. Instead, he shows that when the post-slavery future appeared on Boston's doorstep, racism, among other factors, pushed free non-white labourers from the city.[43] With the abolition of slavery on the agenda, the racial logic underpinning Atlantic slavery was entering a new era in which it would no longer be supported by slave laws but would still be constitutive of social hierarchies.

AFTERLIVES

What scholars have rarely done to date is to consider the long-term legacies of urban slavery and its memorialization in cities around the Atlantic. Abolition singled out slavery as a form of labour mobilization that was no longer permitted and was primarily focused on the plantations and the slave trade.[44] The campaigns to abolish slavery firmly imprinted in the public's mind the image of the slave ship and the plantation as the sites of ultimate terror. The horrors of agricultural slavery and the slave trade became the main argument as to why the institution should be abolished. The policies that accompanied abolition aimed both at providing economic continuity and social stability. The issue of social stability meant that many slave societies at the time of abolition grappled with a transformation of their practices of citizenship and race. Although, most notably in the African context, abolition made it clear that slavery did not need a formal institutional framework to persist. The abolishing states in the Americas were all primarily concerned with how the newly freed population would have a place in the labour process. There was a great fear that abolition would leave former slaves without any motivation to work on plantation estates. This meant that the former slaves would have to

40. Bellamy, "Macon, Georgia, 1823–1860.", p. 298.
41. *Ibid.*, p. 299.
42. David Brion Davis, *Inhuman Bondage: The Rise and Fall of Slavery in the New World* (New York [etc.], 2008), pp. 186–187.
43. See the article by Jared Ross Hardesty in this Special Issue.
44. Frederick Cooper, Thomas C. Holt, and Rebecca J. Scott, *Beyond Slavery: Explorations of Race, Labor, and Citizenship in Postemancipation Societies* (Chapel Hill, NC, 2000), p. 7.

learn to exercise self-discipline rather than being disciplined by an external force or, as Sir James Stephen in the Colonial Office once famously summarized, they had to replace the "dread of being flogged" with the "dread of starving".[45]

There was a great optimism about the post-slavery future at the moments that abolition occurred around the world, and, even if governments were concerned about economic and social stability, the new equality before the law was embraced. The French were asked to "forget all distinctions of origins", and on the British islands it was declared that the law should no longer favour Europeans or be to the "prejudice of persons of African birth or origin".[46] This was not only a view espoused by government officials. In liberated Charleston, the white German population initially held festivities that included and welcomed the active participation of freed Afro-Americans.[47] Despite the initial optimism that surrounded the abolition of slavery, the legacy of slavery returned to haunt post-slavery societies. The upsets of the racial and status hierarchies between slaves and non-slaves would come to be reaffirmed. Former slaves continued to carry a stigma of slavery that classed them lower than those who were freeborn, and post-emancipation racialization protected part of the old social hierarchy between slave and free around the Atlantic.

Restoring the older hierarchy depended on practices of distinction between town and country on the French islands and in Brazil, urban segregation in the United States, as well as, almost everywhere, direct assaults on the civil rights of former slaves. Urban freedmen asserting their newly acquired civil rights were met with great violence during the New Orleans Massacre of 1866 and similar events in Memphis and Charleston that year.[48] This type of violence against former slaves and their offspring continued for decades. Although largely a rural phenomenon, the most iconic of the close to 5,000 lynchings in the post-slavery United States South were staged in towns. The terror was far from over once slavery was abolished. The violence was both physical and cultural. The end of slavery led to an increasingly malicious culture of ridicule and degradation of the former slaves in towns. The black-face minstrel shows were not only mocking rural slaves, but with the character of Zip Coon, sometimes called Urban Coon, racists explicitly targeted the educated,

45. David Eltis, *Economic Growth and the Ending of the Transatlantic Slave Trade* (Oxford, 1987), p. 22.

46. Cooper, Holt, and Scott, *Beyond Slavery*, p. 34.

47. Strickland, Miller, and Harrold, *Unequal Freedoms*, p. 201.

48. J. Illingworth, "Erroneous and Incongruous Notions of Liberty: Urban Unrest and the Origins of Radical Reconstruction in New Orleans, 1865–1868", in Bruce Baker and Brian Kelly (eds), *After Slavery: Race, Labor, and Citizenship in the Reconstruction South* (Gainesville, FL, 2013), pp. 35–57.

cultivated, and upwardly mobile freedmen in cities that were regarded as "uppity".

Cities remained sites of the important struggles around (de)segregation, civil rights, and equality waged around the Atlantic world from the late nineteenth century onwards. Even where rights were won, people of African descent and of slave descent continue to be marginalized. Part of this is reflected in the stark difference between the way the history of slavery is purposefully memorialized in urban spaces.[49] Social marginalization is accompanied by a silencing of the history of slavery. Former slave societies are often very slow to incorporate their past into urban public spaces, and when they do, the history of urban slavery is replaced with that of the slave trade and plantation slavery. Kingston in Jamaica typically makes reference to the abolition of slavery, but the role of the city in the slave trade and its dependence on slave labour is nowhere reflected in the urban landscape. In metropolitan cities, the history of slavery is beginning to surface, taking traces of urban slavery in its wake.[50] As Samuel North shows in this issue in the case of Cape Town, the urban history of slavery has become a contested element in politics and the formation of political identities.[51] Contemporary cities in the United States and Brazil rarely mention the relics of slavery and few of them have monuments commemorating the enslavement that took place in the cities.[52] Places that were built using enslaved labour also do not mention this fact or refer to the revolts that shook the cities. This began to change in important ways during the Obama presidency (the president himself was referred to as uppity – the derogatory reference to the urban freedmen) with the installation of statues of black leaders and acknowledgement of slave labour that was used to build such structures as the Capitol and the White House, and ongoing research into the slaves who worked on the Smithsonian buildings.[53] In New York, the discovery of the "African Burial Ground" just beyond the old city wall forcefully pushed the history of urban slavery into the city's public space. In Philadelphia, no visitor can reach the Liberty Bell without first passing through the ruins of the house of George Washington in which the lives of his house slaves are detailed in writing and on video screens. In Brazil, this is still another matter, although some exceptions exist. In Porto

49. The exception might be Charleston, where domestic slavery is more fully integrated in historic homes that offer tours to tourists. Stephen W. Litvin and Joshua David Brewer, "Charleston, South Carolina Tourism and the Presentation of Urban Slavery in an Historic Southern City", *International Journal of Hospitality & Tourism Administration*, 9:1 (2008), pp. 71–84. Available at: https://doi.org/10.1080/15256480801910541; last accessed January 2020.

50. Dienke Hondius, *Gids Slavernijverleden Amsterdam* (Volendam, 2014); Gert Oostindie and Karwan Fatah-Black, *Sporen van de Slavernij in Leiden* (Leiden, 2017).

51. See the article by Samuel North in this Special Issue.

52. Ana Lucia Araujo, *Shadows of the Slave Past: Memory, Heritage, and Slavery* (London, 2014), p. 118.

53. Araujo, *Shadows of the Slave Past*, p. 124.

Alegre, a sculpture and explanatory sign mark the location of the place where slaves used to be hanged.[54]

Yet, victimization seems the sole gaze through which the history of slavery can be regarded in many of these cities.[55] The image that sites of commemoration project is often informed by abolitionist propaganda, and ignores, among other things, the urban context of slavery, which was one of skilled craftsmen and often predominantly women. In cities, specifically, Araujo has found a form of "memory replacement" in which the general history of the transatlantic slave trade and plantation slavery trade fill the gap in places where specific urban experiences could be placed. Studies of urban slavery and the place of slavery in the history of cities has the potential to connect present-day offspring of slaves and slave owners to their shared slavery history. Thematically, attention to the urban context infuses the memory of slavery with examples of urban revolt and the role of women in slave societies, as well as their agency in shaping life in urban slave and freedmen communities.[56]

CONCLUSION

The study of urban slavery has often only emphasized the greater prosperity and agency of urban slaves. Shifting the focus to the age of abolition, when the institution of slavery was in turmoil, allows for a more nuanced view of urban slavery and its afterlives. In the articles in this Special Issue, the emphasis is on the changes that took place in the cities of the Atlantic world once the abolition of slavery came on the agenda. The beginning of the age of abolition was marked by the intense mobility that accompanied the wars and revolutions of the end of the eighteenth century. The rise of the cotton industry, the belated Brazilian coffee boom, and the expansion of slave-based sugar production on Cuba gave a new lease of life to an institution that many had thought was dying. The reconstitution of political order and the reaffirmation of slavery and race relations in much of the Atlantic world of the nineteenth century greatly impacted slavery in cities. When full abolition came to the societies around the Atlantic, the cities became poles of attraction for former slaves seeking the institutional, economic, and cultural advantages of joining urban communities of freedmen. The state and former slave owners as well as lower-class whites grew increasingly suspicious of communities of former slaves, and combinations of segregation, imprisonment, and violence followed. The history of urban slavery is rarely part of memory cultures around the Atlantic

54. *Ibid.*, p. 123.
55. *Ibid.*, p. 213.
56. Myrian Sepúlveda dos Santos, "The Legacy of Slavery in Contemporary Brazil", in Ana Lucia Araujo (ed.), *African Heritage and Memories of Slavery in Brazil and the South Atlantic World* (Amherst, NY, 2015), pp. 330–331.

world. The legacy of the abolitionist campaigns that focused on slave ships and plantations still dominates our understanding of slavery in the present. For descendants of slaves, the rediscovery of the history and legacy of urban slavery presents a way to connect their identities to the centre of many of our contemporary cities and offer a story of belonging.

IRSH 65 (2020), pp. 15–37 doi:10.1017/S0020859020000097

Comparative Perspectives on the Urban Black Atlantic on the Eve of Abolition

WIM KLOOSTER

Department of History, Clark University
Worcester, MA 01610-1477, USA

E-mail: wklooster@clarku.edu

ABSTRACT: By investigating the place of enslaved Africans and their descendants in the cities of the Atlantic world, this article explores many of the themes of this Special Issue across empires, with an emphasis on the Americas in the late eighteenth century, the eve of abolition. The article finds that, in nearly every manual occupation, slaves were integrated with free laborers and, not infrequently, slaves who had reached the level of journeyman or master directed the work of free apprentices. The limited number of slave insurrections in cities may be explained by the fact that they often worked semi-independently, earning money to supplement the livelihood provided by the master, or sometimes almost entirely on their own. To them, city life offered advantages that would have been inconceivable for their rural counterparts, especially the scope of autonomy they enjoyed and the possibilities to secure manumission.

SLAVERY AND PORT CITIES IN THE ATLANTIC WORLD

What are cities? One historian has called them "concentrations of wealth and power".[1] Another has written that a city is a place "where people do different things, and the more different things they do, the more the place is a city".[2] Cities are sites of specialized activity, variegated employment opportunities, exchange of information, and intermingling of people. Cities in the Atlantic world were in many ways the counterparts of the relatively self-contained rural plantations or haciendas. They were indeed concentrations of wealth and power, as the seat of regional or supra-regional institutions and the preferred dwelling places of absentee planters who craved company and conspicuous consumption. Atlantic cities were also marketplaces, information

1. Marjolein 't Hart, "The Glorious City: Monumentalism and Public Space in Seventeenth-Century Amsterdam", in Patrick O'Brien *et al.* (eds), *Urban Achievement in Early Modern Europe: Golden Ages in Antwerp, Amsterdam and London* (Cambridge, 2001), pp. 128–150, 128.
2. Philip D. Curtin, "Preface", in Franklin W. Knight and Peggy K. Liss (eds), *Atlantic Port Cities: Economy, Culture, and Society in the Atlantic World, 1650–1850* (Knoxville, TN, 1991), p. x.

centers, and venues for discrete activity, in each respect differing from the countryside. That was especially true for *port* cities, which came to display features that distinguished them from ports not located on the Atlantic rim. In this article, which synthesizes much of the recent literature, I investigate the place of enslaved Africans and their descendants in these cities. In which types of work were they involved and how did they contribute to the functioning of port cities? The focus will be on the Americas in the late eighteenth century, the eve of abolition.

What were the main ports in the Atlantic world? There was, of course, plenty of change in the composition of the largest ports by population, but it is possible to get a reliable snapshot for the late eighteenth century. What is striking is that the largest ports in the three continents – Europe, the Americas, and Africa – belonged to different categories of size. The European ports were by far the largest, dwarfing the ports in other parts of the Atlantic world. Even a port like Bordeaux, by no means a European giant, had a population between twice and three times as large as that of the most populous port in the New World, Havana. Similarly, New World ports tended to be quite a bit larger than those in Atlantic Africa. Only two African ports would appear on a joint top-ten list of Africa and the Americas, while the largest African port of Bonny was still smaller than the seven largest New World ports.

Some scholars have argued that applying the concept of "port" to Africa in the days before European colonialism makes little sense. Infrastructural investment was almost entirely absent, while the ports were often not even directly located on the Atlantic. Many towns that have received the label "port" in the Bight of Benin, which was so prominent in the Atlantic slave trade, were situated on an inland lagoon that runs parallel to the coast. Slaves destined for export were taken across the lagoon and then overland to the seashore.[3] I will nevertheless include Africa in my discussion here, despite the lack of port facilities in most areas. The actual distance to the Atlantic does not appear to me to be problematic. Although one of the premier ports in the world, Amsterdam was situated far from the sea. Large seafaring ships could not make it to the town, whose maritime front, marked by shallowness and a gradual silting up, was regularly dredged from the seventeenth century onwards. If Amsterdam can count as an Atlantic port, so can those in western Africa.

Atlantic port cities, from Amsterdam to Luanda, grew in fits and starts over the course of the early modern period and often at a rapid pace in the nineteenth century (Figure 1). By the late eighteenth century, the four largest ports of Atlantic America were Havana, the two Brazilian ports of Rio de

3. Robin Law and Silke Strickrodt, "Introduction", in Robin Law and Silke Strickrodt (eds), *Ports of the Slave Trade (Bights of Benin and Biafra): Papers from a Conference of the Centre of Commonwealth Studies, University of Stirling, June 1998* (Stirling, 1999), pp. 1–11, 3.

Figure 1. Port cities of the Atlantic.

Janeiro and Salvador, and New York, all with populations over 30,000. Ten ports, including Boston, but also little-known Saint-Pierre in Martinique, had a population between 15,000 and 30,000 (Table 1). Only one port on the Atlantic side of Africa had a population that would have qualified it for a place in the top ten New World port cities: Bonny on the coast of Benin with 25,000 inhabitants. The next ports in size were Elmina on the Gold Coast, which boasted 12,000–15,000 people, Luanda with 9,755, Porto

Table 1. *The Twenty Largest Port Cities of Atlantic America, c.1790.*

Port	*Enslaved Africans*	*Enslaved %*	*Free People of Color*	*Whites*	*Total Population*	*Year*
Havana[4]	10,849	*24.5*	9,751	23,737	44,337	1791
Rio de Janeiro	14,986	*34.5*	8,812	19,578	43,376	1789
Salvador	14,695	*43.7*	7,943[5]	10,997	33,635[6]	1775
New York	2,389	*7.2*	1,101	29,661	33,131	1790
Buenos Aires	2,250*	*7.5*			29,920*	1778
Philadelphia	210	*0.7*	1,420	26,892	28,522	1790
Kingston	16,659	*62.9*	3,280	6,539	26,478	1788
Saint-Pierre (Martinique)	3,720	*18.6*			20,000*	1788
Boston	0[7]	*0.0*	766	17,554	18,320	1790
Recife					18,207	1776
Campeche			3,000*[8]		18,000*	1766
Charleston	7,684	*47.0*	586	8,089	16,359	1790
Cap Français	10,000*	*66.7*	1,400*	3,600*	15,000*	1789
Santiago de Cuba					15,000*[9]	1792
Bridgetown (Barbados)					14,000*	1773
Cartagena de Indias	2,584	*18.9*	6,745	4,273[10]	13,690	1777
Baltimore	1,255	*9.3*	323	11,925	13,503	1790
Paramaribo	8,000*	*68.0*	1,760*	2,000*	11,760*	1791
Willemstad (Curaçao)	5,419	*46.9*	2,617	3,507	11,543	1789
Santo Domingo					10,702	1782–3

4. The numbers for Havana are substantially lower than in the 1774 census, which lists 21,281 slaves (28.1 per cent), 10,881 free people of color, and 43,392 whites for a total population of 75,554. Ynaê Lopes dos Santos, "La Habana Bourbônica: Reforma ilustrada e escravidão em Havana (1763–1790)", *Revista de Indias*, 75:269 (2017), pp. 81–113, 99.

5. One historian's numbers add up to 7,837 free people of color: João José Reis, "Slave Resistance in Brazil: Bahia, 1807–1835", *Luso-Brazilian Review*, 25:1 (1988), pp. 111–144, 114.

6. In 1780, 39,209 people were counted.

7. Although slavery was on its way out in Boston, a few slaves remained. They did not end up in the first census of the United States because the whites who owned slaves chose not to stand out. George H. Moore, *Notes on the History of Slavery in Massachusetts* (New York, 1866), p. 247.

8. The total number of enslaved people and free people of color.

9. The city's *district* had 20,761 inhabitants in 1792, including 6,037 enslaved Africans (29.1 per cent) and 6,512 free people of color. Adriana Chira, "Uneasy Intimacies: Race, Family, and Property in Santiago de Cuba, 1803–1868" (Ph.D., University of Michigan, 2016), p. 309.

10. Includes 239 clergy. In addition, the city had eighty-eight indigenous inhabitants.

Note: The population figures with an asterisk are estimates.

Sources: Havana: Alejandro de Humboldt, *Ensayo político sobre la isla de Cuba* (Caracas, 2005), p. 44; Rio de Janeiro: Mary C. Karasch, *Slave Life in Rio de Janeiro, 1808–1850* (Princeton, NJ, 1987), p. 62; Salvador: A.J.R. Russell-Wood, "Ports of Colonial Brazil", in Franklin W. Knight and Peggy K. Liss (eds), *Atlantic Port Cities: Economy, Culture, and Society in the Atlantic World, 1650–1850* (Baltimore, MD, 1991), pp. 196–239, 222; New York: US Bureau of the Census, *Heads of Family at the First Census of the United States Taken in the Year 1790: New York* (Washington, DC, 1908), p. 9; Buenos Aires: Susan M. Socolow, "Buenos Aires: Atlantic Port and Hinterland in the Eighteenth Century", in Knight and Liss, *Atlantic Port Cities*, pp. 240–261, 250. Lyman L. Johnson, "Estimaciones de la población de Buenos Aires en 1744, 1778 y 1810", *Desarrollo Económico*, 19:73 (1979), pp. 107–119; Philadelphia: US Bureau of the Census, *Heads of Family at the First Census of the United States Taken in the Year 1790: Pennsylvania* (Washington, DC, 1908), p. 10; Kingston: Trevor Burnard, "Kingston, Jamaica: Crucible of Modernity", in Jorge Cañizares-Esguerra, Matt D. Childs, and James Sidbury (eds), *The Black Urban Atlantic in the Age of the Slave Trade* (Philadelphia, PA, 2013), pp. 122–144, 127; Saint-Pierre: Léo Elisabeth, *La société martiniquaise aux XVIIe et XVIIIe siècles 1664–1789* (Paris, 2003), p. 101; Frédéric Régent, *La France et ses esclaves. De la colonization aux abolitions (1620–1848)* (Paris, 2007), p. 120; Boston: US Bureau of the Census, *Heads of Family at the First Census of the United States Taken in the Year 1790: Massachusetts* (Washington, DC, 1908), p. 10; Recife: Jacob M. Price, "Summation: The American Panorama of Atlantic Port Cities", in Knight and Liss, *Atlantic Port Cities*, pp. 262–276, 263; Campeche: Adriana Delfina Rocher Salas, "Religiosidad e identidad en San Francisco de Campeche. Siglos XVI y XVII", *Anuario de estudios Americanos*, 63:2 (2006), pp. 27–47, p. 44, n. 39; Charleston: US Bureau of the Census, *Heads of Family at the First Census of the United States Taken in the Year 1790: South Carolina* (Washington, DC, 1908), p. 9; Cap Français: David Geggus, "The Major Port Towns of Saint Domingue in the Later Eighteenth Century", in Knight and Liss, *Atlantic Port Cities*, pp. 87–116, 108; Santiago de Cuba: Leví Marrero, *Cuba; economía y Sociedad. Azúcar, Ilustración y conciencia (1763–1788)* (Madrid, 1983), p. 147; Bridgetown: Pedro L.V. Welch, *Slave Society in the City: Bridgetown, Barbados, 1680–1834* (Kingston [etc.], 2003), p. 53; Cartagena de Indias: María Aguilera Díaz and Adolfo Meisel Roca, *Tres siglos de historia demográfica de Cartagena de Indias* (Cartagena, 2009), p. 22; Baltimore: US Bureau of the Census, *Heads of Family at the First Census of the United States Taken in the Year 1790: Maryland* (Washington, DC, 1908), p. 9; Paramaribo: Cornelis Ch. Goslinga, *The Dutch in the Caribbean and in the Guianas 1680–1791* (Assen [etc.], 1985), p. 519; Willemstad: NAN, Raad van Coloniën 120, "Generaal rapport over Curaçao en onderhorige eylanden", Bijlage no. 16: Opgave der huizen van particulieren [Appendix 16: Indication of private homes]; Santo Domingo: María Rosario Sevilla Soler, *Santo Domingo Tierra de Frontera (1750–1800)* (Seville, 1980), p. 35.

Novo with 7,000–10,000, and Ouidah with 6,000–7,000.[11] However, the largest "African port", arguably, was London, home to 40,000 people of African birth or descent in the late eighteenth century.[12] The story of Africans and their lives in early modern Europe is not well-known. After the Portuguese started to trade in Africans in the mid-fifteenth century, they soon shipped some of their captives to the metropolis. As blacks continued to arrive, they made up around ten percent of Lisbon's population by the mid-sixteenth century, according to a semi-official census.[13] Enslaved blacks were also sold from Lisbon across the Spanish border to Seville, the port town that in the sixteenth century was one of Europe's largest cities, smaller only than Paris and Naples. By 1565, one in fourteen residents of the city was a slave, and most slaves were of African birth or descent. Nor were African slaves a new sight in sixteenth-century Seville, which had received its first black immigrants in the late fourteenth century by way of the trans-Saharan slave trade. Since Seville had become Spain's designated port for trade with and navigation to the Americas, the first slaves to enter the Americas came actually from Seville and not Africa. King Ferdinand, for instance, gave permission in 1510 for 200 slaves to be transported from Seville to the settlers of Hispaniola.[14]

It seems certain that the first blacks to arrive in the Holy Roman Empire and the Dutch Republic also came off Portuguese ships. Blacks living in Amsterdam in the early seventeenth century worked as servants or slaves for Portuguese New Christians and Jews, many of whom must have been unaware of the local ban on slavery.[15] The existence of black slaves has also been documented for the contemporary Jewish communities of Antwerp and Hamburg.[16] In Amsterdam, it is clear, slaves disappeared in the course of the seventeenth century. A Spaniard who had resided in town for twenty-five years could write to a friend in 1685: "Slavery is not allowed

11. Paul E. Lovejoy, "The Urban Background of Enslaved Muslims in the Americas", *Slavery & Abolition: A Journal of Slave and Post-Slave Studies*, 26 (2005), pp. 349–376, 353.
12. Lovejoy, "Urban Background", p. 366.
13. A.C. de C.M. Saunders, *A Social History of Black Slaves and Freedmen in Portugal 1441–1555* (Cambridge, 1982), p. 87.
14. Ruth Pike, *Aristocrats and Traders: Sevillian Society in the Sixteenth Century* (Ithaca, NY [etc.], 1972), pp. 172–175.
15. As in other European cities, the distinction between slavery and domestic service by free people was not always well defined. Cf. Giulia Bonazza, *Abolitionism and the Persistence of Slavery in Italian States, 1750–1850* (Cham, 2019), p. 108.
16. Jan Denucé, *Afrika in de XVIde eeuw en de handel van Antwerpen* (Antwerp, 1937), p. 49; Hans Pohl, *Die Portugiesen in Antwerpen (1567–1648). Zur Geschichte einer Minderheit* (Wiesbaden, 1977), p. 324; Michael Studemund-Halévy, *Biographisches Lexikon der Hamburger Sefarden: Die Grabinschriften des Portugiesenfriedhofs an der Königstrasse in Hamburg-Altona* (Hamburg, 2000), pp. 664–665.

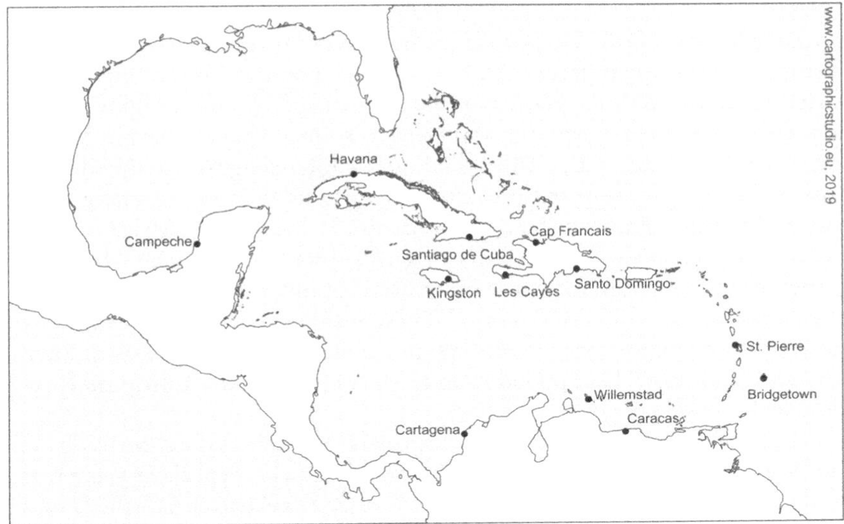

Figure 2. Caribbean ports.

here. Arriving slaves are immediately freed. The many blacks hailing from Brazil and other areas all work for a salary".[17]

The main profession of black slaves in northern European ports was that of servant. Merchants on slaving voyages frequently brought back teenage boys to French ports to serve as household servants. Teenage blacks from Africa served in virtually every household of resident slave traders in such ports, but rarely elsewhere.[18] Although domestic servants were also among the enslaved population of Bordeaux, most blacks residing there were trained in a few crafts in order to serve in specific capacities in the French West Indies. These included cooks, wigmakers, coopers, carpenters, locksmiths, blacksmiths, potters, saddlers, tailors, and seamstresses.[19]

If African slavery in European port cities would always remain a minor phenomenon, African ports involved in the Atlantic slave trade saw a phenomenal rise of their enslaved populations. More than half of Luanda's residents were

17. B.N. Teensma, "Abraham Idaña's beschrijving van Amsterdam, 1685", *Amstelodamum*, 83 (1991), pp. 113–138, 131.

18. Perry Viles, "The Slaving Interest in the Atlantic Ports, 1763–1792", *French Historical Studies* 7 (1972), pp. 529–543, 539–540. About half of all blacks residing in French ports hailed from the French Caribbean: Erick Noël, "Noirs et gens de couleur dans les villes de l'ouest de la France au XVIIIe siècle", in Guy Saupin (ed.), *Villes atlantiques dans l'Europe occidentale du Moyen Âge au XXe siècle* (Rennes, 2015), pp. 217–226, 220.

19. Éric Saugera, *Bordeaux port négrier. Chronologie, économie, idéologie XVIIe–XIXe siècles* (Biarritz [etc.], 1995), p. 296.

enslaved in the 1780s and 1790s, two thirds of the inhabitants of the French slaving port of Gorée in Senegal were slaves in 1767,[20] while slaves in Portuguese-controlled Benguela, one of the main slave-sending ports in Africa, represented three quarters of the population by the late eighteenth century. Crew members of arriving ships saw as soon as they docked in Benguela that "slaves unloaded the ships and carried passengers to the decks".[21] Enslaved labor also featured prominently in Ouidah, another major slaving port in Atlantic Africa on the coast of Benin. It was, writes Africanist Robin Law, "predominantly a community of slaves. In addition to the African personnel of the European forts, the households of indigenous officials and merchants also included many slaves".[22] These resident slaves were distinct from those sold into export, since local law prohibited the sale overseas of anyone born in Dahomey. That applied even to slaves held by the European forts in Ouidah.[23]

In Lagos in present-day Nigeria, the growth of the Atlantic slave trade in the late eighteenth century "led to a dramatic expansion of local slavery as a means of acquiring people and increased in significance relative to these other types of dependency. This change occurred in part as a consequence of the sheer growth in the supply of slaves on the coast and of incomes with which to buy them".[24] By the 1850s, European visitors believed the majority of the population were slaves.

Likewise, ports in the Americas involved in the slave trade came to house large enslaved populations. In some towns, the introduction of slaves rapidly transformed the urban landscape, as it did in Buenos Aires, where blacks and colored people represented more than a quarter of the population by the early nineteenth century after a marked rise of slave imports in the previous quarter-century.[25] In other ports, slaves were present from the outset, their numbers growing along with the general population. Beginning in the closing decades of the sixteenth century, for example, the port of Cartagena de Indias on the

20. Luanda's enslaved accounted for 57.2 per cent of the population in 1781 and an average of 55.3 per cent in 1796–99: José C. Curto and Raymond R. Gervais, "A dinâmica demográfica de Luanda no contexto do tráfico de escravos do Atlântico Sul, 1781–1844", *Topoi* 3:4 (2002), pp. 85–138, 120. The percentage of the enslaved in Gorée (1767) was 68.8: Boubacar Barry, *Senegambia and the Atlantic Slave Trade* (Cambridge, 1998), p. 76.

21. Mariana P. Candido, *An African Slaving Port and the Atlantic World: Benguela and Its Hinterland* (Cambridge, 2013), p. 113, 116.

22. Robin Law, *Ouidah: The Social History of a West African Slaving 'Port', 1727–1892* (Athens, OH, 2004), p. 77.

23. Law, *Ouidah*, p. 78.

24. Kristin Mann, *Slavery and the Birth of an African City: Lagos, 1760–1900* (Bloomington, IN, 2007), p. 72.

25. Lyman L. Johnson, *Workshop of Revolution: Plebeian Buenos Aires and the Atlantic World, 1776–1810* (Durham, NC [etc.], 2011), p. 37.

coast of present-day Colombia already had a black majority.[26] Slave majorities were not exceptional in ports of Atlantic America. In Kingston and the two port cities of Saint Croix, an island belonging to Denmark, slaves accounted for more than sixty per cent of the population, while in Cap Français (Saint-Domingue) and Paramaribo (Suriname), they made up two thirds of the residents.[27] The enslaved share was even eighty-one per cent in Saint-Domingue's port of Les Cayes.[28]

SLAVE OCCUPATIONS IN ATLANTIC PORT CITIES

People of African birth and descent throughout the Atlantic world distinguished themselves in military service, playing a key role, for example, in Havana's almost successful defense against British invasion in 1762, for which the 3,000 enslaved defenders did not receive the recognition they deserved – quite the opposite. In 1807, thousands of slaves joined the free population of Buenos Aires to repel another British invasion. While they failed in regular warfare, their urban guerrilla led to victory.[29] In peaceful years, domestic service was a common profession for New World slaves.[30] Domestic work could denote many different activities, such as spinning yarn, weaving cloth, preparing food, making and mending clothes, making candles, tending livestock, and taking care of children.[31] In some Atlantic port cities, and perhaps the majority, female domestics predominated, as in Cartagena de Indias, where they made up sixty per cent of the enslaved domestic workforce.[32] But whether male or female, domestic slave lives tended to be incorporated in the families of white masters and mistresses. Some enslaved women working in Anglican houses in New York City attended schools, were well fed, and wore clothing as expensive as that of their masters and mistresses.[33] As Charles Foy has observed: "For

26. Antonino Vidal Ortega, *Cartagena de Indias y la región histórica del Caribe, 1580–1640* (Seville, 2002), p. 271.

27. Neville A.T. Hall, *Slave Society in the Danish West Indies: St. Thomas, St. John, and St. Croix*, ed. B.W. Higman (Baltimore, MD [etc.], 1992), p. 87. See also Table 1.

28. Jean Saint-Vil, "Villes et bourgs de Saint-Domingue au XVIIIe siècle (Essai de géographie historique)", *Les cahiers d'outre-mer*, 31 (1978), pp. 251–270, 263.

29. Elena A. Schneider, *The Occupation of Havana: War Trade, and Slavery in the Atlantic World* (Williamsburg, VA [etc.], 2018), pp. 117–120. Johnson, *Workshop of Revolution*, pp. 249–271.

30. Domestic servants in Lima made up over eighty per cent of the enslaved population by the late eighteenth century: Alberto Flores Galindo S., *Aristocracia y plebe. Lima, 1760–1830: Estructura de clases y sociedad colonial* (Lima, 1984), p. 121.

31. Jared Ross Hardesty, *Unfreedom: Slavery and Dependence in Eighteenth-Century Boston* (New York [etc.], 2016), p. 113.

32. Pablo Rodríguez, *Sentimientos y vida familiar en el Nuevo Reino de Granada. Siglo XVIII* (Santa Fe de Bogotá, 1997), p. 47.

33. Graham Russell Hodges, *Root and Branch: African Americans in New York and East Jersey, 1613–1863* (Chapel Hill, NC, 1999), p. 111.

elites [...] house slaves dressed in silk shirts, powdered wigs, white silk stockings, tailored trousers, and shoes with silver buckles, reinforced the elite status of their gentlemen masters".[34] Many a slave would have welcomed this display of refinement – enslaved North American barbers took the initiative themselves to wear fine European-style clothing and to powder their hair like their owners.[35] At the same time, we should be careful not to romanticize the paternalism expressed by white owners vis-à-vis the slaves they considered part of their extended family.[36] Moreover, female enslaved domestic servants were obviously vulnerable to sexual exploitation. In other ways, too, their lives were tenuous. In Bridgetown, Barbados, for example, they were sold or passed on among slave owners' relatives multiple times.[37]

Nor should we ignore the world the slaves made themselves. In Spanish and Portuguese America, they offset the difficulty of starting a family in an environment where fellow blacks were relatively few in number and where slaveholdings were small by joining lay brotherhoods, which served as mutual-aid societies. Black brotherhoods were numerous in Brazil, where they were based on ethnicity or provenience, at least in Rio de Janeiro.[38] In Buenos Aires, brotherhoods provided credit to their members, dowries for those planning to get married or entering a convent, pensions, and even indulgences.[39] Catholic Church services in Willemstad, Curaçao, allowed the resident population of African birth and descent to socialize and forms bonds.[40] Even the small numbers of blacks and people of color in European ports found ways to carve out their own autonomous sphere. In Nantes, epicenter of the

34. Charles R. Foy, "Ports of Slavery, Ports of Freedom: How Slaves Used Northern Seaports' Maritime Industry to Escape and Create Trans-Atlantic Identities" (Ph.D., Rutgers University, 2008), p. 66. See also Mariana L.R. Dantas, *Black Townsmen: Urban Slavery and Freedom in the Eighteenth-Century Americas* (New York, 2008), p. 78.

35. Douglas Walter Bristol, Jr, *Knights of the Razor: Black Barbers in Slavery and Freedom* (Baltimore, MD, 2009), pp. 15–16.

36. Cf. Debra Blumenthal, *Enemies and Familiars: Slavery and Mastery in Fifteenth-Century Valencia* (Ithaca, NY, 2009), p. 268.

37. Marisa J. Fuentes, *Dispossessed Lives: Enslaved Women, Violence, and the Archive* (Philadelphia, PA, 2016), p. 93.

38. Blumenthal, *Enemies and Familiars*, pp. 201–206. Matt D. Childs, "Re-creating African Ethnic Identities in Cuba", in Jorge Cañizares-Esguerra, Matt D. Childs, and James Sidbury (eds), *The Black Urban Atlantic in the Age of the Slave Trade* (Philadelphia, PA, 2013), pp. 85–100, 90. Mariza de Carvalho Soares, *Slavery and African Catholics in Eighteenth-Century Rio de Janeiro* (Durham, NC, 2011), pp. 173–174.

39. Miguel A. Rosal, "La religiosidad católica de los afrodescendientes de Buenos Aires (siglos XVIII–XIX)", *Hispania Sacra* 60:122 (2008), pp. 597–633, 601. In Cuba, Montevideo, and Buenos Aires, the activities of these confraternities declined as African nations emerged. Alex Borucki, *From Shipmates to Soldiers: Emerging Black Identities in the Rio de la Plata* (Albuquerque, NM, 2015), p. 87.

40. Wim Klooster, "Subordinate but Proud: Curaçao's Free Blacks and Mulattoes in the Eighteenth Century", *New West Indian Guide / Nieuwe West-Indische Gids (NWIG)*, 68 (1994), pp. 283–300, 291–293.

French slave trade, they mourned and rejoiced together, and acted as godparents for each other's children. And when they socialized together outside the purview of religious or secular authorities, they caused alarm, just as they did in Cap Français when they held their own church meetings, preaching and catechizing and naming church wardens.[41]

Urban slave insurrections almost never occurred prior to the Age of Revolutions, and even then, they were rare.[42] One explanation may lie in the relative freedom slaves enjoyed, a common trait of Atlantic port cities. Slaves often worked semi-independently, earning money to supplement the livelihood provided by the master, or sometimes almost entirely on their own. Historian Pedro Welch has observed for Bridgetown that "[t]he rhythm of urban occupational life was removed from the regimentation characteristic of the rural field slaves. Skilled slaves, domestic slaves and those involved in self-hire and marketing/selling, all found an ambience which offered 'room to manoeuvre' options".[43] Many a master allowed his or her slave to work on their own, returning to their masters at regular intervals to bring back a share of the income they had earned.[44] We can trace this custom to Greco-Roman times, although the New World practice was rooted in late medieval Spain and Portugal, where masters employed their slaves not only in their own business, but hired them out to others, and let them carry out their own trade, provided the master received part of the slave's income. Not only did many slaveholders thus recuperate the costs of the slave in a short time, the slave's earnings could actually be the only source of income for the master.[45] In Spanish American cities, this phenomenon was observed from the first years of the Spanish conquest onwards.[46]

41. Dwain C. Pruitt, "*Nantes Noir*: Living Race in the City of Slavers" (Ph.D., Emory University, 2005), pp. 224–226, 234–235. David Geggus, "The Slaves and Free People of Color of Cap Français", in Cañizares-Esguerra, Childs, and Sidbury, *Black Urban Atlantic*, pp. 101–121, 118.
42. One conspicuous exception is the revolt in Salvador of 1835: João José Reis, *Slave Rebellion in Brazil: The Muslim Uprising of 1835 in Bahia* (Baltimore, MD, 1993).
43. Pedro L.V. Welch, *Slave Society in the City: Bridgetown, Barbados 1680–1834* (Kingston [etc.], 2003), p. 157.
44. Cf. John Thornton, *Africa and Africans in the Making of the Atlantic World, 1400–1680* (Cambridge, 1992), p. 178; L. Virginia Gould, "Urban Slavery-Urban Freedom: The Manumission of Jacqueline Lemelle", in David Barry Gaspar and Darlene Clark Hine (eds), *More Than Chattel: Black Women and Slavery in the Americas* (Bloomington, IN [etc.], 1996), pp. 298–314, 300, 302. On ethnic interaction in Curaçao, see Linda M. Rupert, "Trading Globally, Speaking Locally: Curaçao's Sephardim in the Making of a Caribbean Creole", in David Cesarani and Gemma Romain (eds), *Jews and Port Cities, 1550–1990: Commerce, Community, and Cosmopolitanism* (London, 2005), pp. 109–122.
45. Deborah Kamen, "Manumission and Slave-Allowances in Classical Athens", *Historia* 65 (2016), pp. 413–426, 421–422. Spain and Portugal: Saunders, *Social History*, pp. 67–68; William D. Phillips, Jr, *Slavery in Medieval and Early Modern Iberia* (Philadelphia, PA, 2014), pp. 109–110.
46. Carmen Bernand, *Negros esclavos y libres en las ciudades hispanoamericanas* (Madrid, 2001), p. 38. Some towns were reputedly more convenient for self-hire than others. For that reason, one slaveholder in Córdoba in the Río de la Plata let her slave work 700 kilometers away in Buenos

It could also be found in other parts of the Americas, as in New York City, where the practice became so common that by 1711, the city's government designated the Meal Market on Wall Street as the authorized place to hire slaves.[47] In Danish Saint Croix, many persons, the island council commented in 1792, had no other property than a few slaves and nothing to live on apart from what these slaves brought in. "Skilled craftsmen, particularly carpenters, and other skilled slaves like seamen, were as important as itinerant vendors as 'sole means of support' for some of the town's whites and freedmen."[48] And in New Orleans, one traveler reported in the early nineteenth century that slave owners encouraged their female slaves "to use their free time in prostitution and to report back each day the amount they have taken".[49]

Hiring out was one of several arrangements slave owners made to guarantee their own income. "Slave-owners who were not self-employed, such as seamen, labourers or stone-masons, sometimes persuaded their employer to take on their slaves as well, so that master and man worked side by side in the same or different capacities."[50] In general, as Emma Hart has noted for Charleston, South Carolina, "[t]he flexibility of slave labor allowed firms to weather difficult economic times and continue their development, where those in an entirely free labor system may have failed".[51] Large numbers of slaves thus made a living. David Geggus has estimated that 2,000 "jobbers" could be found in late colonial Cap Français.[52] Hiring out, or jobbing, also existed in the ports of Atlantic Africa, such as Luanda, where almost half of all slaves of one neighborhood in the 1820s were tailors, seamstresses, barbers, carpenters, and laundresses. Many female slaves were street vendors who hawked dried fish, palm oil, china, and Indian textiles.[53]

Throughout the Atlantic world, then, as jobbers or regular bondspeople, slaves worked in port cities in a variety of occupations. Increasingly, port

Aires in the early years of the nineteenth century: María Verónica Secreto, "Os escravos de Buenos Aires. Do terceiro pátio à rua: a busca do tolerável (1776–1814)", *Tempo* 18:33 (2012), pp. 23–49, 45.

47. Foy, "Ports of Slavery, Ports of Freedom", p. 67.

48. Hall, *Slave Society*, p. 91.

49. C.C. Robin, cited in Rashauna Johnson, *Slavery's Metropolis: Unfree Labor in New Orleans During the Age of Revolutions* (New York, 2016), p. 109.

50. Saunders, *Social History*, p. 75.

51. Emma Hart, *Building Charleston: Town and Society in the Eighteenth-Century British Atlantic World* (Charlottesville, VA [etc.], 2010), p. 111.

52. Geggus, "Slaves and Free People of Color", 115. Whereas slave owners initially hired out their slaves, at least in Guadeloupe's ports it became more common for slaves to find work themselves. Anne Pérotin-Dumon, *La ville aux Iles, la ville dans l'île. Basse-Terre et Pointe-à-Pitre, Guadeloupe, 1650–1820* (Paris, 2000), p. 660.

53. Roquinaldo Ferreira, "Slavery and the Social and Cultural Landscapes of Luanda", in Cañizares-Esguerra, Childs, and Sidbury, *Black Urban Atlantic*, pp. 185–206, 190, 192. See also Roquinaldo Ferreira, *Cross-Cultural Exchange in the Atlantic World: Angola and Brazil during the Era of the Slave Trade* (New York, 2012), pp. 130–135.

city slaves became indispensable in the maritime economy. In Willemstad, black and colored sailors, fishermen, caulkers, dockhands, warehouse workers, and sail makers were all needed to keep the port afloat. Members of Curaçao's ruling council estimated as early as 1741 that two thirds of the sailors were either slaves, or free people of color, a share that only increased in subsequent decades.[54] What set Curaçao apart from most other colonies was its large number of slave fishermen and sailors.[55] These slaves earned a salary on board private vessels and those of the West India Company. The muster of one Curaçaoan vessel included a white (Irish) captain, a white locally born quartermaster, five creole white sailors, and seventeen slave sailors, of whom twelve had been born on the island itself and five in West Africa. Each sailor, irrespective of his legal status, earned ten pesos per month.[56] Of all possible professions, that of sailor undoubtedly lent slaves the most freedom of movement. This life seemed so attractive to some Africans that they borrowed letters of freedom from other sailors, which allowed them to sail on one of the merchant vessels leaving Willemstad every day. This practice was outlawed more than once by a regulation that only allowed free people of color to be recruited with the permission of their masters. Some slave sailors abused this freedom by running away; sailors constituted one sixth of runaways in the eighteenth century.[57] On the other hand, sailors from across the Americas ran a risk if they were free, as some of them found out upon arrival in New Orleans. If they could not produce evidence of their freedom, imprisonment or enslavement may be their fate.[58]

Slaves engaged in a wide range of port-related jobs. One Kingston shipwright owned fifty-two slaves, including twelve shipwrights, ten caulkers, four joiners, three laborers, two blacksmiths, two block-makers, a turner, a pitch boiler, a bellows blower, a lath-wheel turner, a sailor, and a store-and-water man.[59] In Bridgetown, slaves were employed as shipwrights, caulkers, sail makers, ship carpenters, sailors, and boatmen.[60] So many slaves were active as sailors that the island's governor complained in 1786 that "the Numbers of Negro Slaves employed in navigating the Trading Vessels in these Seas [...] seem to me to increase so much as to require the attention of the British Legislature, as it

54. Nationaal Archief, The Netherlands (NAN), Nieuwe West-Indische Compagnie (NWIC) 588, fol. 890, information provided by delegates of the Council of Curaçao, J.G. Pax, Johannes Stuijlingh, and Jan van Schagen, 18 June 1741.

55. Archivo General de Indias (Seville), Santo Domingo 781, examination of Samuel Levi Maduro, Puerto Cabello, 6 September 1730.

56. NAN, NWIC 601, fol. 953.

57. Klooster, "Subordinate but Proud", p. 285.

58. Johnson, *Slavery's Metropolis*, pp. 59–60.

59. B.W. Higman, *Slave Population and Economy in Jamaica, 1807–1834* (Cambridge, 1976), pp. 37–38.

60. Welch, *Slave Society in the City*, p. 82.

throws so many English Seamen out of employment".[61] It was not uncommon for skilled maritime slaves to be bought by Caribbean masters from North American slave owners, who could earn good money from the sale of slave coopers, caulkers, riggers, and sail makers.[62]

Enslaved artisans were also ubiquitous in South American ports. In Havana, they dominated crafts such as blacksmithing, shoemaking, and painting, while in Buenos Aires in 1800, slaves "were present in nearly every artisan trade and were crucial to small retail, managing the stalls in the city's markets and peddling everything from thread to bread and milk door to door".[63] Having bought a newly arriving slave, owners placed him or her with an artisan, where they would be apprenticed for widely varying periods – as short as a few weeks and as long as six years – depending on the skill level sought. In nearly every manual occupation, slaves were integrated with free laborers, and not infrequently did slaves who had reached the level of journeyman or master direct the work of free apprentices.[64] From North America to Brazil, slaves were hired to labor in public works, repairing and paving streets, erecting bridges, and assisting in the construction or maintenance of public buildings.[65] In Charleston, enslaved black and white skilled workers worked side by side in the city's building industry, where they were trained as carpenters, bricklayers, painters, and plasterers.[66] In the Spanish American societies where white honor was of fundamental importance, the mingling of white and black created misgivings among "lowly" whites, who either abandoned their trade, or never engaged in manual labor in the first place. More than a few immigrants from Spain thus lived in abject poverty in Cartagena de Indias.[67] But whites in French New Orleans also refused to engage in heavy and degrading labor, which they associated with slaves.[68]

Much less exerting than public works was the practice of hawking. In Saint Croix,

> [w]hite townsfolk, poor and better-off alike, had their slaves take to the streets hawking a variety of goods. These slaves, mostly women, armed with their passes and trays on their heads [...] were a constant feature of the landscape in

61. Julius Sherrard Scott III, "The Common Wind: Currents of Afro-American Communication in the Era of the Haitian Revolution" (Ph.D., Duke University, 1986), p. 106.
62. Foy, "Ports of Slavery, Ports of Freedom", p. 84.
63. Johnson, *Workshop of Revolution*, p. 38.
64. Schneider, *Occupation of Havana*, pp. 76–77. Johnson, *Workshop of Revolution*, pp. 38–42.
65. Dantas, *Black Townsmen*, p. 88.
66. Hart, *Building Charleston*, p. 79.
67. Luis Felipe Pellicer, *La vivencia del honor en la provincial de Venezuela, 1774–1809. Estudio de casos* (Caracas, 1996), pp. 26, 28, 33, 35–38. Loredana Giolitto, "Esclavitud y libertad en Cartagena de Indias. Reflexiones en torno a un caso de manumisión a finales del periodo colonial", *Fronteras de la historia*, 8 (2003), pp. 65–91, 80.
68. Cécile Vidal, *Caribbean New Orleans: Empire, Race, and the Making of a Slave Society* (Williamsburg, VA [etc.], 2019), pp. 310–311.

> town and country. The stock in trade consisted of such items as bread, butter, coffee beans, fruit, meat, vegetables, candles, cushions and haberdashery notions. Plying their trade on behalf of their masters and mistresses, they were the lifeline of an internal marketing system, complementing the Sunday market of the country slaves.[69]

Such activities offered the slave a measure of autonomy in the workplace. In Boston, Jared Hardesty has argued, slaves carved out "a space in which they could protect the interests of themselves, their families, and their communities. [...] Slavery in this context was not a totalizing system of oppression but a structure that slaves learned to navigate and manipulate to their advantage".[70] Availing themselves of the opportunities offered to them, some slaves in Spanish American ports acquired so much wealth that they became richer than their owners.[71]

Despite the many differences between city and countryside, between port and plantation, these two worlds were highly interconnected.[72] Slaves constantly crossed this divide, most of them forced by their owners who wanted them to perform labor or go on errands, but some of their own volition. Little is still known about rural flight to the cities, although this was by no means a minor phenomenon. One historian has even argued that late eighteenth-century Buenos Aires was turned into "an immense urban *palenque*" (maroon settlement).[73] In the more anonymous urban environments, runaways presented themselves as free men and women – and in many cases, they actually may have been, as their owners did not keep their end of the bargain.[74] Passing for freedmen was not easy, given the scars that were a perpetual reminder of the maroon's slave past.[75] Blending in also meant adopting the material culture of the resident black population.[76]

69. Hall, *Slave Society*, pp. 90–91.
70. Hardesty, *Unfreedom*, pp. 3, 104. See also Johnson, *Slavery's Metropolis*, p. 71.
71. Bernand, *Negros esclavos y libres*, p. 39.
72. Pepijn Brandon, "Between the Plantation and the Port: Racialization and Social Control in Eighteenth-Century Paramaribo", *International Review of Social History*, 64 (2019), pp. 95–124, 99–100.
73. Eduardo Saguier, "La fuga esclava como resistencia rutinaria y cotidiana en el Buenos Aires del siglo XVIII", *Revista de humanidades y ciencias sociales* (Bolivia), 1:2 (1995), pp. 115–184, 134.
74. 285 runaway advertisements in the Saint-Domingue newspaper *Affiches Américaines* in the years 1766–1791 refer to maroons *se disant libre*: "Le marronnage dans le monde atlantique. Sources et trajectoires de vie". Available at: http://www.marronnage.info/fr/corpus.php; last accessed 29 October 2019. Cf. the insistence of one runaway in New York on his freedom in Shane White, *Somewhat More Independent: The End of Slavery in New York City, 1770–1810* (Athens, GA [etc.], 1991), pp. 117–119.
75. Fuentes, *Dispossessed Lives*, p. 19.
76. Vidal, *Caribbean New Orleans*, 125. Pérotin-Dumon, *La ville aux Iles*, p. 665.

We may assume that what may have attracted some of the male maroons was to work on one of the many vessels involved in inter-American trade.[77] Julius Scott has argued that "[l]ife aboard one of the modest vessels which plied the coasts or engaged in small-scale intercolonial commerce presented an attractive alternative to the life of regimental hierarchy to be found aboard a larger ship or ashore on a standard sugar plantation".[78] The future black abolitionist Olaudah Equiano jumped at the chance to serve on a ship in Montserrat in the 1760s, since his new profession enabled him to see other islands, meet new people, earn money, and, as Scott put it, most importantly, look his owner in the eye and demand respect.[79]

Although blacks working in the maritime economy often did not work under the close supervision of their masters, they still longed for more autonomy. Similar to disadvantaged men in Europe who sought a way to abandon their lives, the maritime economy of port cities helped New World blacks escape slavery. Stealing a boat and rowing to a nearby Spanish colony was the main route to freedom, especially since slaves were declared free upon arrival if they announced their willingness to convert to Catholicism. Some black sailors, like the ones from Curaçao, simply absconded during trading voyages.[80] Nor was there a lack of slaves who used employment aboard colonial vessels as a launchpad to freedom. Bondsmen would routinely visit taverns, which served as sites of sociability for white sailors and enslaved workers alike. These were centers of entertainment and celebration, where crime was plotted, but they also served as places of refuge and markets for seamen. Ship captains were usually not interested in a crew member's legal status, but in his skills. Many a runaway slave in North America's Thirteen Colonies thus obtained berths on whaling ships, oyster ships, and merchant vessels.[81]

77. Cf. Flávio Gomes, "Africans and Petit Marronage in Rio de Janeiro, ca.1800–1840", *Luso-Brazilian Review*, 47:2 (2010), pp. 74–99, 75. In Bridgetown, runaways also gathered in the vicinity of a garrison, for which they performed various tasks: Jerome S. Handler, "Escaping Slavery in a Caribbean Plantation Society: Marronage in Barbados, 1650s–1830s", *NWIG*, 71 (1997), pp. 183–225, 195.

78. Scott, "Common Wind", p. 106.

79. Scott, "Common Wind", p. 107.

80. Linda M. Rupert, "Marronage, Manumission and Maritime Trade in the Early Modern Caribbean", *Slavery & Abolition* 30 (2009), pp. 361–382, 364.

81. Foy, "Ports of Slavery, Ports of Freedom", pp. 72–73, 136–137, 142. Gregory E. O'Malley has suggested another motive for some recently arrived Africans to flee from the Carolina Lowcountry to Charleston: they wanted to retrace their steps and perhaps return by ship to their native soil. Gregory E. O'Malley, "Slavery's Converging Ground: Charleston's Slave Trade as the Black Heart of the Lowcountry", *William and Mary Quarterly*, 74 (2017), pp. 271–302, 298–299.

Like slaves with port-related occupations, enslaved musicians were often not satisfied with the relatively large amount of autonomy they must have possessed, making every effort to become free.[82] Musicians attempted to shed their slave status in various American port cities. Thirty-four men listed in Saint-Domingue runaway advertisements in the last quarter-century before the Haitian Revolution played the violin.[83] One in every four skilled runaway slaves from New York City was listed as possessing musical talents: fiddlers, drummers, fifers, singers, and a French horn player.[84] The fugitive slaves who departed from Willemstad, the port of Curaçao, included violinists and one French horn player.[85] Likewise, manumission letters from that island refer to several violinists, an oboist, and – once again – a French horn player.[86] Throughout the Atlantic world, slaves of all backgrounds did indeed seek to obtain freedom through manumission. The most convenient way for slaves to work their way toward obtaining freedom in this way was the Spanish American system of *coartación*, in which slaves could pay the required sum in installments.[87] Field hands in particular had a small chance of becoming free by this process, as has been abundantly shown. Urban slaves, by contrast, stood a better chance, although even for the majority of them, becoming free by such means was no realistic prospect. Even men and women who had saved the right amount of money to secure manumission sometimes faced opposition from their masters and could not induce civil authorities to intervene.[88]

82. The friar of a convent in Mendoza in the Río de la Plata – admittedly not a port – did not hide his surprise about the request for manumission in 1810 of a slave in charge of the monastery's organ and violin. In so many ways, the friar argued, the man was already free, having even been granted the right to teach students outside the convent. The musician in question, Fernando Guzmán, had a different perspective, rooted in natural law: "I have always been convinced that the only thing that can satisfy the slave in his servitude and dark dejection, is the hope to obtain his freedom. Nature resents to see her laws broken by a cruel arbitrariness founded on a tyrannical despotism." Silvia C. Mallo, "La libertad en el discurso del Estado, de amos y esclavos, 1780–1830", *Revista de historia de América*, 112 (1991), pp. 121–146, 132, 136.

83. "Le marronnage dans le monde atlantique". Five different advertisements were published regarding one violinist, a native of Curaçao. I have counted him once. Out of 130 known men who may have participated in concerts in Saint-Domingue, no fewer than 70 were slaves, 60 of them violinists: Bernard Camier, "Les concerts dans les capitales de Saint-Domingue à la fin du XVIIIe siècle", *Revue de Musicologie*, 93 (2007), pp. 75–98, 80.

84. Hodges, *Root and Branch*, p. 115.

85. Klooster, "Subordinate but Proud", p. 285.

86. T. van der Lee, *Curaçaose vrijbrieven 1722–1863. Met indices op namen van vrijgelatenen en hun voormalige eigenaren* (The Hague, 1998), pp. 291 (21 June 1799), 282 (1 June 1798), and 214 (21 February 1783).

87. Manuel Lucena Salmoral, "El derecho de coartación del esclavo en la América española", *Revista de Indias*, 59:216 (1999), pp. 357–374.

88. Lyman L. Johnson, "Manumission in Colonial Buenos Aires, 1776–1810", *The Hispanic American Historical Review*, 59 (1979), pp. 258–279, 261.

TRANSITIONS TO FREEDOM

For those who were manumitted, one historian has suggested, the transition from an enslaved to a free existence may not have been dramatic: "There is every sort of evidence that slaves in the categories most often freed (e.g., domestic servants, soldiers, skilled workers, mistresses), were treated more like free people, even before they were freed."[89] A significant number of slaves in Saint-Domingue even enjoyed de facto freedom, precarious as it was because their owners could withdraw it without notice.[90] Nor was there a vast difference between the jobs of free people and the tasks they had performed as slaves. Free women in Guadeloupe, for example, usually worked as seamstress or laundress, professions however that did not allow them to escape from poverty.[91] Some enterprising men and women began to engage in new activities. In the slave trading center of Cartagena de Indias, this point was already reached by the early seventeenth century, when many of men and women with slave backgrounds ran small inns or businesses renting out houses.[92] In other ports, free people of color did not branch out into such occupations until the second half of the eighteenth century. In Bridgetown, they were merchants, haberdashers, tavern and innkeepers, hucksters, tailors, shoemakers, and jewelers.[93] In Paramaribo, economic prominence of free men of color had to wait until white emigration set in in the 1770s in the wake of an economic crisis. Then, free colored males began to fill positions that had traditionally been occupied by the white population: those of blacksmith, carpenter, tailor, and shoemaker.[94] Most free women of color in Paramaribo worked as seamstresses or housekeepers, while free black women were employed as laundresses and market vendors.[95]

89. Arthur L. Stinchcombe, "Freedom and Oppression of Slaves in the Eighteenth-Century Caribbean", *American Sociological Review*, 59 (1994), pp. 911–929, 914.
90. Jennifer L. Palmer, *Intimate Bonds: Family and Slavery in the French Atlantic* (Philadelphia, PA, 2016), pp. 37, 170.
91. Frédéric Régent, *Esclavage, métissage, liberté. La Révolution française en Guadeloupe, 1789–1802* (Paris, 2004), pp. 167, 181.
92. Antonino Vidal Ortega, *Cartagena de Indias y la región histórica del Caribe, 1580–1640* (Seville, 2002), p. 264. See also Jane Landers, "The African Landscape of Seventeenth-Century Cartagena and Its Hinterlands", in Cañizares-Esguerra, Childs, and Sidbury, *Black Urban Atlantic*, pp. 147–162.
93. Welch, *Slave Society in the City*, p. 166.
94. Rosemarijn Hoefte and Jean Jacques Vrij, "Free Black and Colored Women in Early-Nineteenth-Century Paramaribo, Suriname", in David Barry Gaspar and Darlene Clark Hine (eds), *Beyond Bondage: Free Women of Color in the Americas* (Urbana, IL [etc.], 2004), pp. 145–168, 152. Albert von Sack, *A Narrative of a Voyage to Surinam: Of a Residence there during 1805, 1806, and 1807; and of the Author's Return to Europe by way of North America* (London, 1810), p. 114.
95. Hoefte and Vrij, "Free Black and Colored Women", p. 160.

This trend was not visible in most of North America, where manumission was a rare occurrence.[96] Nor was it easy for freed men and women to find employment. The authorities in Savannah, Georgia, banned free people of African descent from owning or working in liquor stores, doing public work, skilled trades, owning real estate, and teaching.[97] In Brazil and the Caribbean, by contrast, free men and women of color grew in numbers as well as economic power, and as they did, they rose in prominence as slave owners. By the early nineteenth century, freedmen in the Danish West Indies owned some two thirds of all urban slaves. In Kingston, Jamaica, no less than eighty-seven percent of the free people of color owned slaves, a percentage higher than that of local whites.[98] Slave origins did not prevent ambitious men and women from buying and owning slaves. One Bahian ex-slave, who trained his own slaves as barbers and musicians, did free ten of them, but obliged each of them in his will to pay for the recitation of fifty masses for his sold. Twelve other slaves he never set free.[99]

That recently manumitted men and women had no qualms about buying slaves themselves is exemplified by the case of a Curaçaoan woman named Rijna Isabella, unearthed by historian Han Jordaan. When she bought a newly arrived enslaved African woman, it transpired that Rijna Isabella had not yet paid the full amount due for her own manumission, which had been arranged two years earlier. Out of the total sum of 350 pesos, she had only put up 102. When her master died, she signed an IOU, for which two slaves whom she had bought served as collateral. Rijna Isabella thus seems to have preferred having her own slaves earn money by hiring themselves out over

96. In New York and New Jersey, for example, there were only a handful of manumissions before the American Revolution: Hodges, *Root and Branch*, p. 102.

97. Whittington B. Johnson, "Free Blacks in Antebellum Savannah: An Economic Profile", *The Georgia Historical Quarterly*, 64:4 (1980), pp. 418–31, 419.

98. Hall, *Slave Society*, p. 143. Trevor Burnard: "Kingston, Jamaica: Crucible of Modernity", in Cañizares-Esguerra, Childs, and Sidbury, *Black Urban Atlantic*, pp. 122–144, 141. Out of fifty-eight free blacks and people of color in Willemstad who signed a mortgage in the period 1737–1754, thirty-four (58.6 per cent) owned slaves. They put most of their slaves to work on plots of land outside the city. Bernard R. Buddingh', *Otrobanda. 'Aen de Oversijde van deese haven': De geschiedenis van Otrobanda, stadsdeel van Willemstad, Curaçao van 1696 tot 1755* (Curaçao, 2006), pp. 251–253.

99. Hendrik Kraay, "The Politics of Race in Independence-Era Bahia: The Black Militia Officers of Salvador, 1790-1840", in Hendrik Kraay (ed.), *Afro-Brazilian Culture and Politics: Bahia, 1790s to 1990s* (Abingdon [etc.], 1998), pp. 30–56, 34. On the prominence of people of African descent – free and enslaved – among barbers in Brazil, see Beatriz Catão Cruz Santos, "Irmandades, oficias mecânicos e cidadania no Rio de Janeiro do século XVIII", *Varia historia*, 26:43 (2010), pp. 131–153, 140. Mariza de Carvalho Soares, "African Barbeiros in Brazilian Slave Ports", in Cañizares-Esguerra, Childs, and Sidbury, *Black Urban Atlantic*, pp. 207–230. Enslaved barbers were also common in seventeenth-century Livorno. Guillaume Calafat and Cesare Santus, "Les avatars du 'Turc'. Esclaves et commerçants musulmans à Livourne (1600–1750)", in Jocelyne Dakhlia and Bernard Vincent (eds), *Les Musulmans dans l'histoire de l'Europe*, vol. I. *Une intégration invisible* (Paris, 2011), pp. 471–522, 488–489.

paying off her debt, indeed using the money thus made toward her own self-purchase.[100] Outside of Curaçao, a few cases have surfaced of slaves buying other slaves. In 1786, for example, the cook Francisco, slave of a brigadier in Buenos Aires, bought the slave Luis for the amount of 400 pesos.[101]

In Saint-Domingue, free women of color not only owned slaves, but were actively involved in the slave trade, purchasing Africans directly from arriving ships in port, while others attended slave auctions.[102] Similarly, in New Orleans, free black women owned slaves for service and speculation and in higher numbers than did free black men, although not in the same proportion and in the same numbers as their white counterparts.[103] Colored women in Saint-Domingue's port cities also owned an appreciable amount of non-human property, including real estate. The same applied to Bridgetown, where colored women kept small shops, taverns, and "hotels".[104]

As perhaps the world's wealthiest colony by the late eighteenth century, Saint-Domingue was visited by thousands of sailors. According to one contemporary estimate, more than 2,500 sailors found themselves in the busiest port of Cap Français at any given time, outnumbering the resident white and free colored populations.[105] This created a demand for prostitution, a common phenomenon in port cities around the Atlantic world and a profession into which enslaved women were not infrequently forced by their (male and female) owners.[106] The numerous bordellos in Cap Français were filled with free women of color, perhaps as many as 3,000 in all by 1777. Other female *gens de couleur* worked as so-called *ménagères* or housekeepers/concubines. These women received high salaries for the combination of household and sexual services they supplied to their employers, who were invariably

100. Han Jordaan, *Slavernij en vrijheid op Curaçao. De dynamiek van een achttiende-eeuws Atlantisch handelsknooppunt* (Zutphen, 2013), p. 68. An alternative explanation would be that legal freedom was not Rijna Isabella's first priority, which would mirror the mindset of some slaves in Buenos Aires who preferred to use the money they earned to buy real estate instead of their own liberty. Miguel A. Rosal, "Negros y pardos propietarios de bienes raíces y de esclavos en el Buenos Aires de fines del período hispánico", *Anuario de estudios Americanos*, 58:2 (2001), pp. 495–512, 500.

101. Rosal, "Negros y pardos propietarios", p. 509.

102. Susan M. Socolow, "Economic Roles of the Free Women of Color of Cap Français", in David Barry Gaspar and Darlene Clark Hine (eds), *More than Chattel: Black Women and Slavery in the Americas* (Bloomington, IN, 1996), pp. 279–297, 286–288.

103. Kimberly S. Hanger, "Landlords, Shopkeepers, Farmers, and Slave-Owners: Free Black Female Property Owners in Colonial New Orleans", in Gaspar and Hine, *Beyond Bondage*, pp. 219–236, 221, 225.

104. Welch, *Slave Society in the City*, p. 172.

105. Scott, "Common Wind", p. 61.

106. Roquinaldo Ferreira, "Slavery and the Social and Cultural Landscapes of Luanda", in Cañizares-Esguerra, Childs, and Sidbury, *Black Urban Atlantic*, pp. 185–206, 191.

members of the economic elite.[107] It was in this capacity that many women of color amassed the capital that allowed them to start their own business. Like poor black women in Buenos Aires, they must have taken pride in the fruits of their labor.[108]

The achievements of free people of color in Caribbean ports did not go unchallenged. Racist ordinances circumscribed the freedoms of the free black and colored population of Willemstad, Curaçao. Playing loud music was forbidden, as was carrying a stick, or walking the streets after dark. Any white was permitted to punish nonwhite behavior considered impertinent with a cane. Besides, the legal testimony of black or colored witnesses lacked judicial force. Specific legislation discriminating against free nonwhites did not exist, with one important exception. After complaints from less affluent whites, a prohibition was introduced in 1749 for blacks and coloreds to keep a shop in town, although they could continue their commercial dealings in their homes and take merchandise to town during the daytime.[109] Free non-whites of color also faced various legal disabilities in Suriname, where their footwear distinguished them from both the slaves and the whites. Different from slaves, manumitted blacks and colored men and women were allowed to wear shoes, albeit still with no socks. Only the freeborn enjoyed that privilege.[110]

In Spanish American cities, free blacks and people of color were not allowed to live on their own, could not become clergymen, scribes or notaries, and were forbidden from having Indian servants. In Venezuela, females were forbidden from wearing gold, silk or pearls, and males did not have the right to walk side by side with whites in the streets, nor were they to be given a chair in white houses.[111] In order to preserve their honor, white guild members of Buenos Aires' shoemaker guild barred non-white master shoemakers who had the same tasks and obligations as their white colleagues from voting in guild elections in Buenos Aires.[112] In Saint-Domingue, the separate legal

107. Dominique Rogers and Stewart King, "Housekeepers, Merchants, Rentières: Free Women of Color in the Port Cities of Colonial Saint-Domingue, 1750–1790", in Douglas Catterall and Jody Campbell (eds), *Women in Port: Gendering Communities, Economies, and Social Networks in Atlantic Port Cities, 1500–1800* (Leiden [etc.], 2012), pp. 357–397, 361–363.
108. Carmen Bernand, "La plèbe ou le peuple? Buenos Aires, fin XVIIIe-début XIXe siècle", *Caravelle. Cahiers du monde hispanique et luso-brésilien*, 84 (2005), pp. 147–168, 162.
109. Klooster, "Subordinate but Proud", p. 289; Han Jordaan, "Free Blacks and Coloreds and the Administration of Justice in Eighteenth-Century Curaçao", *NWIG*, 84 (2010), pp. 63–86, 82.
110. J.D. Kuniss, *Surinam und seine Bewohner oder Nachrichten über die geographischen, physischen, statistischen, moralischen und politischen Verhältnisse dieses Landes während eines zwanzigjährigen Aufenthalts daselbst* (Erfurt, 1805), pp. 73–74.
111. Marianela Ponce, *El ordenamiento jurídico y el ejercicio del derecho de libertad de los esclavos en la Provincia de Venezuela 1730–1768* (Caracas, 1994), pp. 38–39; Pellicer, *Vivencia del honor*, pp. 42, 116–117. Discrimination of free people of color went back to the early days of Spanish American colonization. In 1577, they were already forced to live with their employers in Peru: Frederick P. Bowser, *The African Slave in Colonial Peru 1524–1650* (Stanford, CA, 1974), p. 303.
112. Secreto, "Escravos de Buenos Aires", pp. 37–38.

status of free blacks and *gens de couleur* was not stressed until the 1760s and 1770s, when they could no longer be surgeons or midwives, ride in coaches, have certain types of household furniture, or adopt the dress or hairstyles of whites.[113] These regulations underscore that whites not only resented economic competition from their non-white neighbors, but they also resented the freedom of free people of color to behave in ways similar to whites. Small wonder, therefore, that they objected vehemently to attempts of these adversaries to whiten themselves in Spanish America after the adoption of a formal royal decree – the *gracias al sacar* – that made it possible to purchase whiteness in the late eighteenth century. Thus, two African-descended families in Caracas faced a storm of indignation when they sought permission to be considered white and to have one of their sons enter the priesthood. Their strategy had been to intermarry with each other generation after generation, which was typical of white families that belonged to the colonial elite.[114] In other ways, too, many free people of color made the upper-class white mentality their own. In Caracas, they deliberately used the caste system to exclude those deemed inferior, just as they themselves were shut out from white elite society, as a certain Juan Bautista Arias found out in 1774. This *caraqueño* failed to meet the racial criteria of the *pardo* (mulatto) militia, which concluded from his genealogy that the man was partly Indian, unlike the militia members who were "growing closer each time more to the whites, while they were distancing themselves from the blacks".[115]

CONCLUSION

In conclusion, we can discern that the increasing rhythm of the Atlantic slave trade did more than simply guarantee a steady supply of enslaved workers to the New World's plantations. In some places earlier than others, but almost universally as the eighteenth century advanced, the urban landscape changed along with the dramatic industrialization of the countryside. In a way, the urban Atlantic and, more specifically, the Atlantic ports on either side of the ocean, internalized slavery. Professions typical for cities that had once been monopolized by Europeans began to be filled by men and women who were formally enslaved. To them, city life offered advantages that would have been inconceivable for their rural counterparts, especially the scope of

113. Gabriel Debien, *Études antillaises (XVIIIe Siècle)* (Paris, 1956), p. 75. Yvan Debbasch, *Couleur et liberté. Le jeu de critère ethnique dans un ordre juridique esclavagiste* (Paris, 1967), pp. 38–39, 53–54, 74–75. John D. Garrigus, *Before Haiti. Race and Citizenship in French Saint-Domingue* (New York, 2006), p. 95.

114. Ann Twinam, *Purchasing Whiteness. Pardos, Mulattos, and the Quest for Social Mobility in the Spanish Indies* (Stanford, CA, 2015), pp. 145–147.

115. Twinam, *Purchasing Whiteness*, pp. 207–208.

autonomy they enjoyed and the possibilities to secure manumission. Consequently, free people of color became a feature of Atlantic ports, often continuing the jobs they had mastered as urban slaves.

IRSH 65 (2020), pp. 39–65 doi:10.1017/S0020859020000073

Slaves and Slavery in Kingston, 1770–1815

Trevor Burnard

Wilberforce Professor of Slavery and Emancipation
University of Hull
Cottingham Road, Hull HU6 7RX, United Kingdom

E-mail: T.G.Burnard@hull.ac.uk

Abstract: Historians have mostly ignored Kingston and its enslaved population, despite it being the fourth largest town in the British Atlantic before the American Revolution and the town with the largest enslaved population in British America before emancipation. The result of such historiographical neglect is a lacuna in scholarship. In this article, I examine one period of the history of slavery in Kingston, from when the slave trade in Jamaica was at its height, from the early 1770s through to the early nineteenth century, and then after the slave trade was abolished but when slavery in the town became especially important. One question I especially want to explore is how Kingston maintained its prosperity even after its major trade – the Atlantic slave trade – was stopped by legislative fiat in 1807.

KINGSTON AND THE MEMORY OF SLAVERY

If you wander down to the waterfront of Kingston's magnificent harbour, you will see no reminder of the most important fact about Kingston's history – that it was the "Ellis Island" of African American life in British America, the place where nearly 900,000 Africans were landed to begin what was usually a miserable existence as mostly plantation slaves and occasionally urban slaves between Kingston's founding in 1692 and the abolition of the slave trade in 1808.[1] Only Rio de Janeiro – a slave port for a much longer period than Kingston – surpasses Kingston as the American location where most Africans became American slaves. Yet, there is no marker among the docks, banks, and commercial buildings that comprise the Kingston waterfront, where, in the eighteenth century – peaking in the decades after the end of the American Revolution – thousands of Africans arrived every year to be sold into slavery, sometimes immediately after disembarkation. Indeed, reminders of Kingston's slave past are virtually absent from the thriving city of over

1. Trevor Burnard and Kenneth Morgan, "The Dynamics of the Slave Market and Slave Purchasing Patterns in Jamaica, 1655–1788", *William and Mary Quarterly*, 58 (2001), pp. 205–228.

one million people. The only public monument to slavery in the city is Laura Facey Cooper's impressive but controversial statue in Emancipation Park in the heart of the city's business district, "Redemption Song", which depicts two naked Afro-Jamaicans looking skyward to celebrate emancipation on 1 August 1834.[2] For the most part, however, the role that slavery, the slave trade, and slaves played in creating the most dynamic city in the English-speaking Caribbean (Figure 1) is largely ignored in contemporary Kingston.

Historians, too, have mostly ignored Kingston and its enslaved population. Apart from a series of articles by this author, an article from 1991 by Barry Higman on Jamaican port towns in which Kingston features heavily, a historical geography by Colin Clarke that covers the history of Kingston from 1692 to the late twentieth century, two unpublished theses by graduates of the University of the West Indies (Wilma Bailey and Lorna Simmonds), and an unpublished PhD by Douglas Mann, the history of Kingston has been neglected within British Atlantic historiography.[3] Despite being the fourth largest town in the British Atlantic before the American Revolution and the town with the largest enslaved population in British America before emancipation, the literature on Kingston is sparse. Indeed, its neighbours – Port

2. For criticism of the large endowments of the figures and of the artist as being more connected to Jamaica's elite than to the mass of the population, see Gary Younge, "Kingston", 14 August 2003, *The Guardian*. Available at: https://www.theguardian.com/world/2003/aug/14/arts.artsnews; last accessed 21 December 2019.

3. Colin G. Clarke, *Kingston, Jamaica: Urban Development and Social Change, 1692–1962* (Berkeley, CA, 1975); B.W. Higman, "Jamaican Port Towns in the Early Nineteenth Century", in Franklin W. Knight and Peggy K. Liss (eds), *Atlantic Port Cities: Economy, Culture, and Society in the Atlantic Worlds, 1650–1850* (Knoxville, TN, 1991), pp. 117–148. For works that pertain to Kingston, see also Trevor Burnard, "'The Grand Mart of the Island': The Economic Function of Kingston, Jamaica in the Mid-Eighteenth Century", in Kathleen E. A. Monteith and Glen Richards (eds), *Jamaica in Slavery and Freedom: History, Heritage, and Culture* (Kingston, 2002), pp. 225–241; *idem*, "'Gay and Agreeable Ladies': White Women in Mid-Eighteenth-Century Kingston, Jamaica", *Wadabagei*, 9:3 (2006), pp. 27–49; *idem*, "Kingston, Jamaica: A Crucible of Modernity", in Jorge Canizares-Esguerra, Matt D. Childs and James Sidbury (eds), *The Black Urban Atlantic in the Age of the Slave Trade* (Philadelphia, PA, 2013), pp. 123–146; *idem* and Emma Hart, "Kingston, Jamaica and Charleston, South Carolina: A New Look at Comparative Urbanization in Plantation Colonial British America", *Journal of Urban History*, 39 (2013), pp. 214–234; Wilma Bailey, "Kingston 1692–1843: A Colonial City" (Ph.D., University of the West Indies, 1974); Sheena Boa, "Urban Free Black and Coloured Women: Jamaica 1760–1834", *Jamaican Historical Review*, 18 (1993), pp. 1–6; Lorna Simmonds, "'That Little Shadow of Property and Freedom': Urban Slave Society in Jamaica, 1780–1834" (MA thesis, the University of the West Indies, Mona, 1987); Douglas F. Mann, "Becoming Creole: Material Life and Society in Eighteenth-Century Kingston, Jamaica" (unpublished Ph.D. thesis, University of Georgia, 2005); and James Robertson, "A 1748 'Petition of Negro Slaves' and the Local Politics of Slavery in Jamaica", *William and Mary Quarterly*, 67 (2010), pp. 319–346.

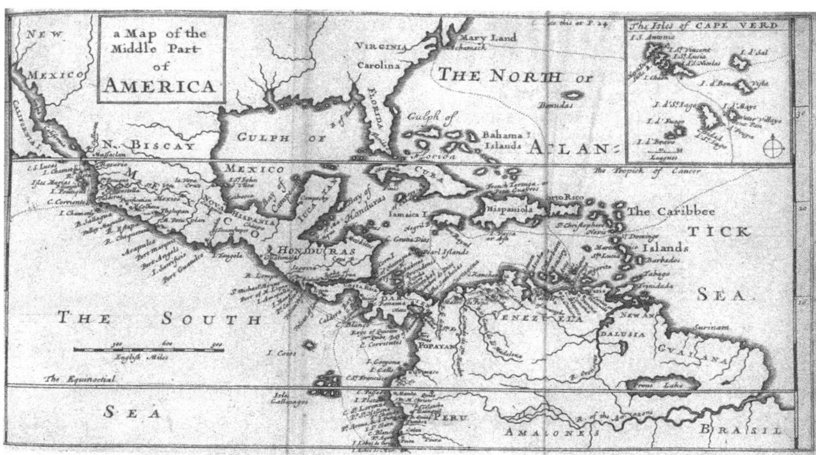

Figure 1. "A Map of the Middle Part of America", in William Dampier, *A New Voyage around the World…* (London, 1697).
JBC Map Collection, 30840–1. John Carter Brown Library, Providence, Rhode Island, USA.

Royal and Spanishtown – are better served by historians.[4] The result of such historiographical neglect is a lacuna in scholarship. We know too little about the role of slavery in shaping Kingston and even less about the lives of the enslaved population who thronged its streets, not least on the waterfront, where in 1832 a large percentage of slaves lived and worked and where, on King Street, near the harbour, every week 10,000 people from town and country attended a "Negro market".[5]

In this article, I examine one period of the history of slavery in Kingston, from when the slave trade in Jamaica was at its height, from the early 1770s through to the early nineteenth century, and then after the slave trade was abolished but when slavery in the town became especially important. One question I especially want to explore is how Kingston maintained its prosperity even after its major trade – the Atlantic slave trade – was stopped by legislative fiat in 1807. In 1793, a committee set up by the Jamaican House of Assembly to enquire into the effects of a possible abolition of the slave trade declared that the abolition of the slave trade "would gradually diminish the number of white inhabitants in the island, and thereby lessen its security"

4. For Spanishtown, see James Robertson, *Gone Is the Ancient Glory: Spanish Town, Jamaica, 1534–2000* (Kingston, 2005). For Port Royal, see Michael Pawson, David Buisseret and Matthew Mulcahy, "'That fatall spott': The Rise and Fall – and Rise and Fall Again – of Port Royal, Jamaica", in Carole Shammas (ed.), *Investing in the Early Modern Built Environment: Europeans, Asians, Settlers and Indigenous Societies* (Leiden, 2012), pp. 191–218.
5. Higman, "Jamaican Port Towns", pp. 137, 139.

and "would cause bankruptcies, create discontents" and that in Kingston "such merchants as have already acquired fortunes by trade, seeing no probability of employing their money to advantage in the purchase of lands in Jamaica, would quit the country, and carry away their capitals; and the traders and shopkeepers, being their customers, would not be able to make their annual remittances, either to their correspondents or to the manufacturers in Great-Britain".[6] Yet, these grim prognostications did not come to pass.

Among the parishes in Jamaica after 1807, Kingston alone did not suffer economic decline. Indeed, if real estate transactions are one guide, Kingston enjoyed an economic boom before and after the abolition of the slave trade. Ahmed Reid and David B. Ryden show that between 1800 and 1810, the price of land continued to soar in Kingston while property prices in the hinterland collapsed: Kingston land prices increased in this period by nearly a quarter, while prices in the interior fell by over forty per cent, returning to levels not seen since before the 1740s.[7] Its boom was testimony to the inventiveness of Kingston residents, who moved seemingly painlessly from providing the slave labour that was the lifeblood of the plantation system to being the fulcrum of British trade with Latin America during the Napoleonic wars.[8] Yet, this move at the top levels of mercantile activity did not reduce the town's commitment to slavery. Indeed, urban slavery, which had been in relative decline in the last years of the eighteenth century, picked up pace after 1807, meaning that by 1815 the percentage of Jamaica's enslaved population that lived in Kingston was higher than at any time since the early eighteenth century.[9]

THE DEMOGRAPHY OF SLAVERY IN KINGSTON

How many enslaved people were there in Kingston and how important were they within the Jamaican slave population? As is often the case for population statistics for this period, the data is confusing and conflicting. There are three ways of establishing the size of the enslaved population: an annual poll tax on slaves for the purposes of revenue collection; occasional censuses (as in 1774 and 1788); and figures derived from the registration of slaves legislation implemented as part of British amelioration of slavery policies from 1817. In most parts of Jamaica, the differences between the numbers of enslaved people enumerated in poll tax records and censuses or slave registration records

6. *Journals of the Assembly of Jamaica*, 9:146–147 (1792).
7. Ahmed Reid and David Ryden, "Sugar, Land Markets, and the Williams Thesis: Evidence from Jamaica's Property Sales, 1750–1810", *Slavery and Abolition*, 34 (2013), pp. 401–424.
8. Dorothy Burne Goebel, "British Trade to the Spanish Colonies, 1796–1823", *American Historical Review*, 43 (1938), pp. 289–294; Frances Armytage, *The Free Port System in the British West Indies: A Study in Commercial Policy, 1766–1822* (London, 1953), pp. 52–71; and Adrian Pearce, *British Trade with Spanish America, 1763–1808* (Liverpool, 2007), chs 4–6.
9. B.W. Higman, *Slave Population and Economy in Jamaica, 1807–1834* (Cambridge, 1976), p. 58.

were not that great. In Jamaica, excluding Kingston, the poll tax numbers of enslaved people enumerated in 1817 were ninety-four per cent of enslaved people registered under the Slave Registration Act of the same year. In Kingston, however, the poll tax recorded only 45.4 per cent of enslaved people resident in the town. In 1788, the percentage was even lower. The number of enslaved people enumerated in the poll tax for that year was just thirty-seven per cent of the enslaved people noted as living in Kingston in a census taken that year.[10]

Edward Long, writing in 1774, claimed that the tax lists were very accurate, arguing that "we have no data so simple, so intelligible, & so certain as the poll Tax returns". But, as he admitted, a "small and limited number [of whites who were exempted] from the payment of the Taxes and Negroes were left out", including such people as overseers and people who did not own land but who rented out their slaves to planters. In the countryside, such exempted persons and their slaves were relatively few in number: Having carefully compared the poll tax records with the actual numbers of slaves in Westmoreland Parish in south-west Jamaica, Long estimated that one seventh of the slave population was not accounted for in the tax records (a somewhat higher percentage than in 1817, where 92.8 per cent of Westmoreland slaves were included in poll tax data). From this investigation, he asserted that although the tax lists do "not shew the whole numbers of Negroes actually on the island [...] the exemption is uniform and cannot affect the list much more at one period than another". The problem was that slavery in Kingston did not accord with these assumptions. The large number of men and women who owned just one or two slaves and who were renters rather than owners of land meant that many slave owners and their slaves were exempted from the poll tax. In 1832, 1,843 of 2,557 slave owners in Kingston (72.1 per cent) owned between one and five enslaved people and just 254 slave owners owned more than ten enslaved people.[11] In addition, as will be discussed below, many enslaved people were kept in merchant yards ready for sale to retail purchasers. It is possible that such enslaved people were not counted as permanent residents of the town. Consequently, as Table 1 shows, the differences in population size between enslaved people listed in poll tax lists and those noted in censuses or under the Slave Registration Act were considerable.

It needs to be noted that although Table 1 looks authoritative, the figures are based on very weak data. I have extrapolated from Long's assessment of the accuracy of the poll tax to make assumptions regarding the total enslaved population both in Kingston and in Jamaica, applying that dubious measure

10. For population figures and explanations of how they are derived, see, for 1807–1834, Higman, *Slave Population and Economy*, pp. 255–256. For the eighteenth century, see David B. Ryden, *West Indian Slavery and British Abolition, 1783–1807* (New York, 2009), pp. 299–302.
11. Higman, *Slave Population and Economy*, p. 275.

Table 1. *Estimates of Jamaica's Slave Population, 1745–1834.*

Year	Poll Tax	Total Slaves	Jamaican Slaves	% Ja. Slaves
1740	4,534	7,556	105,573	7.2
1745	4,649	7,749	119,604	6.5
1769	5,779	9,632	177,557	5.4
1774	5,400	9,000	205,092	4.4
1788	6,162	16,659	224,355	7.4
1797	5,556	13,890	290,898	4.8
1798	5,534	13,835	294,398	4.7
1800	5,996	14,990	320,148	4.7
1801	6,351	15,878	326,695	4.9
1805	6,984	17,460	308,775	5.7
1810	5,847	12,713	333,705	4.4
1815	6,499	14,128	330,984	3.8
1817	8,157	17,954	345,252	5.2
1834	5,764	12,531	309,167	4.1

NB. Between 1797 and 1815, it is assumed that the poll tax accounted for ninety-four per cent of Jamaican slaves and forty-six per cent of slaves in Kingston. Between 1740 and 1774, it is assumed that the poll tax accounted for sixty per cent of slaves in Kingston. Figures have been adjusted accordingly.
Sources: Higman, *Slave Population and Economy*, pp. 255–256; Burnard, "Crucible of Modernity", p. 127; Ryden, *West Indian Slavery and British Abolition*, p. 301.

called "common sense" in order to determine some ratios and using the data from 1788 and 1817 as controls over any wild inferences. The figures need further rationalization and should be treated as extremely tentative. Nevertheless, they do provide a rough guide to population patterns in Kingston over nearly a century.

From this imperfect data, we can make some assumptions about trends in the enslaved population of Kingston over time. Firstly, the enslaved population was considerable by British Atlantic standards. Indeed, Kingston had more slaves and free people of colour than any town in eighteenth-century British America. Between them Boston, Philadelphia, and New York contained 5,343 black people in the 1770s, accounting for less than seven per cent of the total population. Charleston had 6,300 black people, almost all slaves, amounting to fifty-five per cent of the population. Kingston had around 9,000 slaves in 1774 from a population of 14,200, and 16,659 slaves from a population of 26,478 in 1788 (nearly sixty-three per cent of the total population). There were also more enslaved people in Kingston than in Bridgetown, Barbados, by the start of the American Revolution. Bridgetown had 5,600 enslaved residents in 1773, which was forty per cent of a total population estimated at 14,000.[12]

12. Burnard and Hart, "Kingston and Charleston", pp. 217, 219.

Secondly, the size of the enslaved population in Kingston varied over time, changing in accord with developments in the wider society. Overall, the enslaved population in Kingston increased in line with Jamaica's population growth, reaching a peak of 17,940 in 1817, when it was 5.2 per cent of the enslaved population. It was nearly as large in 1805, when there were 17,460 enslaved people in Kingston. If we take the difference between the numbers of slaves enumerated in the poll tax and the real numbers listed in 1788 to be indicative of numbers in 1805 rather than the preferred ratio from 1817, then the actual numbers in 1805 might have been as high as 18,876. Usually, the enslaved population in Kingston was between 4.5 and 5.5 per cent of the Jamaican enslaved population. There was a spike in 1788, when Kingston accounted for 7.4 per cent of Jamaica's slave population. This spike was probably due to the influx of loyalists and their slaves from the newly independent United States.[13] Most of these loyalists settled in Kingston. A report in 1784 to the Assembly of Jamaica noted that of 877 certificates of freedom offered to white foreigners between 1777 and 1784, 495 went to people living in Kingston.[14] A further spike after 1800 probably reflects the influx of refugees and their slaves from Saint-Domingue, most bound by their certificates of residence to remain in Kingston.[15] Possibly, although the population data for 1774 is very much guesswork, the lowest percentage of slaves in Jamaica living in Kingston may have been just before the American Revolution, when the plantation economy was especially prosperous.

Thirdly, enslaved people were always a majority of Kingston's population. Detailed figures from 1788 recorded in the local vestry minutes and tabulated in Tables 2, 3, and 4 show that enslaved people made up 62.9 per cent of the total population. Although, as was true in the Jamaican slave population overall, male slaves made up a slight majority of the enslaved population (52.3 per cent), female slaves were a greater proportion of all females in Kingston than male slaves were of all males. Female slaves were 69.8 per cent of the female population in 1788 and if we include free women of colour in this group, then this percentage increases to 84.6. By contrast, reflecting the

13. Maya Jasanoff, *Liberty's Exiles: American Loyalists in the Revolutionary World* (New York, 2011), p. 257.
14. 8 December 1784, *Journals of the Assembly of Jamaica*, 7:48.
15. Complaints from authorities in Kingston about the burden of caring for refugees from Saint-Domingue and their slaves were constant from 1793, peaking from 1798 to 1800. In 1798, for example, a petition from Kingston residents was presented to the House of Assembly, stating that the French people of colour were a problem in a town suffering under high prices for provisions, the urgent necessities of the poor, and with food in short supply. Kingston found it impossible to cope with a huge influx of enslaved people from Saint-Domingue slaves and was not allowed to send French slaves into the interior. Of the 1,512 French slaves on the island, 1,486 were in Kingston. The petitioners declared that the parishes of Kingston and Port Royal needed relief as they "have equal rights to protection with any other part of the island". 11 December 1798, *Journals of the Assembly of Jamaica*, 10:220.

Table 2. *Kingston's Slave Population by Sex and Colour, 1788.*

Sex	Total Population	Coloured Slaves	Black Slaves	Total Slaves	% Total Population
Male	15,105	498	8,217	8,715	57.7
Female	11,373	581	7,363	7,944	69.8
Total	26,478	1,079	15,580	16,659	62.9

Source: Kingston Vestry Minutes, 28 February 1788, Jamaica Archives.

disproportionate number of white males in the white population, male slaves made up 57.7 per cent of all males and, when free males of colour are included, 68.3 per cent of all males.[16]

The large numbers of black and coloured women over white women may have contributed to a distinctive feature of life in Kingston, which is the extensive and open practice of concubinage of white men with black or coloured mistresses. Concubinage is too benign a word for what was often sexual exploitation. J.B. Moreton was most open on the matter, declaring in 1790 that even the most "honourable gentlemen" had slaves and even coloured daughters who were "lamblike lasses" available for "sport" after social occasions. He made the ribald comment that "when the ball or rigadoon is over" then a man can "escort her to your house or lodging and taste all the wanton and warm endearments she can yield before morning". He also expanded upon the common trope of overtly lascivious coloured women, arguing that such women would be very upset if their male lovers showed restraint in their dealings with them.[17] There was a practical reason, also, why white men preferred concubinage with black or coloured women rather than entering into marriage with a white woman. Christer Petley argues that choosing a white wife was costly, as it meant having to provide the wife with an expensively equipped household in order to keep up "appearances". "Keeping" a black or coloured "housekeeper" was cheaper, allowing a white man to live a more relaxed and moderate lifestyle in a less properly appointed house.[18]

Finally, the enslaved population of Kingston was lighter skinned and possibly more likely to be native-born than the enslaved population as a whole.

16. The data does not allow us to isolate adults from children. The white population was likely dominated by adult men with few children and few adult women, and the population of free people of colour probably had an excess of adult women, making the disproportion of adult women who were slaves or free people of colour greater in this section of the population than in the population overall.

17. J.B. Moreton, *Manners and Customs in the West India Islands* (London, 1790), p. 129.

18. Christer Petley, "Plantations and Homes: The Material Culture of the Early Nineteenth-Century Jamaican Elite", *Slavery & Abolition*, 35 (2014), pp. 446–448.

Table 3. *Kingston's Population by Status, 1788.*

Sex	Slaves	% Total	Freeds	% Total	Whites	% Total
Male	8,715	52.3	1,597	10.6	4,793	31.7
Female	7,944	47.7	1,683	14.8	1,746	15.4
Total	16,659	62.9	3,280	12.4	6,539	24.7

Source: Kingston Vestry Minutes, 28 February 1788, Jamaica Archives.

Table 4. *Kingston's Population by Colour, 1788.*

Sex	Black	% Total	Coloured	% Total	White	% Total
Male	8,500	56.3	1,812	12.0	4,793	31.7
Female	7,670	67.4	1,957	17.2	1,746	15.4
Total	16,170	61.1	3,769	14.2	6,539	24.7

Source: Kingston Vestry Minutes, 28 February 1788, Jamaica Archives.

Most slaves (93.5 per cent) were listed in 1788 as "black" or of fully African descent. A proportion of enslaved people and a majority of free people of colour were described as "coloured", meaning that they fitted into the complex hierarchy of various shades of colour that were characterized in Jamaica by terms such as "mulatto", "sambo", and "quadroon".[19] In 1788, there were 1,079 enslaved persons (6.5 per cent of all slaves) and 2,690 free people of colour (eighty-two per cent in that category) who were coloured, making up 14.2 per cent of the total population and 18.9 per cent of the non-white population. The percentage of enslaved people who were coloured corresponds closely to what Higman and Gisela Eisner believe was the Jamaican norm at the end of slavery – about seven per cent or 23,000 slaves in 1834. Given that the percentage of Jamaican slaves in 1788 who were coloured rather than black would have been appreciably lower than in 1834, as a result of high mortality among slaves and a vibrant Atlantic slave trade, this high figure of coloured enslaved people confirms Higman's contention that slaves of colour were concentrated in Kingston.[20] If we add in the large numbers of coloured free people, the majority of whom were women, Kingston can be viewed as very much the centre of free coloured life in eighteenth- as well as nineteenth-century Jamaica.[21]

19. Moreton, *Manners and Customs*, p. 123.
20. Higman, *Slave Population and Economy in Jamaica*, p. 142; Gisela Eisner, *Jamaica: 1830–1930* (Manchester, 1961), pp. 129, 152.
21. Trevor Burnard, "'Une Véritable Nuisance pour la Communauté'. La Place ambivalent des libres de couleur dans la société libre de la Jamäique au XVIIIe siècle", in Boris Lesueur and Dominque Rogers (eds), *Libres de Couleur dans les Americas* (Paris, 2016).

ENSLAVED POPULATIONS

Kingston had two enslaved populations. One was the resident enslaved population who worked as domestics, tradesmen, boatsmen, and petty traders. The other population comprised transient Africans who arrived in Kingston having endured the Middle Passage and who were sold to local merchants and then resold to purchasers, mostly from the countryside, and who were then sent to work on plantations.[22] These transients may have numbered in their thousands at any one time. New scholarship has altered our views about how these Africans experienced their relatively brief but transformative time spent in Kingston – a period when they underwent the process of being commodified and made into enslaved people. Relatively little attention has customarily been given to this process of transformation, and usually scholars have relied on sensational texts such as that by Alexander Falconbridge, which depicted slave sales as riotous occasions – or "scrambles" – where African captives were the object of a frenzy of over-attention from buyers desperate to acquire their share of human flesh.[23]

In a scramble, the so-called captain or factor set aside the upper deck of the slave ship, sheltered by canvas sails. The Africans stood in rows and, at a signal, prospective buyers rushed the slaves and marked out those they preferred. Falconbridge described purchasers rushing, "with all the ferocity of brutes", taking hold of Africans with their hands or handkerchiefs or ropes. "It is scarcely possible", he lamented, "to describe the confusion of which this mode of selling is productive [...] The poor astonished negroes were so much terrified by these proceedings, that several of them, through fear, climbed over the walls of the court yard, and ran wild about the town; but were soon hunted down and retaken".[24] Falconbridge's account came from the early 1790s, when demand for slaves far outstripped supply. It was, as he suggested, a dangerous way of selling slaves, likely to damage valuable "produce". John Tailyour, the second largest "Guinea factor" selling slaves in Kingston between 1785 and 1796, told a correspondent that if he allowed a person to choose slaves before the date of the sale, "you have made an agreement which would undoubtedly ruin the sale of your Cargo, and when such a thing was insisted on, I would not choose to sell the Cargo".[25] And it never worked in normal times, when ship captains and factors often had to bargain

22. Nicholas Radburn, "Guinea Factors, Slave Sales, and the Profits of the Transatlantic Slave Trade in Late Eighteenth-Century Jamaica: The Case of John Tailyour", *William and Mary Quarterly*, 72 (2015), pp. 243–286.

23. For South Carolina, see Sean Kelley, "Scrambling for Slaves: Captive Sales in Colonial South Carolina", *Slavery & Abolition*, 34 (2013), pp. 1–21.

24. Christopher Fyfe (ed.), *Anna Maria Falconbridge, Narrative of Two Voyages ...* (Liverpool, 2000), pp. 216–217.

25. Tailyour to Thomas Jones, 17 February 1798, John Tailyour Letterbook 1788–1790, Box 9, Tailyour Papers, William L. Clements Library, University of Michigan, Ann Arbor.

hard with purchasers and work out complicated credit terms to get rid of all their enslaved people. "Refuse" enslaved people – the old, sick, and diseased – were especially difficult to sell and occasionally were unceremoniously dumped on the waterfront, dying without medical attention in front of uncaring spectators.[26] It was an altogether unedifying process. As Kenneth Morgan notes, "the process involved the commodification of people, selling off the remaining slaves at the end of a sale rather like a shop-owner marking down the price of damaged fruit in order to sell his produce".[27]

Over time, however, ship captains came to favour selling wholesale to merchants who then sold on enslaved Africans at retail prices from their merchant houses in town. As early as the start of the eighteenth century, the Royal African Company sold slaves in Kingston from a building in the town rather than from the decks of ships. When Olaudah Equiano was delivered to Bridgetown at mid-century this practice was common. Equiano described being taken ashore to "the merchant's yard" where "we were all pent up together without regard to age or sex".[28] One way in which we can see the evolution of slave-trading practices is how, by the mid-eighteenth century, most enslaved people were sold to merchants, rather than to planters, and in much larger lots than in the seventeenth century, usually between ten and forty but sometimes as many as 100 or more.[29] Path-breaking research by Louis Nelson into the architecture of slave traders' houses, such as Hibbert House, a surviving eighteenth-century house once owned by Kingston's largest slave trader, reveals that the cellars of merchant houses were designed to be containment cells, secured by a single strong door with ventilation from a single barred window opening. Slaves were kept there for some time before being moved from the cellar and paraded in the rear yard and gallery.[30] These sales were painful. John Tailyour related to his cousin Simon Taylor, who had bought one sister but left the other – "a girl with one eye" – in Tailyour's

26. J.B. Moreton claimed that, in the 1780s, "dead bodies" were "concealed in the hold" of ships and then thrown overboard "least any report should circulate of the cargo's being sickly". Moreton, *West India Custom and Manners*, p. 145.

27. Kenneth Morgan, *Transatlantic Slavery* (London, 2016), p. 53. For the importance of credit in the trade, see Robin Pearson and David Richardson, "Social Capital, Institutional Innovation and Atlantic Trade before 1800", *Business History*, 50 (2008), pp. 765–780; Kenneth Morgan, "Merchant Networks, the Guarantee System and the British Slave Trade to Jamaica in the 1790s", *Slavery & Abolition*, 37 (2016), pp. 334–352; and Nicholas Radburn, "Keeping 'the wheel in motion': Trans-Atlantic Credit Terms, Slave Prices, and the Geography of Slavery in the British Americas, 1755–1807", *Journal of Economic History*, 75 (2015), pp. 660–689.

28. Olaudah Equiano, *The Interesting Narrative of the Life of Olaudah Equiano* ... ed. Vincent Carretta, *Unchained Voices: An Anthology of Black Voices in the English-Speaking World in the Eighteenth Century* (London: [1996], 2004), p. 206.

29. Burnard and Morgan, "Dynamics of the Slave Market", pp. 206–207.

30. Louis P. Nelson, *Architecture and Empire in Jamaica* (New Haven, CT, 2016), pp. 30–34; and James Robertson, "Eighteenth-Century Jamaica's Ambivalent Cosmopolitanism", *History*, 99 (2014), pp. 607–631.

store, that the girl was "crying most dreadfully" on account of being separated from her sibling.[31]

The move away from selling aboard ship was codified in 1792 by the Assembly of Jamaica, who ordered that the sale of all newly arrived Africans "shall be conducted on shore".[32] It made the process a very public one and connected it more closely to the commercial rhythms of Kingston. Buyers purchasing enslaved people at Hibbert's house likely collected their property from the rear piazza and then escorted them out via the side gate and down Duke Street. The newly purchased slaves would then be displayed to the public as they were transferred from town to countryside. Some observers were shocked by the way in which this was done. The editor of the *Royal Gazette* tut-tutted in 1791 that "the indecency of parading newly purchased Negroes through the streets has been frequently noticed". He was outraged by a recent parade in which "a full-grown negro fellow in a very infirm state was led along Harbour Street without the least covering".[33]

The Atlantic slave trade to Kingston reached its peak in the thirty years before abolition took effect in 1808. As Table 5 shows, Kingston received 358,369 slaves through 1,200 slave voyages between 1770 and 1808. This accounted for 40.5 per cent of the 885,545 Africans sent to the British Caribbean in this period and 34.8 per cent of all British slave voyages. Kingston was far and away the largest port of slave importation in Jamaica, accounting for eighty-nine per cent of all shipments.[34] "Guinea merchants" were doubtful that other ports in Jamaica had the infrastructure necessary to sell enslaved people. John Tailyour warned a correspondent not to sell except at Kingston for "experience has shown the danger of making sales at the outports, and I would not wish to make the trial myself [...] I would not sell at Port Morant as no-one would come to a trade there".[35] Only a proportion of these African captives remained in Jamaica. Many slaves were re-exported in the 1780s and 1790s, notably to Cuba, but also to Saint-Domingue, Louisiana, Savanna, Providence, Cartagena, and Trinidad. Between 1786 and 1788, Alexandre Lindo, the leading slave broker in Kingston, brought in 7,873 Africans and sold 7,510 as slaves, with 4,780 (73.6 per cent)

31. Tailyour to Simon Taylor, 6 January 1790, Simon Taylor Papers, XIV/51, Institute of Commonwealth Studies, London.

32. Bryan Edwards, *The History, Civil and Commercial, of the British Colonies in the West Indies* (London, 1801), vol. II, pp. 115–116.

33. *Royal Gazette*, 15 July 1791.

34. *Transatlantic Slave Trade Database* http://slavevoyages.org/. The figures in this database accord closely to data collected by Jamaicans in this period. A report to the House of Assembly noted 85,528 slaves landed between November 1792 and November 1799, with, for example, 20,355 slaves landed in 1793. The database records 20,507 slaves landed in Kingston in 1793. "Account of the Number of Slaves Imported into Kingston from Africa, November 1792–November 1799", 13 December 1799, *Journals of the Assembly of Jamaica*, 10:367–372.

35. John Tailyour to Thomas Jones, 17 February 1788, Letterbook 1788–1790, Tailyour Papers.

Table 5. *The Atlantic Slave Trade to Kingston, 1770–1808.*

Years	Voyages	Slaves Landed	Average Size Cargo
1770–72	76	20,104	264.5
1773–75	194	46,906	241.8
1776–78	84	24,092	286.8
1779–81	40	14,688	367.2
1782–84	67	29,519	440.6
1785–87	60	22,700	378.3
1788–90	86	21,987	255.7
1791–93	154	41,764	271.2
1794–96	100	32,322	323.2
1797–99	95	33,526	352.9
1800–02	115	36,165	314.5
1804–06	61	16,771	274.9
1807–08	68	17,825	262.1
Total	1,200	358,369	298.6

Source: Transatlantic Slave Trade Database. Available at: http://slavevoyages.org/; last accessed 25 November 2019.

re-exported. The percentage of enslaved people who died between arrival and sale was 4.6, close to mortality in the Middle Passage by the 1780s.[36] The percentages re-exported varied per ship, with all 180 slaves on the *Snow John*, which arrived in Kingston on 9 April 1787, being sold off the island. Similarly, in the 1790s, the numbers of slaves re-exported varied widely from year to year. Overall, 11,616 slaves, from among 85,258 Africans arriving in Kingston between November 1792 and November 1799, were sold to foreign buyers, mostly Cuban. But while virtually no enslaved people were re-exported in the booming years of 1793 and 1798 (215 and 655 respectively), many enslaved people were sold off the island between 1795 and 1797. In 1795, 4,214 slaves or 36.8 per cent of all enslaved people imported into Kingston were sent off the island on ninety-five ships.[37]

Africans arriving in Kingston came from every slave exporting region of Africa, except the southern tip of the continent. The biggest region of exportation was the Bight of Biafra, which accounted for 43.8 per cent of enslaved people landed in Jamaica between 1776 and 1800 and 51.2 per cent between 1801 and 1808. The Gold Coast and Angola were sizeable areas of exportation to Jamaica, comprising nearly a quarter of slaves landed in the case of the Gold Coast between 1776 and 1800 and 17.6 per cent in the case of Angola. But enslaved people also came from Benin, the Windward Coast, Sierra Leone,

36. Herbert S. Klein and Stanley L. Engerman, "Slave Mortality in the British Slave Trade 1791–1797", in Roger Anstey and P.E.H. Hair (eds), *Liverpool, the African Slave Trade and Abolition* (Liverpool, 1989), pp. 113–122.

37. *Ibid.*; 4 February 1800, *Journals of the Assembly of Jamaica*, 1799, 10:433.

and Senegambia.[38] Thus, the ethnic origins of enslaved people arriving in Kingston were diverse. That diversity was enhanced by how enslaved people were sold, gathered together from many nations in merchant yards and containment cells. It is thought that Jamaicans had strong preferences in favour of slaves from the Gold Coast and the Bight of Benin and were antagonistic to slaves from Old Calabar (Biafra), but slave price data from merchants' accounts does not support such claims.[39] Winde and Allardyce (1773–1775) and Watt and Allardyce (1775–1776) opened up to the House of Assembly their records of twenty-nine slave shipments from six regions of Africa. As Table 6 shows, slaves from Benin, Senegambia, and the Gold Coast fetched a premium over slaves from Biafra and Sierra Leone. Nevertheless, the differences in price by ethnicity must be calibrated against a greater price differential by year. The seven slave shipments that they brokered in 1773 and 1774 (including two from the Gold Coast and three from Benin) fetched an average price of £58.79, but that price fell to £54.94 for seven shipments in 1775 and plummeted to £46.30 per slave for twelve slave sales in the war-plagued year of 1776. After war broke out between Britain and America in July 1776, Watt and Allardyce did not receive more than £48.11 per slave for any shipment and had four shipments that had "average prices" below, sometimes well below their average for the three years recorded of £47.31.[40]

An even more pronounced pattern of relatively small differences by ethnicity and great differences by year can be found for thirty slave sales brokered by Barrett and Parkinson, William Ross, Allan and White, and William Daggers between 1789 and 1792. Between 1789 and 1791, slaves from the Gold Coast (1,355 slaves sold for an average price of £67.27) and Sierra Leone (131 slaves at £68.42) were more expensive than slaves from Biafra (3,826 at £65.72) and from the Windward Coast (£64.20). But these differences were much less than the differences between sales made between 1789 and 1791, when slaves were bought at an average price of £65.94 currency (£47.13 sterling) and seven slave sales made in 1792 (three from Biafra and three from the Gold Coast), when the price jumped by 26.7 per cent from the previous three years to reach £83.43 or £59.59 sterling per slave.[41] In other words, differences in price were more significant over time than differences in the ethnicity of captives. An enslaved person from the Bight of Biafra cost more to purchase in 1792 than an enslaved person from the Gold Coast did two years previously, even though Gold Coast

38. Trevor Burnard, *Planters, Merchants, and Slaves: Plantation Societies in British America, 1650–1820* (Chicago, IL, 2015), p. 171.

39. Morgan, *Transatlantic Slavery*, p. 53. For statements favouring Gold Coast slaves and not favouring Ebo slaves from Biafra, see John Tailyour to William Miles, 3 October 1789 and 22 November 1789, Letterbook 1788–1790, Tailyour Papers.

40. *Journals of the Assembly of Jamaica*, 1793, 9:149.

41. *Ibid.*

Table 6. *Slave Sales by Year and Ethnicity, 1773–1776, Winde and Allardyce, Watt and Allardyce.*

Region/Year	No. Slaves	Ave. Price Currency	Ave. Price Sterling
Senegambia	280	£51.35	£36.68
Sierra Leone	716	46.24	33.02
Windward Coast	838	50.11	35.79
Gold Coast	1,476	50.91	36.36
Bight of Benin	2,453	52.68	37.63
Bight of Biafra	1,753	45.99	32.85
1773/4	1,777	58.79	41.99
1775	2,133	54.94	39.24
1776	3,961	46.30	33.07

NB. Jamaica currency converts to sterling at a rate of 1.4:1.
Source: Journals of the Assembly of Jamaica, 1793, 9:149.

slaves appear to have been more desirable to purchase than enslaved people from the Bight of Biafra.

All parties involved in the complex business of the Atlantic slave trade were highly sensitive to trade conditions, such as war, or the availability of credit, or the prices fetched for enslaved people at certain ports. There were surges and collapses in the slave trade to individual colonies based on merchants' reaction to a host of separate pieces of business information.[42] They were especially sensitive to price changes. It is not accidental that high prices in 1773 and 1774 led to a surge in shipments to Kingston between 1774 and 1776. And a rapid decline in prices once the American War of Independence had broken out contributed to the number of slave voyages to Kingston reducing from an average of sixty-five between 1774 and 1776 to just fourteen per annum between 1777 and 1782. The extraordinary jump in prices after the Saint-Domingue revolt, started in 1792, made Kingston an attractive destination for slaving captains, especially as sugar prices increased and as planters made large excess profits. The wealthy Kingston-based planter Simon Taylor, for example, saw his net profits from sugar jump following the start of the French Revolution from £17,639 in 1788 to an average of £32,635 per annum between 1789 and 1792, with a peak of £42,555.65 net profit in 1791.[43] To cater to this growing wealth, the number of slave voyages into

42. Sheryllynne Haggerty, "Risk and Risk Management in the Liverpool Slave Trade", *Business History*, 51 (2009), pp. 817–834; Kenneth Morgan, "Remittance Procedures in the Eighteenth-Century British Slave Trade", *Business History Review*, 79 (2005), pp. 715–749; and Stephen D. Behrendt, "Markets, Transaction Cycles, and Profits: Merchant Decision Making in the British Slave Trade", *William and Mary Quarterly*, 58 (2001), pp. 171–204.

43. Christer Petley, *White Fury: A Jamaican Slaveholder and the Age of Revolution* (Oxford, 2018).

Kingston increased from thirty-five to seventy-five from 1792 to 1793 while the numbers of the enslaved landed jumped from 9,791 to 20,507. Similarly, slave imports jumped from 13,384 in 1799 to 19,019 in 1800 when slave prices increased from £58.54 in 1798 to £72.24 in 1799, according to data from the books of Aspinall and Hardy and Hardy, Pennock and Brittan.[44]

Table 5 shows frequent surges and slumps in the slave trade: it was buoyant before the American Revolution and then experienced a dramatic drop during the American War of Independence. 1780 marked the nadir, with just 4,091 slaves arriving on the island. War-related problems were one reason for the decline. Another problem reducing slave traffic to Jamaica was extremely low prices. In 1779, for example, 258 enslaved people from the Gold Coast on board the *Rumbold* fetched just £32.75 per slave, a decline of eighty-five per cent from what Winde and Allardyce had received for 410 Gold Coast enslaved people arriving in 1775.[45] Slave traders tried to deal with war problems by sending enslaved people in much larger shipments – the average size of slave shipments was 440 slaves between 1782 and 1784, compared with 241 between 1773 and 1775. The end of the war saw a spurt in slave voyages, with 14,654 enslaved people landed in 1784. This was followed by a decline as competition for slaves from Saint-Domingue in the late 1780s proved too intense for Jamaicans to cope with. Between 1786 and 1790, the prices that traders achieved in Saint-Domingue – prime adult male slaves fetched 40.8 per cent more than in Jamaica – reached levels that were not to be surpassed until the mid-1840s in Cuba.[46] Consequently, the supply of enslaved people to Kingston reached a post-Seven Years' War low in 1788 when only 3,613 enslaved people were landed. Nevertheless, slave prices were very high, perhaps because supply was so short, especially in 1792. A trader commented that "even indifferent negroes command very high prices" and that slave prices were at their highest point for seventy-five years.[47]

The response to high prices in 1792, as we have seen, was a spurt in slave trade numbers in 1793. This boom resulted from three interrelated things – turbulence in the Saint-Domingue coffee and sugar markets as slave rebellion threatened white control; the sudden emergence of abolitionism as a political force, making fearful planters stock up on enslaved people in case the trade was suddenly stopped; and, most of all, booming sugar prices, as Britain took

44. *Journals of the Assembly of Jamaica*, 1799, 10:436.

45. *Journals of the Assembly of Jamaica*, 1793, 9:149; Trevor Burnard and John Garrigus, *The Plantation Machine: Atlantic Capitalism in French Saint-Domingue and British Jamaica* (Philadelphia, PA, 2016).

46. David Eltis and David Richardson, "Prices of African Slaves Newly Arrived in the Americas, 1673–1865: New Evidence on Long-Run Trends and Regional Differentials", in David Eltis, Frank D. Lewis, and Kenneth L. Sokoloff (eds), *Slavery in the Development of the Americas* (Cambridge, 2004), pp. 201, 208.

47. Seymour Drescher, "The Shocking Birth of British Abolitionism", *Slavery & Abolition*, 33 (2012), p. 583.

advantage of French disarray by opening up re-exportation to foreign markets. But the boom ended almost as soon as it started. The immense importation of enslaved people into Kingston led to a glut, and by July 1793 "the rage for selling Guinea cargoes" had "considerably subsided". Moreover, slave-trading merchants in Britain were afflicted by a major credit crunch in Britain beginning in February 1793. The outbreak of the French Revolution also raised costs of shipping and insurance from Africa, while yellow fever raged throughout the island and throughout the Americas. Slave sale prices quickly declined. Nevertheless, the numbers of enslaved people entering Kingston only fell slightly, to an average of 12,124 enslaved people imported per annum between 1794 and 1800.[48]

Planters continued to prosper in the 1790s thanks to high sugar prices and beneficial trade investments. The boom led planters to invest heavily in land, machinery, and enslaved people to take advantage of rising prices through dramatically increasing productivity. At the same time, foreign powers, notably Spanish Cuba (the principal beneficiary of Saint-Domingue's collapse), took advantage of high sugar prices and more extensive and more fertile lands as well as investment in industrial plant to ramp up their sugar-producing capacity. Kingston merchants benefited for a time, as we have seen, exporting increasing numbers of enslaved people to Cuba and other foreign places. But rising Cuban sugar output eventually led to falling prices for overextended Jamaican planters who, David Ryden argues, were trapped in an upward cycle of "irrational exuberance" in the 1790s. Economic reality, however, caught up with overproducing and over-indebted planters, who were paying over the odds for fresh inputs of African workers to grow more sugar than a glutted British market could handle. Jamaican planters, who specialized in low-grade sugar, were especially badly affected by the end of the sugar boom. A crash in the speculative market for sugar in Hamburg in 1799 led to a bust in sugar prices and the collapse of European sugar markets. Planter income plummeted and many could no longer afford slaves. Between 1804 and 1806, annual slave sales were just 5,590, with only 4,473 slaves landing in Kingston in 1805. The imminent abolition of the slave trade meant that sales picked up in 1806 and especially in 1807, as planters took their last opportunity to buy enslaved people before such purchases became impossible. Jamaican estates were still profitable if well run, but the overextension of the 1790s led to many planters

48. Morgan, "Merchant Networks", p. 343; *idem*, "James Rogers and the Bristol Slave Trade", *Historical Research*, 76 (2003), pp. 189–216; Radburn, "Keeping the 'Wheel in Motion'", pp. 680–682; *idem*, "Guinea Factors", pp. 277–278. For how quickly the market turned from boom to bust, see Bruce L. Mouser (ed.), *A Slaving Voyage to Africa and Jamaica: The Log of the Sandown, 1793–1794* (Bloomington, IN, 2002), pp. 111–117. For yellow fever, see John McNeill, *Mosquito Empire: Ecology and War in the Greater Caribbean, 1620–1914* (New York, 2010); and David Patrick Geggus, *Slavery, War, and Revolution: The British Occupation of Saint Domingue 1793–1798* (Oxford, 1982), p. 121.

struggling in the 1800s. One indication of their struggles was a decline in land prices outside Kingston, which reduced by seventeen per cent between 1800 and 1805 and by a calamitous twenty-nine per cent between 1805 and 1810.[49]

THE PROFITABILITY OF SLAVE TRADING

The slave trade was large and very lucrative for those involved. Morgan notes that the commissions that John Tailyour received from "Guinea trading" were £36,792 sterling between 1785 and 1792, allowing him to retire in comfort to his native Scotland, where he died on 11 February 1816 with a net worth of nearly £100,000. He made an annual profit of between £5,000 and £6,000 sterling. His partners, Peter Ballantine and James Fairlie, died around the same time, with £26,025 and £46,294 respectively in non-landed property.[50] Tailyour's peak years of slave trading were in 1793 and 1794, when he was factor for twenty-eight slave voyages and 9,262 slaves. In these years, his firm sold twenty-two per cent of all slaves landed in Jamaica. Between 1786 and 1796, they sold eleven per cent of Jamaican slave cargoes.[51] Alexandre Lindo, the most substantial slave trader in Kingston, was so wealthy that he could arrange to lend the amazing sum (most of it gained through credit, of course, which was to be a problem when Napoleon reneged on the deal) of £500,000 to Napoleon for his campaign in Haiti in 1802 and 1803. Thomas Hibbert, Lindo's predecessor as Kingston's biggest slave trader, rose from nothing (his family had been weavers in Manchester) to great wealth during his forty-six-year residence in Kingston. When he died, he left three nephews £215,000 each. They later also became involved in slave trading.[52]

Yet, in 1788, Kingston merchants realized that there was a growing abolitionist movement in Britain with massive public support whose adherents were determined to abolish the trade in slaves with Africa. Taylor was appalled that Britain could even consider ending the slave trade, thinking in 1788 that the discussion about this matter showed that a "general madness has pervaded all ranks of People in Britain", encouraging them to "interfere with a Trade they seem not to understand and to pass laws to Rob their fellow subjects in the West Indies of their property". Writing on the eve of the fall of the Bastille in Paris, he lamented that "I cannot think it possible a trade so

49. Ryden, *West Indian Slavery and British Abolition*, pp. 234–239; Reid and Ryden, "Sugar, Land Markets and the Williams Thesis", p. 16.

50. Morgan, "Merchant Networks", p. 345.

51. Radburn, "Guinea Factors", p. 261.

52. *Ibid.*, p. 283; Jackie Ranston, *The Lindo Legacy* (London, 2000), pp. 50–63; Katie Donington, "Transforming Capital: Slavery, Family, Commerce and the Making of the Hibbert Family", in Catherine Hall *et al.*, *Legacies of British Slaveholding: Colonial Slavery and the Formation of Victorian Britain* (Cambridge, 2014), pp. 203–249; *idem*, *The Bonds of Family: Slavery, Commerce, and Culture in the British Atlantic World* (Manchester, 2019).

profitable to Britain and necessary to the Colony's can be thrown away to please a parcel of Rogues and Fools". Abolitionist actions, he noted, had an unintended effect. News of movements to abolish the slave trade alarmed planters and "the fear of it makes Slaves in very great demand and greater averages are made now than were ever known before".[53]

Kingston merchants had no reason, therefore, to believe that they would participate in what proponents of the abolition of the slave trade argued was a sensible readjustment of the Jamaican plantation economy to make planters care for their existing enslaved people. Supporters of abolition in the House of Lords, such as the Duke of Gloucester, thought that planters would not be harmed by abolition as they had been lured into bad business practices by their reliance on the slave trade. Without fresh inputs of slave labour encouraging bad behaviour, he argued, planters would be forced to treat their workers more humanely.[54] In the debates on abolition, however, Kingston slave traders were condemned for their willingness to sell enslaved people in wartime to enemies who were increasing their enslaved populations and plantation output at Britain's expense. The British parliament passed an act in 1806 forbidding merchants from trading enslaved people with foreigners. And, unlike what happened in 1834, when slave owners were compensated for their losses from their property being freed, no Kingston merchant was given money to compensate for the loss of a very lucrative business.[55] While there was some concern about what would happen to the £2,641,200 that Liverpool reputedly had at stake in the Atlantic slave trade in 1807, the losses of Kingston merchants from slave abolition were not considered.[56]

What happened to Kingston slave factors when the abolition of the slave trade occurred is an unstudied topic. Thus, the conclusions offered below are very tentative. It seems, however, that the ending of the slave trade in 1807 did not dampen economic growth in Kingston. Land prices, as we have noted, continued to rise in the first decade of the 1800s and mansions belonging to merchant princes continued to be built in Kingston's suburbs. The commercial life of Kingston remained buoyant despite the closing of its most significant trade. What seems to have happened is that Kingston merchants used their contacts in Spanish America to whom they had sold enslaved

53. Taylor to J. and A. Alexander, 7 September 1788 and 12 July 1789, Letterbook 1788–90, Tailyour Papers.

54. Ryden, *West Indian Slavery and British Abolition*, pp. 257–258.

55. David Richardson, "The Ending of the British Slave Trade in 1807: The Economic Context", in Stephen Farrell *et al.* (eds), *The British Slave Trade: Abolition, Parliament and People* (Edinburgh, 2007), pp. 127–140. George Hibbert (1757–1837), nephew of the Kingston slave trader Thomas (1710–1780), was a leader of the West India interest and argued for compensation for traders affected by the events of 1807. He met with no success. Donington, "Transforming Capital", p. 214.

56. Kenneth Morgan, "Liverpool's Dominance in the British Slave Trade, 1740–1807", in David Richardson *et al.* (eds), *Liverpool and Transatlantic Slavery* (Liverpool, 2007), p. 15.

people in the 1790s to undermine Spanish commerce by importing cheap and desirable manufactured goods acquired out of Britain from its initial burst into industrialization. Adrian Pearce calculates that, in 1807, the value of British exports to Spanish America, mostly going through free ports in the Caribbean, of which Jamaica's was by far the most important, was in the region of £3–4 million (or 13 million pesos), making up about six per cent of total British exports. It is difficult to know how much of this money was routed through Kingston, but Pearce suggests that the town was the major entrepôt through which British goods reached Spanish America.

This market was a rich field for British manufactured goods, helping to stimulate industrialization in Britain and providing streams of money, including precious bullion, for Kingston middlemen. As Pearce suggests, this trade was especially important between 1806 and 1808, when exports, legal and illegal, to Spanish America peaked and helped to compensate for the wartime crisis in British trade with Europe in these years. The exact amount of trade and bullion that passed through Kingston to Spanish America is unclear, but it must have been of the order of £1–2 million sterling per annum in the first decade of the 1800s. That amount of money was of an order of magnitude greater than the value of the slave trade, which probably brought in around £1 million in a year only in 1793, when slave imports topped 20,000, and £300,000–400,000 in the dead years of the mid-1800s.[57] As Reid and Ryden explain, Kingston's "nimble" traders quickly readjusted to the changing imperial economy by transferring their capital from slave-trading ventures into conveying manufactured goods from Britain to Latin America. Thus, they argue, it was not the merchants who organized the slave trade who suffered most from its abolition, but the planter class, whose fixed investment depended upon slavery, who were especially financially affected.[58]

THE ENSLAVED EXPERIENCE

The records that survive from Kingston contain little information about how slaves lived, except when they are written about as accessories or impediments to how whites went about their lives. We have no direct testimony from an enslaved person from Kingston in this period and not much data about how slaves worked, how they spent their relatively limited leisure time, or what they thought or felt. All of the evidence we have about enslaved life in Kingston between 1770 and 1815 comes from white-created sources. These sources tend to be highly negative about black Jamaicans' capacity. Occasionally, a slave is treated favourably in the white press, as in 1791

57. Pearce, *British Trade with Spanish America*, pp. 236–250; Goebel, "British Trade to the Spanish Colonies".
58. Reid and Ryden, "Sugar, Land Markets and the Williams' Thesis", p. 20.

when it was noted how "a negro fellow who died last week" had amassed a small fortune of £200 "following the very opposite professions of Bucher and chimney sweep, Cook and Gardener". The report concluded, however, that the slave had bequeathed this large sum to his mistress – a statement that stretches plausibility.[59]

More often, however, slaves are mentioned only as being public nuisances, such as the slaves who turned up to every funeral procession to "insult the feelings of those who occupy the succeeding chaise" and who disrupt religious services by talking loudly. The author thought that the most suitable punishment for such people would be flagellation.[60] The underlying tone in which slaves were discussed was one approaching contempt. The *Royal Gazette* complained that it had been reported that "the body of a negro, in a putrid and offensive state", had been lying on the road for several days without being removed by legislative fiat. The newspaper expressed little sympathy with the dead man but did think that he should have been removed from the road as he was "offensive to decency".[61] Instead, writers to the paper tended to congratulate themselves for taking the amelioration of slavery seriously. One writer noted how a "woman was prosecuted for her severities against her negroes" and concluded from this not that slaves were badly treated but that Jamaicans were willing to prosecute whites when they did not act as they should.[62] Assumptions about the character of the urban enslaved from white sources, however, show unremitting hostility. White hostility to enslaved people in Kingston was aggravated not only by the constant contact they had with enslaved people, but by the nature of urban slavery, in which enslaved people tended to be relatively well-treated and independent domestics or skilled tradesmen and in which the gap between the enslaved and the free coloured populations was much smaller than on the plantations. The enslaved had more possibilities in Kingston than on the plantation not only to acquire competence through self-hiring, but to challenge, through their comparative affluence and ability to create lives for themselves separate to those imagined for them by their owners, the underlying principles of white supremacy. The *Royal Gazette* argued ten years earlier, for example, against slaves being able to hire themselves out for wages because they felt slaves would not work for money but instead were satisfied with "Idleness, Drunkenness, Gaming and thievery".[63]

Urban slavery was different from slavery in general because the jobs that urban enslaved people did were different from those on the plantation. They were engaged in a variety of artisanal activities but were concentrated mainly

59. *Royal Gazette*, 20 August 1791.
60. *Ibid.*, 2 September 1791.
61. *Ibid.*, 7 July 1791.
62. *Ibid.*, 30 July 1791.
63. *Ibid.*, 3 November 1781.

in ship carpentry, building and road construction, furniture making, coppering, smithing, tailoring and seamstressing, cobbling, and some limited processing of agricultural products. The urban enslaved were much more likely than plantation slaves to be skilled in a number of occupations and described in runaway ads as "jack of all trades".[64] An example of the multiple skills the urban enslaved had can be seen in an advertisement by Stephen Prosser in 1780 seeking to sell "a young negroe wench" in which he described his enslaved property as being not only "a good cook", but as someone who could also "wash and iron, and is a little of a semptress and used to marketing".[65] Visitors to Jamaica were occasionally impressed at the skills of urban enslaved people. Johann Waldeck, a German traveller who spent some time in Kingston during the American War of Independence, marvelled at how the nineteen enslaved people owned by his friend, a master carpenter, "finish the finest cabinet work, mostly from mahogany". They had been trained so well, he asserted, that they did "the most excellent cabinet work", allowing his German friend to "no longer work" and amass enough money to become a real estate speculator. Waldeck "was surprised at how competent the black slaves could be".[66]

Some of these jobs brought enslaved people money and made them closer in function to the jobs done by free people of colour. But some jobs were very unpleasant and even less desired than working as a plantation slave. A fairly large number of enslaved people were employed by the government in public works schemes doing hard repetitive work while being organized in gangs under the supervision of slave drivers. For example, in August 1805, enslaved people from the heavily populated Kingston workhouse were engaged in digging "the foundations of the new bridge to be thrown over the town gully". Some enslaved people were also employed as sailors. A newspaper advertisement in 1800 asked for owners to provide "sailor negroes in such Gangs as may be required with Tickets". Most enslaved people, however, especially female slaves, worked as domestics. Lorna Simmonds estimates that two thirds of Kingston slaves in the early nineteenth century worked within urban households or in adjoining "negro yards" as housekeepers, in transport or as waiting men or cooks.[67]

What is striking about all these jobs is that they were public facing. Few urban enslaved people experienced the anonymity common in the countryside for most field hands, who could avoid contact with whites most of the time.[68]

64. Mann, "Beyond Creole", p. 180.

65. *Royal Gazette*, 13 May 1780.

66. Johann Waldeck. "Hessian Accounts of America", Ms. 2006, National Library of Jamaica, Kingston, 21–122 ff.

67. Simmonds, "'That Little Shadow of Property and Freedom'", pp. 129, 152, 164–165, 175–180; *Royal Gazette*, 3–10 February 1781, 27 September–4 October 1800, 3–10 August 1805.

68. Trevor Burnard, *Mastery, Tyranny, and Desire: Thomas Thistlewood and His Slaves in the Anglo-Jamaican World* (Chapel Hill, NC, 2004), p. 192.

Urban enslaved people were constantly present, either as workers or as participants in the flourishing urban slave markets. Such markets were formally regulated in 1781 by an Act of Assembly. They operated daily and were accompanied by hawking or peddling in the street. Enslaved people formed a counterpoint, perhaps an opposition to regular shopkeepers, operating on the fringes of legality. Many lived close to the edge and were thought by white observers to have to resort to thievery out of desperation. A report in the *Columbian* magazine for 1797 argued that Kingston slaves got so little money or food that they were required "to commit any depredations on the community when the toils of the day are done, for mere subsistence".[69] Nevertheless, the real difference between work done by the urban enslaved and plantation slaves was that in Kingston enslaved people had multiple opportunities to self-hire. Indeed, in the essential and lucrative maritime trades, self-hiring by enslaved people was customary practice. The nature of enslaved work in the Kingston port was to enhance the fluidity of enslaved life, as enslaved port workers tended to work for themselves as much as for their owners. A writer noted in 1790 that most work relating to shipping, including that to do with naval ships of war, was "all under the care of negroes". He concluded that in every case, "one is a chief who has two other negroes, being the property of some of the inhabitants of Kingston or Port Royal". These masters "let then out to hire to themselves; that is they expect a certain sum from them daily or weekly, for six bitts to a dollar a day for each negro".[70] Enslaved workers were thus able to make a bit of money on the side from their self-hire, meaning that urban slavery was more permeable and more variegated than slavery elsewhere on the island.

As in antebellum New York City, Kingston enslaved people developed an oppositional culture to that of whites.[71] Many whites found slaves' attitudes to authority worrying. Kingston enslaved people lived violent lives: ninety-five published coroners' reports in the early nineteenth century detail twenty-four accidental drownings, twenty-two cases of sick Africans thrown overboard when entering Kingston harbour to be sold as slaves, nineteen suicides, and sixteen murders. Whites were concerned that violence might be directed against them. It was not – there were no slave uprisings in the town in the nineteenth century. But there were at least two conspiracies discovered before they could be implemented, as well as a mutiny on 27 May 1808 of fifty-four African recruits to the 2nd Regiment, mainly from the Gold Coast. The mutineers killed two white officers. Retaliation was brutal, with ten mutineers killed and several shot by court martial and others transported to British

69. Simmonds, "'That Little Shadow of Property and Freedom'", pp. 186–191; *Columbian Magazine*, 3 (1798), p. 78.

70. Anon., *Short Journey in the West Indies …* (London, 1790), pp. 24–25.

71. Shane White, "'It Was a Proud Day': African Americans, Festivals, and Parades in the North, 1741–1834", *Journal of American History*, 81 (1994), pp. 13–50.

Honduras. The slaves suspected as plotters in two conspiracies discovered in 1803 and 1809 were also executed. The most dangerous plot appears to have been that of 1809, where "creole boys" were thought to have plotted with Africans, black soldiers, and French and Spanish refugees to "get rid of the whites" and have enslaved people "turn on their masters". Such plots were extremely dangerous in the immediate aftermath of Haiti. And this plot also resulted in harsh retribution against the ringleaders.[72]

Oppositional culture also featured in what became by the end of slavery one of the most characteristic forms of black culture: the carnivalesque black mimicry of white authority represented in the Jonkonnu or John Canoe ceremonies, held around Christmastime each year (Figure 2).[73] They are pictured beautifully in Isaac Belisario's *Sketches of Character* prints published just before the end of the four year period of apprenticeship of ex-slaves in 1838.[74] John Canoes were popular black entertainers who paraded around Kingston wearing outlandish masks and costumes, which included skirts, wigs, fans, plumes, and whips. As Kay Dian Kriz notes, these "[a]ctor-Boys satirize the very notion of maintaining boundaries in a place like Jamaica", criss-crossing racial, class, and gender divisions that white creoles usually maintained through force and legislation.[75] Whites liked to pretend that John Canoes were creatures of fun and harmless entertainers, but written and visual depictions suggest that these performers were often aggressive and faintly menacing. In a popular memoir, *Tom Cringle's Log*, published in 1833, Michael Scott noted that the Kingston militia was called out "in case any of the John Canoes should take a small fancy to pillage the town, or to rise and cut the throats of their masters, or any innocent recreation of the kind".

John Canoes and Set Girls were distinctly urban creatures. John Stewart noted in 1823 how "the Negro girls of the town (who conceive themselves far superior to those on the estates, in point of *taste, manners* and fashion)" joined together in groups called the blues and the reds in their finery, "sometimes at the expense of the white or brown mistress who took a pride in shewing them off to the greatest advantage".[76] These "actor-boys" embodied disorder. The first visual depiction of them in William Elmes' *Adventures of Johnny Newcome* (1812) is at a "negro ball". The John Canoe character is

72. Simmonds, "'That Little Shadow of Property and Freedom'", pp. 275, 369–385.

73. Michael Craton, "Decoding Pitchy-Patchy: The Roots, Branches and Essence of Junkanoo", *Slavery & Abolition*, 16 (1995), pp. 14–44.

74. T.J. Barringer, Gillian Forrester, and Barbaro Martinez-Ruiz, *Art and Emancipation in Jamaica* (New Haven, CT, 2007).

75. Kay Dian Kriz, *Slavery, Sugar, and the Culture of Refinement* (New Haven, CT, 2008), p. 136.

76. [Michael Scott], *Tom Cringle's Log*, 2 vols (Edinburgh, 1833), vol. 1, p. 353; John Stewart, *An Account of Jamaica and its Inhabitants …* (Edinburgh, 1823), p. 263.

Figure 2. "Jaw-Bone, or House John-Canoe".
Slavery Images: A Visual Record of the African Slave Trade and Slave Life in the Early African Diaspora. *Available at: http://slaveryimages.org/s/slaveryimages/item/2311; last accessed 3 December 2019.*

ludicrously caricatured as a parody of long-gone British male fashion and is a vaguely menacing figure among grinning, dancing, indolent blacks. Belisario, painting for a middle-class audience at the moment of emancipation, tones down the menace, but even so, his Set Girls and Actor-Boys or John Canoes are decked out in outrageous military garb.[77]

One significant difference between urban enslavement and plantation slavery was that enslaved people in Kingston lived cheek by jowl with white people. Residential segregation was limited until near the end of slavery, when concentrations of enslaved peoples' residences began appearing at the edge of the town. Enslaved people were often housed with their owners, or in closely adjacent "negro" yards. Whites complained that they could never escape the attention of enslaved people. The black presence was hard to disguise in the town, in ways that made the town more obviously a mixture of black and white than, ironically, the plantation, where enslaved people worked and lived often at quite a distance from the great house. As Ann Appleton Storrow noted in 1792, "the Town of Kingston has some beautiful houses in it, [and] was it uniformly well-built it would be an elegant one, but you often see between two handsome houses, an obscene negro yard, which spoils the effect entirely". Another writer was more direct in his condemnation of enslaved spatial presence alongside whites: Kingston was "a wretched mixture of handsome and spacious houses, with vile hovels and disgraceful sheds".[78]

The principal disruption that was practised by John Canoes was to transform the spatial location in which enslaved people resided. Kingston enslaved people often lived with white people but were generally invisible in the homes in which they dwelled: the street was their normal locale. During the Jonkonnu festival, however, a spatial inversion occurred, during which black entertainers invaded the spaces of white authority. Not only did John Canoes and Set Girls dress up and address whites with great familiarity, singing "satirical philippics" against masters that whites may have thought were still within the bounds of "decorum" but which may have had a more spirited edge, they also invaded the houses of white merchants, drinking with the owners in ways that "annihilated the distance" between white and black. Some whites found this threatening. One observer wrote that the performers "completely besieged my room" and that she was then "forced to listen to their rude songs, which I should fancy must be very like the wild yelling and screaming that we read of in African travels".[79] The invasion of the house was pointed. The lead performer, as Belisario pictured in an especially fine print, wore an elaborate model of a house on his head (Figure 2) that may have been destroyed (as it is in contemporary re-creations) at the end of festivities. The house on the head of the enslaved person was highly symbolic. Nelson

77. Kriz, *Slavery, Sugar, and the Culture of Refinement*, pp. 136–140.

78. Ann Appleton Storrow to Miss Butler, Kingston, 23 September 1792, Ann Appleton Storrow Papers, Folder 1790–92, Massachusetts Historical Society; Anon., *An Account of Jamaica and its Inhabitants, by a Gentleman long Resident in the West Indies* (London, 1808), p. 14.

79. Craton, "Pitchy-Patchy", p. 28; and Cynric R. Williams, *A Tour through the Island of Jamaica … in the Year 1823* (London, 1826), pp. 21–27.

suggests it was a visual representation of what enslaved people believed – that the whole edifice of white power, as represented in merchants' tall buildings in Kingston, rested on the heads of enslaved people.[80] Kingston was a wealthy and flourishing town. But black people knew that its prosperity rested squarely upon slavery and the slave trade and, at bottom, upon the bodies of enslaved people.

80. Nelson, *Architecture and Empire in Jamaica*, p. 186.

IRSH 65 (2020), pp. 67–92 doi:10.1017/S0020859020000140

The Expansion of Slavery in Benguela During the Nineteenth Century

Mariana P. Candido

Department of History, University of Notre Dame
219 O'Shaughnessy, Notre Dame, IN 46556 USA

E-mail: mcandido@nd.edu

Abstract: This article explores the nature and expansion of slavery in Benguela, in West Central Africa, during the nineteenth century, engaging with the scholarship on second slavery. Robert Palmer, Eric Hobsbawm, and Janet Polasky have framed the nineteenth century as the age of contagious liberty, yet, in Benguela, and elsewhere along the African coast, the institution of slavery expanded, in part to attend to the European and North American demand for natural resources. In the wake of the end of the slave trade, plantation slavery spread along the African coast to supply the growing demand in Europe and North America for cotton, sugar, and natural resources such as wax, ivory, rubber, and gum copal. In Portuguese territories in West Central Africa, slavery remained alive until 1869, when enslaved people were put into systems of apprenticeship very similar to labor regimes elsewhere in the Atlantic world. For the thousands of people who remained in captivity in Benguela, the nineteenth century continued to be a moment of oppression, forced labor, and extreme violence, not an age of abolition.

After the 1836 abolition of slave exports, local merchants and recently arrived immigrants from Portugal and Brazil set up plantations around Benguela making extensive use of unfree labor. In this article, I examine how abolition, colonialism, and economic exploitation were part of the same process in Benguela, which resulted in new zones of slavery responding to industrialization and market competition. Looking at individual cases, wherever possible, this study examines the kinds of activities enslaved people performed and the nature of slave labor. Moreover, it examines how free and enslaved people interacted and the differences that existed in terms of gender, analyzing the type of labor performed by enslaved men and women. And it questions the limitations of the "age of abolition".

INTRODUCTION

Urbanization and slavery have a long and intertwined history in West Central Africa and predate the early contact with Europeans in the late fifteenth century. Urban areas were located inland, away from the coast, yet they were important spaces of interaction and exchange, acting as political and economic centers.[1] With the expansion of the Atlantic world, smaller settlements along the African coast became important commercial centers and new towns emerged, linked to internal markets and European cities and ports in the Americas. These new towns included the ports of Saint Louis and Gorée in Senegambia; Elmina and Anomabu along the Gold Coast; Cacheu on the Upper Guinea Coast; Ouidah, Porto Novo, and Lagos in the Bight of Benin; Bonny and Old Calabar in the Bight of Biafra; and Luanda, Cabinda, and Benguela in West Central Africa.[2] The population of all these towns grew in the context of engagement with the Atlantic world and the expansion of the transatlantic slave trade. However, it is important to stress that urbanization in Africa predated the arrival of Europeans and the transatlantic slave trade, although further archeological research is necessary to provide more information on the nature and importance of West Central African urban centers.

In the era of Atlantic commerce, urban spaces on the African coast became centers of wealth concentration with the emergence of new commercial elites that profited from the sale of human beings along with ivory and gold. Several African ports had a sizable female population due to the pressures and dynamics of the slave trade but also the opportunities available in coastal towns. During the eighteenth century, population estimates indicate that women constituted the majority in coastal centers. For example, in the town of Cacheu on the Upper Guinea Coast there were 514 women and 386 men in 1731.[3] Luanda had 5,647 women and 4,108 men among its residents in

1. Jan Vansina, *How Societies Are Born: Governance in West Central Africa before 1600* (Charlottesville, VA, 2004); John K. Thornton, *A Cultural History of the Atlantic World, 1250–1820* (New York, 2012).

2. Space does not permit me to list all sources that deal with urbanization along Western Africa and the transatlantic slave trade, but key among them are George E. Brooks, *Landlords and Strangers: Ecology, Society, and Trade in Western Africa, 1000–1630* (Boulder, CO, 1993); Toby Green, "Building Slavery in the Atlantic World: Atlantic Connections and the Changing Institution of Slavery in Cabo Verde, Fifteenth–Sixteenth Centuries", *Slavery & Abolition*, 32 (2011), pp. 227–245; Filipa Ribeiro Da Silva, "Dutch Trade with Senegambia, Guinea, and Cape Verde, c.1590–1674", in Toby Green (ed.), *Brokers of Change: Atlantic Commerce and Cultures in Precolonial Western Africa* (Oxford, 2012), pp. 125–147; Lorelle Semley, *To Be Free and French: Citizenship in France's Atlantic Empire*, Critical Perspectives on Empire (Cambridge, 2017); Rebecca Shumway, "Castle Slaves of the Eighteenth-Century Gold Coast (Ghana)", *Slavery & Abolition*, 35 (2014), pp. 84–98; Pernille Ipsen, *Daughters of the Trade: Atlantic Slavers and Interracial Marriage on the Gold Coast, Early Modern Americas* (Philadelphia, PA, 2015); Kristin Mann, *Slavery and the Birth of an African City: Lagos, 1760–1900* (Bloomington, IN, 2010); Stacey Sommerdyk, "Rivalry on the Loango Coast: A Re-Examination of the Dutch in the Atlantic Slave Trade", in Arlindo Manuel Caldeira (ed.), *Trabalho Forçado Africano. O Caminho de Ida* (Porto, 2009), pp. 105–118; Mariana P. Candido, *An African Slaving Port and the Atlantic World: Benguela and Its Hinterland* (New York, 2013).

3. Havik, *Silences and Soundbites*, Table 2, "Population Census 1731".

1781.[4] There were 1,352 women and 892 men in Benguela in 1797.[5] More information is available for port towns in the nineteenth century, as for the towns of Ouidah and Accra where women comprised the majority of the population.[6] Free and enslaved women played important economic roles in these coastal centers as traders, farmers, shopkeepers, and nurses, among other activities.[7] Similar to urban centers elsewhere along the Atlantic basin, slavery was central to the organization of the space and production of goods that attended populations in transit.[8] Unlike other ports on the African coast, in West Central Africa the expansion of slavery was also intimately linked to the consolidation of the Portuguese colonial establishment in Luanda, Benguela, and inland fortresses. The construction of colonial infrastructure, including administrative centers, fortresses, and ports, relied on the exploitation of unfree labor, as I have discussed elsewhere.[9]

This study examines the expansion of slavery in Benguela during the nineteenth century. This period was a moment of profound transformation along the African coast, with the decline and abolition of slave exports as well as the expansion of slave labor in coastal and inland urban centers. Despite a historiography that celebrates the nineteenth century as the age of emancipation, liberty, and democratic revolutions, as framed by Robert Palmer, Eric Hobsbawm, and Janet Polasky, this study stresses the expansion and strengthening of the institution of slavery rather than its decline.[10] The eighteenth- and

4. José C. Curto and Raymond R. Gervais, "The Population History of Luanda during the Late Atlantic Slave Trade, 1781–1844", *African Economic History*, 29 (2001), pp. 1–59, 55.

5. Arquivo Histórico Ultramarino (AHU), Angola, box 87, document 51, "Mapa das Pessoas Livres e escravos, empregos, e os oficios que varios tem", 1 January 1798. See Mariana P. Candido, *Fronteras de esclavización. Esclavitud, comercio e identidad en Benguela, 1780–1850* (Mexico City, 2011), pp. 76–99.

6. Law, *Ouidah*, p. 76; John Parker, *Making the Town: Ga State and Society in Early Colonial Accra* (Portsmouth, NH, 2000), p. 190.

7. Claire C. Robertson, "We Must Overcome: Genealogy and Evolution of Female Slavery in West Africa", *Journal of West African History*, 1:1 (2015), pp. 59–92; Vanessa S. Oliveira, "Gender, Foodstuff Production and Trade in Late-Eighteenth Century Luanda", *African Economic History*, 43 (2015), pp. 57–81; Kristin Mann, "Women, Landed Property, and the Accumulation of Wealth in Early Colonial Lagos", *Signs*, 16 (1991), pp. 682–706; Semley, *To Be Free and French*.

8. For other Atlantic ports see Mary C. Karasch, *Slave Life in Rio de Janeiro, 1808–1850* (Princeton, NJ, 1987); David Barry Gaspar and Darlene Clark Hine, *More Than Chattel: Black Women and Slavery in the Americas* (Bloomington, IN, 1996); Alejandro de la Fuente, *Havana and the Atlantic in the Sixteenth Century* (Chapel Hill, NC, 2008); Mann, *Slavery and the Birth of an African City*; Jane Landers, "Founding Mothers: Female Rebels in Colonial New Granada and Spanish Florida", *Journal of African American History*, 98 (2013), pp. 7–23.

9. See Candido, *An African Slaving Port*.

10. For studies that celebrate the late eighteenth and early nineteenth century as the "Age of Revolution and Liberty" see Eric Hobsbawm, *Age of Revolution 1789–1848* (London, 2010); Robert Roswell Palmer, *The Age of the Democratic Revolution: The Challenge* (Princeton, NJ, 1969); Janet L. Polasky, *Revolutions without Borders: The Call to Liberty in the Atlantic World*

nineteenth-century liberal revolutions that swept the North Atlantic did not represent the end of African labor exploitation or even of slavery in West Central Africa. In fact, during the nineteenth century, slavery expanded in Luanda and Benguela as well as in other African urban centers, related to the transition to the so-called legitimate trade in natural resources such as ivory, and cash crops such as coffee, cocoa beans, and cotton.[11] Regaining, acquiring, or consolidating freedom became even more difficult for those who remained in bondage in West Central Africa. Individuals who petitioned for emancipation did not necessarily encounter supportive colonial officials or individuals who could help them in their quest for freedom.[12] In many ways,

(New Haven, CT, 2015). The scholarship on the Portuguese empire, however, stresses that slavery not only continued to exist but also thrived during the nineteenth century. See, for example, João Pedro Marques, "Uma Cosmética Demorada. As Cortes Perante O Problema Da Escravidão (1836–1875)", *Análise Social*, 36:158–159 (2001), pp. 209–247; Valentim Alexandre and Jill Dias, *O Império Africano* (Lisbon, 1998); Roquinaldo Ferreira, "Abolicionismo versus Colonialismo. Rupturas e Continuidades em Angola (Século XIX)", in Roberto Guedes (ed.), *África. Brasileiros e portugueses, séculos XVI–XIX* (Rio de Janeiro, 2013), pp. 95–112; Vanessa S. Oliveira, "Trabalho escravo e ocupações urbanas em Luanda na segunda metade do século XIX", in Selma Pantoja and Estevam C. Thompson (eds), *Em torno de Angola. Narrativas, identidades e conexões atlânticas* (São Paulo, 2014), pp. 265–267.

11. For more on this, see Paul E. Lovejoy and Jan S. Hogendorn, *Slow Death for Slavery: The Course of Abolition in Northern Nigeria, 1897–1936* (Cambridge, 1993); W.G. Clarence-Smith, "Runaway Slaves and Social Bandits in Southern Angola, 1875–1913", *Slavery & Abolition*, 6:3 (1985), pp. 23–33; Sandra E. Greene, *Slave Owners of West Africa: Decision Making in the Age of Abolition* (Bloomington, IN, 2017); Trevor R. Getz, *Slavery and Reform in West Africa: Toward Emancipation in Nineteenth-Century Senegal and the Gold Coast* (Athens, OH, 2004); Samuël Cöghe, "The Problem of Freedom in a Mid-Nineteenth-Century Atlantic Slave Society: The Liberated Africans of the Anglo-Portuguese Mixed Commission in Luanda (1844–1870)", *Slavery & Abolition*, 33 (2012), pp. 479–500; Jelmer Vos, "Work in Times of Slavery, Colonialism, and Civil War: Labor Relations in Angola from 1800 to 2000", *History in Africa*, 41 (2014), pp. 363–385; Roquinaldo Amaral Ferreira, "Agricultural Enterprise and Unfree Labour in Nineteenth Century Angola", in Robin Law, Suzanne Schwarz, and Silke Strickrodt (eds), *Commercial Agriculture, the Slave Trade and Slavery in Atlantic Africa* (Woodbridge, 2013), pp. 225–242; Suzanne Schwarz, "'A Just and Honourable Commerce': Abolitionist Experimentation in Sierra Leone in the Late Eighteenth and Early Nineteenth Centuries", *African Economic History*, 45:1 (2017), pp. 1–45.

12. See, for example, José C. Curto, "Un Butin Illégitime. Razzias d'esclaves et relations luso-africaines dans la région des fleuves Kwanza et Kwango en 1805", in Isabel de Castro Henriques and Louis Sala-Molins (eds), *Déraison, Esclavage et Droit: Les fondements idéologiques et juridiques de la traite négrière et de l'esclavage* (Paris, 2002), pp. 315–327; José C. Curto, "Struggling against Enslavement: The Case of José Manuel in Benguela, 1816–20", *Canadian Journal of African Studies*, 39 (2005), pp. 96–122; José C. Curto, "Experiences of Enslavement in West Central Africa", *Histoire Sociale/Social History*, 41:82 (2008), pp. 381–415; Roquinaldo Ferreira, "Slaving and Resistance to Slaving in West Central Africa", in David Eltis and Stanley L. Engerman (eds), *The Cambridge World History of Slavery*, vol. 3 (Cambridge, 2011), pp. 111–131; Mariana P. Candido, "African Freedom Suits and Portuguese Vassal Status: Legal Mechanisms for Fighting Enslavement in Benguela, Angola, 1800–1830", *Slavery & Abolition*, 32 (2011), pp. 447–459; Mariana P. Candido, "O limite tênue entre a liberdade e

urban centers were not about opportunities and freedom but were threatening spaces. Several studies indicate that free Africans were kidnapped, enslaved, and deported to the Americas while conducting business, visiting friends or relatives, or transiting alone through coastal towns.[13]

The Portuguese empire abolished slave exports from West Central Africa in 1836, yet the use of local enslaved people expanded after this date. Local merchants and recently arrived immigrants from Portugal and Brazil set up plantations around Benguela, making extensive use of unfree labor. Cotton and sugarcane plantations were established in order to meet international demand for raw materials in the context of industrialization. In urban centers such as Benguela, enslaved labor use also expanded until slavery was abolished in 1869, and a system of apprenticeship was put in place.[14] This process of the "slow death" of slavery has received some scholarly attention for other locations in Africa, but not much has been written about this transition in West Central Africa.[15] While in recent decades Roquinaldo Ferreira, Samuël Cöghe, Jelmer Vos, and Vanessa S. Oliveira have published important studies

escravidão em Benguela durante a era do comércio transatlântico", *Afro-Ásia*, 47 (2013), pp. 239–268.

13. See Catarina Madeira Santos, "Esclavage africain et traite atlantique confrontés: transactions langagières et juridiques (à propos du tribunal de mucanos dans l'Angola des xviie et xviiie siècles)", *Brésil(s). Sciences Humaines et Sociales*, 1 (2012), pp. 127–148; Mariana P. Candido, "The Transatlantic Slave Trade and the Vulnerability of Free Blacks in Benguela, Angola, 1780–1830", in Mark Meuwese and Jeffrey A. Fortin (eds), *Atlantic Biographies: Individuals and Peoples in the Atlantic World* (Leiden, 2013), pp. 193–210; Enrique Martino, "Panya: Economies of Deception and the Discontinuities of Indentured Labour Recruitment and the Slave Trade, Nigeria and Fernando Pó, 1890s–1940s", *African Economic History*, 44 (2016), pp. 91–129.

14. José de Almada, *Apontamentos históricos sobre a escravatura e o trabalho indígena nas colónias portuguesas* (Lisbon, 1932), pp. 39–41. For studies on the transformation of slavery into new forms of exploitation in West Central Africa, see Maria da Conceição Neto, "De escravos a serviçais, de serviçais a contratados. Omissões, percepções e equívocos na história do trabalho africano na Angola colonial", *Cadernos de Estudos Africanos*, 33 (2017), pp. 107–129; Aida Freudenthal, "Os quilombos de Angola no século XIX. A recusa da escravidão", *Estudos Afro-Asiáticos*, 32 (1997), pp. 109–134; Jelmer Vos, "Child Slaves and Freemen at the Spiritan Mission in Soyo, 1880–1885", *Journal of Family History*, 35:1 (2010), pp. 71–90; Vos, "Work in Times of Slavery"; Ferreira, "Agricultural Enterprise".

15. For example, see Lovejoy, *Slow Death for Slavery: The Course of Abolition in Northern Nigeria, 1897–1936* (Cambridge, 1993); Martin A. Klein, *Slavery and Colonial Rule in French West Africa* (New York, 1998); Martin A. Klein, Alice Bellagamba, and Sandra E. Greene (eds), *Bitter Legacy: African Slavery Past and Present* (Princeton, NJ, 2011); Frederick Cooper, *From Slaves to Squatters: Plantation Labor and Agriculture in Zanzibar and Coastal Kenya, 1890–1925* (New Haven, CT, 1980); Mohammed Bashir Salau, *The West African Slave Plantation: A Case Study*, 1st edn (New York, 2011); Richard L. Roberts, *Litigants and Households: African Disputes and Colonial Courts in the French Soudan, 1895–1912* (Portsmouth, NH, 2005); Pamela Scully, *Liberating the Family?: Gender and British Slave Emancipation in the Rural Western Cape, South Africa, 1823–1853* (Portsmouth, NH, 1997); Elisabeth McMahon, *Slavery and Emancipation in Islamic East Africa: From Honor to Respectability* (New York, 2013).

on the end of the slave trade and the expansion of unfree labor in commercial agriculture in Angola, much more research is needed, particularly regarding areas away from coastal centers and on the experiences of individuals in resisting forced labor.[16] In addition to exploring the expansion of slavery, this study examines the activities enslaved people performed and the nature of slave labor and resistance in Benguela. By looking at individual cases it is possible to interrogate the differences that existed in terms of gender, analyzing the type of labor performed by enslaved men and women, and how slavery changed over time. Relying on primary sources from the Arquivo Nacional de Angola, the Tribunal da Comarca de Benguela (both in Angola), and the Arquivo Histórico Ultramarino (Portugal), this study discusses slavery in Benguela, helping us to analyze its meaning and limitations to the "age of liberty", and slavery's direct relationship with colonialism on the African coast.[17]

BENGUELA AND THE AGE OF ABOLITION

The nineteenth century was a period of profound transformations.[18] Although the French, American, and Saint Domingue revolutions led to the reorganization of states, economies, and labor in different spaces, it was not a period of liberty everywhere and to everyone in the Atlantic world.[19] The "universal cry of liberty"[20] did not reach West Central Africa until the end of the nineteenth century, and it certainly did not endorse political emancipation for Africans. In the colony of Angola, which also included the administration of the town of Benguela and its interior, arguments about slave exporting and its consequences for the stagnation of local agricultural production occupied some of the debate between metropolis and colony in the early decades of the nineteenth century. Different colonial authorities reported that the growing slave trade in the early nineteenth century affected the consolidation of agricultural production and local industries. In 1805, for example, the

16. Ferreira, "Agricultural Enterprise"; Cöghe, "Problem of Freedom"; Vos, "Work in Times of Slavery"; Paulo Teodoro de Matos and Jelmer Vos, "Demografia e relações de trabalho em Angola c.1800. Um ensaio metodológico", *Diálogos*, 17:3 (2014), pp. 807–834; Roquinaldo Ferreira, "A supressão do tráfico de escravos em Angola (ca. 1830–ca. 1860)", *História Unisinos*, 15:1 (2011), pp. 3–13; Oliveira, "Trabalho escravo"; Vanessa S. Oliveira, *Women and Slavery in Luanda* (Madison, WI, forthcoming).

17. On the nineteenth century as the height of Enlightenment and freedom, see Hobsbawm, *Age of Revolution*; David Brion Davis, *Slavery and Human Progress* (New York, 1986).

18. Hobsbawm, *Age of Revolution*; Jeremy Adelman, *Sovereignty and Revolution in the Iberian Atlantic* (Princeton, NJ, 2006).

19. On contagious liberty see David Brion Davis, *The Problem of Slavery in the Age of Revolution, 1770–1823* (New York, 1999); Laurent Dubois, *Avengers of the New World the Story of the Haitian Revolution* (Cambridge, MA, 2004); Polasky, *Revolutions without Borders*, among others.

20. Polasky, *Revolutions without Borders*, p. 5.

Catholic priest Boaventura José de Melo reported that the colonies of Benguela and Angola exported people who could produce food locally "due to the surplus of land and propitious environment".[21] The governor of Angola in 1826, Nicolau Abreu Castelo Branco, personally encouraged the production of sugarcane to replace the export of captives, and recommended that the Portuguese Crown reward any trader engaged in new economic activities with an honorary induction into the Order of Christ.[22] The Portuguese empire envisioned exploiting the production of cotton and indigo in addition to sugarcane, but also tapping into natural resources such as beeswax, gum copal, and orchil lichen – products in high demand from industries in Europe and North America.[23] In all these industries coerced labor would respond to the demand for increased production.

Despite British pressure to bring the slave trade to an end and the progressive abolition of slavery in the Americas, there were protests that without enslavement it would be very difficult to maintain production since the local population was considered "unwilling to cooperate" and rebellious; it was claimed that the only way to obtain labor was through force and violence.[24] The debates about colonialism, agricultural expansion, and new economic plans after the 1836 slave export ban continued into the 1840s, despite the fact that the slave trade remained alive in part due to the demand in markets such as Cuba and Brazil. In 1844, José Joaquim Lopes de Lima, the colonial administrator in Goa and Timor, claimed "the infamous trade hurt our interest in Africa, stealing our hands who are employed in strange lands", making reference to the use of African enslaved labor in Brazil.[25] Pamphlets and booklets were published to advance the idea that enslaved people should remain in West Central Africa to help consolidate Portuguese colonialism and agricultural production.[26] Projects were approved to financially support agricultural expansion, relying, ironically, on the labor of enslaved people. For example, the Projeto de Regulamento da Companhia de Agricultura e Indústria de Angola e Benguela (Project to Regulate the Agriculture and Industry

21. AHU, Angola, box. 114, doc. 30, 23 November 1805 (old classification).

22. AHU, Angola, Codex 542, fol. 111v, 30 December 1826. New attempts were made in 1839; see Arquivo Nacional de Angola (ANA), Codex 221, fol. 17, 10 December 1839.

23. AHU, Angola, Codex 452, fol. 130v, 5 May 1827; AHU, Angola, Correspondência dos Governadores, Folder 2, 12 December 1836.

24. AHU, Angola, Correspondência dos Governadores, Folder 2 C, 30 September 1839; AHU, Angola, Correspondência dos Governadores, Folder 18, 15 December 1852.

25. Lopes de Lima cited in Roquinaldo Ferreira, "Escravidão e revoltas de escravos em Angola (1830–1860)", *Afro-Ásia*, 21–22 (1998), p. 14.

26. Joaquim Antonio de Carvalho e Menezes, *Memoria geográfica, e política das possessões portuguezas n'Affrica occidental, que diz respeito aos reinos de Angola, Benguela, e suas dependências* (Lisbon, 1834), pp. 27–52; Arsênio P.P. de Carpo, *Projecto de uma Companhia para o Melhoramento do Commércio, agricultura e indústria na Província de Angola* (Lisbon, 1848).

Companies of Angola and Benguela) suggested shifting the focus from captive exports to a less lucrative though "noble" economic enterprise: the production of coffee, sugarcane, and natural resources within the Portuguese colonies in Africa.[27] In many ways, the 1836 slave export ban led to the expansion of slavery locally, similar to what happened elsewhere in the Atlantic world, and leading to what historians have called the second slavery period.[28] Plantations spread in Benguela and surrounding areas, such as Catumbela, Dombe Grande, and Cuio, as can be seen in Figure 1.[29]

In the 1850s, the newly appointed governor of Benguela, Vicente Ferrer Barruncho, was particularly interested in the development of a cash crop economy. In an 1856 report written a few months after his arrival in Benguela, he described the region of Dombe Grande as "excellent for agriculture. It could be even better if the heathens [*gentio*] were not so devoted to their customs and habits and neglectful of hard labor. [...] All the flour consumed in Benguela comes from this location". He observed that one example of prosperity was the Equimina farm, owned by Ignácio Teixeira Xavier, whom he described as an entrepreneur. In Equimina, Barruncho claimed, Teixeira Xavier

> produced *aguardente*, but not sugar. [...] Labor was employed in the production of manioc, potato and maize. [...] I saw how the slaves are well employed and treated. Only 46 slaves were used, which included carpenters and a blacksmith. In the production of orchil lichen, 63 slaves are employed. In the coast town of Lucira, Teixeira Xavier employs 52 of his slaves in fishing.[30]

The governor suggested that Benguela residents should follow Teixeira Xavier's business model, employing enslaved and free labor for the advancement of plantation agriculture.

Barruncho's suggestions conformed with Portuguese colonial policies. With the end of transatlantic slave exports, the Portuguese administration encouraged the diversification of the economy, favoring the export of local staples such as orchil lichen. However, Barruncho's model entrepreneur, Teixeira

27. AHU, Angola, Correspondência dos Governadores, Folder 2, 8 April 1836.

28. Ada Ferrer, "Cuban Slavery and Atlantic Antislavery", *Review (Fernand Braudel Center)*, 31 (2008), pp. 267–295; Dale Tomich and Michael Zeuske, "Introduction, the Second Slavery: Mass Slavery, World-Economy, and Comparative Microhistories", *Review (Fernand Braudel Center)*, 31 (2008), pp. 91–100.

29. W.G. Clarence-Smith, *The Third Portuguese Empire, 1825–1975* (Manchester, 1985); W.G. Clarence-Smith, *Slaves, Peasants, and Capitalists in Southern Angola, 1840–1926* (Cambridge, 1979); Ai Freudenthal, *Arimos e fazenda. A transição agrária em Angola, 1850-1880* (Luanda: Chá de Caxinde, 2005); Oliveira, "Trabalho escravo".

30. Boletim Oficial do Governo Geral da Província de Angola (BOGGPA), no. 585, 13 December 1856, pp. 3–6, 26 November 1856. On the importance of orchil weed, see Maria Emília Madeira Santos (ed.), *Viagens e Apontamentos de um Portuense em África. O Diário de Silva Porto* (Coimbra, 1986), p. 75; Maria Cristina Cortez Wissenbach, "As feitorias de urzela e o tráfico de escravos. Georg Tams, José Ribeiro dos Santos e os negócios da África Centro-Ocidental na década de 1840", *Afro-Ásia*, 43 (2011), pp. 43–90.

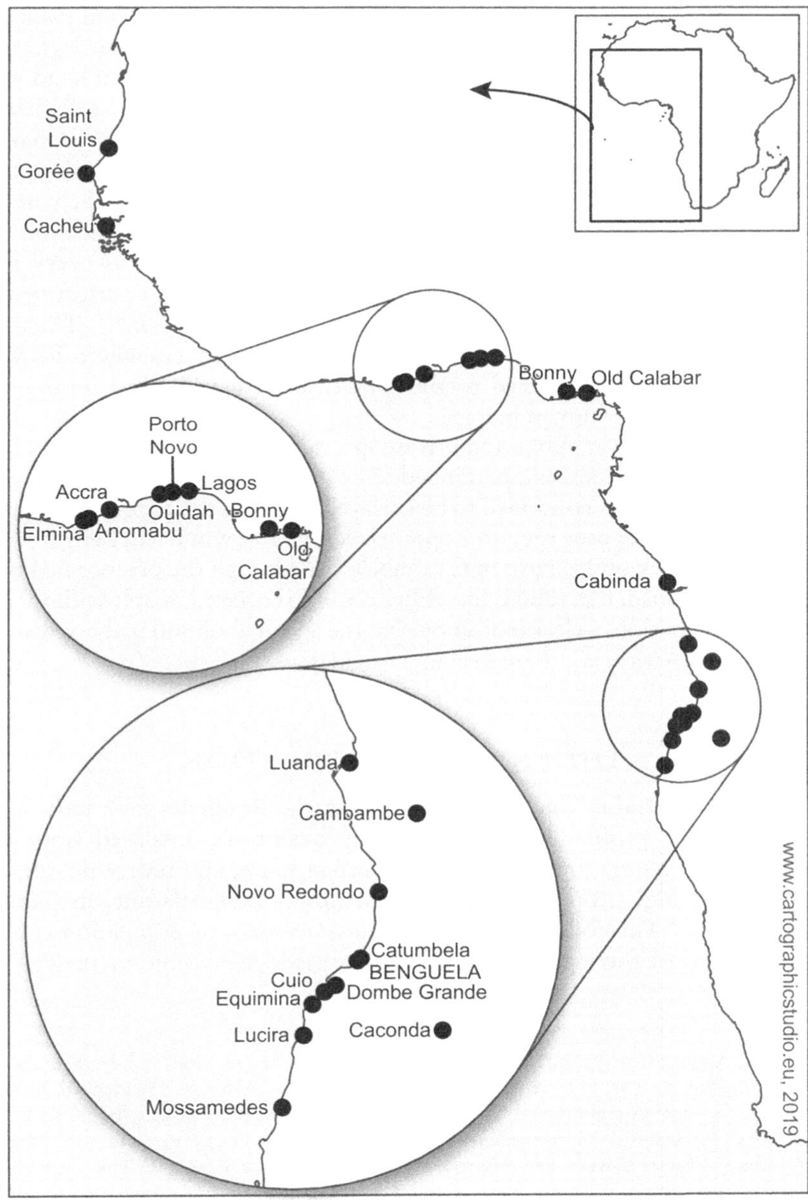

Figure 1. The Western African coast, with details to locations mentioned in the text.

Xavier, was later accused of smuggling enslaved labor overseas and using his plantations as a façade for his illegal business. This case shows how legitimate commerce in raw materials and tropical goods developed hand in hand with the smuggling of human beings. The governor of Angola, José Sobrinho Coelho do Amaral, accused Barruncho of involvement in the illegal slaving scheme, suggesting that Teixeira Xavier's legal activity camouflaged contraband trade in slaves.[31] The trader John Monteiro, who visited Benguela a few years later, argued that "only a very large number of cruisers on the Angolan coast could have prevented the shipment of slaves, as every man and woman, white or black, was interested in the trade, and a perfect system of communication existed from all points, overland and by sea".[32] Thus, the expansion of agricultural production in Benguela and elsewhere in West Central Africa was connected to the growth of enslaved labor locally and contraband trade in human beings.

Slavery expanded in public and private spaces, including in official economic and household activities, and continued to exist as a legal institution until 1869. However, individuals continued to be enslaved well into the 1870s. In 1873, for example, Bento Augusto Ribeiro Lopes seized two free women in Benguela and put them to work on his farm in Catumbela.[33] Although the practice had been officially abolished, individuals like Ribeiro Lopes enslaved people without fear of any reprehension, a clear indication that the age of abolition had not reached West Central Africa, and Benguela in particular.

THE ENSLAVED POPULATION

Slavery was central to the economy of Benguela. Residents took part in the slave trade and profited from the auxiliary businesses. Enslaved labor was also vital to the organization of colonial urban space, and unfree people had represented a high proportion of the population of Benguela since its foundation in 1617.[34] The collection of *mapas populacionais*, or population counts, since the end of the eighteenth century has made it possible to analyze the

31. AHU, Angola, Correspondência dos Governadores, Folder 22A, doc. 15 July 1856; see also BOGGPA, 1865, no. 585, 13 December 1856, pp. 3–6. For more on this, see Freudenthal, *Arimos e Fazendas*, 189–190; Alexandre and Dias, *O Império Africano*, pp. 398–402; Isabel de Castro Henriques, *Percursos da Modernidade em Angola* (Lisbon, 1997), pp. 532–550; Mariana P. Candido, "Trade, Slavery and Migration in the Interior of Benguela: The Case of the Caconda, 1830–1870", in Beatrix Heintze and Achim von Oppen (eds), *Angola on the Move: Transport Routes, Communications, and History* (Frankfurt am Main, 2008), pp. 69–72.

32. Joachim John Monteiro, *Angola and the River Congo* (London, 1876), p. 267.

33. ANA, box 1322, Catumbela, 15 February 1873.

34. Adriano Parreira, "A Primeira Conquista de Benguela", *História, Lisboa*, 12:128 (1990), pp. 64–68; Aida Freudenthal, "Benguela. Da feitoria à cidade colonial", *Fontes & Estudos*, 6–7 (2011), pp. 197–229; Candido, *An African Slaving Port*.

size of the free and unfree populations of Benguela. In 1798, for example, there were 1,185 enslaved people in Benguela out of a total population of 3,023 people (see Figure 2). In 1804, the first population account available for the nineteenth century indicates a decline in the overall population, with 889 free people and 1,118 enslaved people identified as living in Benguela. The higher proportion of enslaved individuals than free people continued until the end of the decade. In 1811, the population count identified a surprisingly small free population of 351 individuals, compared to 1,081 enslaved people in the urban center. The population estimates do not include captives in transit, only those who resided in Benguela. These figures lead to questions about the violence and security necessary to control uprisings and flights.[35]

By 1813, the ratio of free and unfree people was more balanced, as can be seen in Figure 2. By then, the free population was calculated at 1,010 people, while the unfree was 1,141 – a ratio of almost 1:1 that continued until 1826. In the last population counts available prior to the 1836 slave export ban, 796 free and 741 enslaved people lived in Benguela.

Both free and enslaved populations declined in the 1833 population estimate, probably as a result of rearrangements in the slave trade, including the British ban on slave exports in 1808, the ban north of the equator in 1814, and the first attempt to bring slave imports to an end in Brazil in 1826.[36] Despite these efforts, people continued to be captured, enslaved, and exported from West Central Africa, and Benguela was no exception. However, the shifts in Atlantic commerce did affect the organization of the population of Benguela.

35. AHU, Angola, box 89, doc. 88. On Benguela household organization, see Instituto Histórico Geográfico Brasileiro (IHGB), DL32,02.02 and DL32,02.03. For a discussion on the slave population, see Candido, *Fronteras de esclavización*, pp. 91–99. On the importance of population counts to West Central African history, see José C. Curto, "The Anatomy of a Demographic Explosion: Luanda, 1844–1850", *International Journal of African Historical Studies*, 32:2–3 (1999), pp. 381–405; Candido, "Trade, Slavery and Migration", pp. 63–84; Paulo Teodoro de Matos, "Population Censuses in the Portuguese Empire", *Romanian Journal of Population Studies*, 1 (2013), pp. 5–26; Matos and Vos, "Demografia e relações de trabalho"; Daniel B. Domingues da Silva, *The Atlantic Slave Trade from West Central Africa, 1780–1867* (Cambridge, 2017).

36. On the legislation related to the gradual abolition of the slave trade in the Portuguese empire, see Ferreira, "Supressão do tráfico de escravos"; Roquinaldo Ferreira, "Abolicionismo versus colonialismo. Rupturas e continuidades em Angola (século XIX)", in Roberto Guedes (ed.), *África. Brasileiros e Portugueses, séculos XVI–XIX* (Rio de Janeiro, 2013), pp. 95–112; Roquinaldo Ferreira, "Measuring Short- and Long-Term Impacts of Abolitionism in the South Atlantic, 1807–1860s", in David Richardson and Filipa Ribeiro da Silva (eds), *Networks and Trans-Cultural Exchange: Slave Trading in the South Atlantic, 1590–1867* (Leiden, 2014), pp. 221–237; Arlindo Manuel Caldeira, *Escravos e traficantes no império português. O comércio negreiro português no Atlântico durante os séculos XV a XIX* (Lisbon, 2013); Domingues da Silva, *Atlantic Slave Trade*, pp. 16–37; Vanessa S. Oliveira, "Slavery and the Forgotten Women Slave Owners of Luanda (1846–1876)", in Paul E. Lovejoy and Vanessa S. Oliveira (eds), *Slavery, Memory and Citizenship* (Trenton, NJ, 2016), pp. 129–147.

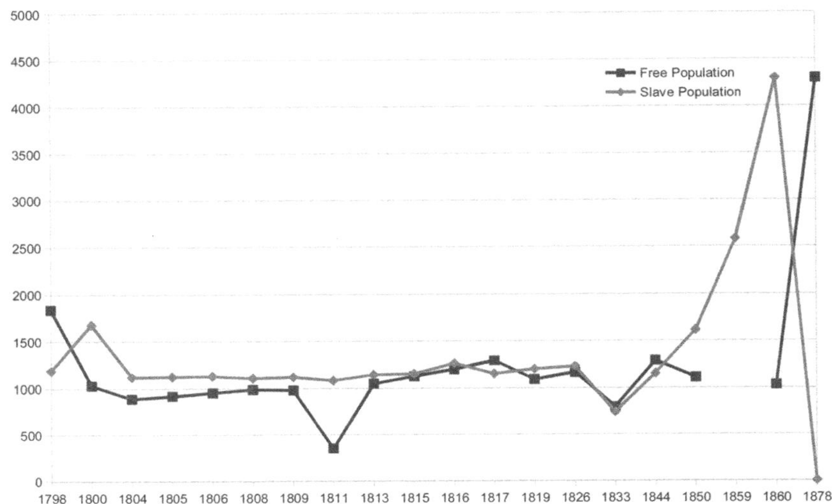

Figure 2. Benguela population by status, 1798–1833.
Sources: AHU, Angola, 1 section, box 88, document 46; ANA, Codex 442, fols. 161v–162; AHU, Angola, 1 section, box 113, document 6; AHU, Angola, 1 section, box 116, document 87; AHU, Angola, 1 section, box 118, document 21; AHU, Angola, 1 section, box 120, document 21; AHU, Angola, 1 section, box 121, document 32; AHU, Angola, 1 section, box 124, document 8.; AHU, Angola, 1 section, box 127, document 59; AHU, Angola, 1 section, box 131, document 45; AHU, Angola, 1 section, box 133, document 32; AHU, Angola, 1 section, box 136, document 19; AHU, Angola, 1 section, box 138, document 1; AHU, Angola, 1 section, box 156, document 16; AHU, Angola, 1 section, box 176, document 17.

As can be seen in Figure 2, there was an increase in the number of enslaved people in Benguela after the 1836 ban. In 1844, 1,288 and 1,150 free and enslaved people lived in Benguela respectively. While there was a decline in the number of free people (1,106), mainly fewer men, the unfree population jumped to 1,614 people in 1850, representing a ratio of 1:1.5. The size of the slave population in 1859 is derived from the slave register rather than a specific population count, and thus the size of the free population is not certain, but it is important to remember that the end of slave imports in Brazil in 1850 provoked a major population reconfiguration in Luanda.[37] A similar process seems to have occurred in Benguela, as suggested by the 1860 population count that shows 1,029 free people and 4,298 enslaved people in the town. With the abolition of slavery in Portuguese possessions in 1869, information about enslaved people was no longer collected in the population count.

37. On the population of Luanda, see Curto, "Anatomy of a Demographic Explosion"; Vanessa S. Oliveira, "The Donas of Luanda, c.1770–1867: From Atlantic Slave Trading to 'Legitimate' Commerce" (Ph.D., York University, 2016).

After 1869, the category "slave" disappeared from the estimates, giving the illusion that all people who lived in territories under Portuguese control were free. This masks the fact that slavery remained alive under the name of *contrato* in the Portuguese empire well into the twentieth century.[38] By 1878, the Benguela population count listed only free people, numbering 4,298, creating the illusion that everyone enjoyed the same degree of freedom.

THE INSTITUTION OF SLAVERY IN BENGUELA

Since the 1960s, scholars have often discussed the nature of slavery in Africa, with some emphasizing how the institution differed from what developed in the Americas and elsewhere, in terms of skin-color classification, social stigma, and social insertion of slave descendants.[39] Recent scholarship has emphasized the ways in which slavery continues to shape political and economic access to modern societies, and that slavery in Africa was much closer to slavery in the Americas than scholars were willing to recognize in the 1970s.[40] There is no

38. Eric Allina, "Modern Slavery and Latter Day Pawns under Colonial Rule in Central Mozambique", in Joel Quirk and Darshan Vigneswaran (eds), *Slavery, Migration and Contemporary Bondage in Africa* (Trenton, NJ, 2013), pp. 37–63; Eric Allina, *Slavery by Any Other Name: African Life under Company Rule in Colonial Mozambique* (Charlottesville, VA, 2012).

39. On the debate over the nature of slavery in Angola, see Isabel de Castro Henriques, *Percursos da Modernidade em Angola. Dinâmicas comerciais e transformações sociais no século XIX* (Lisbon: Instituto de Investigação Científica Tropical, 1997); W.G. Clarence-Smith, "Slavery in Coastal Southern Angola, 1875–1913", *Journal of Southern African Studies*, 2 (1976), pp. 214–223; Joseph C. Miller, "The Paradoxes of Impoverishment in the Atlantic Zone", in David Birmingham and Phyllis Martin (eds), *History of Central Africa*, vol. 1 (London, 1983), pp. 118–159; John Thornton, "The Slave Trade in Eighteenth Century Angola: Effects of Demographic Structure", *Canadian Journal of African Studies*, 14 (1980), pp. 417– 427. For the historiographical debate on the nature of slavery in Africa, see Suzanne Miers and Igor Kopytoff (eds), *Slavery in Africa: Historical and Anthropological Perspectives* (Madison, WI, 1977); Walter Rodney, *History of the Upper Guinea Coast: 1545–1800* (New York: Monthly Review Press, 1980); Joseph C. Miller, "Imbangala Lineage Slavery", in Miers and Kopytoff, *Slavery in Africa*, pp. 205–233; Paul E. Lovejoy, *Transformations in Slavery* (New York, 2000); Suzanne Miers and Richard Roberts (eds), *The End of Slavery in Africa* (Madison, WI, 1988), pp. 3–58; Klein, Bellagamba, and Greene, *Bitter Legacy*, pp. 1–19; Daniel B. Domingues da Silva, "The Supply of Slaves from Luanda, 1768–1806: Records of Anselmo Da Fonseca Coutinho", *African Economic History*, 38 (2009), pp. 53–76; Roquinaldo Ferreira, "Slavery and the Social and Cultural Landscape of Luanda", in Jorge Cañizares-Esguerra, Matt Childs, and James Sidbury (eds), *The Black Urban Atlantic in the Age of the Slave Trade* (Philadelphia, PA, 2013), pp. 185–205.

40. Green, "Building Slavery in the Atlantic World"; Chouki El Hamel, *Black Morocco: A History of Slavery, Race, and Islam* (New York, 2013); Bruce S. Hall, *A History of Race in Muslim West Africa, 1600–1960*, African Studies Series (Cambridge, 2011); Jennifer Lofkrantz, "Idealism and Pragmatism: The Related Muslim West African Discourses on Identity, Captivity and Ransoming", *African Economic History*, 42 (2015), pp. 87–107; Klein, Bellagamba, and Greene, *Bitter*

doubt that the form of slavery that developed in Angola was shaped by local societies, but also by the fact that the territories were part of the Portuguese empire. In some respects, particularly notions of skin-color classification and emancipation, slavery in Angola had more in common with experiences in Brazil than elsewhere on the continent. During the nineteenth century, the apprenticeship regimes, notions of social mobility, and status and racial classification corresponded to what was happening in Brazil and in the Caribbean during the same period.[41] This also shows how ideas circulated in the Atlantic world, influencing how colonial officials perceived and operated within legal slave systems.[42]

Enslaved labor was essential to running the colonial center of Benguela. In 1800, for example, the Brazilian-born governor Félix Xavier Pinheiro de Lacerda owned four enslaved children employed as domestic servants. Also serving in his house were an enslaved man called Eusébio and a freed black man, José, who worked as a cook, showing that free and enslaved people worked side by side.[43] In 1811, the governor of Benguela, António Rebello de Andrade Vasconcelos e Souza, had at least two young girls working as domestic slaves.[44] In Benguela and in the interior, colonial authorities and

Legacy; Benedetta Rossi (ed.), *Reconfiguring Slavery: West African Trajectories* (Liverpool, 2009); Marie Rodet, "Escaping Slavery and Building Diasporic Communities in French Soudan and Senegal, ca. 1880–1940", *International Journal of African Historical Studies*, 48:2 (2015), pp. 363–386.

41. See, for example, Hebe Maria Mattos de Castro, *Das cores do silêncio. Os significados da liberdade no sudeste escravista: Brasil século XIX* (Rio de Janeiro, 1995); Beatriz G. Mamigonian, "In the Name of Freedom: Slave Trade Abolition, the Law and the Brazilian Branch of the African Emigration Scheme (Brazil–British West Indies, 1830s–1850s)", *Slavery & Abolition*, 30 (2009), pp. 41–66; Douglas Libby, "A Culture of Colors Representational Identities and Afro-Brazilians in Minas Gerais in the Eighteenth and Nineteenth Centuries", *Luso-Brazilian Review*, 50:1 (2013), pp. 26–52; B.W. Higman, *Plantation Jamaica, 1750–1850: Capital and Control in a Colonial Economy* (Kingston, Jamaica, 2005); Rebecca J. Scott, *Slave Emancipation in Cuba the Transition to Free Labor, 1860–1899* (Pittsburgh, PA, 2000).

42. On the circulation of colonial officers between Brazil and Angola and Benguela see Hebe Mattos, "'Black Troops' and Hierarchies of Color in the Portuguese Atlantic World: The Case of Henrique Dias and His Black Regiment", *Luso-Brazilian Review*, 45:1 (2008), pp. 6–29; Mariana P. Candido, "South Atlantic Exchanges: The Role of Brazilian-Born Agents in Benguela, 1650–1850", *Luso-Brazilian Review*, 50:1 (2013), pp. 53–82; Roberto Guedes and Caroline S. Pontes, "Notícias do presídio de Caconda (1797). Moradores, escravatura, tutores e órfãos", in Eduardo França Paiva and Vanicléia Santos (eds), *África e Brasil no Mundo Moderno* (Belo Horizonte, 2013), pp. 153–180; Flávia Maria de Carvalho, *Sobas e homens do rei. Relações de poder e escravidão em Angola (séculos XVII e XVIII)* (Maceió, Alagoas, 2015).

43. Arquivo Nacional da Torre do Tombo (ANTT), Feitos Findos (FF), Justificações Ultramarinas (JU), África, bundle 12, no. 9, 28 July 1800. On the importance of slavery in Benguela, see Candido, *An African Slaving Port*; Roquinaldo Ferreira, "Biografia, mobilidade e Cultura Atlântica: A Micro-Escala do Tráfico de escravos em Benguela, séculos XVIII–XIX", *Tempo*, 10:2 (2006); Freudenthal, "Benguela".

44. ANA, Codex 323, fol. 28–29, 19 August 1811; ANA, Codex 323, fol. 30–31, 20 August 1811.

residents employed enslaved people, both male and female, in house gardens, especially in the cultivation of maize, beans, manioc, and pumpkin to provide the town's food supply.[45] Besides these domestic uses within household compounds, enslaved people were also employed as soldiers under Portuguese and African law. In the case of the Portuguese forces, officials employed enslaved males to march in front of the battalion; the military considered them dispensable soldiers. Despite their status as unfree persons, they carried weapons and were used to protect the free population who lived within the colonial centers as well as the long-distance trade caravans traveling inland.[46]

Before and after the 1836 slave export ban, enslaved people worked in mines in West Central Africa. In the interior of Angola, the Cambambe mines required a large number of workers, some of them with skilled training as blacksmiths.[47] In Benguela, the most important mines were those that extracted sulfur as well as salt. These relied on laborers provided by local authorities, the *sobas*, who were forced to provide free and coercive labor to the colonial state as a tribute. While sulfur was mined for export, salt was shipped inland and utilized as currency to acquire products such as ivory or wax.[48] Salt produced in the Benguela region was also exported to

45. IHGB, DL32,02.01 "Relação dos moradores da cidade de São Filipe de Benguela", 1789; IHGB, DL81,02.28, "Mapas feitos por Alexandre José Botelho de Vasconcelos, contendo censo das pessoas livres, escravos, casas, terras e senzalas", 1796. For the use of enslaved people in farming in Bihé, see ANA, Codex 445, fol. 57–58, 21 April 1810. On the use of slave labor in gardens in Angola, see Selma Pantoja, "Donas de 'arimos'. Um negócio feminino no abastecimento de gêneros alimentícios em Luanda (séculos XVIII e XIX)", in Selma Pantoja (ed.), *Entre Áfricas e Brasis* (Brasilia, 2001), pp. 35–49; Mariana P. Candido, "Aguida Gonçalves da Silva, une dona à Benguela à fin du XVIIIe siècle", *Brésil(s). Sciences Humaines et Sociales*, 1 (2012), pp. 33–54; Vanessa S. Oliveira, "Gender, Foodstuff Production and Trade in Late-Eighteenth Century Luanda", *African Economic History*, 43 (2015), pp. 57–81.

46. On the use of slaves in the military, see AHU, Angola, box 88, doc. 8, 10 June 1798. For some cases, see ANA, Codex 510, fol. 9v, 20 May 1847; João Carlos Feo Cardoso de Castello Branco e Torres, *Memórias Contendo a Biographia Do Vice-Almirante Luiz Da Motta Feo e Torres* (Paris, 1825), p. 344; Jean-Baptiste Douville, *Voyage au Congo et dans l'interieus de l'Afrique Equinoxiale. Fait dans les années 1828, 1829 et 1830* (Paris, 1832), vol. 1, p. 18. See also Roquinaldo Ferreira, "O Brasil e a arte da guerra em Angola (sécs. XVII e XVIII)", *Estudos Historicos*, 1:39 (2007), pp. 3–23; Sean Arnold Stilwell, *Paradoxes of Power: The Kano "mamluks" and Male Royal Slavery in the Sokoto Caliphate, 1804–1903* (Portsmouth, NH, 2004); Sparks, *Where the Negroes Are Masters*; Rudolph T. Ware, *The Walking Qur'an Islamic Education, Embodied Knowledge, and History in West Africa* (Chapel Hill, NC, 2014); Jennifer Lofkrantz, "Protecting Freeborn Muslims: The Sokoto Caliphate's Attempts to Prevent Illegal Enslavement and Its Acceptance of the Strategy of Ransoming", *Slavery & Abolition*, 32 (2011), pp. 109–127; Paul E. Lovejoy, "Jihad and the Era of the Second Slavery", *Journal of Global Slavery*, 1 (2016), pp. 28–43.

47. Beatrix Heintze, *Fontes para a história de Angola no século XVII*, 2 vols (Stuttgart, 1985); Crislayne Alfagali, *Ferreiros e fundidores da Ilamba. Uma história social da fabricação do ferro e da Real Fábrica de Nova Oeiras (Angola, segunda metade do século XVIII)* (Luanda, 2018).

48. Thomas Edward Bowdich, *An Account of the Discoveries of the Portuguese in the Interior of Angola and Mozambique* (London, 1824), p. 21; see also *Almanak Statistico da Provincia de*

Luanda, where it supplied local needs in addition to vessels departing for the Americas.[49]

In a town where no animal transport existed, the colonial state employed enslaved people to convey all kinds of products and people.[50] Groups of three or four enslaved men carried people in palanquins, unloaded the cargo from anchored ships, and carried both loads and passengers to the decks.[51] The movement of a passenger to or from a boat required the labor of four slaves to prevent the passenger from getting his or her clothes wet.[52] Porters provided transportation inside the town and carried all sort of products, including toilet waste.[53] Porters also carried the luggage of Portuguese administrators and ecclesiastical leaders who were moving to the interior.[54] Enslaved men and women served as porters for the transportation of weapons, gunpowder, food, and military supplies for expeditions.[55] In some cases, captives belonged to the administration, but Benguela residents were compelled to provide their own enslaved men, women, and children for colonial expeditions.[56] These requisitions were not always popular. Masters wanted to avoid losing their labor and tried to get out of sending their captives, even by lying about their state of fitness.[57]

Angola, xix. On salt mines, see Antonio de Saldanha da Gama, *Memória sobre as colônias de Portugal. Situadas na costa occidental d'Africa* (Paris, 1839), p. 71; Miller, *Way of Death*, p. 56. On the labor extracted from local authorities, see Beatrix Heintze, "The Angolan Vassal Tributes of the 17th Century", *Revista de História Económica e Social*, 6 (1980), pp. 57–78; Carvalho, *Sobas e homens do rei*.

49. Miller, *Way of Death*, p. 274.

50. "Relatório do Governo de D. Miguel António de Mello," *Boletim da Sociedade de Geografia de Lisboa*, 5:9 (1885), p. 550.

51. On the use of slaves as palanquin carriers, see ANA, Codex 447, fol. 30v–34, 6 October 1818; ANA, Codex 507, fol. 129v–132v, 18 January 1819. Carrying someone on a palanquin was an activity restricted to slaves throughout the South Atlantic world. See Miller, *Way of Death*, pp. 191–192, 293; Karasch, "From Porterage to Proprietorship: African Occupations in Rio de Janeiro, 1808-1850", in *Race and Slavery in the Western Hemisphere: Quantitative Studies*, ed. Stanley L. Engerman and Eugene D. Genovese (Princeton, N.J., 1975), pp. 377–379. On portage and prestige, see Magyar, *Reisen in Süd-Afrika*, ch. 1, "Estadia em Benguela", p. 22; ch. 2, "Partida para o Interior de África", p. 1. On reactions to this practice, see Da Gama, *Memória sobre as colonias de Portugal*, p. 75.

52. Feo Torres, *Memórias Contendo a Biographia*, p. 364.

53. László Magyar, *Reisen in Süd-Afrika in den Jahren 1849 bis 1857* (Leipzig, 1859), ch. 1, "Estadia em Benguela", p. 23. I would like to thank Conceição Neto for providing the Portuguese translation of the German edition of Magyar's diary.

54. See letters written by D. Miguel Antonio de Melo, governor of Angola, which stressed that internal journeys to Caconda could be costly; AHU, Angola, box 101, doc. 3, 26 March 1801; AHU, Angola, box 121 A, doc. 16, 9 December 1810; ANA, Codex 445, fol. 111v, 1 December 1811; ANA, Codex 517, fol. 56v, 7 January 1796. See also Feo Torres, *Memórias Contendo a Biographia*, p. 303.

55. Douville, *Voyage au Congo*, vol. 2, p. 117; A. J. R. Russell-Wood, *The Black Man in Slavery and Freedom in Colonial Brazil* (New York, 1982).

56. ANA, Codex 441, fol. 5, 27 July 1796.

57. ANA, Codex 455, fol. 267, 1 December 1846.

The enslaved population also did most of the work in town as bakers, fishers, and tailors. Enslaved men and women employed in skilled positions enjoyed social status and some level of monetary compensation, which allowed them to save toward manumission.[58] At the turn of the nineteenth century, António Pascoal was an enslaved blacksmith who belonged to Inés, a black woman. In 1796, Pascoal acquired the support of Benguela's governor to establish a workshop in Benguela with his apprentice, António Felipe, thus becoming the only blacksmith in town.[59] Fifteen years later, in 1811, Francisco, Dona Maria Domingos de Barros's slave, worked in the royal iron workshop and received a small sum of money for his work.[60]

Although enslaved people were everywhere in Benguela, the official correspondence provides little detail about the nature of their lives, their housing conditions, their family and religious experiences, or their daily lives (Figure 3).

SLAVERY AFTER THE END OF SLAVE EXPORTS

According to a report by the traveler Carlos José Caldeira, who visited Benguela in the late 1840s, the houses along the Morena beach served as gathering points for the ivory, wax, gum copal, leather, and orchil exported from the port. Caldeira reported that more than 1,000 enslaved individuals were employed in the cultivation of orchil lichen at different plantations stretching from Benguela to the port of Mossamedes further south.[61] The use of enslaved labor in major public construction projects such as the building of administrative houses or streets also continued after the slave export ban. To compensate for the physically demanding tasks and to avoid the possibility of escapes that would delay the progress of work, Portuguese agents offered compensation in the form of tobacco or alcohol to the enslaved men and women employed in urban infrastructure construction.[62]

In the 1840s and 1850s, Benguela was a town in transition, moving away from slave exports and toward the use of enslaved labor locally, although smuggling continued to occur. Colonial authorities denounced attempts to embark captives illegally, in part because the continuing export of human

58. On cases of skilled slaves manumitted by slaveholders, see ANTT, FF, JU, África, bundle. 2, no. 3 A; ANTT, FF, JU, África, bundle 2, no. 3 B; ANTT, FF, JU, África, bundle. 21, no. 12; ANTT, FF, JU, África, bundle. 22, no. 5. On cases in Luanda, see Oliveira, "Trabalho escravo".
59. ANA, Codex 442, fol. 21, 31 October 1796.
60. ANA, Codex 445, fol. 123v, 1 February 1812.
61. Carlos José Caldeira, *Apontamentos d'uma viagem de Lisboa à China e da China a Lisboa* (Lisbon, 1852), pp. 174–176. See also Monteiro, *Angola and the River Congo*, pp. 267–268. On the importance of wax in Benguela in the post-1850s, see Candido, "Trade, Slavery and Migration", p. 74.
62. ANA, Codex 453, fol. 15v, 24 November 1842.

Figure 3. "A Portrait of a Slave in the Portuguese settlement of Benguela, on the western coast of Africa. (One of the many unhappy objects of cruelty, in that part of the world) guarding sheep, he has an Iron Collar fastened round his neck, which would entangle him in the bushes, if he attempted to escape to his relations. The wounds on his body were inflicted by the whip. This miserable being was purchased & made free, by a British Naval Officer, for Sixty Dollars, who brought him to England in 1813, and had him Christened at Norwich when he was 14 years old, where he is now at School by the name of Charles Fortunatus Freeman." Published by Edward Orme, Bond Street, London, July 20th 1813.
National Maritime Museum, Greenwich, London, Michael Graham-Stewart Slavery Collection.

beings threatened the expansion of local agricultural enterprise.[63] In 1854, for example, 194 captives were located in Equimina, a beach south of Benguela, where slave traders planned to export them clandestinely. Among them were fifty-three men, thirty-three women, thirty-seven young girls, sixty-nine young boys, and five babies. The large number of children caught in this single operation underlines the large number of young people deported from West Central Africa in the nineteenth century.[64] On the farms in Equimina, enslaved

63. AHU, 2 Section, Folder 30, 2 February 1862.
64. Tribunal da Comarca de Benguela (TCB), "Translado de uns autos de tomada e apreensão [...] José Luis da Silva Viana e Ignácio Teixeira Xavier, como abaixo se declara", 19 December 1854. For

people, while secured with chains, iron collars, and shackles, produced, among other items, sugar and *aguardente*, a distilled sugarcane alcohol.[65]

In the 1860s, the traveler John Monteiro described "the houses [of Benguela] having large walled gardens and enclosures for slaves".[66] The visitors reported encountering enslaved people in the streets, in part due to the increase in the enslaved population in the wake of the 1836 slave export ban, the 1850 closure of the Brazilian market, and the local consolidation of the plantation economy, such as the establishment of large farms dedicated to the cultivation of sugarcane.[67] The 1859 slave register provides some clues about the type of labor performed by unfree people. Male captives were listed with skilled positions including masons, fishermen, carpenters, cooks, and tailors. They also served as barbers, shoemakers, bakers, and sailors.[68] There are few references to the occupations of enslaved women in the colonial documents, yet the slave register reveals that women also performed skilled labor as seamstresses, cooks, launderers, and street vendors.[69] All of these urban activities benefited their masters, who profited from their street work. One of the main activities enslaved women performed in Benguela was to supply food and water to a population in constant movement. The concentration of many enslaved street vendors belonging to the same owner indicates that specific residents dominated some urban trade activities. António da Costa Covelo, a Benguela resident, owned thirty enslaved individuals, two-thirds of whom were women. While Covelo employed his male captives mainly in fishing and copper activities, eighteen out of his twenty enslaved women were street vendors. Covelo had only two female captives who were not *quitandeiras*: Sebastiana, an eight-year-old girl, and Joaquina, a one-year-old toddler.[70]

the literature on enslaved children in the nineteenth century, see David Eltis and Stanley L. Engerman, "Was the Slave Trade Dominated by Men?" *Journal of Interdisciplinary History*, 23 (1992), pp. 237–257; Audra Diptee, *From Africa to Jamaica: The Making of an Atlantic Slave Society, 1775–1807* (Gainsville, FL, 2012); Benjamin Nicholas Lawrance, *Amistad's Orphans: An Atlantic Story of Children, Slavery, and Smuggling* (New Haven, CT, 2015).

65. ANA, Codex 475, fol. 1, 7 November 1865; Monteiro, *Angola and the River Congo*, p. 281. This episode was also reported by the British Department of Foreign Affairs; see Lewis Hertslet, *A Collection of Treaties and Conventions, Between Great Britain and Foreign Powers*, vol. X (London, 1859), pp. 488–489.

66. Monteiro, *Angola and the River Congo*, p. 265.

67. W.G. Clarence-Smith, "Capitalist Penetration among the Nyaneka of Southern Angola, 1760 to 1920s", *African Studies*, 37 (1978); W.G. Clarence-Smith, *Slaves, Peasants, and Capitalists in Southern Angola, 1840–1926*, African Studies Series 27 (Cambridge, 1979); Freudenthal, *Arimos e fazendas*; Freudenthal, "Benguela."

68. The Benguela slave register lists ninety fishermen, 124 carpenters, fifty male cooks, and thirty tailors, among other occupations. See ANA, Codex 3160.

69. ANA, Codex 3160; *Almanak statistico da Provincia d'Angola e suas dependencias para o anno de 1852* (Luanda: Imprensa do Governo, 1851), p. 54.

70. ANA, Codex 3160. On enslaved women labor, see Robertson, "We Must Overcome"; Vanessa S. Oliveira, "Notas preliminares sobre punição de escravos em Luanda (século XIX)",

At different times in the nineteenth century, women formed most of the enslaved population in Benguela, as can be seen in Figure 4. As in the pre-1836 period, enslaved women worked on domestic tasks or in the house gardens, but also took part in urban commercial activities.[71] When employed in domestic tasks, enslaved women cleaned, took care of the house, and cooked; they also acted as nurses, performed many tasks in the house for the slave masters, and met their sexual demands.[72]

With the decline of slave exports and the expansion of legitimate commerce in ivory, beeswax, and then wild rubber, enslaved people were also put to work on the new farms and plantations established around Benguela and in Dombe Grande. There, they provided much of the labor needed for the cultivation of cotton and sugarcane, and for orchil lichen collection.[73] The businesswoman Teresa de Jesus Barruncho established plantations in Benguela, Cuio, and Dombe Grande. By 1861, she had three different plantations in Dombe Grande; on one of her plantations she had more than 300 captives, many of them women. As a result, Barruncho became the leading exporter of cotton and wax from the port of Benguela.[74]

Reports indicate that, during the 1860s, the landscape was transformed by the expansion of agriculture and the plantation economy as "the great plains that used to be covered by dense woods and served as refuge for wild animals, are now clear of trees, and almost all of the land along the coast is now plantations of cotton and sugarcane".[75] By the second half of the nineteenth century, slavery in Benguela resembled the plantation economy in the Americas. While urban slavery continued to be important, many of Benguela's wealthy residents expanded their business activities in surrounding areas by investing in

in *O colonialismo português. Novos rumos da historiografia dos PALOP* (Porto, 2013), pp. 155–176; Oliveira, "Slavery and the Forgotten Women Slave Owners"; Oliveira, "Trabalho escravo".

71. See Selma Pantoja, "As Fontes Escritas do Século XVII e o Estudo da Representação do Feminino em Luanda", in *Construindo o passado Angolano. As fontes e a sua interpretação. Actas do II* Seminário internacional sobre a história de Angola (Lisbon, 2000), pp. 583–596.

72. Magyar, *Reisen in Süd-Afrika*, ch. 1: "Estadia em Benguela", p. 10. I am very grateful to Maria da Conceição Neto, who shared her Portuguese translation of the original Hungarian. On the sexual exploitation of enslaved women in Benguela, see Mariana P. Candido, "Concubinage and Slavery in Benguela, c.1750–1850", in Olatunji Ojo and Nadine Hunt (eds), *Slavery in Africa and the Caribbean: A History of Enslavement and Identity Since the 18th Century* (London, 2012), pp. 65–84.

73. AHU, Angola, Codex 542, fol. 111v, 30 December 1826; Feo Torres, *Memórias Contendo a Biographia*, pp. 334–335; da Gama, *Memória sobre as colônias de Portugal*, p. 8; *Almanak Statistico da Provincia de Angola*, p. 50.

74. BOGGPA, 1862, no. 894, 22 November 1862, fol. 333–334; BOGGPA, 1864, no. 6, 6 February 1864, fol. 55. See also Freudenthal, *Arimos e Fazendas*, p. 213; Alexandre and Dias, *O Império Africano*, p. 450.

75. AHU, Correspondência dos Governadores, Folder 38, 21 December 1868, document "Relatório do Governo de Benguela referente a 1864–68".

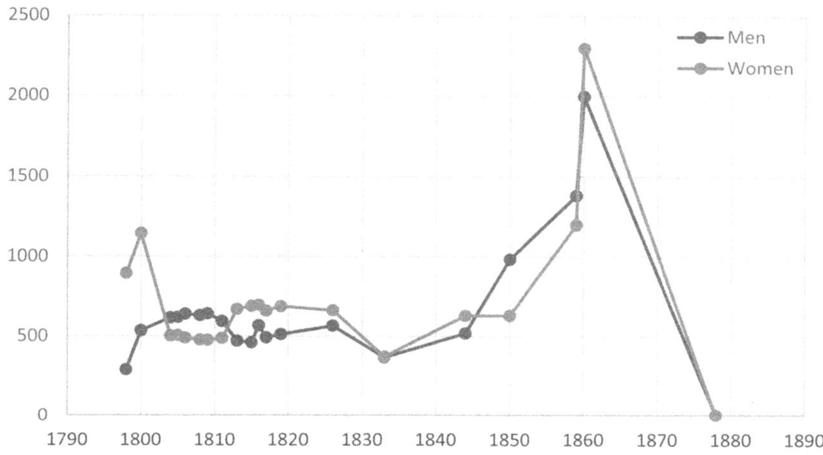

Figure 4. Benguela enslaved population by gender, 1800–1880.
Sources: AHU, Angola, 1 section, box 88, document 46; ANA, Codex 442, fols. 161v–162; AHU, Angola, 1 section, box 113, document 6; AHU, Angola, 1 section, box 116, document 87; AHU, Angola, 1 section, box 118, document 21; AHU, Angola, 1 section, box 120, document 21; AHU, Angola, 1 section, box 121, document 32; AHU, Angola, 1 section, box 124, document 8.; AHU, Angola, 1 section, box 127, document 59; AHU, Angola, 1 section, box 131, document 45; AHU, Angola, 1 section, box 133, document 32; AHU, Angola, 1 section, box 136, document 19; AHU, Angola, 1 section, box 138, document 1; AHU, Angola, 1 section, box 156, document 16; AHU, Angola, 1 section, box 176, document 17.

the agricultural economy to export its crops to growing industrialized countries in Europe and North America.

RESISTANCE

Slavery was not mild in West Central Africa, and evidence suggests its violent nature. Severe physical punishment or the threat of being sent to the Americas may have prevented some slave resistance and uprisings, yet they did occur.[76] The same violence that generated slaves and maintained control over them

76. On slave resistance and flight in Angola, see Clarence-Smith, "Runaway Slaves"; Freudenthal, "Os quilombos de Angola"; Beatrix Heintze, *Asilo ameaçado. Oportunidades e consequências da fuga de escravos em Angola no século XVII* (Luanda, 1995); Roquinaldo Ferreira, "Escravidão e revoltas de escravos em Angola (1830–1860)", *Afro-Ásia*, 21–22 (1998), pp. 9–44; Roquinaldo Ferreira, "Slave Flights and Runaway Communities in Angola (17th–19th Centuries)", *Anos 90*, 21:40 (2014), pp. 65–90; Roquinaldo Ferreira, "Slavery and the Social and Cultural Landscape of Luanda", in Jorge Cañizares-Esguerra, Matt Childs, and James Sidbury (eds), *The Black Urban Atlantic in the Age of the Slave Trade* (Philadelphia, PA, 2013), pp. 185–205.

could also trigger resistance.[77] The historical registers did not record acts of daily resistance such as working at a slow pace, sabotaging tasks, or breaking tools; the authorities only recorded instances of violent resistance that demonstrated a physical clash with the system.

Events taking place in the Atlantic world and in the interior of Benguela shaped the ways captives viewed their slavery, inclining them to resist, negotiate, or integrate into the host society. Continuous warfare or political turbulence in the interior as well as social insecurity may have led enslaved individuals to negotiate their labor conditions. Moments of change in the Atlantic world or instability after the death of slave masters encouraged many to run away, as scholars have pointed out.[78] The authorities feared assembled groups of enslaved individuals, perceived as especially dangerous to social stability particularly in a port town with a large enslaved population. When groups of captives confronted each other in the streets, slaveholders and military personnel feared the consequences. In 1814, a group of enslaved men who belonged to Justiniano José dos Regos, a Benguela trader, physically attacked the captives of two other merchants, António Lopes Araújo and Francisco Ferreira Gomes. Colonial soldiers had to intervene to control the street fight and were wounded.[79] These street fights posed a serious threat to Benguela's colonial administration. In the mid-eighteenth century, any enslaved person caught using a knife against a free person could be punished with 105 lashes plus two months of forced labor at the disposal of the colonial state. On the second infraction the enslaved person faced double punishment, and after the third time he or she could be deported to Brazil. However, by the early nineteenth century, the authorities had changed this last punishment since it would affect the slave owner, who could lose his property overnight. Authorities instead imposed a new penalty: fifty lashes in a public space.[80]

Running away was an effective way to resist slavery. Colonial records suggest enslaved individuals often escaped and moved inland by following the paths of long-distance trade routes, which may have led them back to their homeland or to inland markets to look for help or follow a trail. In 1808, a team led by António headed toward the slave market in Caconda, more than 250 kilometers inland of Benguela, in search of captives who had fled their slaveowners in Benguela. Rumors spread in Benguela that some of António's enslaved females had urged other urban slaves to run away.

77. João José Reis and Eduardo Silva, *Negociação e Conflito. A resistência Negra no Brasil Escravista* (São Paulo, 1999), pp. 13–20; Heintze, *Asilo ameaçado.*

78. Freudenthal, "Os quilombos de Angola"; Clarence-Smith, "Runaway Slaves", pp. 23–33.

79. AHU, Angola, box 146, doc. 13, 9 November 1814. On Ferreira Gomes family, see Roquinaldo Ferreira, "Biografia como história social. O clã Ferreira Gomes e os mundos da escravização no Atlântico Sul", *Varia Historia,* 29:51 (2013), pp. 679–719.

80. See AHU, Angola, box 36, doc. 8, 27 March 1748; AHU, Angola, box 101, doc. 38, 25 August 1801.

Feeling responsible, António led a team of armed guards, but it is not clear if they ever located the runaway group.[81]

Free people offering help to runaway slaves could be arrested, as happened with dona Ana José Aranha, a black female trader who moved goods and people between inland markets and Benguela in the first decades of the nineteenth century. A resident in the market of Caconda, dona Aranha was one of the largest slave owners and food producers in the inland fortress. In her compound dona Aranha controlled 266 people, including eighty-four enslaved people who cultivated beans and manioc in her fields. Part of her production was probably destined to supply the Benguela population's demand for food. On one of her journeys to Benguela, another trader reported seeing some Benguela runaway captives employed in dona Aranha's caravan. The governor of Benguela ordered her arrest, alleging she was offering protection to runaway slaves and colonial soldiers who had abandoned their positions.[82] Four decades later, offering asylum to runaway slaves was punished not with arrest but with a fine. In 1846, Rita, a free black woman and resident of Benguela, received a fine of 100,000 *reis* for hiding two runaway captives. Two runaway women found refuge in Rita's compound after escaping their master's establishment in Benguela. Rita lived close by, and it is not clear if she participated in the escape. Since she had offered asylum and was caught, she was required to pay the fine imposed by the governor.[83]

Although some people were successful in fleeing captivity, the fear of being recaptured was real. This may explain why some individuals would return to Benguela and buy their manumission even after years spent living as a free person. This was the case with José Eleutério, who belonged to the Santa Casa da Misericórdia, the Holy House of Mercy, a Catholic lay institution intimately linked with Portuguese colonialism that operated a hospital in Benguela. When José Eleutério ran away the administrator of the hospital agreed to free him in exchange for 300,000 *reis*. Over three years later, Eleutério returned to Benguela, paid his manumission, and received his freedom letter in August 1817.[84] Cases in the Tribunal da Comarca de Benguela, the courthouse of Benguela, reveal that slave masters resisted freeing their captives even if they managed to save the money to buy their freedom.[85] Unlike Eleutério,

81. ANA, Codex 443, fol. 171, 25 January 1808.
82. On D. Aranha's case and her arrest see ANA, Codex 443, fol. 109v–110, 15 June 1802. For more on her, see Candido, *An African Slaving Port*, pp. 169–270.
83. ANA, Codex 444, fol. 116, 9 October 1846; ANA, Codex 455, fol. 238v, 14 October 1846; ANA, Codex 460, fol. 11v, 5 October 1846.
84. ANA, Codex 155, fol. 1v, 30 April 1817; ANA, Codex 155, fol. 5, 28 August 1817.
85. See, for example, TCB, "Autos crimes de reclamação de liberdade. Ministério Público vs António Martins Bastos, 1850", "Reinvindicação de liberdade. Teresa vs Joana Mendes de Moraes, 1860", and "Reinvindicação de liberdade. Júlia vs Josefa Manuel Pereira, 1860", among others. On masters' reluctance to free people, see José C. Curto, "'As If from a Free Womb': Baptismal Manumissions in the Conceição Parish, Luanda, 1778–1807", *Portuguese Studies*

Dorotéia, a runaway enslaved woman, was not able to buy her manumission after escaping her master. She served in the house of Lieutenant José Rodriguez Guimarães for many years until 1837, when she finally found an opportunity to flee. It appears she was able to escape north to the port of Novo Redondo, where she lived as a free trader. However, nine years later in 1846 a colonial officer identified her and informed Guimarães of her location.[86] It is unclear whether Dorotéia was recaptured. This case clearly reveals that colonial officers kept track of runaway individuals and searched for them even years after their flight.

The fear of runaway captives was constant in Benguela, in part because African rulers could easily offer refuge. The records suggest that running away was a successful strategy for most of the nineteenth century.[87] Only on very few occasions were colonial forces successful in locating and recapturing runaway individuals.[88] Under African rulers' jurisdiction, unfree people found mechanisms to escape, even committing crimes to be re-enslaved by someone else who became their new master. Cases like these, known as *tumbikar*, are rare in the Portuguese documentation since such events occurred beyond the Portuguese scope, but some itinerant merchants reported encountering cases of enslaved people willing to change masters. These cases are only attested for the period after the 1850s when these accounts were recorded.[89]

The existence of maroon communities in areas surrounding Benguela demonstrates that successful escapes were more common than the colonial sources indicate.[90] Anyone who offered asylum to runaway slaves could face severe retaliation. In the 1840s and 1850s, authorities and slave owners sometimes accused free or freed blacks of helping runaway slaves with promises of better and safer lives. The Benguela trader António Joaquim Monteiro accused Matias, also known as Matias *do sertão*, of convincing Monteiro's captives to run away in 1848. Sixteen of Monteiro's enslaved individuals planned to escape to the interior, but only three succeeded. With the collaboration of colonial

Review, 10:1 (2002), pp. 26–57; Oliveira, "Slavery and the Forgotten Women Slave Owners of Luanda".

86. ANA, Codex 166, fol. 134v, 17 July 1846.

87. ANA, Codex 443, fol. 156, 27 October 1807; ANA, Codex 509, fol. 256v–257, 7 December 1837; AHU, Angola, Correspondência dos Governadores, Folder 5 B, 24 December 1842; ANA, Codex 456, fol. 108v, 31 October 1844; ANA, Codex 461, fol. 33, 4 June 1847; ANA, Codex 463, fol. 114v, 31 May 1848.

88. BOGGPA, no. 513, 28 July 1855.

89. Magyar, *Reisen in Süd-Afrika*, ch. 7: "A Nação dos Quimbundos e seus Costumes", p. 19; Heintze, *Asilo ameaçado*.

90. Portuguese agents used the term *quilombo* to refer to maroon communities during the nineteenth century; see ANA, Codex 455, fol. 251–251v, 2 November 1846. For a discussion of the term, see Freudenthal, "Os quilombos de Angola", pp. 109–134; Maria Conceição Neto, "Kilombo, Quilombos, Ocilombo", *Revista Mensagem (Luanda)*, 4 (1989), pp. 5–19. For more on *quilombos* in Benguela see Ralph Delgado, *Ao Sul do Cuanza (ocupação e aproveitamento do Antigo Reino de Benguela)* (Lisbon, 1944), pp. 2, 623.

forces, Monteiro later apprehended all of them, including one in Matias's company. All of them quickly blamed Matias for their actions.[91] Free black people helped runaway slaves, usually leading them toward the interior in search of the protection of African rulers. Zambo, a free black man from the Dombe region, helped an enslaved woman belonging to dona Margarida to escape. In 1847, Portuguese agents pursued and captured both in the interior.[92] Occasionally, African rulers returned the runaway individuals to the Portuguese authorities, as in the case of the *soba* Marango from Ganda who recaptured a portion of the 130 runaway captives who had escaped from Marques Esteves, a resident of Catumbela. For his cooperation, the *soba* received ten firearms, gunpowder, textiles, and alcohol. However, *soba* Marango also wanted a cash reward beyond the goods he received.[93] One can only imagine the punishment that recaptured runaway enslaved individuals endured, since the historical documents provide little information.

Running away was relatively easy and offered a greater chance of success than more aggressive alternatives such as violent attacks against slave owners or uprisings. It also offered quicker access to freedom than negotiating access to manumission. The colonial records are limited and problematic and provide few clues about daily resistance. For example, unlike the case of Luanda, no information has been located on runaway slave announcements.[94] The number of escaped captives who were never recaptured is unknown. The sources are also limited to enslaved individuals under Portuguese jurisdiction, so little information is available on the nature of resistance of enslaved individuals who lived under the jurisdiction of African rulers.

CONCLUSION

The nineteenth century can only be considered the age of emancipation if we ignore the fact that the slave trade expanded after 1801 in the South Atlantic world. Unlike other places in the Atlantic world, in Benguela the nineteenth century was not a moment of freedom but a period when slavery expanded dramatically. Although slave exports were prohibited in 1836, the trade in human beings continued until the 1860s. In fact, the use of slave labor expanded after 1836 and the number of enslaved people in Benguela increased. In the colonial center enslaved people performed most of the work, both public and private. In the wake of the end of the slave trade, so-called legitimate trade expanded. Ironically, the legitimate commerce relied on forced labor to

91. ANA, Codex 461, fol. 71–72, 5 June 1848; ANA, Codex 462, fol. 108–110, 9 June 1848.
92. ANA, Codex 463, fol. 27, 27 November 1847.
93. Delgado, *Ao Sul do Cuanza*, pp. 1, 544–545.
94. José C. Curto, "Resistência à escravidão na África. O caso dos escravos fugitivos recapturados em Angola, 1846-1876", *Afro-Ásia*, 33 (2005), pp. 1–21.

supply the growing demand in Europe and North America for cotton, sugar, and natural resources such as wax, ivory, rubber, and gum copal. Thus, any attempt to portray the nineteenth century as an age of freedom and liberty excludes not only West Central Africa, but also events in other parts of the Atlantic world such as Brazil or Cuba.

In Portuguese territories in West Central Africa, slavery remained alive until 1869, when enslaved people were put into systems of apprenticeship very similar to labor regimes elsewhere in the Atlantic world. For the thousands of people who remained in captivity in Benguela, the nineteenth century continued to be a time of oppression, forced labor, and extreme violence. Yet, enslaved individuals resisted through flight and small acts of resistance that sabotaged masters and the colonial economy. Their resistance indicates that slavery in West Central Africa was as violent and oppressive as anywhere else in the Atlantic world.

IRSH 65 (2020), pp. 93–115 doi:10.1017/S0020859020000103

Freedom of Movement, Access to the Urban Centres, and Abolition of Slavery in the French Caribbean

Marion Pluskota

Institute for History, Leiden University
Johan Huizinga, Doelensteeg 16,
2311 VL Leiden, The Netherlands

E-mail: m.pluskota@hum.leidenuniv.nl

Abstract: How did the abolition of slavery influence the relations between urban centres and rural areas? How did "new" French citizens experience access to the urban environment? Based on the archives of the correctional courts, this article focuses on how race and citizenship determined the accessibility of French colonial urban spaces and institutions after 1848. The abolition of slavery in the French Antilles on 27 April 1848 led to a modification of the legal and judicial systems: the changing legal status of former slaves gave them new opportunities to move around the colonies, at least on paper. In theory, after 1848, everyone should have had freedom of social and spatial mobility and access to the urban centres and their institutions; what happened in practice, however, still needs to be researched. This article shows that the abolition exacerbated two dynamics already at play since the beginning of the nineteenth century: the control of the population and the attraction of the urban environment for the elite. The plantation system in the mid-nineteenth century was suffering both economically and politically: the newly acquired freedom and possible migration of former slaves to the towns (Saint-Pierre and Fort-de-France in Martinique, Pointe-à-Pitre and Basse-Terre in Guadeloupe) threatened to destabilize the system of private justice as well as the economic apparatus. To counteract these legal changes, vagrancy laws were implemented to restrict citizens' mobility while, at the same time, the white elite's discourse on urban spaces changed from them being seen as a hotbed for revolutionary ideas to representing a safe environment to which access needed to be restricted.

INTRODUCTION

Controlling, and criminalizing if necessary, the mobility of colonial subjects was an early priority for early modern colonial authorities. The colonies had been used as a safety valve by some states, such as Portugal and the UK, to send vagrants from Europe to work, and labour shortage dictated where they were to be sent.[1] The idea that colonial subjects could move where and when they chose was greatly undermined by the eighteenth century. Sarah Nicolazzo has shown how, in the eighteenth century, vagrancy took on a new meaning in the British colonies as labour became an essential value to the developing economy.[2] Vagrancy acts, originally copied from the metropoles, multiplied in the colonies to meet various purposes. The authorities used vagrancy laws to: control work supply; supervise the population; prevent the use of "non-conformist culture" such as obeah;[3] and as a form of social control to "improve" the nature of the population living in these territories. Some historians have suggested that, before emancipation and abolition, vagrancy laws were mostly aimed at "undesirable" Europeans, who were not carrying their weight in the development of the colony.[4] In port cities such as Calcutta and Zanzibar, vagrancy acts were used to get rid of drunk and disorderly Europeans, who were seen as a bad influence to the local communities whose labour was essential for economic development.[5] The means for sanctions against these subjects were however limited: it was not always possible to make them leave the colony, especially if they had been sent there as a punishment for vagrancy from their home country. In the nineteenth century and from the emancipation era onwards, vagrancy laws became a tool to force freed people to work in colonies relying mostly on an agricultural economy: studies on South African legislations against vagrants during the emancipation or on the West Indian British colonies and the United States after the civil war have shown how vagrancy laws were used to prevent freed people's mobility.[6] Vagrancy acts in the Caribbean colonies have often

1. A.L. Bier and Paul Ocobock (ed.), *Cast Out: Vagrancy and Homelessness in Global and Historical Perspectives* (Athens, OH, 2008), pp. 12–13; Muiris MacGiollabhui, "'Carrying the Green Bough': The Transnational Exile of the United Irishman, 1791–1806", in Thomas Adam (ed.), *Yearbook of Transnational History*, vol. 2 (Vancouver, 2019), pp. 51–76, 57.
2. Sarah Nicolazzo, "Vagrant Figures: Law, Labor, and Refusal in the Eighteenth-Century Atlantic World" (Ph.D., Penn University, 2014). Available at: http://repository.upenn.edu/edissertations/1386; last accessed 1 November 2019.
3. Danielle Boaz, "Fraud, Vagrancy and the Pretended Exercise of Supernatural Powers in England, South Africa and Jamaica", *Law and History*, 5:1 (2018), pp. 54–84; Danielle N. Boaz, "Obeah, Vagrancy, and the Boundaries of Religious Freedom: Analyzing the Proscription of 'Pretending to Possess Supernatural Powers' in the Anglophone Caribbean", *Journal of Law and Religion*, 32 (2017), pp. 423–448.
4. Bier and Ocobock, *Cast Out*, p. 13.
5. *Ibid.*
6. Richard Lyess Watson, *Slave Emancipation and Racial Attitudes in Nineteenth-Century South Africa* (Cambridge, 2012), pp. 48–50; Elizabeth Elbourne, "Freedom at Issue: Vagrancy Legislation and the Meaning of Freedom in Britain and the Cape Colony, 1799 to 1842", *Slavery & Abolition*, 15 (1994), pp. 114–150; Richard K. Fleischman, David Oldroyd, and Thomas N. Tyson, "The Efficacy/Inefficacy of Accounting in Controlling Labour During the Transition from Slavery in the United States and British West Indies", *Accounting, Auditing & Accountability Journal*, 24 (2011), pp. 751–780.

been seen as distinct from legislations and practices against marronage; however, as suggested by Robert Bancroft Cummings,[7] the distinction between the two is more subtle than initially thought. Before the nineteenth century, policing of vagrancy and marronage was carried out by masters and civilians, as were the punishments against runaway slaves. Control was thus exercised first and foremost by the plantation owners and their intendants, with help, if possible, of the local authorities. The ad hoc construction of justice in the colonies, especially in the British and French Caribbean colonies, which followed a proto-national model of development, meant that discretion on the side of the prosecutors was relatively large. Nicolazzo demonstrates how, in the eighteenth century, the "unpredictable mobility" of certain people, not easily identifiable, became synonymous with social and economic threats and therefore justified the extension of policing powers, as did marronage.[8] Viola Müller argues in this Special Issue that a more nuanced understanding of marronage is necessary to fathom the reality experienced by runaway slaves. Likewise, this article on vagrancy in the French colonies argues that the study of vagrancy acts against the new French citizens reveals more than a willingness by the local elite to prevent the mobility of the workforce. It highlights their attempts to create white urban enclaves by limiting access to the urban territory and urban institutions by freed people. The premises of racial segregation and urbanization control in colonial cities, which have usually been studied from the perspective of British colonies,[9] appear to have been well established in the agricultural colonies of the French Caribbean.

In theory, everyone after 1848 should have had freedom of social and spatial mobility and access to the judicial system and the urban market; but what happened in practice still needs to be researched. The question of former slaves' mobility has never been framed by historians of the French Caribbean in relation to the changing perception of the urban environment in a predominantly agricultural system. How did these legal changes impact freemen and freewomen and former slaves' access to the urban environment? The changing legal status of former slaves gave them new opportunities to move around the colonies, at least on paper. And having access to the urban environment also meant having access to the highest institutions of the colonies, particularly the courts of justice. Based on the archives of the

7. Robert Bancroft Cummings, "Queer Marronage and Caribbean Writing" (Ph.D., Leeds University, 2012), p. 46.

8. Nicolazzo, "Vagrant Figures", p. 35.

9. Andrew Burton, *African Underclass: Urbanisation, Crime and Colonial Order in Dar es Salaam* (Oxford, 2005), pp. 16–23; Jocelyn Alexander, "Hooligans, Spivs and Loafers"?: The Politics of Vagrancy in 1960s Southern Rhodesia", *The Journal of African History*, 53 (2012), pp. 345–366, 346–347.

correctional courts, this article focuses on how race and citizenship[10] determined the accessibility of French colonial urban spaces and institutions after 1848.

URBANIZATION IN THE FRENCH ANTILLES

The development of the sugar economy in the French Caribbean territories since the seventeenth century led to a relatively high population density in the most favourable islands.[11] Calm bays such as Fort-Royal (now Fort-de-France) and Saint-Pierre in Martinique, Port-au-Prince and Cap-Français in Haiti, or Basse-Terre and Pointe-à-Pitre in Guadeloupe became important ports of commerce, growing thanks to the colonial trades of, among others, slaves, sugar, indigo, and cotton.[12] These towns, which developed out of the port and/or military defences, followed an orthogonal street plan, often bordered by drainage canals or rivers, as in Fort-de-France, creating "natural" borders to the urban enclaves.[13] Saint-Pierre was surrounded by volcanic slopes that prevented its development towards the east and was also crossed by a river on its northern side (Figure 1).[14] These canals, rivers, and hills became a border between the colonial town and the *faubourgs*, which grew in connection with the port economy, but were not yet subject to urban planning.[15] Other French settlements of military origins in the Caribbean remained relatively small, such as Marigot in Saint Martin or Cayenne in French Guyana.[16] Despite being a strong contender in the eighteenth-century slave trade, with more than 500,000 men and women being transported to the French Antilles, the French settlements experienced limited urban development until the nineteenth century. Small parishes or *bourgs* were, however,

10. "Citizen" in this article refers to a person with civil rights, not political rights. On the possibility of being a "French man" without being a "French citizen", see Silyane Larcher, *L'Autre citoyen. L'Idéal républicain et les Antilles après l'esclavage* (Paris, 2014), pp. 163–65.

11. For instance, in 1789, Martinique counted roughly 99,100 inhabitants, for a surface of 1,128 km^2, in other words, eighty-eight inhabitants per km^2. See J.H. Galloway, *The Sugar Cane Industry: An Historical Geography from Its Origins to 1914* (Cambridge, 2005), p. 114.

12. Paul Butel, *Histoire des Antilles françaises* (Paris, 2003).

13. Nicolas Rey, *Lakou et ghetto. Les quartiers périphériques aux Antilles françaises* (Paris, 2001), pp. 54–57.

14. See the map of Saint-Pierre, 1824, by M. Monnier. Available at: http://gallica.bnf.fr/ark:/12148/btv1b6700416m/f7.item.zoom; last accessed 10 January 2017.

15. Rey, *Lakou et ghetto*, p. 56.

16. Due to the carceral nature of the town of Saint-Laurent-du-Maroni in French Guyana and its specific development in relation to the prison, it will not be included in this study. On the difficulty of settling in French Guyana, see Marie-Louise Marchand-Thébault, "L'esclavage en Guyane française sous l'ancien régime", *Revue française d'histoire d'outre-mer*, 47:166 (1960), pp. 5–75.

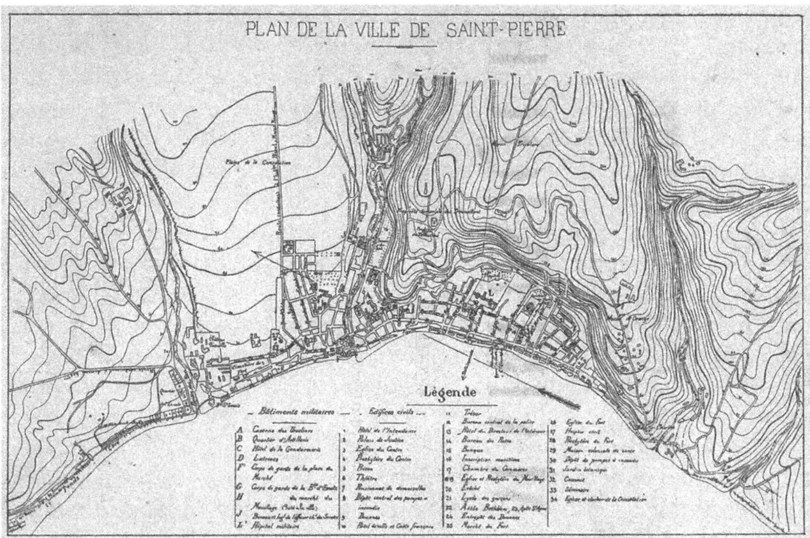

Figure 1. Map of Saint-Pierre, Martinique, 1902.

dotted along the coast.[17] Transport connections between the parishes in Martinique were relatively well established and frequent, but the geographical landscape of Guadeloupe made travel between the two sides of the island more difficult. The development of Pointe-à-Pitre, as a link between Basse-Terre and Grande-Terre, really started only with the British occupation of the island during the Seven Year's War. Drainage of the swampy grounds was necessary before any settlement was made possible.[18] The distinction between urban and rural was sharpened in the French Antillean colonies:[19] the model of economic development followed in Martinique and Guadeloupe meant that most of the workforce was spread in the rural areas to cultivate and harvest crops. The urban centres provided seats for the governmental, military, and judicial institutions, as well as some forms of entertainment for the elite and, for some, a place of residence. The number of inhabitants in the countryside was therefore much higher than in the urban centres, with an important concentration of slaves. Urban slavery may have

17. See, for instance, the map of Martinique in 1848, in Gilbert Pago, *Les femmes et la liquidation du système esclavagiste à la Martinique, 1848–1852* (Matoury, 1998), p. 20.
18. Rey, *Lakou et ghetto*, p. 55.
19. Malcolm Cross, *Urbanization and Urban Growth in the Caribbean: An Essay on Social Change in Dependent Societies* (Cambridge, 1979), p. 25.

been more limited than in the rural areas, but it did exist:[20] domestics,[21] laundresses, and day labourers lived in the urban centres or in their immediate proximity and were more numerous than the white population. The rest of the white planters resided on their plantations, the *habitations sucrerie*, which started to decline in the second half of the nineteenth century.[22]

The main towns in the French Caribbean were located on the largest French islands: Martinique (Figure 2) and Guadeloupe (Figure 3), which, after the Napoleonic episode and an English invasion, continued to be governed by the French. Martinique was the official centre of the French Antilles, with the governor residing in Fort-Royal since 1790. Both Guadeloupe and Martinique's economies turned towards the production of sugar in the seventeenth century and the labour-intensive monoculture of sugar cane had a strong impact on the demographics of the islands: sixty to seventy per cent of the population were still working in the rural areas by the mid-nineteenth century.[23] The urban centres of Saint-Pierre, Fort-Royal,[24] and those of Basse-Terre and Pointe-à-Pitre developed thanks to the colonial economy and the importance of maritime trade.[25] The population living in what can be defined as *villes et bourgs* was therefore rather limited: twenty-three per cent of the inhabitants of Guadeloupe (without dependencies) lived in a town or large village in 1847; in Martinique this was 26.5 per cent. White people accounted for eight per cent of the total population in Martinique in 1847. The administration of Guadeloupe claimed that they could not give a precise number for the "white/coloured" ratio in 1847 but assumed it to be the same as in Martinique, and claimed that the class of freemen/freewomen was four times higher than the white class.[26] A further note in 1849 explained that white people constituted one-twelfth, or 8.3 per cent, of the total population.[27]

20. Anne Pérotin-Dumon, *La ville aux îles, la ville dans l'île* (Paris, 2002), p. 551.
21. Bernard Moitt, *Women and Slavery in the French Antilles, 1635–1848* (Bloomington, IN, 2001), pp. 61–62.
22. Christian Schnakenbourg, "La disparition des 'habitation-sucreries' en Guadeloupe (1848–1906). Recherche sur la désagrégation des structures préindustrielles de la production sucrière antillaise après l'abolition de l'esclavage', *Revue française d'histoire d'outre-mer*, 74:276 (1987), pp. 257–309.
23. Myriam Cottias, "Droit, justice et dépendance dans le Antilles françaises (1848–1852)", *Annales. Histoire, sciences sociales*, 59 (2004), pp. 547–567, 548.
24. Roughly 24,000 inhabitants in Saint-Pierre in 1850 and 13,130 inhabitants in Fort-de-France in 1853: *Des villages de Cassini aux communes d'aujourd'hui*. Available at : http://cassini.ehess.fr/cassini/fr/html/1_navigation.php; last accessed 18 December 2019.
25. In 1846, Basse-Terre and its suburbs counted 6,800 inhabitants; Pointe-à-Pitre and suburbs 13,300 inhabitants according to *Tableaux de population, de culture, de commerce et de navigation* (Paris, 1846), p. 15. Note that Pointe-à-Pitre was badly destroyed in 1843 after an earthquake that killed an estimated 3,000 people.
26. *Tableaux de population, de culture, de commerce et de navigation* (Paris, 1851), pp. 12–15.
27. *Tableaux de population, de culture, de commerce et de navigation* (Paris, 1852), pp. 14–15.

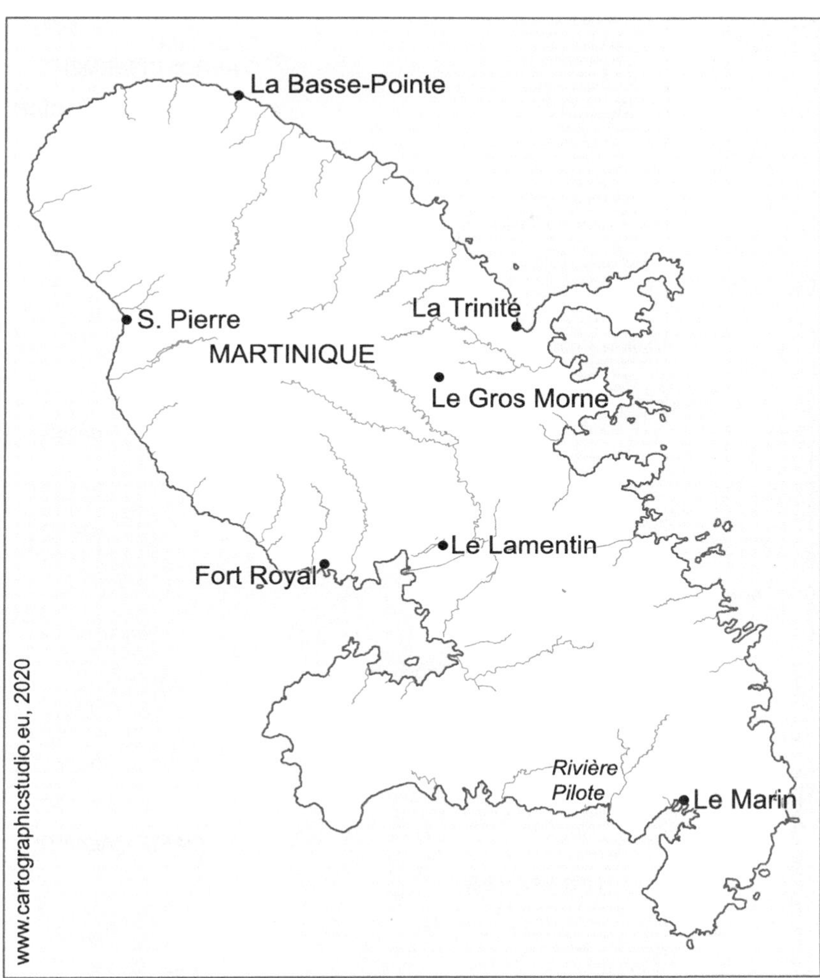

Figure 2. Map of Martinique and its main towns and villages, 1835.

The urban centres (the *bourgs*, large villages, and towns) of the French Antilles were dominated thus by the free population consisting of the white elite (comprising settlers, or *colons*, and creoles), poor whites, the mixed-races, foreigners, and black freemen and freewomen.[28] In Martinique before the abolition, the *villes et bourgs* counted around 23,800 free people and 8,200 slaves. In Guadeloupe and its dependencies, 19,500 free people and 10,000 slaves lived

28. This category includes free-born blacks and freedmen and freedwomen.

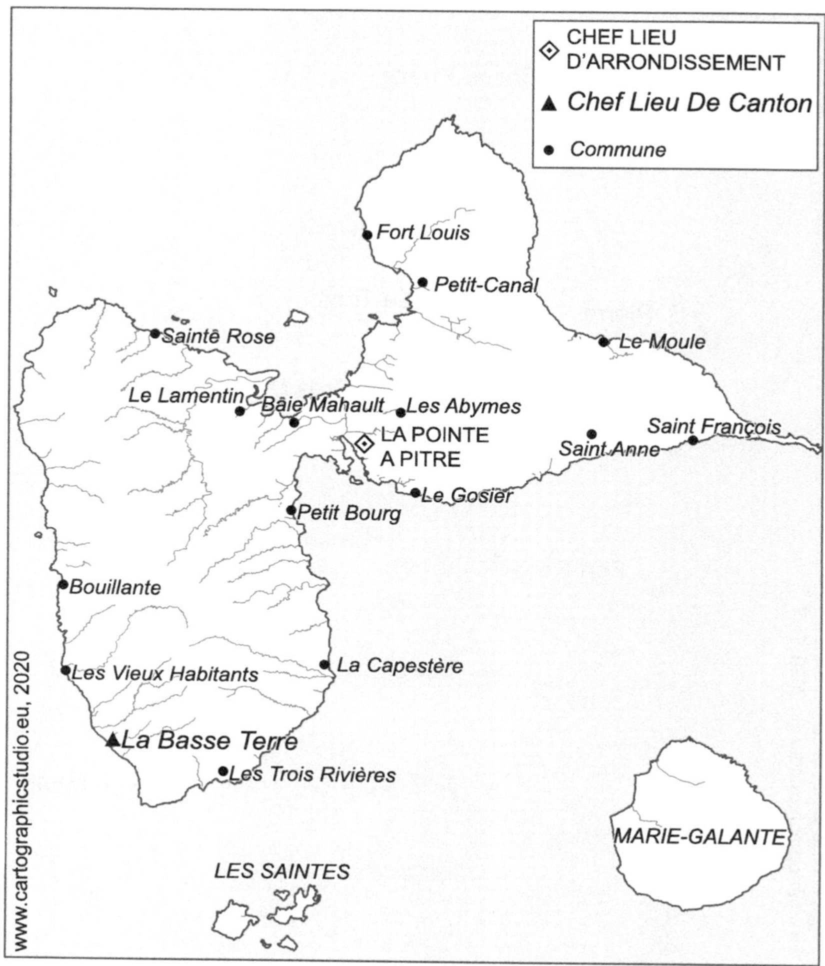

Figure 3. Map of Guadeloupe, based on an etching by Morin, 1835.

in the towns and large villages. In contrast, rural Martinique had 24,400 free people and 64,600 slaves in 1846, while Guadeloupe had a larger share of slaves, with around 77,800 slaves and 21,800 free people (Table 1).[29] The settlement of the official colonial government in the urban centres also brought with it a certain number of metropolitan civil servants and officials who resided close to the seat of the government. Many white *colon* families settled in these towns, but also freed blacks who had been manumitted and left their

29. *Tableaux de population, de culture, de commerce et de navigation* (Paris, 1851), pp. 12–15.

Table 1. *Urban population in Martinique and Guadeloupe in the mid-nineteenth century.*

Islands	Urban population in 1847	Rural population in 1847	Total population in 1847
Martinique	Slaves: 8,210 Free: 23,861 26.5%	Slaves: 64,640 Free: 24,410 73.5%	121,130
Guadeloupe	Slaves: 9,975 Free: 19,528 23%	Slaves: 77,777 Free: 21,829 77%	129,109

Source: Tableaux de population, de culture, de commerce et de navigation (Paris, 1851), pp. 12–15.

former masters to work in towns.[30] Before 1848, slaves formed seventy-five per cent of the population in the French Antilles[31] and although most of them were employed in the plantations, some were living in the towns as domestics for white and freemen's families, and they could also be seen working in the *ateliers* adjoining the port.[32] According to the 1847 census in Guadeloupe, sixty-five per cent of urban families had between one and three slaves working in their household, most of them women, employed to cook, wash, and generally run the house.[33] A list of 218 slaves from the French Caribbean colonies and La Réunion, whose slaves received their freedom in 1847, gives an example of the role of urban domesticity in slaves' occupations. Domestics counted for roughly forty per cent of the occupations of the urban slaves, along with manual labouring and working as a field hand, a much higher percentage than in the countryside.[34] At the beginning of the nineteenth century, some urban slaves were also employed as day labourers and were hired out by their masters and mistresses (notably impoverished creole women)[35] who were living in town.[36] Overall, the ratio of "whites" to "people of colour" was therefore less disproportionate in the urban centres than in the countryside, especially on the sites of original settlement, which

30. Butel, *Histoire des Antilles françaises*, p. 307.
31. For Guadeloupe, see Pérotin-Dumon, *La ville aux îles*, pp. 330–331. For Martinique, see Arlette Gautier, "Les Familles Esclaves Aux Antilles Françaises, 1635–1848." *Population*, 55 (2000), pp. 975–1001, p. 981.
32. Josette Fallope, "Les occupations d'esclaves à la Guadeloupe dans la première moitié du XIXe siècle", *Revue française d'histoire d'outre-mer*, 74:275 (1987), pp. 189–205.
33. Raymond Boutin, *Petit-Canal. Une commune de la Guadeloupe au XIXe siècle* (Paris, 1983).
34. Moitt, *Women and Slavery*, p. 61.
35. Pago, *Les femmes et la liquidation du système esclavagiste*, pp. 36–37.
36. Rebecca Hartkopf Schloss, *Sweet Liberty: The Final Days of Slavery in Martinique* (Philadelphia, PA, 2009), p. 11.

were the richest and best built.[37] Before the abolition of slavery, the demography of the towns changed little, although the first half of the nineteenth century saw an increase of freedmen and freedwomen moving to the towns, linking urban development with the increase of free people.[38]

"BEING MOBILE" IN THE FRENCH COLONIES

Following the expansion of the colonial society from the seventeenth century, the socio-economic positions and the mobility (both social and spatial) of people inhabiting the Antillean islands were strongly defined by their colour, gender, and civil status.[39] How one was to behave would depend on these criteria and going against prescribed behaviours, such as being absent from the master's house for too long or not taking care of one's family, would lead to various punishments for both white and black people.[40] These could include fines, being shunned by the community, and even official expulsion from the colony.[41] However, slaves and freemen and freewomen had to endure much harsher punishments than white people, rich or poor. Slaves were regularly whipped and sometimes tortured for bad behaviour against their masters or against another white person. The society was strictly divided and people who did not belong to the two well-defined categories of black slaves or white elite often struggled to find their place and, more importantly, their rights in this colonial society. Black freemen and freewomen, mixed-race children and adults, and poor white people, also known as *petit-blancs*, were constantly negotiating their position in society, in relation to each other and under the control of the elite.

Despite these strict divides between classes, members of the free black and slave classes experienced a degree of social and spatial mobility before the abolition; and opportunities for mobility could often be found in the urban centres. Since the eighteenth century, some masters ignored the colonial legislation regarding slaves' work and freedom of movement by giving them substantial responsibilities in their business or by letting them carry out tasks away from the master's household and with little supervision. Indeed, in order to maximize their assets, some masters provided their slaves with an education and allowed them to keep small shops or take care of the accounts, or even gave them "managerial" responsibilities that, according to Coquille, the procurer of Guadeloupe, made them particularly "arrogant".[42]

37. For instance, the parish of the Fort in Saint-Pierre, which contrasted strongly with its poorer *faubourgs*. Or the poor district of Terres-de-Sainville in Fort-Royal, which grew after 1832.
38. Pérotin-Dumon, *La ville aux îles*, pp. 330–332.
39. Hartkopf Schloss, *Sweet Liberty*, p. 116.
40. *Ibid.*
41. *Ibid.*, pp. 117–119.
42. Pérotin-Dumon, *La ville aux îles*, p. 663.

In receiving permission to rent a room in town as long as they share their wages with their master, the comings and goings of slaves in the urban environment were a common sight. Their role in the urban merchant economy was thus clearly visible. Some slaves were free to sail between villages to sell their master's products; one was trained as a jeweller and permitted by his master to roam the colony.[43] The attitude of the masters towards marronage during the *ancien régime* sheds a similar light on the mobility of slaves: marronage was considered a problem only when slaves deserted in groups and formed "gangs", thus becoming a threat to the general order. *Petit marronage*, defined as the absence of a single individual or very small group for a few days, was often treated casually by the planter or his manager.[44] Likewise, the punishment for a long period of time spent away from the plantation was contingent on the amount of time the slaves had already spent on the island: a newcomer accused of marronage was less likely to be branded than a slave who had already had the opportunity to build a network in and outside the plantation.[45] This led to situations where maroon slaves were only reported missing after a few weeks or even a couple of months.[46] Price notes that creole maroons were more likely to run away to the cities, where they knew they would be less likely to be questioned about their whereabouts, being surrounded by other people of colour, freemen, and freewomen, but also slaves, and thus experiencing a certain freedom of movement.[47]

Thus, the economic interests of planters encouraged a certain mobility of slaves to and from the urban centres. But the judicial system also unwittingly aided the connection between rural areas and urban centres by pushing certain victims to seek justice against their master in urban institutions. The slavery system led to the development of a particularly cruel private justice in the hands of the white masters. Slaves brought to or born in the French colonies were subject to the Code Noir, implemented in 1685 by Jean-Baptiste Colbert. The Code Noir was meant to cover the possession, transaction, and legal status of slaves in the French colonies. One of its paradoxes resided in the legal status of a slave; whereas they were considered movable possessions (for instance they could be inherited by the children of their owner), they were still legally responsible if they committed a crime.[48] This situation meant that they could be tried by the judicial system in place in the colony and sent to prison: this

43. Archives Nationales d'Outre-Mer (ANOM), Dépôt des fortifications des colonies, 130; Pérotin-Dumon, *La ville aux îles*, pp. 663–666; S. Larcher, *L'Autre citoyen*, pp. 93–94.

44. Richard Price, *Maroon Societies: Rebel Slaves Communities in the Americas*, 3rd edn (Baltimore, MD, 1996), pp. 111–112.

45. Price, *Maroon Societies*, p. 114.

46. Pérotin-Dumon, *La ville aux îles*, pp. 875–876; Moitt, *Women and Slavery*, p. 160.

47. Price, *Maroon Societies*, 125.

48. Frédéric Charlin, "La condition juridique de l'esclave sous la Monarchie de Juillet", *Droits*, 52:2 (2010), pp. 45–74, 63.

sentence had a direct impact on the owner of the slave, as he was losing for a certain amount of time a member of his workforce. To counteract this loss of revenue, the colonial system developed specific regulations concerning punishment, which allowed the master to punish them privately.[49]

Although most cases of mutilations and violence by owners went unpunished, a small number of slaves succeeded in getting their master condemned for excessive punishments.[50] This was made possible by the fact that slaves had a legal identity even if they were considered movable possessions. Therefore, they could access the court of justice to seek reparation. The courts of justice in the colonies were located in the urban centres and gaining access to them could be difficult if the slaves were not allowed to leave the property. However the number of freemen and freewomen had increased since the eighteenth century and they could serve as intermediaries with officials to transfer the slaves' complaints or to help them buy their freedom.[51] Slaves could benefit – after the imposition of the Penal Code in 1828 – from the *pourvoi en cassation* (appeal to have the legality of a judgment assessed by the highest judicial court in Paris) if they were involved in the same criminal affair as a freeman or freewoman; by 1838 they could do it by themselves.[52] Thus, a network of information and assistance was created between rural slaves, rural freemen and freewomen, and the urban environment, and this network was strengthened by their meetings during balls, festivities, and urban processions.[53] Unwittingly, the flawed colonial justice system in Martinique and Guadeloupe helped create links between people from the lower classes, which then produced networks of information about rural and urban concerns. Likewise, the relative mobility between plantations and the urban environment afforded to certain slaves helped facilitate the exchange of political news from other countries and the metropole.[54] Urban domestics who heard and repeated their masters' discussions during dinner were often complained about by officials, especially in times of rebellion.[55] As such, the links between slaves, former

49. For instance, see Pago, *Les femmes et la liquidation du système esclavagiste*, pp. 39–42.

50. John Savage, "Between Colonial Fact and French Law: Slave Poisoners and the Provostial Court in Restoration-Era Martinique", *French Historical Studies*, 29:4 (2006), pp. 565–594, 570–71; Price, *Maroon Societies*, p. 114.

51. Anne Pérotin-Dumon, *Etre patriote sous les Tropiques* (Basse-Terre, 1985); Pérotin-Dumon, *La ville aux îles*, pp. 877–878.

52. *Collection complète des lois, décrets d'intérêt général, traités internationaux, arrêtés, circulaires, instructions, etc.*, vol. 35 (Paris, 1836), p. 149; Crim. 17 août 1838, *Bulletins Criminels*, no. 43, p. 405, v. annexes, no. 3, quoted in Charlin, "La condition juridique de l'esclave", p. 64, n. 87; R. Montgomery Martin (ed.), *The Colonial Magazine and Commercial-Maritime Journal*, vol. 1 (London, January–April 1840), p. 465.

53. Larcher, *L'Esclave et le citoyen*, p. 94.

54. Julian S. Scott, "The Common Wind: Currents of Afro-American Communication in the Era of the Haitian Revolution" (Ph.D., Duke University, 1986), pp. 34–35.

55. Larcher, *L'Esclave et le citoyen*, p. 101.

slaves, and pro-abolitionist white people were strengthened thanks to the judicial identity of the slaves and the economic possibilities of the towns, this dynamic being most visible in the urban environment where contact between people of different backgrounds was regularly observed.

POPULATION CONTROL AND RESTRICTED MOBILITY IN THE NINETEENTH CENTURY

The question of mobility became particularly conspicuous after the abolition of slavery in 1848, when the codes that regulated the travelling and movement of people (for instance the sale of a slave to another planter) officially disappeared. The abolition brought a new legal and social status to the former slaves: more than 162,000 inhabitants of Martinique and Guadeloupe became freemen and freewomen and French citizens, now deserving of treatment equal to that of white French citizens.[56] With the abolition of slavery, every citizen was given the right to travel throughout the colony, as long as he or she could prove a place of residence and means of subsistence. This meant that citizens should have been allowed to settle where they wished, also in the urban areas. The reality was very different, however. Historians have shown that the white elite in French plantation colonies refused for a long time to submit to legal and judicial changes imposed by the metropole.[57] There are several reasons for this. First, the white elite feared a loss of power and identity. Second, they were afraid of losing the opportunity to punish their slaves privately; up until that point the responsibility of punishing slaves had been controlled by private justice. In reality, restrictions on mobility had already begun after the return of slavery in 1802. Access to urban areas became more and more restricted after the Napoleonic wars with the development of vagrancy laws and an increased police and militia presence in both towns and the countryside. Indeed, the nineteenth century changed the dynamic at play during the *ancien régime*, with the creation of a "slave police" after the reinstatement of slavery in the colonies in 1802. Police *commissaires* were appointed in every town and were charged with keeping the peace and forcing ex-slaves to return to their masters.[58] Officials focused on urban areas in order to limit the apparent freedom enjoyed by certain slaves and frustrate their attempts to pass as freemen and freewomen in the urban economy.

56. Jean-Pierre Sainton, "De l'état d'esclave à 'l'état de citoyen'. Modalités du passage de l'esclavage à la citoyenneté aux Antilles françaises sous la Seconde République (1848–1850)', *Outre-mers*, 90:338 (2003), pp. 47–82, 53.

57. John Savage, "Unwanted Slaves: The Punishment of Transportation and the Making of Legal Subjects in Early Nineteenth-Century Martinique", *Citizenship Studies*, 10:1 (2006), pp. 35–53; Savage, "Between Colonial Fact and French Law"; Hartkopf Schloss, *Sweet Liberty*.

58. Pérotin-Dumon, *La ville aux îles*, p. 668.

During the discussions that preceded the abolition of slavery, the commission for the abolition of slavery, presided by Victor Schoelcher, advised the Ministère de la Marine et des Colonies (Ministry of the Navy and Colonies) to implement new legislation against vagrancy to prevent former slaves leaving for another planter.[59] The influence of the British colonies is perceptible in Schoelcher's legal provisions: in Barbados, for instance, during the apprenticeship period, vagrancy laws were designed to prevent "idleness" and used to complicate the search for a new job by former slaves. Former slaves were forced to stay in the countryside to work for their former masters to avoid arrest. The vagrancy laws in the British islands in the 1830s formed part of the white attempt to prolong the plantation system and sustain its economic development despite the abolition of slave labour.[60] In the French islands of Martinique and Guadeloupe, where economic resources were also based on the plantation system, preventing the new French citizens from leaving the countryside also became a necessity for the creoles. The abolition of slavery on 27 April 1848 led to a modification of the legal system in the Antillean colonies regarding mobility and the right to work: in order to maintain and eventually reinforce their governmental powers, local authorities quickly imposed new regulations on the movement of the new French citizens. The plantation system suffered economically and politically: the migration of former slaves to the urban centres (Saint-Pierre and Fort-de-France in Martinique, Pointe-à-Pitre and Basse-Terre in Guadeloupe) destabilized the system of private justice as much as their newly acquired freedom. In July and August 1848, various decrees were published to prevent vagrancy and idleness. The definition of vagrant was very broad: it included people who had no precise address; those who had a home but no job; those who were eating in someone else's house; those who built an *ajoupa* (a cabin or wooden shack); and those who had temporary employment but no home.[61] In order to tighten control of the population, the authorities encouraged the development of a (rural) police force to patrol the colonies.[62] In addition to this police force, the governor of Guadeloupe encouraged the use of militia constituted by citizens, "to protect people and property" and specifically to arrest vagrants.[63] The militia was meant to "forget all distinctions of origins", however Schoelcher himself, during the first elections organized around universal suffrage in 1849, denounced

59. *Recueil de la législation nouvelle* (Basse-Terre, 1848), p. 8.

60. Anthony de V. Philips, "Emancipation Betrayed: Social Control Legislation in the British Caribbean (with Special Reference to Barbados), 1834–1876 – Freedom: Beyond the USA", *Chicago-Kent Law Review*, 70 (1995), pp. 1349–1372.

61. Josette Fallope, *Esclaves et citoyens. Les noirs a la Guadeloupe au XIXe siècle dans le processus de resistance et d'integration (1802–1910)* (Basse-Terre, 1992), p. 400.

62. Adolphe Gatine, *Abolition de l'esclavage à la Guadeloupe: Quatre mois de gouvernement dans cette colonie* (Paris, 1849), pp. 65–66.

63. *Ibid.*, p. 65.

the discrimination suffered by black people at the hands of the militia and gendarmerie. They did not hesitate to shoot black citizens who tried to free a man unjustly accused.[64] This was followed in February 1852 by the creation of the *livret de travail* (work pass) for labourers employed for less than a year, and new restrictions "to combat vagrancy".[65] Eventually, on 10 September 1855, the governor of Martinique Louis Henri de Gueydon passed an edict making it compulsory to have a passport to move between parishes for everyone over sixteen years old.[66] This local legislation, published under the title *Police du travail*, went against the French rules of free movement but it was not until 1870 that its repeal became a subject of discussion in the assembly.[67]

The increase in prosecutions against "vagrants" was not, in itself, unique to the colonies. Parallel to the bureaucratization and professionalization of the police system at the beginning of the nineteenth century (in the city but also in the countryside with the gendarmerie), a more efficient control of the population was imposed by officials from the metropole. The prosecution of vagrancy was defined by Article 270 of the 1810 Penal Code as being without a permanent address, travelling with no means of subsistence, and having no regular employment. It became an offence (*délit*) to be tried by the Tribunal of First Instance.[68] This legislation was officially applied in the Caribbean colonies in 1828.[69] However, as Philips has shown in the case of Barbados, where the vagrancy laws in place followed the wording of their British domestic counterparts but had very different purposes,[70] the practice of the law was much more radical in Martinique and Guadeloupe than in the metropole. The Antillean colonies could still be ruled by gubernatorial decrees and had therefore developed specific legislation on labour and vagrancy, in place until 1878. Although in the judicial archives we see an attempt by the clerk to delete any form of discrimination by not mentioning the colour or (ex-) civil status of the suspect, it becomes obvious that the law was discriminatory in practice. Indeed, in the duplicates of sentencing papers sent to Paris, the mention of colour or origins (*mulatto*, "mixed-race"; *capresse*, child born from a mixed-race person and a black person) disappeared, giving the

64. Victor Schoelcher, quoted in *Bulletin colonial. Supplément à la revue du XIXe siècle* (Paris, 1849), n.p.
65. Butel, *Histoire des Antilles françaises*, p. 308; Bruno Maillard, "'Ils sortiront des hommes'. Les enfants du pénitencier de l'Ilet à Guillaume (île de la Réunion) 1864–1879", *Criminocorpus. Revue hypermédia*. Available at: http://criminocorpus.revues.org/1770; last accessed 12 June 2017.
66. Anne Girollet, *Victor Schoelcher. Abolitionniste et républicain* (Paris, 2000), pp. 266–267.
67. Victor Schoelcher, *L'arrêté Gueydon à la Martinique et l'arrêté Husson à la Guadeloupe* (Paris, 1872).
68. Available at: http://ledroitcriminel.fr/la_legislation_criminelle/anciens_textes/code_penal_1810/code_penal_1810_2.htm; last accessed 13 June 2017.
69. *Recueil d'ordonnances royales concernant la Guadeloupe, 1824–1828*, vol. 2, pp. 72–73. Available at: https://issuu.com/scduag/docs/adg18154-2/73; last accessed 8 November 2019.
70. Philips, "Emancipation Betrayed".

impression that the suspects were treated equally. In reality, numerous former slaves did not have a surname and were still registered without one, giving away their origins.[71] The judicial archives thus show the specific focus set by the administration on these former slaves. It is interesting indeed to see that, except in two cases, the vagrancy cases brought to the court only concerned black people.[72]

In the early months after abolition, the number of vagrants arrested by the gendarmerie was still relatively low: in August 1848, in Guadeloupe, only six vagrants among fifty-eight suspects were arrested, and at the end of the year, an average of fifteen prisoners were sent to the *ateliers de discipline* (type of forced labour).[73] In the session of January 1851 of the Guadeloupe Court of Appeal, ten cases referred to the *délit* of vagrancy.[74] It appears, however, that all of the suspects arrested for vagrancy could give an address where they lived and slept. By definition, they were therefore not vagrants but had come to town to look for work. For instance, Marcelin, a young carpenter apprentice, was born in Les Anses d'Arlet in the south of the island but came to Saint-Pierre to find employment:[75] as he was paid by the task, his work migration was legitimate and even if he had meagre resources, he could not, if they were to follow the wording of the original Penal Code, be considered a vagrant. He was, however, arrested when he decided to settle in the old town of Saint-Pierre to look for work. Multiple accounts reveal similar experiences in the years following abolition; the suspects gave their place of birth and residence but were still tried for vagrancy due to the fact that they were moving and walking within the region, searching for employment.

In the first semester of 1855, in Saint-Pierre, out of ninety-one cases tried in the Tribunal of First Instance, thirty-two were related to accusations of vagrancy (twenty men and twelve women).[76] Julie's case is representative of the treatment received by "vagrants". She was born in Africa and lived in Grand'Rivière, working as a *faiseuse de bouts* (cigarette maker), but was arrested in Saint-Pierre while at work. She was then sentenced to six months in prison, the usual sentence in Martinique against vagrancy, whereas the Penal Code required a three-to-six-month sentence.[77] Had she been a man she would have been sent to work on the public roads or sent to an *atelier*

71. Certain former slaves were registered in the *état civil* (registry office) up to fifteen years after the abolition of slavery. See Larcher, *L'Autre citoyen*, p. 191; Guillaume Durand, 'Spécificités anthroponymiques Antillaises. Les noms de famille des Martiniquais d'ascendance servile', *Nouvelle revue d'onomastique*, 39–40 (2002), pp. 307–329.
72. ANOM, 6DPPC/115.
73. *Ibid.*, pp. 67–68.
74. *Gazette officielle de la Guadeloupe*, 20 February 1851, pp. 1–3.
75. ANOM, 6DPPC/115.
76. *Ibid.*
77. *Ibid.*

de discipline, which were created to put vagrants to work.[78] Five *ateliers de discipline* were created in Guadeloupe: two in Basse-Terre and Pointe-à-Pitre and three others in the islands of Saintes, Saint-Martin, and Marie-Galante, where urbanization was almost null. Prisoners were forced to do public work, often outside the urban enclaves, but they could also be sentenced to work for a planter.

The mobility and access to urban areas of former slaves were not only limited by vagrancy laws, but also by the restructuring of the judicial system. As we discussed previously, the way the judicial system worked during the *ancien régime* encouraged the development of links between rural and urban areas, essential to gaining access to official institutions. However, the reorganization of the judicial system that occurred in 1828, with the imposition of the *Code d'Instruction Criminelle* and the *Code Pénal*, and the bureaucratization of the justice system from the Revolution onwards led to the creation of local courts (*juges de paix* and *tribunal cantonal*) in the more rural areas to deal with conflicts between employers and employees; in a similar fashion to the appointment of local *commissaires*, the judicial system was brought closer to the rural population, but it mostly benefited the white employers. Likewise, the existence of local courts prevented former slaves from going to the cities to seek redress as it was not possible to bypass the local judge, meaning that one very important reason to go to the city (to access formal institutions) became obsolete after 1789.[79]

Finally, the economic opportunities offered by the towns before abolition did not increase sufficiently to provide enough outlets for the newly freed population, at least according to the government. The fact that the economic resources of the islands remained the same in the three decades following abolition suggests that the planters did not take the opportunity to change their economic model. The culture of sugar cane continued – many former slaves were now being employed as day labourers. Urbanization continued to increase but at a relatively slow pace compared to European cities.[80] Indeed, the new factories that opened for the transformation of the sugar cane economy were located close to the fields and did not encroach on the urban landscape. Thus, as various historians have shown, many socio-economic aspects of the pre-abolition Antillean society prevailed even after the abolition of slavery and the process of restraining citizens' mobility continued.[81]

78. Gatine, *Abolition de l'esclavage à la Guadeloupe*, p. 66; *Recueil de la législation nouvelle*, p. 23; Nelly Schmidt, "1848 dans les colonies françaises des Caraïbes. Ambitions républicaines et ordre colonial", *Revue française d'histoire d'outre-mer*, 85:320 (1998), pp. 33–69, 52–53.

79. Ministère de la Marine et des Colonies, *Les colonies françaises en 1883* (Paris, 1883), pp. 36–40.

80. *Tableaux de population, de culture, de commerce et de navigation* (Paris, 1846), p. 12 for Martinique.

81. Gilbert Pago, *L'Insurrection du sud. Contribution à l'étude sociale de la Martinique* (Fort-de-France, 1974), pp. 5–34; Nelly Schmidt, *La France a-t-elle aboli l'esclavage?* (Paris, 2009).

Access to the urban environment during slavery was also linked to economic opportunities but the job market in the towns after abolition remained limited, agricultural labour still providing most of the employment.[82] Skilled artisans were sought after, but most of the new citizens were unskilled labourers and many former slaves chose to become owners of their cabins and small gardens, if they were successful in gaining ownership from planters. Likewise, more than 2,000 cabins were said to have been built in the Guadeloupian countryside between 1848 and 1852, and in Rivière-Pilote in Martinique, on the slopes of the mountain, former slaves joined freemen and freewomen in cultivating vegetables for domestic and market consumption.[83] In addition to the risk of being arrested as a vagrant, a heavy tax (*impôt personnel*) was imposed on each worker: fifteen francs per year for someone leaving a town, ten francs for a villager (living in a *bourg*), and five francs for a countryside inhabitant. This tax was initially imposed in 1846 in order to prevent the *affranchis* from leaving the plantations, where their labour was needed, and was increased in 1848.[84]

The newly acquired freedom created fear in the white population (due to the large number of former slaves, the fear of riots and demands for redress, the reduction in employment opportunities as new workers entered the market) and the white elites actively blocked the migration and potential settlement of former slaves in the towns. Again, contradictory dynamics were at play in the practice of the law: on the one hand, freedom of movement had to be given to every citizen, as long as they could claim a residential address and employment (per task or per contract), but on the other hand, mobility towards the urban centres was strongly limited by the misuse of vagrancy laws in an attempt to prevent the loss of workforce on the plantations. Mobility from one plantation to another was not the main issue, however; when looking at the way the laws were used, it appears that it was mobility towards and settlement within the towns that were criminalized.

WHITE TOWNS, BLACK COUNTRYSIDE?

The white elite's efforts to hold back former slaves in the rural plantations through the strong use of vagrancy laws reveal another facet of their concerns, which was not directly linked to the possible loss of income. By strengthening the repression against "idle" or seemingly "vagrant" citizens (who did nevertheless have a place of residence), the elite also tried to limit the migration of former slaves to the urban enclaves. The cases brought to the judge of the

82. Rosamunde Renard, "Labour Relations in Martinique and Guadeloupe, 1848–1870", *Journal of Caribbean History*, 26:1 (1992), pp. 37–61, 39.

83. Fallope, *Esclaves et citoyens*, p. 413; Larcher, *L'Autre citoyen*, p. 277.

84. Gatine, *Abolition de l'esclavage à la Guadeloupe*, p. 76.

Tribunal of First Instance reveal a strong focus on former rural slaves crossing the "border" of the urban environment, the town and its *faubourgs*. The records that survive show mostly suspects arrested for vagrancy and idleness who were residing in rural areas but came to Saint-Pierre or Fort-de-France to find work. "Idle" men and women who were already living in town before the abolition were very rarely reported in these archives and if they were, they were likewise condemned to six months' imprisonment, in an *atelier* in the suburbs or even outside the city limits.

An interesting case was sent to the highest French judicial court, which shows the willingness of the local court to drop vagrancy charges if the suspect decided to settle on a plantation. In 1852 the cassation court in Paris broke the judgment of the appeal court of Martinique, which had dropped the case against Louis, suspected of vagrancy, who had agreed to work and live on Ducoulange's land. The cassation court claimed that Louis had indeed been in a state of vagrancy before Ducoulange's offer to work for him; therefore, the prosecution fees should not have been settled by the colony, nor should the case have been dropped. The state had the right to force Louis to carry out three months of public work, as defined by the laws of 1828 and 1848.[85] It seems that this case reveals divergent points of view on the role of regulated mobility in the colonies: whereas the local authorities were satisfied with Louis settling in the countryside to work and therefore dismissed the case against him, Parisian judges, less aware of the local situation, argued against dismissing the case.

The regulation of mobility after the abolition, however, reveals more than a simple concern over a potential lack of employees: sugar production levels in the years following the abolition did drop, but the period 1817–1882 remains a period of expansion for sugar export. Likewise, the production of secondary crops such as cotton, coffee, and cacao increased regularly after the abolition.[86] The colonies were also aware of their need to develop a more industrialized production to compete with European beet sugar, and this many years before the abolition of slavery.[87] This specific legislation on vagrancy and labour mirrors a more or less conscious attempt to limit access to the urban environment to the white, "deserving" population and prevent a rural exodus that would see the towns being taken over by former slaves. Indeed, the restrictions imposed upon black people were already seen in the treatment of freemen and freewomen before the abolition of slavery. A petition from "free men of colour",

85. Désiré Dalloz (ed.), *Jurisprudence générale du royaume. Année 1852*, p. 32; see also Martine Fabre, "Le rôle de la Cour de cassation dans l'élaboration du droit colonial", *Histoire de la justice*, 16:1 (2005), pp. 75–92.

86. Fallope, *Esclaves et citoyens*, pp. 358–361; Nelly Schmidt, "Les paradoxes du développement industriel des colonies françaises des Caraïbes pendant la seconde moitié du XIXe siècle, perspectives comparatives", *Histoire, économie et société*, 8 (1989), pp. 313–333, 327.

87. Schmidt, "Les paradoxes', p. 314.

merchants, and landowners, was sent to the French parliament in 1829 to complain about the fact that official positions in the French administration and in public office, generally located in the urban centres, were forbidden to them, in contradiction with what the old Code Noir prescribed (a freeman or freewomen would have the same right as a French citizen).[88] Preventing access to administrative positions was a means of denying them access to the "white class" and to social mobility, but it also gave them an incentive to leave the town if they could not find employment.

The abolition of slavery and the disorder that ensued had a strong impact on planters' feeling of safety. The abolition brought hundreds of white planters to the cities. But the migration of planters to the towns in troubled times, and to Saint-Pierre in particular, is an odd reaction when compared to the first abolition of slavery in 1794. The pro-abolitionist planters of Martinique addressed planters in the Antilles by claiming that the pro-abolitionist riots in Saint-Pierre since 1790 were misrepresented by the anti-abolitionist planters as a "war between the planters and the town of Saint-Pierre".[89] The colonial assembly in Martinique, seated in Fort-Royal since 1790 and strongly anti-abolitionist, argued that it was the people of the towns who wanted to establish equality, setting them up in opposition to the more practical people of the countryside.[90] The cleavage between the planters and merchants and *petit-blancs* of Saint-Pierre appeared patent in this pamphlet and certain officials played upon these dissensions to impose their views. A similar attempt by urban patriots in 1789–1792 to abolish slavery was thwarted in Guadeloupe by the community of the rural elite.[91] In February 1831, a slave uprising aimed to torch and pillage the city of Saint-Pierre: cane fields were burned, planters' families were shipped to France or the United States for refuge, and a letter published in a French newspaper described Saint-Pierre as the "most miserable place on earth due to its succession of bankruptcies and interest rates of 50 per cent on loans".[92] During this episode, planters' families did not reach Saint-Pierre to find refuge but instead escaped to the metropole or to foreign countries.

In the middle of the century, the discourse had changed, both in the words of the administration and of the elite. First, the tax mentioned above and imposed on urban inhabitants was meant to "drive away from the towns the inhabitants of the countryside". Likewise, small merchants and artisans had

88. *Pétition des hommes de couleur de la Guadeloupe* (Paris, 1830).
89. *Adresse des planteurs réfugiés dans la ville de St Pierre Martinique, aux Planteurs des Antilles* (Saint-Pierre-Martinique, 1790).
90. Jacques Adélaïde-Merlande, *La Caraïbe et la Guyane au temps de la Révolution et de l'Empire, 1789–1804* (Paris, 1992), pp. 55–56.
91. Frédéric Régent, "Révoltes, factions, catégories juridiques et sociales en Guadeloupe (1789–1794)", *Cahiers d'histoire: Revue d'histoire critique*, 94–95 (2005), pp. 87–99.
92. Moitt, *Women and Slavery*, pp. 130–131.

to pay a specific tax to do their trade, in order to "reduce the number of parasitic and miserable industries carried out by the idle men who ran away from the cultivation of the land".[93] The government was actively pushing away anyone who was not welcome in the cities. Second, by 1848, the elite had developed a new understanding of the city: it appears that the creole elite sought help and refuge in the urbanized environment and their discourse about the urban environment changed dramatically. The written testimonies of rural planters who experienced slave riots demonstrate their logical search for help where the island official powers resided, in Saint-Pierre or Fort-de-France, and at the same time reframed their view of the urban environment as a place of safety.

Irmisse de Lalung, a creole white planter and aristocrat living with her family in Le Prêcheur, wrote in her diary in 1848:

> We were expecting a serious event at Prêcheur; many scared women withdrew to Saint-Pierre. Our kin from the town asked us to join them; my uncle insisted that we moved [...] we were sorry not to have M. Dujon with us [...] his wife, frightened by the situation, forced him a few days before to take her to Saint-Pierre.[94]

In addition to seeking the support of the governor or influential officials, the white rural elite could also count on the presence of the militia and army, and the possibility, in extreme situations, to board a boat. To the elite, the towns came to represent the safest environment in a tense situation. Seeing the streets in these towns taken over by former slaves, who publicly showed their joy when slavery was abolished, was particularly despised and feared by the anti-abolitionist elite:

> From the edge of the ambush, we could see the town festivities [...] the negroes, who had taken all the horses, donkeys, and carts of their former masters, roamed the streets in cavalcade, insulting the whites.[95]

Dessalles, who opposed the abolition, wrote on 24 May 1848: "The streets are full of screaming and yelling negroes stopping passers-by and forcing them to shout 'Vive la République! Vive la liberté!'".[96]

Various episodes of such violence were reported by pro-planter newspapers surrounding the 1849 elections: people of colour from Port-Louis were described as "cannibals willing to eat the flesh and drink the blood of

93. Fallope, *Esclaves et citoyens*, pp. 400–401.

94. In "Notes sur les évènements du Prêcheur et émigration à Puerto Rico", Saint-Pierre, 1849; see ANOM, box 153, folder 1275, quoted in Pago, *Les femmes et la liquidation du système esclavagiste*, p. 103. Unless otherwise stated, all quotations from French sources rendered in English are my translation. My translation.

95. Pago, *Les femmes et la liquidation du système esclavagiste*, p. 114. My translation.

96. Pierre Dessalles, magistrate and Conseiller Supérieur of Martinique from 1808 to 1831, wrote a long diary recording his life in Martinique between 1808 and 1856, quoted in Pago, *Les femmes et la liquidation du système esclavagiste*, p. 113.

Bissette".[97] Similar rhetoric was used in a letter written by Bissette about the "mulâtres"[98] in Fort-de-France: "I know that there is in the town of Fort de France, more than one mulatto [...] who would like to see the heads of my children at the end of a spike".[99] In Martinique, men of colour were chosen to sit in the administration of the two main cities in September 1848, but one year later the atmosphere had soured and pro-planters took back control of the government. Rumours circulated that the former slaves were trying to repeat what had happened in Saint-Domingue and the whites started to fear the "natural barbarity of Africans".[100] The purging of the administrations, dissolution of (urban) political clubs, and stricter control over the black population thus followed. In Guadeloupe in March 1850, after legal and administrative changes, only eight of the thirty-two mayors on the islands were of colour.[101] At the same time, a general fear of riots grew among the planters: politically engaged leaders of colour promised retribution to the former slaves, for instance in the village of Petit-Canal in Guadeloupe, the story of which is published in the *Causes célèbres des colonies*.[102] In addition to violent threats against the planters heard in the countryside, some rural habitations of former masters were burned and white people were forced to flee to the main towns.[103] Arson of planters' houses in the countryside was common until 1860 and the administration blamed these fires on the "malice" of the "creole workers", "indigenous workers", and other "autochthone workers".[104] An anecdote related by the abolitionist Jean-Baptiste Colson reveals the tension that existed in the countryside at the time: while visiting the surroundings of Case-Pilote in Martinique, he came across a woman, a former slave, who asked him, a *béqué*,[105] what he was doing there. When he asked for a glass of water, she told him to move on, sending him towards a house where she knew white people "like him" were still living. Colson explains that only thanks to the Republican symbols he was carrying and the egalitarian relations he had established from the start with the woman was he able to win her confidence and a glass of water.[106] Many members of the rural elites were still anti-abolition, and it is clear from this anecdote why they changed their views about the traditionally pro-abolition cities, moved to the urban areas for protection, and tried to prevent "the fall" of what they would consider their last bastions of power.

97. *Bulletin colonial. Supplément à la revue du XIXe siècle* (Paris, 1849), n.p.
98. *Mulâtre*, "mulatto", mixed-race.
99. Bissette quoted in *Bulletin colonial. Supplément à la revue du XIXe siècle* (Paris, 1849), n.p.
100. Fallope, *Esclaves et citoyens*, pp. 384–387.
101. *Ibid.*, p. 386.
102. *Causes célèbres des colonies, t. 2 affaire du petit/canal.*
103. Larcher, *L'Autre citoyen*, p. 175.
104. ANOM, Martinique folder 12 D 118.
105. *Béqué* or *béké*: descendant of the first *colons* and/or slave masters.
106. Anecdote quoted in Larcher, *L'Autre citoyen*, pp. 179–181.

CONCLUSION

Urban slavery in the largest French Caribbean islands remained limited due to the fact that the agricultural land needed most work from the men and women. The towns were inhabited by the government elite, some white artisans, and many freemen and freewomen who participated in the development of the port and took advantage of the comings and goings of crews and goods. The slaves who lived in the towns were employed in domestic tasks within the household of a white or black family. Even if the number of urban slaves was limited, seeing rural slaves walking the urban streets was not a rare phenomenon. They would be sent to the nearest town by their owner to carry out certain tasks and had, if they were not runaway slaves, relatively easy access to the town, within the limits set by their owner. The nineteenth century and especially the abolition of slavery changed this dynamic: journeys that were once allowed and irregularly checked became a threat to both the town and rural elites, who feared losing their plantation workforce, their legal supremacy, and their access to the best positions. The elites, to which the magistrates presiding in the Tribunal of First Instance belonged, quickly responded to this "unchecked" mobility of the new citizens of the colonies. They misused the racially neutral legislation of the Penal Code on vagrancy to limit the mobility of former slaves towards the towns. In the metropolitan cities, vagrancy laws had the double aim of enforcing strict control of the population, while allowing and securing free movement of the "respectable/controlled population" (people who had a permanent address and means of survival). The practice of the law in the colonies, however, went against the movement of a certain category of people, who were deemed undesirable in the towns but were needed in the rural areas. The fact that they had a place of residence did not prevent them from being arrested and tried. As such, the decrees relative to the colonies and eventually the Penal Code itself became economic and migratory tools in the hands of the creole elite whose main economic resources were the plantation system and export of colonial products. The fear of losing income in an already struggling economy forced officials to find new ways to control the newly freed population and prevent their settling in more urbanized areas, especially if their hands and skills were not needed.

The towns thus became sites of contestation between the white elite and people of colour; the creoles did their utmost to keep these urban enclaves from growing even further. By twisting the meaning of the law, the elite succeeded in creating invisible barriers to the urban landscape in order to preserve it, as much as possible, as a "safe haven", controlled and inhabited by white people, leading the way to unwritten forms of segregation.

IRSH 65 (2020), pp. 117–144 doi:10.1017/S0020859020000152

Families, Manumission, and Freed People in Urban Minas Gerais in the Era of Atlantic Abolitionism

MARIANA L.R. DANTAS

College of Arts and Sciences
Wilson Hall Administrative, second floor, 204
Ohio University, USA

E-mail: dantas@ohio.edu

DOUGLAS C. LIBBY

Departamento de História
Av. Antônio Carlos, 6627
Universidade Federal de Minas Gerais, Belo Horizonte, Brazil

E-mail: dlibby.bh@gmail.com

ABSTRACT: Late eighteenth- and early nineteenth-century Minas Gerais was heavily reliant on its slave labor force and invested in the social order shaped by slavery. The main systematic challenge to slavery was discrete negotiations of manumission that resulted in the freedom of a few individual slaves. This practice fueled the expansion of a free population of African descendants, who congregated most visibly in the captaincy's urban centers. Through an examination of manumission stories from two African-descendant families in the towns of Sabará and São José, this article underscores the relevance of family ties and social networks to the pursuit and experience of freedom in the region. As slavery remained entrenched in Brazil, despite Atlantic abolitionist efforts elsewhere, urban families' pursuit and negotiation of manumissions shaped a historical process that naturalized the idea and possibility of black freedom.

INTRODUCTION

From its inception, the economy of the captaincy, later province, of Minas Gerais was dependent on slave labor. The earliest regiment that regulated land grants in the mining district tied the size of mining concessions to the number of enslaved workers: prospectors received 5.5 square meters of land per slave, for a maximum of sixty-six square meters.[1] Demand for slave

1. Waldemar de Almeida Barbosa, *Dicionário da terra e da gente de Minas* (Belo Horizonte, 1985), pp. 76–77; Luciano Figueiredo (ed.), *Códice Costa Matoso* (Belo Horizonte, 1999), pp. 311–324.

labor led to a rapid growth of the captaincy's enslaved population. The development of ancillary economic activities, equally reliant on slave labor, further contributed to a regional population that, by the mid-eighteenth century, was predominantly made up of the enslaved. As the century progressed, declining gold yields were not enough to undermine Minas Gerais's or Brazil's commitment to slavery. The development of new export crops, the revival of sugar production in Brazil's coastal regions, and the consolidation of food production aimed at domestic markets had, like mining, relied on the labor of slaves.[2]

The wave of abolitionist thinking and efforts that swept the Atlantic world at the turn of the eighteenth to nineteenth century barely impinged upon the prevalence of slavery in Brazil.[3] While events in Saint-Domingue, the northern United States, and the Spanish Americas challenged the ubiquity of slavery in the Americas, property holders and political leaders in Brazil, as well as in Cuba and the southern United States, remained convinced that their economic well-being and the stability of their societies relied on the preservation of slavery as a labor system and social order.[4] Ironically, the suppression of Danish, British, and American transatlantic slave trades helped to ensure a larger supply of African slaves to Brazil at a time when new agricultural exploits intensified demand for slave labor, thus strengthening the institution of slavery.[5] In Minas Gerais, population data from 1786 and 1808 seem to suggest slavery's slow decline: while the overall population of the captaincy increased by almost twenty per cent, its enslaved population decreased by nearly fifteen per cent. However, by 1821, on the eve of independence, the size of the regional slave force was on the rebound.

Population data for Minas Gerais in the late eighteenth and early nineteenth century reveal another relevant demographic shift. While the percentage of enslaved residents fell from forty-nine in 1786 to thirty-three in 1821, the population of free(d) African descendants rose from thirty-three per cent in 1786 to forty per cent in 1821. Similarly, the white population grew steadily

2. Angelo Alves Carrara, *Minas e currais. Produção rural e mercado interno em Minas Gerais, 1674–1807* (Juiz de Fora, 2007).

3. Public debates and efforts to abolish the slave trade to Brazil date from the late 1830s, and to abolish slavery altogether from the 1860s or later. Wlamyra Ribeiro de Albuquerque, *O jogo da dissimulação. Abolição e cidadania negra no Brasil* (São Paulo, 2009); Dale Graden, *Disease, Resistance, and Lies: The Demise of the Transatlantic Slave Trade to Brazil and Cuba* (Baton Rouge, LA, 2014); Celso Castilho, *Slave Emancipation and Transformations in Brazilian Political Citizenship* (Pittsburgh, PA, 2016); Beatriz Mamigonian, *Africanos livres. A abolição do tráfico de escravos no Brasil* (São Paulo, 2017).

4. Laird Bergad, *The Comparative Histories of Slavery in Brazil, Cuba, and the United States* (New York, 2007); Ada Ferrer, *Freedom's Mirror: Cuba and Haiti in the Age of Revolution* (New York, 2014); Aline Helg, *Slaves No More: Self-Liberation before Abolitionism in the Americas* (Chapel Hill, NC, 2019).

5. Dauril Alden, "Late Colonial Brazil, 1750–1808", in Leslie Bethell (ed.), *Colonial Brazil* (Cambridge, 1987), pp. 310–336; Jobson de Arruda Andrade, *O Brasil no comércio colonial* (São Paulo, 1980).

and was significantly larger in 1821 than it had been thirty-five years earlier.[6] Late colonial Minas Gerais's population was becoming freer. These numbers suggest that, at a time of growing abolitionist efforts in the North Atlantic, the Spanish Americas, and the Caribbean, the pursuit of legal freedom for Africans and their descendants in late colonial Brazil, and Minas Gerais more specifically, may have had its own unique form. Rather than targeting the trade or slavery itself, efforts in support of the enslaved focused on freeing individuals through the practice of manumission.[7]

This article investigates the idiosyncratic way legal and final freedom from enslavement for Africans and their descendants was conceived of, articulated, and experienced in one of the strongholds of slavery during an era of Atlantic abolitionist efforts. In late eighteenth- and early nineteenth-century Minas Gerais, the main systematic challenge to slavery was discrete negotiations of manumission that resulted in the freedom of a few individual slaves. These manumissions, or legal grants of freedom, were often secured through monetary compensation or negotiated labor expectations; occasionally, they were the product of an owner, parent, or relative's gift of freedom.[8] They fueled the expansion of a free population of African descendants, who congregated most visibly in the captaincy's urban centers, where they became small property holders and, whenever possible, slave owners.[9] This group's social transition from enslaved to freed property holders, their economic survival, and pursuit of further social upward mobility, relied on their participation in the diverse craft, service, and commercial activities that marked late colonial urban life in Minas Gerais. But it was often their ability to count on local family and social networks to help them integrate into the urban environment and navigate existing hierarchies of socio-racial categories that shaped their access to manumission and experience of freedom. This article examines manumission stories from two African-descendant families in the towns of Sabará and São José (Figure 1) to underscore urban families as key agents of individual freedom in late colonial Minas Gerais.

6. The number of white inhabitants in Minas Gerais grew from 65,664 individuals in 1786 to 136,690 in 1821, and from eighteen per cent to twenty-seven per cent of the captaincy's population. See Arquivo Público Mineiro, Belo Horizonte (hereafter APM), Mapas de População de Minas Gerais, Coleção Arquivo Casa dos Contos, microfilm 512, spreadsheet 30009/ item 2.

7. Aline Helg has recently argued that manumission remained the most viable and indeed almost exclusive path to freedom for enslaved Africans and African descendants in Brazil, Cuba, and the southern United States in this era. Helg, *Slaves No More*, pp. 221–244.

8. Stuart Schwartz, "The Manumission of Slaves in Colonial Brazil: Bahia, 1684–1745", *The Hispanic American Historical Review*, 54 (1974), pp. 603–635; Rafael de Bivar Marquese, "A dinâmica da escravidão no Brasil. Resistência, tráfico negreiro e alforrias, séculos XVII a XIX", *Novos Estudos – CEBRAP*, 74 (2006), pp. 107–123; Márcio de Sousa Soares, *A remissão do cativeiro. A dádiva da alforria e o governo dos escravos nos Campos dos Goitacases, c.1750–c.1830* (Rio de Janeiro, 2009), pp. 106–115.

9. Herbert S. Klein and Francisco Vidal Luna, *Slavery in Brazil* (Cambridge, 2010), pp. 141–148.

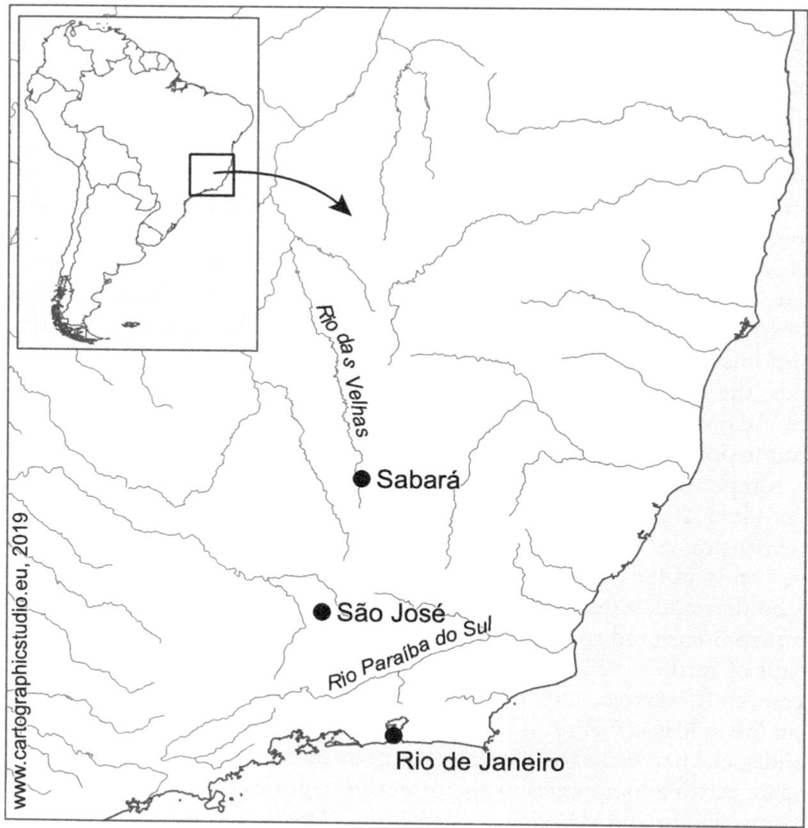

Figure 1. The location of the towns of Sabará and São José in Brazil.

In his now classic *Slavery and Social Death*, Orlando Patterson argues that manumission contributed to strengthening rather than weakening the power dynamic created by slavery. Similarly, Brazilian historian Márcio Soares asserts that, established as a gift rather than a right, manumission restructured and reaffirmed ex-slaves' obligations toward members of the slave-owning class. Freed people, in this sense, formed a category of individuals whose social status was subordinate to that of freeborn slaveholders.[10] Additionally, because self-purchase or the purchase of family members were widespread, manumissions facilitated the acquisition of new Africans and renewal of the slave force. Ultimately, the possibility of freedom through manumission helped to

10. Orlando Patterson, *Slavery and Social Death: A Comparative Study* (Cambridge, MA, 1982); Soares, *A remissão do cativeiro*, pp. 137–178.

alleviate conflictive master–slave relations, reinforce the use of slave labor, and strengthen slave society's control over freed people and even freeborn African descendants.

Yet, manumission practices may have also helped to erode the foundations of slavery in Brazil. Individual and family strategies revealed in notarial and parish records from Sabará and São José indicate that some slaves and their relatives viewed the pursuit of freedom through manumission as a de facto if not de jure right. They initiated negotiations, bypassed their masters, and appealed directly to the courts, and expected freedom to be available for purchase if they had the means to buy it. Their actions notably shaped a fast-growing population of free African descendants whose visibility reinforced freedom as a condition within reach. Occasionally the product of family efforts, manumission could also challenge power relationships between white slaveholders and African descendants. Slaves freed by family members were afforded the chance to integrate a social network on terms of relative equality; manumission itself did not reaffirm their subordination to the authority of their former masters. The fragments of family history discussed in this article thus undermine the notion that acts of manumission merely reframed the power relationship between African descendants and white slaveholders. They also illuminate how manumission practices may have fostered public and state intervention in the process of securing the freedom of slaves.

SABARÁ, SÃO JOSÉ, AND THE RISE OF A FREE AFRICAN-DESCENDANT POPULATION IN MINAS GERAIS

The towns of colonial Minas Gerais emerged as a result of the development of gold mining during the late seventeenth and early eighteenth centuries. Sabará was incorporated in 1711 and formed by conjoined mining settlements at the confluence of the rivers Sabará and das Velhas. The hamlets' location on the route to the city of Bahia, then the seat of the colonial government, and its concentration of Portuguese settlers made them the ideal site for a new town.[11] Sabará's rich mines and its political elevation to the seat of its township (the town proper plus its adjacent rural parishes) and judicial district, the Comarca do Rio das Velhas, quickly attracted a large urban population. By the second half of the eighteenth century it boasted thousands of inhabitants.[12] The town of São José similarly owed its early settlement to explorers searching

11. Diogo Pereira de Vasconcellos, *História antiga de Minas Gerais* (Ouro Preto, 1901); Cláudia Damasceno Fonseca, *Arraiais e vilas d'el rei. Espaço e poder nas Minas setecentistas* (Belo Horizonte, 2011), pp. 144–149.

12. APM, Mapa de população de 1776 das freguesias da Comarca do Rio das Velhas, Coleção Arquivo Histórico Ultramarino (hereafter AHU), box 112, doc. 11; APM, Mapa dos Habitantes atuais da Capitania de Minas Gerais (1776), AHU, box 110, doc. 59.

for precious metals.[13] Starting as a crossing station on the banks of the das Mortes river, the hamlet was incorporated as the town of São José in 1718. São José also benefited from its location on a main route, in this case linking the central mining districts to the city of Rio de Janeiro. Unlike Sabará, however, it never became the seat of its judicial district, the Comarca do Rio das Mortes; the town of São João was chosen instead.

If Sabará and São José's beginnings were connected to gold mining, their later economic trajectory was more closely tied to Brazil's growing internal consumer markets. In Sabará and the Comarca do Rio das Velhas, extraction of gold remained a relevant activity throughout the eighteenth and into the early nineteenth century. Yet, already in 1756, a list of the wealthiest men in the captaincy reveals that three out of four elite men in the township pursued other investments. In the Comarca do Rio das Velhas more broadly, merchants were as numerous as miners, while farmers comprised a quarter of the men listed.[14] São José and the Comarca do Rio das Mortes were never major mining centers.[15] In 1756, only ten per cent of the captaincy's wealthiest individuals resided in the comarca; among them, less than a third were listed as miners. São José had proportionally more merchants and agriculturists among its residents than anywhere else in Minas Gerais.[16]

By the late eighteenth century, farming had become the predominant economic activity in the two judicial districts. A 1766 count of economic units in Rio das Velhas reveals 1,396 farms and 174 plantations, but only 571 mining sites.[17] Mining still concentrated a larger enslaved labor force than farming (11,189 slaves versus 9,374, respectively), but by 1804 nearly half of the comarca's enslaved population belonged to farming households.[18] The Comarca do Rio das Velhas thus contributed to the shift from mining to provisioning local and regional markets that marked the economy of nineteenth-century Minas Gerais.

13. Olinto Barbosa dos Santos Filho, *Guia da cidade de Tiradentes. História e arte* (Tiradentes, [1977] 2012); Herculano Velloso, *Ligeiras memórias sobre a Vila de São José nos tempos coloniais* (Tiradentes, 2013).

14. APM, Relação dos homens abastados das Comarcas de Minas (24 July 1756), AHU, box 70, doc. 40.

15. The 1735–1749 *capitação*, or head tax, records reveal that only about fifteen per cent of the captaincy's slaves were in the Comarcar do Rio das Mortes. Figueiredo, *Códice Costa Matoso*, pp. 407–414.

16. APM, Relação dos homens abastados das Comarcas de Minas (24 July 1756), AHU, box 70, doc. 40.

17. APM, Resumo geral de roças, lavras, fazendas e escravos da Capitania de Minas Gerais (1766), AHU, box 03, doc. 58.

18. Instituto Brasileiro de Museus, Museu do Ouro de Sabará/Arquivo Casa Borga Gato, Sabará (hereafter MOS/ACBG), Mapa da população da comarca do Sabará menos do termo da Vila de Paracatu do Príncipe feito em observância da ordem do Illmo Exmo Sñr e Capitão General (23 July 1804).

Most Comarca do Rio das Mortes slaves were engaged in farming activities by the mid-century, if not earlier. The 1766 survey shows more than two thirds of Rio das Mortes's enslaved labor employed on farms and ranches. Additionally, slaveholdings in agriculture averaged 9.5 individuals, as opposed to 6.5 in other comarcas. As farming became economically more prominent in the captaincy, the Comarca do Rio das Mortes's share of Minas Gerais's slave population increased from fifteen to 21.3 per cent between the 1730s and 1760s.[19] Declining gold output and expanding agricultural activities refocused, moreover, Minas Gerais's provisioning economy as the Rio das Mortes region led the captaincy's efforts to supply the port city of Rio de Janeiro and its lively coastwise trade.[20]

Early nineteenth-century Sabará and São José could therefore be described as farm towns. While the farms of the Comarca do Rio das Velhas, which accounted for twenty-eight per cent of regional households in 1804, were mostly located in rural areas, they nevertheless maintained important economic ties with their urban counterparts (a quarter of all comarca households). Urban merchants, service providers, and small manufacturers provided commercial and material support for farming activities. Conversely, ten per cent of households engaged in urban activities also produced foodstuffs like corn, beans, rice, and manioc.[21] In the town of São José, 49.1 per cent of all households surveyed in 1806 were headed by craftsmen, small manufacturers, and service providers; another 33.8 per cent were headed by agriculturists.[22] These economic surveys reveal regional economies that had moved beyond the mining settlements of the early eighteenth century. They further depict urban populations engaged in economic activities that supported local farming and ranching and the provisioning of domestic markets near and far.

The economic history of the towns of Sabará and São José and their respective comarcas was invariably connected to the formation and rapid growth of regional slave populations. Within a few decades after settlement, the Comarca do Rio das Velhas already counted 12,000 enslaved residents.[23] The connection between slave ownership and gold mining led to the adoption of the *capitação*, a slave head tax, as a form of collecting the royal fifth (the crown's share) of gold yields. *Capitação* records show that slaves in Rio das

19. APM, Resumo geral de roças, lavras, fazendas e escravos da Capitania de Minas Gerais (1766), AHU, box 03, doc. 58.

20. Afonso de Alencastro Graça Filho, *A princesa do Oeste e o mito da decadência de Minas Gerais. São João del Rei, 1831–1888* (São Paulo, 2002), pp. 36–38.

21. MOS/ACBG, Mapa da população da comarca do Sabará menos do termo da Vila de Paracatu do Príncipe feito em observância da ordem do Illmo Exmo Sñr e Capitão General (23 July 1804).

22. APM, Mapa de população, mineração, comercio e cultura da Villa de São Jozé, e seo termo no anno de 1806, AHU, box 180, doc. 59. Curiously, no merchants except for cattle dealers were included in this tally.

23. Number recorded in a 1729 tax record. Barbosa, *Dicionário da terra*, p. 85.

Velhas doubled in number between 1729 and 1750.[24] By 1767, another 17,290 slaves were added to the regional population, making it the largest enslaved population in the captaincy.[25] During this period, the township of Sabará concentrated a large proportion of enslaved residents of the Comarca do Rio das Velhas: 7,000 out of 12,000, or fifty-eight per cent, in 1729; and 21,267 out of 49,156, or forty-three per cent, in 1776.[26] Moreover, the urban parish of Sabará held proportionally more slaves (sixty per cent of all residents) than the judicial district as a whole (forty-nine per cent of all residents) in 1776.[27]

By the early nineteenth century, as gold output declined in Sabará and the Comarca of Rio das Velhas, so did the enslaved population.[28] Rather than admit to the depletion of gold deposits, local officials argued that a shortage of labor, caused by competition for slave imports from the captaincy of Rio de Janeiro and the Rio de la Plata region, had triggered a general economic slowdown.[29] It is indeed possible that growing demand for slaves elsewhere affected Sabará slaveholders' access to enslaved Africans, even though Atlantic slave trading and slave prices were quite stable at the time.[30] Eventually, Sabará's enslaved population recovered slightly, but it never again accounted for three fifths of town dwellers, as it had in 1776. Between 1796 and 1819, slaves never amounted to more than thirty-five per cent of the urban population.[31]

The declining numbers and diminished relevance of Sabará's enslaved urban population was followed closely by the rise in the numbers of its free African-descendant residents. When, in 1776, census takers counted the

24. Figueiredo, *Códice Costa Matoso*, pp. 406–413.

25. APM, Mapas geral de Fogos, Filhos, Filhas, Escravos, Pardos, Forros e Pretos (1767), AHU, box 93, doc. 58. Studies of the slave trade to Minas Gerais include Manolo Florentino, *Em Costas Negras. Uma história do tráfico de escravos entre a África e o Rio de Janeiro* (São Paulo, 1997), pp. 37–44; Daniel Barros Domingues and David Eltis, "The Slave Trade to Pernambuco, 1561–1851", in David Eltis and David Richardson Silva (eds), *Extending the Frontiers: Essays on the New Transatlantic Slave Trade Database*, (New Haven, CT, 2008), pp. 95–155.

26. Barbosa, *Dicionário da terra*, p. 85; APM, Mapas da Capitania remetidos pelo governador de Minas D. Antônio de Noronha (28 January 1776), AHU, box 112, doc. 11.

27. APM, Mapas da Capitania remetidos pelo governador de Minas D. Antônio de Noronha (28 January 1776), AHU, box 112, doc. 11.

28. APM, Mapa da população que neste ano de 1796 contem esta Freguesia da Senhora da Conceição da Vila Real do Sabará (1796), Acervo da Secretária do Governo da Capitania (hereafter SC), box 31, doc. 25; APM, Mapa da população do termo da Vila Real de Nossa Senhora da Conceição de Sabará em o ano de 1809, SC, box 80, doc. 40.

29. APM, Senado da Câmara da Vila de Sabará to Príncipe Regente (4 January 1806), Acervo Câmara Municipal de Sabará (hereafter CMS), codex 126, fo. 133.

30. Laird W. Bergad, *Slavery and the Demographic and Economic History of Minas Gerais, 1720–1888* (Cambridge, 1999), pp. 164–165.

31. APM, Mapa da população do termo da Vila Real de Nossa Senhora da Conceição de Sabará em o ano de 1809, SC, box 80, doc. 40; APM, Mapa da População do termo da Vila Real do Sabará em o ano de 1816, SC, box 100, doc. 87; APM, Mapa da população do termo de Sabará em 1819, elaborado pelo capitão José de Araújo de Silva Alvarenga, Acervo Casa dos Contos, box 87, doc. 20255.

township's population of free *pretos* (persons solely of African descent) and free *pardos* (persons of mixed European and African descent), it totaled 12,062 individuals and represented one third of the overall population.[32] By the early nineteenth century, free African descendants had become the largest segment of the population of both the township and the urban parish of Sabará (31,307 and 4,318 respectively), representing in both cases fifty-one per cent of the overall population.[33] This demographic shift, from a predominantly enslaved to a predominantly free black population, suggests that the town was experiencing more than lack of access to Atlantic slave markets. The urban population had become progressively freer.

In contrast to Sabará, the enslaved population of the township of São José grew steadily during the late eighteenth century, helping to transform the Comarca do Rio das Mortes into the most populated of all four judicial districts in Minas Gerais. The region's dynamic agricultural complex attracted free and freed immigrants and new African slaves in such numbers that its residents, who represented less than a quarter of the captaincy's population in 1776, accounted for 35.8 per cent of Minas Gerais's inhabitants in 1808, and 41.6 per cent in 1821.[34] The relevance of slaves within this population is clearly evident in the 1795 *Rol de Confessados* (ecclesiastical nominal list) of the parish of São José. Slaves accounted for 48.2 per cent of the total parish population and 51.9 per cent of residents in the parish's urban seat, a high proportion that is reminiscent of Sabará's earlier demographic profile and attests to a continued local dependence on slave labor.[35] The significant presence of Africans among the parish slaves (three fifths of all enslaved residents) suggests, moreover, that São José had yet to be affected by any slowdown in the transatlantic slave trade.

São José's enslaved residents, unlike Sabará's, maintained a strong presence through 1808, when they represented 41.8 per cent of the township's total population.[36] But by 1831, the trajectory of the two enslaved populations were converging again. Having experienced only moderate population growth between 1795 and 1831, the enslaved proportion of the São José parish's residents dropped notably from 48.2 to 39.6 per cent, and in the urban seat of the

32. APM, Mapa de população de 1776 das freguesias da Comarca do Rio das Velhas, AHU, box 112, doc. 11.

33. APM, Mapa da população do termo da Vila Real de Nossa Senhora da Conceição de Sabará em o ano de 1809, SC, box 80, doc. 40.

34. *Revista do Arquivo Público Mineiro*, 2 (1897), p. 511; APM Arquivo Casa dos Contos, microfilm 512, spreadsheet 30009/ item 2; Wilhelm Ludwig von Eschwege, "Notícias e reflexões estatísticas sobre a Província de Minas Gerais", *Revista do Arquivo Público Mineiro*, 4 (1899), pp. 732–762.

35. Instituto Histórico e Geográfico de Tiradentes, Rol dos Confessados dezta Freguesia de Santo Antonio de São Jozé do Rio das Mortes neste prezente anno de 1795. The *Rol* tallied individuals who had confessed during the Lent of 1795; since children under seven years of age were not included, these slaveholdings may have been larger than recorded.

36. APM, Secretaria de Governo, box 77, doc. 63.

parish from 51.9 to 38.5 per cent.[37] Nevertheless, these numbers remained high for a region not directly involved in export agriculture; the parish's economic pursuits continued to support São José's commitment to slave labor.

The 1795 *Rol of Confessados* also reveals a noticeable presence of manumitted persons who accounted for thirteen per cent of the parish residents. Among this group, 57.7 per cent were described as being of mixed descent (through the terms *pardos*, *cabras*, etc.), 26.5 per cent as Brazilian-born African descendants (*crioulos*), and the rest as Africans. Additionally, 26.8 per cent of parish slaveholders were listed as manumitted, owning mostly from one to five bondspeople. The population of the São José parish also included a group of freeborn *pardos* and *crioulos* who comprised 7.6 per cent of local slave owners. Within the urban parish seat, the proportion of manumitted and free blacks among slaveholders rested at just over thirty per cent and over ten per cent, respectively. The specific reference to freed people in the *Rol of Confessados* reveals São José as a remarkable example of how eighteenth-century manumission practices shaped slave society in Minas Gerais. It also highlights how African-descendant townspeople broadened the social basis of slavery and contributed to its perpetuation.

Between 1795 and 1831, the free(d) population of African descent of the township and parish of São José continued to grow proportionally more significant, exceeding the numbers found for Sabará. In 1808, thirteen per cent of the township's residents were labeled *pretos* (of pure African descent), and 33.6 per cent were of mixed African and European descent.[38] By 1831, the majority of the residents in the parish of São José (roughly fifty-seven per cent) were free persons of African descent, while another 2.8 per cent were designated as freedmen. More notably, African descendants accounted for seventy-two per cent of the free population within the parish's urban seat. Unfortunately, the omission or inconsistent use in early nineteenth-century documents of the terms *forro* or *liberto*, to designate freed or manumitted, respectively, obscures the relevance of manumission to the shift from slave to free status of São José's African-descendant population. It is possible that such omission merely reflects the tendency to simplify legal stature to a dichotomy between free and slave noticeable in official documentation around the independence of the Brazilian empire in 1822.[39] It is also possible that the decline in references to freed people (*forros*) reflects the growing challenges slaves faced to secure their freedom at a time when abolitionist pressures

37. Núcleo de Pesquisa em História Econômica e Demográfica do Centro de Desenvolvimento e Planejamento Regional/Universidade Federal de Minas Gerais, Listas de 1831 and Listas de 1838, Listas nominativas da década de 1830.

38. APM, Secretaria de Governo, box 77, doc. 63.

39. Douglas Cole Libby, "A empiria das cores. Representações identitárias nas Minas Gerais dos séculos XVIII e XIX", in Eduardo França Paiva, Isnara Pereira Ivo, and Ilton César Martins (eds), *Escravidão, mestiçagens, populações e identidades culturais* (São Paulo, 2010), pp. 41–62.

and Brazil's efforts to outlaw and end the illegal Atlantic slave trade raised the price of slaves and, consequently, the price of freedom. The description of a *forro* population in earlier population lists, tax records, and nominal lists implies, though, that the nineteenth-century prevalence of African descendants among the free population of São José and Sabará was ultimately a product of earlier manumission practices.

FAMILY, MANUMISSION, AND BLACK FREEDOM IN SABARÁ AND SÃO JOSÉ

Enslaved Africans and their descendants in eighteenth- and early nineteenth-century Minas Gerais repeatedly rejected their condition through acts of resistance, flight, and efforts to form runaway slave communities. Their actions produced a freedom that was often fleeting and inexorably fragile because it was not recognized as legitimate by colonial authorities and property holders.[40] The formation and growth of the free African-descendant population of Sabará, São José, and Minas Gerais more broadly was closely tied, instead, to the practice of manumission. From the onset, the labor environment created by the mining economy afforded slaves different opportunities to negotiate the purchase of their freedom. Mining sites often hired enslaved workers who were not owned by the holder of the land concession. These slaves, left sometimes to their own devices, were expected to deliver a certain amount in wages to their owners, but could keep part of their earnings.[41] Similarly, slave women, who were forced to peddle goods and often sexual favors around mining sites to generate income for their owners, were occasionally able to accumulate gold or credit.[42] In this manner, some slaves secured financial resources to purchase their manumission, usually through payments made over a period of three to five years (a practice referred to as *quartação*). Such arrangements suited slaveholders, who had little trouble replacing hands thanks to steady supplies of newly arrived Africans. In not a few cases, persons

40. Waldemar de Almeida Barbosa, *Negros e quilombos em Minas Gerais* (Belo Horizonte, 1972); Carlos Magno Guimarães, *Uma negação da ordem escravista. Quilombos em Minas Gerais no século XVIII* (São Paulo, 1988); Marcos Ferreira de Andrade, "Rebelião escrava na Comarca do Rio das Mortes, Minas Gerais. O caso Carrancas", *Afro-Asia*, 20–21 (1998–1999), pp. 45–82; Luiz Carlos Villalta, "O *encoberto* da Vila do Príncipe (1744–1756). Milenarismo-messianismo e ensaio de revolta contra brancos em Minas Gerais", *Revista de História e Estudos Culturais*, 4:4 (2007). Available at: http://www.revistafenix.pro.br/vol13Villalta.php; last accessed 18 December 2019.

41. Kathleen J. Higgins, *'Licentious Liberty' in a Brazilian Gold-Mining Region: Slavery, Gender, and Social Control in Eighteenth-Century Sabará, Minas Gerais* (University Park, PA, 1999), pp. 68–70.

42. Mariana L.R. Dantas, "Market Women of African Descent and the Making of a Colonial Town in Eighteenth-Century Minas Gerais, Brazil", *Colonial Latin American Historical Review*, Second Series 2:1 (2014), pp. 1–24.

representing slave owners or their family's interests, such as estate executors or legal agents, defended the benefits of offering slaves an opportunity to purchase their freedom. Consequently, in eighteenth-century Minas Gerais the idea that freedom could be within the reach of productive or industrious slaves spread and supported the growth of a free population of African origin and descent even as the enslaved population continued to increase.

The marked gender imbalance of Minas Gerais's early free population, combined with the endemic sexual exploitation of enslaved women, shaped further manumission practices and the formation of a population of free African descendants. The mining district was notorious in the early eighteenth century for its chronic shortage of free white women. In this environment, sexual encounters between free men and enslaved women, though inevitably the product of the coercive and violent dynamic of the slave–master relationship, occasionally led to long-term liaisons, intimate ties, and offspring.[43] These colonial relationships, forged in the shadow of slavery, rarely resulted in marriages between white men and black women, or in the automatic integration of mixed-descendant individuals into the ranks of free colonial subjects. Nevertheless, they sometimes inspired a sense of moral or familial obligation that led to the manumission of an enslaved child, relative, or sexual partner. This practice became common enough to concern colonial officials that a class of *pardos* might attempt to claim for themselves the economic and political entitlements enjoyed by their white fathers.[44] As freed individuals became more numerous in Minas Gerais, and mobilized resources to pursue the manumission of other members of their family and intimate circles, they normalized further the practice of manumission. The large numbers of free African descendants listed in population maps of colonial Minas Gerais reflect more than the economic ingenuity of individual slaves. They also point to a social culture in which manumission had become a family obligation that one generation owed to the next as, together, family members sought to end their enslavement.[45]

43. Luciano Raposo de Almeida Figueiredo, *O avesso da memória. Cotidiano e trabalho da mulher em Minas Gerais no século XVIII* (Rio de Janeiro [etc.], 1993); Rangel Cerceau Netto, *Um em casa do outro* (São Paulo [etc.], 2008).

44. Higgins, *'Licentious Liberty'*, pp. 209–218; Júnia Ferreira Furtado, "The Journey Home: A Freed Mulatto Priest, Cipriano Pires Sardinha, and his Religious Mission to Dahomey", in Stephen Hodkinson and Dick Geary (eds), *Slaves and Religions in Graeco-Roman Antiquity and Modern Brazil* (Newcastle, 2012), pp. 149–173.

45. For an overview of manumission as a family effort in the eighteenth and nineteenth centuries, see Andréa Lisly Gonçalves, *As margens da liberdade. Estudo sobre a prática de alforrias em Minas colonial e provincial* (Belo Horizonte, 2011), pp. 258–263; Klein, *Slavery in Brazil*, pp. 250–292; Enidelce Bertin, *Alforrias na São Paulo do século XIX. Liberdade e dominação* (São Paulo, 2004); Paulo Roberto Staudt Moreira, *Faces da liberdade, mascaras do cativeiro. Experiências de liberdade e escravidão percebidas através das cartas de alforria – Porto Alegre (1858–1888)* (Porto Alegre, 1996); Mieko Nishida, "Manumission and Ethnicity in Urban Slavery: Salvador, Brazil 1808–1888", *Hispanic American Historical Review*, 73 (1993), pp. 361–391; Marcus J. M. de Carvalho, *Liberdade. Rotinas e rupturas do escravismo no Recife, 1822–1850* (Recife, 1998),

* * *

A comparison between manumission records issued in the township of Sabará during the second half of the eighteenth century – referred to as letters of freedom in notarial books – and existing demographic data for that same period suggests that approximately two per cent of the local enslaved population became freed every year. Though a relatively small group, these *forros* (freed slaves) helped to normalize the practice of manumission. Their access to freedom was similarly achieved through the granting and recording of their letters of freedom by public notaries. Their path to freedom, however, often depended on their place of birth (Africa or Brazil) and racial make-up; their gender and age; and the extent of their economic and social integration. Still, taken together, the experiences of these former slaves helped to define and eventually shape what was possible and expected as other slaves sought a path to freedom.

Two distinct groups stand out among slaves who successfully negotiated their manumission in Sabará. The first were *pardo* slaves, who represented almost one third of slaves freed between 1750 and 1810 even though they formed only seventeen per cent of the town's slaves in 1776 and seven per cent in 1810. Often descended from a white progenitor, many *pardo* slaves benefited from their social connections and economic resources to negotiate their freedom. The second noteworthy group were African women. While enslaved women in general attained manumission more frequently than enslaved men, that was particularly true of African women: though only eight per cent of the slaves listed in inventories produced between 1750 and 1810, they corresponded to a quarter of the slaves manumitted during that same period of time in Sabará. The majority of these women, moreover, purchased their freedom, relying on their successful economic endeavors to secure manumission rather than on the circumstances of their birth.[46]

The manumission records of some African women reveal, nevertheless, that their purchased freedom was not merely a financial transaction but a social one as well. Manumission regularly involved the mobilization of the enslaved party's personal or even emotional ties to free or freed persons. The example of Joana, an enslaved Mina, who purchased her freedom from store owner Francisco Gonçalves Machado, is a case in point.[47] According to her letter of freedom Machado had purchased Joana from a previous owner "for the

pp. 213–235; Antônio Henrique Duarte Lacerda, *Os padrões das alforrias em um município cafeeira em expansão (Juiz de Fora, Zona da Mata de Minas Gerais, 1844–1888)* (São Paulo, 2006), pp. 71–72, 81–83, 100–102.

46. Mariana Dantas, *Black Townsmen: Urban Slavery and Freedom in the Eighteenth-Century Americas* (New York, 2008), pp. 97–125; Dantas, "Market Women", pp. 9–13.

47. Mina was a descriptor denoting the place and people of origin (the *nação*) of a slave and referred to a region in western Africa that corresponds to present-day Benin. See James Sweet, *Recreating Africa: Culture, Kinship, and Religion in the African-Portuguese World, 1441–1770*

purpose of her securing the gold with which to buy her freedom".[48] The two were *compadres*, meaning one was godparent to the other's child. That connection seemingly paved the way for the arrangement that allowed Joana to purchase her freedom. In the case of the enslaved Mina Inácia, her owners Belchior Rodrigues Teixeira and Ana Ribeiro Marinho freed her in exchange for the gold she paid and because she had "served [them] well and raised [their] children with much love".[49] Inácia's ties to the Teixeira-Marinho family, perceived by them as love, helped her to negotiate the purchase of her freedom. Finally, Romana, also a Mina slave, purchased her freedom from João da Costa Lima, the father of her son. Despite their shared parentage of Manuel, Romana still had to pay for her freedom. But perhaps their connection made Lima more willing to grant her manumission – as well as to allow the father of Romana's other child, Maria, to purchase the girl's freedom.[50]

As freed slaves became property and slave owners in their own right, the dynamics that had supported their pursuit of freedom informed their decisions about their own slaves. In a sample of twenty-six wills of freed black women collected for the period of 1740 to 1808 in Sabará, eighteen referred to slave owners, and eleven contained the details of one or more manumissions. Good service and some claim of affection or intimacy appear in these documents as justification for manumissions that, nevertheless, almost inevitably were *quartações*, and thus required payment. Common exceptions were the gratuitous manumissions of enslaved children, the daughters or sons of enslaved women owned by the manumitters. Inácia Pacheca, identified as a freed Mina woman, granted her African slave woman Antônia freedom if she paid the executors of Inácia's will 128 *oitavas* over three years. Yet, Inácia freed Antônia's daughter, Rosa, without requiring any payment, leaving her "free from all slavery as if free from birth".[51] These manumissions suggest a few common trends in negotiations of freedom. First, slave owners occasionally exchanged freedom for a slave's sustained service or the means to renew one's labor force by, for instance, purchasing a new slave with the manumission payments of another. Second, it was not rare for owners to willingly offer slaves the chance to buy their way out of captivity. Finally, access to freedom was more commonly extended to an enslaved member of the second

(Chapel Hill, NC, 2003), pp. 13–30; Mariza de Carvalho Soares, *People of Faith: Slavery and African Catholics in Eighteenth-Century Rio de Janeiro* (Durham, NC, 2011), pp. 67–100.

48. MOS/ACBG, Letter of freedom, Francisco Gonçalves Machado to Joana (30 July 1757), Livro de Notas 56. All translations into English of archival sources are the authors' unless otherwise specified.

49. MOS/ACBG, Letter of freedom, Belchior Rodrigues Teixeira and Ana Ribeiro Marinho to Inácia (11 September 1758), Livro de Notas 41.

50. Letter of freedom found in Lima's probate record. MOS/ACBG, Inventário de João da Costa Lima (15 March 1762), Cartório de Segundo Ofício, box 23, doc. 206.

51. APM, Testamento de Inácia Pacheca (27 January 1740), CMS, codex 20, fo. 115.

generation of one's household, who was linked to the slave owner by perceived ties of affection or a sense of kinship-like obligation.

The trajectory of the Vieira da Costa family further suggests that kinship played a role in emerging manumission practices in eighteenth century in Sabará. The Vieira da Costas had lived in and around the urban parish of Sabará since the beginning of the eighteenth century, where many still resided in the early nineteenth century. The family was headed by Jacinto Vieira da Costa, an unmarried Portuguese man, gold miner, and sugar producer. Jacinto died in 1760, after nominating as heirs to his extensive wealth the eight *pardo* children he fathered with six different enslaved women. The formation of this family was deeply entangled with the manumission practices of the time. Its first generation comprised parents connected, most likely, by the sexual exploitation that often characterized the male master–female slave relationship. Its second generation was made up of children born in slavery, but who, after being legally recognized by their father as his offspring, were freed and allowed to inherit his wealth. The children's mothers were in most cases also able to pursue their freedom as a result of their intimate connection to Jacinto's household – though none formally joined the family nucleus through marriage. Finally, a makeshift third generation emerges through the letters of manumission: slaves owned by members of the family who were freed in exchange for monetary compensation. From one generation to the next, the Vieira da Costas and their extended household exemplified the possibility of freedom. Their example reified the notion, if not the reality, that freedom was accessible, even if for a price, to those who were linked by ties of affection or familial obligation to free and freed people.[52]

The origins of the Vieira da Costa family resemble that of many other families formed in Minas Gerais during the early eighteenth century. Male Portuguese settlers, empowered by the slave order, pursued sexual contact with slave women they owned or to whom they had access. Those relationships often produced mixed-descendant children born out of wedlock. Occasionally, they resulted in a series of manumissions. The first recorded manumission in the Vieira da Costa family was Jacinto's daughter Ana. Her 1745 baptismal record, which was appended to her father's estate documents, described her as the *mulata* and natural child of Maria *crioula*, a slave of Jacinto Vieira da Costa.[53] It also stated that her godfather had declared her freed. Like many mixed-descendant children, Ana was manumitted at the baptismal font, apparently with no additional conditions imposed on her labor. Jacinto's son

52. Mariana Dantas, "Picturing Families in Black and White: Race, Family, and Social Mobility in 18th-Century Minas Gerais, Brazil", *The Americas*, 74 (2016), pp. 405–426.

53. Natural is a legal term used in colonial Brazil, and the Portuguese empire more broadly, to designate children born out of wedlock from single parents who were eligible to marry. Linda Lewin, *Surprise Heirs I: Illegitimacy, Patrimonial Rights, and Legal Nationalism in Luso-Brazilian Inheritance, 1750–1821* (Stanford, CA, 2003), pp. 42–70.

Antônio *pardo* was freed in the same manner in 1751; he was the natural son of Rita, the slave of Maria Fernandes (herself a resident on one of Jacinto's properties). A third child, Ana, the natural daughter of Jacinto's slave Antônia, was also freed at the baptismal font in 1756.[54] Before his death, Jacinto freed all his other children in his will, drawn up on 9 May 1760, and named them his heirs "for the love I have for them and the assumption that they are mine". Additionally, he granted them "their freedom manumitting them from now to all eternity as if they had been born free from their mother's womb, that is, those who already do not have their letter of freedom".[55] The gratuitous manumission at baptism or in one's will of an enslaved mixed-descendant, the child of a white male father and a black enslaved mother, was relatively common in early eighteenth-century colonial Minas Gerais.[56] Occasionally, slave owners used the same strategy to free a young or second-generation enslaved member of their household for whom they felt particular affection, responsibility, or even kinship – whether real, suspected, or fictive.

Indeed, Jacinto Vieira da Costa did not limit manumissions to immediate members of his makeshift family. By the time of his death, most of the mothers of Jacinto's children were freed. Jacinto's will does not mention any gift of freedom to these women. Instead, the letter of freedom of Joana Mina, Jacinto's slave and likely the mother of two of his sons, indicates that she paid for her freedom.[57] Mothering his children may have paved the way to freedom for these women, but they seemingly still had to purchase their manumission. In 1756, when he freed his daughter Ana at baptism, Jacinto also freed Maria *crioula* in exchange for a "certain amount of gold".[58] Maria was the daughter of Inácia Courana or Mina, and possibly the half-sister of Jacinto's oldest son, Antônio Vieira da Costa. It would appear that Jacinto was willing to extend the possibility of freedom to his children's other enslaved kin, but in exchange for compensation.

Antônio Vieira da Costa, like his father, granted a few manumissions during his lifetime. He, however, died a bachelor with no known heirs, including no enslaved descendants. His willingness to free Cecília Mina and Leonarda *crioula* suggests nevertheless that personal, even intimate ties guided his decisions about manumission. According to Cecília's 1796 letter of freedom, Antônio had inherited her from his mother, Inácia Vieira da Costa; he declared

54. MOS/ACBG, Inventário de Jacinto Vieira da Costa (10 June 1760), Cartório do Segundo Ofício, box 21, doc. 189, fos. 20–24.

55. MOS/ACBG, Testamento de Jacinto Vieira da Costa (9 May 1760), Cartório do Primeiro Ofício, codex 14 (20), fos. 77–83.

56. Higgins, *'Licentious Liberty'*, pp. 145–174.

57. MOS/ACBG, Letter of freedom, Jacinto Vieira da Costa to Joana Mina (29 November 1756), Cartório do Segundo Ofício, Livro de Notas 118, fo. 56.

58. MOS/ACBG, Letter of freedom, Jacinto Vieira da Costa to Maria Crioula (4 October 1756), Cartório do Segundo Ofício, Livro de Notas 56, fo. 49.

he freed Cecília in recognition of her good services and a payment of 100 *oitavas* of gold.[59] Leonarda, on the other hand, was the daughter of Antônio's slave, Maria Pereira Angola; Antônio received 100,000 *réis* in exchange for her freedom.[60] Both women purchased their freedom. But the place they held within Antônio's household, one as his mother's contemporary and the other as a dependent born to his estate, may also explain his decision to manumit them. Familiarity, intimacy, and maybe even some sense of obligation toward them could have led Antônio to agree to their freedom.

Isabel Vieira da Costa, a *preta forra* (freed black woman) and most likely the mother of Jacinto's oldest daughter Antônia Maria and of his son João, was also on the list of Vieira da Costa manumissions. In the late 1770s, a few decades after achieving her freedom, Isabel, then a slaveholder, agreed to manumit her slaves Clemente and Tomé in exchange for payment in gold.[61] Isabel, like many slave owners before her, used manumission strategically and applied the product of her slaves' labor to renewing her slave labor force. The economic incentive for these manumissions is undeniable, but was there another reasoning informing Isabel's actions? There were no apparent family ties between her and these men, both of whom were African and designated as Mina. It is possible, however, that Isabel's own experience with freedom, and awareness of the self-purchased freedom of others around her, made her more inclined to offer these men the same opportunity. In other words, in the absence of family or intimate ties, a shared understanding that slaves who had the means to purchase freedom should be given the chance to do so may have moved some slave owners to release their human property.

Slaves themselves seem to have developed an understanding that the pursuit of freedom was a benefit to which they were entitled. In 1780, Nicácio *crioulo*, the slave of the alferes José Carvalho de Barros, took advantage of his master's death to negotiate his freedom directly with the judge in charge of the settlement of Barros's estate. In his petition to the court, Nicácio argued that he wanted "to give the just amount for his freedom, which was doubly advantageous to the inheritance or the deceased's creditors" since his advanced state of illness would quickly render him valueless. Barros's widow, who was not consulted during the process of manumission that ensued, later protested the transaction. She claimed that Nicácio had acted in bad faith, negotiated his manumission behind her back, and stolen farming equipment to pay for his

59. MOS/ACBG, Letter of freedom, Antônio Vieira da Costa to Cecília Mina (31 May 1796), Cartório do Primeiro Ofício, Livro de Notas 34, fo. 39.

60. MOS/ACBG, Letter of freedom, Antônio Vieira da Costa to Leonarda Crioula (20 March 1789), Cartório do Primeiro Ofício, Livro de Notas 10(73), fo. 63.

61. Isabel received 100 *oitavas* of gold from each man. MOS/ACBG, Letter of freedom, Isabel Vieira da Costa to Clemente Mina (9 October 1777), Cartório do Segundo Ofício, Livro 67, fo. 49; MOS/ACBG, Letter of freedom, Isabel Vieira da Costa to Tomé Mina (21 July 1779), Cartório do Segundo Ofício, Livro 13(63), fo. 99.

freedom. But by the time her complaint was recorded and the manumission rescinded Nicácio was long gone, enjoying the freedom he and the judge of the Orphans Court had assumed he had the right to purchase.[62] Similarly, slaves of the entailed estate of deceased captain Antônio de Abreu Guimarães also assumed that it was their right to purchase their freedom. In an 1805 consultation with the King's Overseas Council, the entailment's governing board declared itself "perplexed by a question raised by some of the *preto* and *pardo* slaves of that estate who asked for their freedom offering the price for which they were valued". The board recognized the economic advantages of selling slaves their freedom to generate funds for the purchase of new slaves. But they were concerned that the terms of the entailment may prevent disposing of the estate's property in this manner. The Council, perhaps to the relief of the board, replied that such manumissions were advantageous and, in fact, recommended.[63] The Overseas Council, an important branch of the colonial administration, was thus adding its voice to those of local judges, slaves owners, and indeed the enslaved in Sabará, who understood that given the right circumstances slaves should be allowed to bargain for their freedom.

* * *

Sometime during the 1730s or 1740s, two enslaved West Africans, generically designated as Mina, arrived in the town of São José. José (Fernandes da Silva) and Quitéria (Moreira de Carvalho) became slaves to different owners, as the distinct surnames they adopted in freedom suggest. By the late 1740s, they were joined in a union unsanctioned by the Church.[64] The couple formally married between 1759 and 1764. But a 1775 manumission record, in which José assumed paternity of a son who was born around 1748, attests to the couple's long-standing intimate relationship.[65] From this initial evidence,

62. MOS/ACBG, Inventário de José Carvalho de Barros (5 December 1780), Cartório de Segundo Ofício, box 50, doc. 379, fo. 81–84.

63. APM, Petição da Mesa Administrativa do Vínculo do Jagoara ao Rei D. João VI (29 August 1805), AHU, box 177, doc. 24.

64. Slave couples were rarely able to formalize their union through a Church-sanctioned marriage. A Church ruling that slave owners who separated an enslaved couple enjoined in matrimony were committing a mortal sin led owners, who were unwilling to surrender control over future sales of their property, to prevent such marriages. D. Sebastião Monteiro da Vide, *Constituições Primeiras do Arcebispado da Bahia* (Brasília, [1707] 2007), p. 125.

65. Escritório Técnico do Instituto do Patrimônio Histórico e Artístico Nacional-São João del Rei, São João del Rei (hereafter ETIPHAN-SJR), Letter of freedom, Livro de Notas do Segundo Ofício, 1773–1775, fo. 126. In January of 1764 the formally wedded couple José (Fernandes) da Silva and Quitéria Moreira (de Carvalho) baptized a legitimate son who received his father's given name. Arquivo Parochial de Santo Antônio de São José do Rio das Mortes, Tiradentes (hereafter APSASJRM), Baptismal record (27 January 1764), Livro 7, fo. 205.

it has been possible to piece together a complex family history that spans seven generations and was inextricably tied to a series of manumissions. The example of the Moreira da Silva family, as we have chosen to designate them, lends credence to the argument that family formation and paths to freedom were strongly connected in eighteenth and nineteenth-century Minas Gerais. That connection, moreover, framed manumission as an acquired right rather than a benevolent act on the part of slaveholders and fed the incessant growth of the freed and slave-descended Afro-Brazilian population up to and beyond final emancipation in 1888.

The earliest records of the Moreira da Silva family appear in parish baptismal registers. In 1754 and 1757, Quitéria, an enslaved Mina belonging to Antônio Moreira de Carvalho, baptized two natural daughters, Ana and Antônia, respectively, whose father(s) went unnamed (Figure 2).[66] In 1759, Quitéria, still unmarried but by then a freedwoman, baptized her son Joaquim. Sometime between March of 1757 and June of 1759, Quitéria (still registered without a surname) had gained her freedom.[67] It seems relevant that Joaquim's godmother was Rosa Moreira, a *preta* Mina *forra* (black West African freedwoman) and the known sexual partner of Quitéria's former owner Antônio Moreira de Carvalho. Born in Lisbon, Moreira de Carvalho appeared on the 1756 list of São José's wealthiest residents.[68] Like Jacinto Vieira da Costa and numerous other white male slaveholders in colonial Brazil, he pursued a sexual relationship with his enslaved black woman without ever contracting matrimony. He nevertheless acknowledged his illegitimate family: when the couple baptized the youngest of their seven children, a daughter named Rosa, he was listed as the father.[69] Antônio Moreira de Carvalho must have granted a few manumissions, including that of Rosa.[70] Repeated acts of manumission, paired with Rosa's appearance as godmother to one of Quitéria's children, suggest that the formation of these two families overlapped to some extent. The context in which Quitéria and three of her children received

Because São José marriage records from before the 1780s have not survived, it is impossible to determine the exact date the couple married.

66. APSASJRM, Baptismal record (19 May 1754), Livro 7, fo. 34; APSASJRM, Baptismal record (30 March 1757), Livro 7, fo. 92.

67. APSASJRM, Baptismal record (23 June 1759), Livro 7, fo. 131. No letters of freedom have been found for Quitéria or for José.

68. APM, Relação dos homens abastados das Comarcas de Minas (24 July 1756), AHU, box 70, doc. 40. APSASJRM, Livro 80, fo. 28v.

69. APSASJRM, Baptismal record, Livro 7, fo. 54. For a more detailed look at this couple and their extensive family, see Douglas Cole Libby and Afonso de Alencastro Graça Filho, "Reconstruindo a liberdade. Alforrias e forros na freguesia de São José do Rio das Mortes, 1750–1850", *Varia História*, 30 (2003), pp. 135–145.

70. From 1753 to 1762, Moreira de Carvalho appeared at the baptismal font as the owner of eleven slave infants and he or his estate were listed as owners of more than a hundred bondspeople in their respective burial records.

Figure 2. "Negresses Allant a L'Eglise, Pour Etre Baptisées" (black females going to church to be baptized), Jean Baptiste Debret, *Voyage Pittoresque et Historique au Bresil* (Paris, 1834–39), vol. 3, plate 8, p. 129.
Source info: "Baptism in a Catholic Church, Brazil,1816–1831", Slavery Images: A Visual Record of the African Slave Trade and Slave Life in the Early African Diaspora. Available at: http://www.slaveryimages.org/s/slaveryimages/item/1833; last accessed 3 December 2019.

their respective manumissions was thus indelibly marked by familial and fictive kinship relations.[71]

The terms of the manumission of two of Quitéria's daughters reveal that she was the main force driving her family's transition from slavery to freedom. In January 1771, Quitéria Moreira, described simply as an African freedwoman, registered the letters of freedom of her daughters Antônia and Ana. The document explains that the actual manumissions had taken place earlier, a few years after Antônio Moreira de Carvalho's death: Antônia was freed in May 1767, when she was ten years old, and Ana in July 1769, when she was fifteen. The two girls' freedom had been purchased through payments in kind and the estate of Moreira de Carvalho received two recently enslaved Africans in

71. The choice of Manoel Fernandes dos Santos, a son-in-law of Antônio and Rosa Moreira de Carvalho, for the godfather of José and Quitéria's first daughter, baptized in 1754, further underscores how familial and kinship relationships intervened in the affairs of both masters and slaves.

exchange for Antônia and Ana's liberty.[72] At the time when this document was drawn up, Quitéria and José were already a formally married couple. Yet, only Quitéria appeared as the legal agent seeking to notarize the letters of freedom. José's absence from the record suggests that it was she who had negotiated some sort of agreement relative to the girls' manumissions, likely before the death of their owner. In the absence of Moreira de Carvalho's inheritance papers, we can only speculate how that negotiation unfolded. It is not inconceivable, however, that Quitéria considered the purchasing of her daughters' freedom as a matter of course; a right she had earned during her years of servitude, and one that Moreira de Carvalho seems to have recognized. Just the same, the girls' manumissions were not merely the product of their owner's goodwill. The exchange of two young females for two adult male Africans represented a profitable and highly appealing deal for the Moreira de Carvalho estate. It is also suggestive of Quitéria's commercial acumen. Like many other slave and freed black women in colonial urban Brazil, Quitéria may have worked as a street vendor. But whether or not that was her main economic activity, Quitéria managed to procure the credit and connections with which to negotiate the purchase of two African male slaves.[73]

In July 1775, José Fernandes Silva appeared with his wife Quitéria Moreira (de Carvalho) when the couple notarized the letter of freedom of their oldest son, Severino. The notarial register specifies that they had purchased Severino for the purpose of freeing him from Luiz Francisco de Carvalho, presumably an heir of Antônio Moreira de Carvalho. Then twenty-seven years of age, Severino was a prime slave and his parents almost certainly paid the going market price or more.[74] It is hard to imagine that Carvalho felt economically inclined to yield a slave at the height of his productive life to immediate relatives. Nevertheless, a refusal to do so may have met with disapproval within the São José community where Quitéria and José were surely well-known and where family ties were respected. Through their hard work and cultivation of social ties, the Moreira da Silva family, parents and children, successfully raised the necessary funds and capitalized on the local social environment to secure the manumission of Severino. Their overall trajectory to freedom, one that likely started with Quitéria's self-purchase, then José's, the couple's

72. ETIPHAN-SJR, Letter of freedom, Livro de Notas do Segundo Ofício (1773–1775), fos. 10, 11.
73. Mina women were considered to be particularly skilled vendors. See Sheila de Castro Faria, "Damas mercadoras. As *pretas minas* no Rio de Janeiro", in Mariza de Carvalho Soares (ed.), *Rotas atlânticas da diáspora africana. Da Baía do Benim ao Rio de Janeiro* (Niterói, 2007), pp. 101–134; Carlos Eugênio Líbano Soares and Flávio dos Santos Gomes, "Negras minas no Rio de Janeiro: Gênero, nação e trabalho urbano no século XIX," in Mariza de Carvalho Soares (ed.), *Rotas atlânticas da diáspora africana. Da Baía do Benim ao Rio de Janeiro* (Niterói, 2007), pp. 191–222.
74. ETIPHAN-SJR, Letter of freedom, Livro de Notas do Segundo Ofício, 1773–1775, fos. 126.

formal union, and finally their collective efforts to free family members born into slavery, may well have played out among many slave families.

As the Moreira da Silvas pursued their family's freedom and sought to become property holders and slave owners in their own right, their family trajectory became intertwined with that of other enslaved African-descendant families. In 1772, Josefa Mina, slave of José Fernandes da Silva, inscribed as an African freedman, baptized her daughter Tereza: the godmother was Ana Moreira, José and Quitéria's daughter.[75] In 1779, Joana Angola, another slave listed as belonging to José Fernandes da Silva, baptized a boy named Joaquim whose godparents were Antônia Moreiras da Silva's husband and, again, Ana Moreira.[76] Four years later, in 1783, Josefa Mina baptized another daughter, Francisca; José and Quitéria's son Joaquim and his fiancé Genoveva were the godparents.[77] Finally, in 1790, a slave owned by one of José and Quitéria's sons-in-law baptized an infant boy; again, members of the Moreira da Silva family were the godparents.[78] Repeating the pattern of entangled slave–master family relationships that Quitéria had experienced while still a slave, the Moreira da Silva formed fictive kinship ties with their own slaves.

The *Rol de Confessados* of 1795 further illustrates the ways in which now slave-owning members of the Moreira da Silva family developed complex relationships with their slaves and slave families. The then widowed head of household Quitéria Moreira de Carvalho lived with her unmarried son Severino and four adult slaves. Among those were Joana and her fourteen-year-old son Joaquim, whose 1779 baptismal entry is mentioned above. Also residing in the household was Josefa Moreira, designated as Mina *quartada*, meaning that, although still legally bound to Quitéria, she was in the process of purchasing her freedom. Quitéria, it seems, was giving Josefa the same path to liberty she herself had taken several decades earlier, possibly perceiving it not only as natural but perhaps as a right she had no reason to deny.

Some of Quitéria's children, by then adults, also appear in the 1795 nominal list as heads of independent households and slave owners. Quitéria and José's daughter Antônia Moreira da Silva and her husband Lieutenant Joaquim Martins de Souza formed a household comprising three of the couple's children and two young adult male slaves designated as Benguelas (a common, generic West Central African label of origin).[79] Absent from the couple's household was Ana, the slave mother whose son was baptized in 1790, and who may have become freed along with her son in the interim. Quitéria and

75. APSASJRM, Baptismal record, Livro 7, fo. 387.

76. *Ibid.*, fo. 595.

77. APSASJRM, Baptismal record, Livro 8, fo. 103.

78. *Ibid.*, fo. 319. Severino Moreira da Silva stood as godfather and Josefa, the enslaved woman of Quitéria Moreira de Carvalho, as godmother.

79. Martins de Souza was an *alferes* or second lieutenant in a local black militia company, a post of some prestige in the community.

José's son Joaquim Moreira da Silva and his wife Genoveva Maria de Santana formed another household along with Genoveva's brother, a household dependent, and at least two slaves.[80] The slaves were a twenty-one year old Angola man named Antônio and Francisca, an eleven-year-old *crioula* and clearly the daughter of Josefa Mina, who was in the process of purchasing her freedom from matriarch Quitéria, as just seen. Josefa's eldest daughter, Tereza, however, resided in another Moreira da Silva household, that of Ana Moreira da Silva and her husband Pedro da Silva Lourenço. This was a simple question of keeping things in the family: recall that Joaquim and Genoveva had stood as godparents for Francisca and Ana Moreira as godmother for Tereza in the respective 1783 and 1772 baptismal acts.[81]

According to the *Rol de Confessados*, Pedro da Silva Lourenço and Ana Moreira da Silva also owned two African males in their twenties. Additionally, Tereza baptized a son in January of 1795.[82] Two years later, she bore another son.[83] It is conceivable that the father of Tereza's children was one of the two enslaved men also owned by Pedro and Ana. It is also possible that she had found a partner elsewhere in the town of São José. Whether the product of disparate sexual encounters or an enduring but unsanctioned union, Tereza's young family helped to increase Pedro and Ana's slaveholding as the turn of the century approached.

A couple of patterns can be gleaned from the 1795 *Rol de Confessados* and the data examined thus far. Not surprisingly, given the demography of the transatlantic slave trade, all the Africans purchased by members of the Moreira da Silva family appear to have been young adults when the respective transactions took place. Excluding infants encountered at the baptismal font, the four Moreira da Silva slaveholdings described above were composed of six African men, one *crioulo*, two African women, and three native *crioulas*. All of the women appeared as mothers in the São José baptismal registers.[84] These findings are not enough to assert that slave-owning families actively encouraged natural reproduction among their slaves. They nevertheless illustrate how these families benefited from the increase in their enslaved property as a result of the formation of occult, informal families among the enslaved, similar to that of José Fernandes da Silva and Quitéria Moreira de Carvalho up to

80. The couple also had a daughter, who would have been too young to confess and thus does not appear in the *Rol*. For the respective baptism see APSASJRM, Baptismal record, Livro 8, fo. 308.
81. APSASJRM, Baptismal record, Livro 7, fo. 387; APSASJRM, Baptismal record, Livro 8, fo. 103.
82. APSASJRM, Baptismal record, Livro 9, fo. 446v. Quitéria Maria de Souza, a granddaughter of matriarch Quitéria and the daughter of Antônia Moreira da Silva, stood as godmother for the infant slave boy.
83. APSASJRM, Baptismal record, Livro 9, fo. 530v.
84. In 1799, Francisca, who belonged to Joaquim Moreira da Silva, gave birth to a girl. APSASJRM, Baptismal record, Livro 9, fos. 592v–593.

the 1760s.[85] Finally, the reference to the Mina slave Josefa's *quartação* points to a repetition among the Moreira da Silva households of the negotiations of manumission that decades earlier had secured Quitéria and José's liberation from the yoke of slavery.

The third generation of Moreira da Silvas came of age at the turn of the century. The early nineteenth century corresponded to the peak of stable slave prices and the widespread dissemination of slaveholdings.[86] Not surprisingly, three of these third-generation family members were slave owners. The oldest grandchild, Esméria, was married in November of 1800 and baptized her only daughter in January of 1802.[87] Two years later, the couple's enslaved woman Juliana appeared in the parish registers baptizing her infant boy.[88] Esméria herself went on to give birth and baptize three sons between 1805 and 1808.[89] The timing of these baptisms points to the possibility that, aside from being responsible for most of the housework, Juliana served as a wet nurse to Esméria's boys. Other sources reveal that earlier in her marriage Esméria was a shopkeeper while her husband was a tailor – he also held minor positions in local government right up to his death.[90] The possibility of relying on Juliana to nurse and look after her children would have freed Esméria to take up spinning or weaving, at the time fast-growing and respectable female occupations.[91] Ultimately, what stands out is the unmistakable intimacy of the two young families residing together in a single urban household. Neither the slave Juliana nor her son turns up in later sources, so nothing is known of their fate in life. When Esméria and her husband, João Patrício, were inscribed in two nominal lists from the 1830s their household no longer included any slaves.

Manoel Martins Coimbra, like all members of the second and third generations of the Moreira da Silva family, is often described as a *crioulo* in archival sources. Notwithstanding his African descent, Manoel was ordained a priest sometime in the 1810s. By 1825 Manoel began appearing in the São José parish

85. The lack of formal Church (and, by definition, state) sanctioning of the unions that generated these families makes them difficult to trace in the archives, thus keeping them occult from historians, even though at the time they were recognized and condoned within local communities.

86. Zephyr Frank, "Wealth Holding in Southeastern Brazil, 1815–1860", *Hispanic American Historical Review*, 85 (2005), pp. 221–255.

87. APSASJRM, Baptismal record, Livro 24, fo. 143; APSASJRM, Baptismal record, Livro 10, fo. 48.

88. APSASJRM, Baptismal record, Livro 10, fo. 141.

89. *Ibid.*, fos. 162, 229, 281.

90. Arquivo Municipal de Tiradentes (hereafter AMT), Listas de vendas, Fundo Câmara da Vila de São José, Livro 1, fos. 1v–5v; AMT, Documentação Interna, box 1, package 97, fos. 46–47; AMT, Documentação Interna, box 1, package 118, fos. 8–9; AMT, Lançamentos de Fianças, Autos e Contratos e Arrematações, Livro 1, fos. 2–4, 6, 11v–13v, 16v, 19–20v, 22v, 24. For João Patrício's 1851 burial register, see APSASJRM, Death record, Livro 85, fo. 97v.

91. Douglas Cole Libby, "Proto-Industrialisation in a Slave Society: The Case of Minas Gerais", *Journal of Latin American Studies*, 23 (1991), pp. 1–35.

registers as *coajuntor*, or adjunct to the parish priest.[92] Clerics tended to be well-off in eighteenth and nineteenth-century Brazil and Father Manoel was no exception.[93] He and his spinster sister, Quitéria Maria de Souza, co-owned a townhouse, known as Três Cantos, located on the prestigious Rua Direita. The 1831 nominal list of São José shows Manoel as head of a household that included his sister, a niece, two male and one female enslaved Africans, one *crioula* and three *crioulo* slaves.[94] The following year Manoel passed away. His last will and testament listed one of the African male slaves as his and bequeathed the slave to his sister. It also listed all the native-born *crioulo* slaves, who were manumitted pending various terms of service to the heirs (Quitéria Maria and their other sister, Esméria).[95] Three of the *crioulos* were linked by familial ties: Antônio and Efigênia, recorded as married in the nominal list of 1831, were referred to as man and wife in their owner's will; Vitoriano was revealed to be the natural son of Efigênia in 1854 when, as a freedman, he got married.[96] Father Manoel's slaveholding thus included a family whose members were all eventually freed, notwithstanding the burdens of years of continued service to his heirs. By the 1830s, the transatlantic slave trade and a golden age of small and widespread slaveholdings were increasingly under threat. Yet, this slave family's example suggests that the connections between family formation and manumission practices constituted a common tradition that Father Manoel felt beholden to honor.

For another two decades, Quitéria Maria de Souza lived in the Três Cantos townhouse along with her niece Bárbara Patrícia Lopes and Bárbara's many children.[97] Over those years, Quitéria Maria, along with her sister Esméria Martins dos Passos, benefited from the services of the slaves Manoel Martins Coimbra had bequeathed them. Indeed, in the nominal list of 1838 Vitoriano (who later adopted the surname Martins Coimbra) figured simply as a slave belonging to Quitéria Maria in addition to the Africans Maria,

92. APSASJRM, Baptismal record, Livro 15, fo. 35.

93. For an interesting look at how men of color could become priests and accumulate both power and wealth, see Anderson José Machado de Oliveira, "Os processos de habilitação sacerdotal dos homens de cor. Perspectivas metodológicos para uma História Social do catolicismo na América portuguesa", in João Fragoso, Roberto Guedes, and Antônio Carlos Jucá de Sampaio (eds), *Arquivos paroquiais e História Social na América lusa. Métodos e técnicas de pesquisa na reinvenção de um corpus documental* (Rio de Janeiro, 2014), pp. 329–362.

94. Núcleo de Pesquisa em História Econômica e Demográfica do Centro de Desenvolvimento e Planejamento Regional/Universidade Federal de Minas Gerais, Lista de 1831.

95. ETIPHAN-SJR, Last will and testament, Cartório JO, box 512, fos. 6–7.

96. ASASJRM, Baptismal record, Livro 27, fo. 164.

97. For an analysis of Bárbara Patrícia's long-standing "occult" relationship with a member of the local white elite see Douglas Libby, "Family, Stability, and Respectability: Seven Generations of Africans and Afro-descendants in Eighteenth- and Nineteenth-Century Minas Gerais", *The Americas*, 73 (2016), pp. 371–390.

twenty-two years old, and Manoel, forty years old. In the urban setting of São José, these slaves were likely hired out or hired themselves out in order to generate income for the household. In 1842, the slave Maria gave birth to a daughter whose father went unnamed.[98] Typically for Moreira da Silva slaveholdings, Quitéria Maria came to own a slave family. When she died in 1852 the transatlantic slave trade had come to an end. Although she was probably not aware of it, the slave regime she had known for better than seventy years was about to be fundamentally altered by the disappearance of smallholders and, later, by abolitionist threats to the very institution of slavery. In making out her last will and testament, nevertheless, Quitéria Maria followed tradition. The African slave Maria and her daughter were granted manumissions conditioned upon terms of service to Bárbara Patrícia, executor of the estate.[99] Right to the very end, then, the entangled lives of slave and slaveholding families seemed almost inevitably to lead to manumission.

CONCLUSION

The experiences with manumission shared by the Vieira da Costa and Moreira da Silva families, and slaves in Sabará and São José more broadly, unfolded against Brazil's continued commitment to slavery. During this period, criticisms of the practice of slavery were limited to religious and legal tracts that focused mostly on the nature of masters' treatment of, responsibilities to, and expectations for their slaves. Authors like Jorge Benci, André João Antonil, and Nuno Marques Pereira encouraged slave owners to show mercy to their slaves and to convert them to Christianity. They sought a moral middle ground, where metropolitan and colonial need for labor could continue to be met by a brutal labor system that destroyed the bodies but, religious thinkers hoped, saved the souls of the enslaved.[100] The Jesuit priest Manuel Ribeiro Rocha pushed that agenda further. He argued that African slaves, once rescued from paganism, educated in Christian ways, and made to compensate owners for the cost of their redemption, should be given their freedom. Their liberation could happen in four ways: by serving their owners for a period of twenty years; by paying their owners an amount equivalent to twenty years of service; by being freed upon their owner's death; and finally, through their own death, which would accomplish their liberation in the afterlife.[101] Rocha, however,

98. APSASJRM, Baptismal record, Livro 14, fo. 230.

99. ETIPHAN-SJR, Last will and testament, Cartório JO, box 271, doc. 138.

100. Jorge Benci, *Economia cristã dos senhores no governo dos escravos* (São Paulo, 1977); André João Antonil, *Cultura e opulência do Brasil* (Belo Horizonte [etc.], 1982); Nuno Marques Pereira, *O peregrine das Américas* (Rio de Janeiro, 1933).

101. Manuel Ribeiro da Rocha, *Etíope resgatado, empenhado, sustentado, corrigido, instruído e libertado. Discurso teológico-jurídico sobre a libertação dos escravos no Brazil* (Petrópolis, 1992).

never called for the indiscriminate emancipation of slaves or end to the enslavement of Africans and their descendants.

Rocha's work was poorly known at the time of its publication. But its discussion of manumission was neatly reflected in the practices of eighteenth and early nineteenth-century slave owners in Minas Gerais. Different manumission records from the captaincy reveal that freedom often resulted from kinship ties between master and slave, from labor negotiations sometimes initiated by slaves themselves, and from the notion that slaves should be allowed to purchase their freedom when able to do so. The development of these manumission practices unfolded, to be sure, at a time when abolitionist views were emerging and influencing policies and struggles around the Atlantic world. Ironically, those broader abolitionist tendencies converged to fortify the Brazilian slave system. The fall of Haiti severely reduced the scope of the French slave trade while the successive suppression of the trade by Denmark (1803), Britain and the United States (1808), and the Netherlands (1814) greatly reduced demand for slaves on the western coast of Africa.[102] The trade to Brazil, consequently, maintained ample supplies and prices remained stable and low for almost half a century, benefiting agricultural expansion and the multiplication of small slaveholdings.[103] Notable, as well, was the social dissemination of slave ownership among freed and free African descendants.[104] Atlantic abolitionism may have thus contributed to black freedom in Minas Gerais mostly by stabilizing slave prices. The availability and affordability of newly trafficked enslaved workers made manumission a low risk transaction for masters, facilitated the purchase of freedom, and fed hopes among the enslaved that negotiating an end to their own or a relative's captivity was possible.

The discussions and eventual laws that constrained and then abolished the trafficking of slaves and enslavement of African descendants in the Atlantic world at the turn of the eighteenth to the nineteenth century would take several decades to develop in Brazil. Indeed, it was not until the 1860s that discernible popular support for full and immediate abolition of slavery emerged.[105] It may be fair to argue, therefore, that in its long-standing absence

102. Bergad, *The Comparative Histories*, pp. 251–290; Johannes Postma, *The Dutch in the Atlantic Slave Trade* (Cambridge, 2008), pp. 284–304; Seymour Drescher, *Abolition: A History of Slavery and Anti-Slavery* (New York, 2009), pp. 205–266; James Walvin, *Crossings: Africa, the Americas, and the Atlantic Slave Trade* (London, 2013), pp. 169–215; Erik Gobel, *The Danish Slave Trade and Its Abolition* (Leiden, 2016), pp. 138–182.

103. While slave price series are difficult to reconstitute, using evaluations found in inventories from various parts of Minas Gerais, Bergad found that valuations of male slaves from the turn of the century up to the 1820s fluctuated only slightly from mid-eighteenth-century values. Bergad, *Slavery*, pp. 263–265.

104. Zephyr L. Frank, *Dutra's World: Wealth and Family in Nineteenth-Century Rio de Janeiro* (Albuquerque, NM, 2004).

105. Leslie Bethell, *The Abolition of the Brazilian Slave Trade: Britain, Brazil, and the Slave Trade Question, 1807–1869* (Cambridge, 1970); Robert Conrad, *The Destruction of*

of any meaningful opposition, the Brazilian slave system was by far the most consolidated and stable among those surviving into the nineteenth century. An intrinsic part of that slave system was a series of practices which were perceived as contributing to the overall order, morality, and tranquility of the slave society. Among those practices were manumission, acceptance or encouragement of family formation among slaves, and eventually ad hoc support for slaves' right to purchase, or have purchased, their freedom.[106] In time, slaves became more adept at mobilizing the support of family and community members in manumission negotiations, and even at redirecting their claims to the right to freedom away from their masters and to courts of justice and the state. The introduction of an outside advocate into negotiations of freedom helped to undermine the absolute power their masters held over them.[107] As historians of that period, and those practices, we can delight in the slave master class' complacency and inability or unwillingness to comprehend the subversive nature social relations can acquire over time.

Brazilian Slavery, 1850–1888 (Berkeley, CA, 1972); Angela Alonso, *Flores, votos e balas. O movimento abolicionista brasileiro (1868–1888)* (São Paulo, 2015); Albuquerque, *O jogo da dissimulação*, pp. 45–93; Castilho, *Slave Emancipation*, pp. 22–52.

106. Marco Antônio Silveira, "Luta pela alforria e demandas políticas na capitania de Minas Gerais (1750–1808)", *Revista de História*, 158 (2008), pp. 131–156; Arno Wehling, "Uma solução setecentista ousada e inovadora para a escravidão no Brasil", *História*, 34:2 (2015), pp. 146–164.

107. Manuela Carneiro da Cunha, "Silences of the Law: Customary Law and Positive Law on the Manumission of Slaves in Nineteenth Century Brazil", *History and Anthropology*, 2 (1986), pp. 427–443; Keila Grinberg, *Liberata, a lei da ambiguidade. As ações de liberdade da Corte de Apelação do Rio de Janeiro no século XIX* (Rio de Janeiro, 2010); Camillia Cowling, *Conceiving Freedom: Women of Color, Gender, and the Abolition of Slavery in Havana and Rio de Janeiro* (Chapel Hill, NC, 2013).

IRSH 65 (2020), pp. 145–168 doi:10.1017/S0020859020000176

Disappearing from Abolitionism's Heartland: The Legacy of Slavery and Emancipation in Boston

Jared Ross Hardesty

History Department
Western Washington University
Bond Hall (BH) 364, Bellingham, WA, USA

E-mail: hardesj2@wwu.edu

Abstract: This article examines why Boston's slave and free black population consisted of more than 1,500 people in 1750, but by 1790 Boston was home to only 766 people of African descent. This disappearing act, where the town's black population declined by at least fifty per cent between 1763 and 1790, can only be explained by exploring slavery, abolition, and their legacies in Boston. Slaves were vital to the town's economy, filling skilled positions and providing labor for numerous industries. Using the skills acquired to challenge their enslavement, Afro-Bostonians found freedom during the American revolutionary era. Nevertheless, as New England's rural economy collapsed, young white men and women from all over the region flooded Boston looking for work, driving down wages, and competing with black people for menial employment. Forced out of the labor market, many former slaves and their descendants left the region entirely. Others joined the Continental or British armies and never returned home. Moreover, many slave owners, knowing that slavery was coming to an end in Massachusetts, sold their bondsmen and women to other colonies in the Americas where slavery was still legal and profitable. Thus, the long-term legacy of abolition for black Bostonians was that Boston's original enslaved population largely disappeared, while the city became a hub of abolitionism by the 1830s. Boston's abolitionist community – many the descendants of slaveholders – did not have to live with their forefathers' sins. Instead, they crafted a narrative of a free Boston, making it an attractive destination for runaway slaves from across the Atlantic world.

At the age of fourteen, in 1775, Charles Bowles enlisted in the Massachusetts militia during the Siege of Boston. Two years later, Bowles decided "to risk his life in defense of the holy cause of liberty" and joined the Continental army where he would serve until the end of the War of Independence in 1783. After seeing hell during the war, Bowles retired from military life and settled in New Hampshire where he took up "agricultural pursuits", became a Baptist preacher, and drew a pension, dying at the age of eighty-two in 1843.

Given Bowles's seemingly traditional English name, his patriotic fervor, and his relocating to the frontier, his story echoes that of many Americans in the aftermath of the American Revolution. Yet, Bowles had been born a slave in Boston, his father an African and his mother a creole, or locally born, black woman, and used his service in the army to find freedom. His life was more reflective of an enslaved Bostonian during the American Revolution than a white frontiersman. Born in 1761, Bowles grew up in a world where slavery was under assault, but still common. The slavery Bowles experienced in Boston meant he would have most likely grown up learning a skilled trade, traveled around town with his parents and master, and attended religious services. All of these factors ultimately shaped his freedom as Bowles used his mobility and skills to escape to the army, move to New Hampshire, take up farming, and become a minister. In that sense, the experience of Bowles was like that of so many other enslaved and freed Bostonians. Whether voluntary or involuntary, abolition in Boston coincided with the exodus of a large percentage of the black population.[1]

This article explores the lives of men like Charles Bowles to better understand why Boston's black population, which consisted of more than 1,500 people or more than ten per cent of the town's population in 1750, declined precipitously over the course of the revolutionary era. The town's black population declined by at least fifty per cent between 1760 and 1790 and even in 1850 consisted of only 1,999 people, only 400 more than during its colonial zenith. This disappearing act was the product of four decades of warfare, revolution, economic transformation, and ideological development spanning from roughly the end of the Seven Year's War in 1763 to the early nineteenth century.[2]

Scholars have been studying slavery and emancipation in Boston and New England since the 1860s and the literature tends to fall into two broad camps. The first are works exploring slavery in the region, which explore slavery on its own terms in a specific time period. These works usually only contain a short chapter or epilogue on abolition.[3] Second are the studies examining abolition

1. For more on Bowles, see William Cooper Nell, *The Colored Patriots of the American Revolution with Sketches of Several Distinguished Colored Persons...* (Boston, MA, 1855), pp. 28–29.

2. George Levesque, a historian of black Boston, argues against this trend, noting that when observers described the declining black population in the city, they were actually noting how the population declined as a total percentage of Boston's population. Instead, Boston's black population did grow slowly during the early nineteenth century. While technically correct, Levesque's data barely acknowledges the colonial and revolutionary periods and his attempts to quantify only really begin in 1820. By that point, Boston's black population had begun to increase following the events described here. See George A. Levesque, *Black Boston: African American Life and Culture in Urban America* (New York, 1994), ch. 2.

3. For the latest examples, see Wendy Anne Warren, *New England Bound: Slavery and Colonization in Early America* (New York, 2016); Margaret Ellen Newell, *Brethren by Nature:*

and emancipation in New England, which tend to only have a short introductory chapter on slavery. This scholarship also emphasizes change over continuity when dealing with the impact of abolition on black lives.[4] Thus, there is a disconnect in the literature and little overlap outside of a few citations of one another.[5] This article bridges that gap by placing how slavery functioned in Boston in conversation with the process and legacy of abolition in the town and how Boston came to fashion itself as an abolitionist city.

It is important to note that the argument put forth here is not without controversy in the historiography of slavery and abolition in New England. The idea that abolition was a process is at odds with an older historical tradition. Beginning in the 1860s, scholars argued that a 1783 court case, *Commonwealth v. Jennison*, brought an effective end to slavery and that by 1790, there were no slaves in Massachusetts. Upheld as an exceptional decision made by an activist judge looking to destroy slavery, the case appears in triumphalist accounts of the end of slavery in Massachusetts. There are many problems with this analysis, however. The argument made by the judge that slavery was incompatible with the Massachusetts Constitution of 1780 were only in his instructions to the jury, never published, and only cited as precedent more than two decades after the decision. Moreover, even though the United States census of 1790 did not enumerate any slaves in Massachusetts, there is evidence that census takers deliberately avoided recording slaves. Meanwhile, probate and notarial records document the persistence of slavery in Boston into the mid-1790s. By embracing 1783 and 1790 as definitive dates, past historians have obfuscated the troubled, ambiguous abolition in Boston, especially the legacies of slavery in that process.[6]

This article is therefore divided into three parts. First, it explores slavery in Boston (Figure 1). Slaves were vital to Boston's economy, filling skilled positions and providing labor for numerous industries. Second, slaves found

New England Indians, Colonists, and the Origins of American Slavery (Ithaca, NY, 2015); and Jared Ross Hardesty, *Unfreedom: Slavery and Dependence in Eighteenth-Century Boston* (New York, 2016).

4. Work in this camp tends to be slightly older starting with Leon Litwack, *North of Slavery: The Negro in the Free States, 1790–1860* (Chicago, IL, 1969). Other works include Joanne Pope Melish, *Disowning Slavery: Gradual Emancipation and "Race" in New England, 1780–1860* (Ithaca, NY, 1997) and James Oliver Horton and Lois E. Horton, *In Hope of Liberty: Culture, Community and Protest among Northern Free Blacks, 1700–1860* (New York, 1998), which ostensibly looks at a longer sweep of history, but only includes two short chapters on the pre-Revolutionary period.

5. One exception to this rule takes a longue durée approach to slavery and its legacies in Rhode Island, although it also explores the "business of slavery" in addition to the experiences of enslaved people. See Christy Clark-Pujara, *Dark Work: The Business of Slavery in Rhode Island* (New York, 2016).

6. For more on this debate and the problems with using *Commonwealth v. Jennison* and the 1790 Census, see Margot Minardi, *Making Slavery History: Abolitionism and the Politics of Memory in Massachusetts* (New York, 2010), esp. pp. 17–19. Minardi largely agrees with my analysis here.

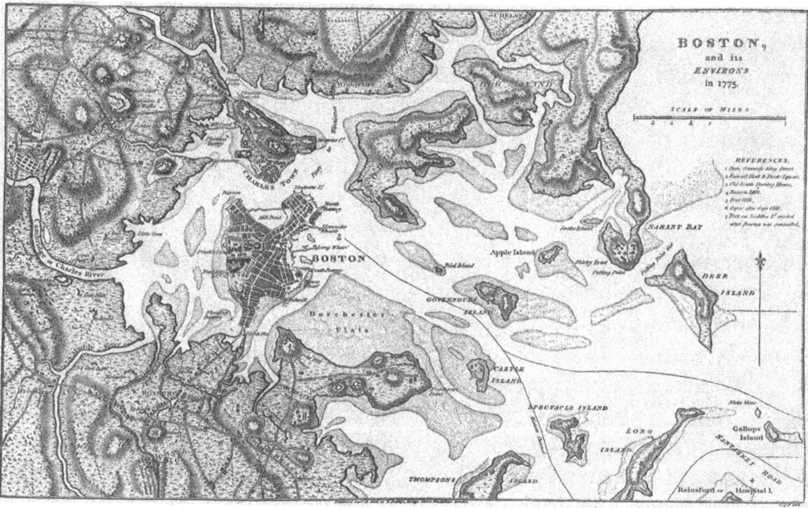

Figure 1. Boston and its Environs, 1775.
Source: Pictures Now/Alamy Stock Photo. Image ID: MM011D.

freedom during the American Revolution using the skills they developed earlier to challenge slavery. They joined the military, absconded, found themselves the target of kidnapping, and were increasingly locked out of Boston's labor market. In short, many former slaves and their descendants left the region entirely. Finally, the legacy of abolition for black Bostonians was that Boston's original enslaved population disappeared, while the city became a hub of abolitionism in the 1820s. No longer having to deal with the living legacies of slavery, abolitionists crafted a narrative of a free Boston, making it an attractive destination for runaway slaves from across the Atlantic world.

SLAVERY IN BOSTON

Slavery in Boston laid the foundation for the town's ambivalent abolition. Only by exploring how slavery functioned and the lives of enslaved people can we better understand why slavery ended the way it did. Enslaved Bostonians faced myriad challenges, but during the eighteenth century, they lived in a dynamic urban environment that valued their labor. Although largely male, enslaved people living in Boston were skilled, mobile, and experts at using local institutions to their advantage. These traits meant slaves understood their value, could read, and sometimes write, and had intimate knowledge of geography, law, politics, and larger intellectual trends. Exploring three themes related to the lived experience of enslaved Bostonians – labor, mobility, and institutional appropriation – demonstrates how they had skillsets that allowed them to resist the quotidian dehumanization of slavery. While still human chattel, Boston's slaves eventually used these skills to forge their own freedom.

During the eighteenth century, Boston's economy, while on a nasty boom-and-bust cycle, grew rapidly, often far exceeding the town's labor capacity.[7] To address the labor shortage, Bostonians of every economic class turned to slave labor. Indeed, by the 1740s, Boston's enslaved population numbered more than 1,500 people or roughly ten per cent of the town's total population. Yet, this number is deceptive as masters often hid slaves – classified as taxable property – from census takers. More likely, African slaves comprised closer to twelve to fifteen per cent of the town's total population. And Bostonians bought these people to work. They served as seamstresses, cooks, and valets in homes and laborers in workshops, distilleries, and shipyards.

What is most striking about enslaved Bostonians, however, is just how many were trained craftsmen. They were carpenters, coopers, bakers, blacksmiths, masons, and printers. Many of them arrived in town as children, became the property of local artisans, and, in addition to living in their masters' households, served as apprentices, learning a trade as they grew. Viewed as a long-term investment by their masters, enslaved tradesmen were central features of Boston's manufacturing sector, building houses and ships, distilling rum, and making rope. Moreover, Boston's skilled slaves held value for the town at large, providing vital labor that kept the town's economy running. Skilled jobs were not easy to fill given eighteenth-century labor structures, and enslaved people could help make up for those shortages.[8]

Skilled and valued, enslaved Bostonians were able to convert these traits into autonomy and mobility, affording enslaved men and women an incredible degree of independence to define their place in eighteenth-century Boston and beyond. Likewise, Boston's enslaved population was highly mobile both within the town and across the Atlantic world. Many enslaved Bostonians found themselves free to go to the market, hire themselves out around the town and surrounding communities, or ply the sea on oceangoing ships. Others self-hired, negotiating their own contracts and work conditions, often with the explicit permission of their masters. Many slaveholders condoned bondsmen and women working independently, hoping to preserve domestic tranquility while still generating revenue. Enslaved men and women, however, took full advantage of these opportunities and used them to carve out spaces for themselves.

7. Gary Nash, *The Urban Crucible: Social Change, Political Consciousness, and the Origins of the American Revolution* (Cambridge, MA, 1979).

8. Jared Ross Hardesty, "'The Negro at the Gate': Enslaved Labor in Eighteenth-Century Boston", *The New England Quarterly*, 87 (2014), pp. 72–98.

Facilitated by their mobility and skillsets, many slaves acquired knowledge and understanding of the world around them. Most importantly, they were accomplished appropriators, learning how to use and navigate local institutions, namely the law and religion.[9] They used these institutions to gain tangible and ultimately useful skills such as literacy and legal knowledge. Literacy came mainly from the adoption of Protestant Christianity. While it is impossible to determine if enslaved Bostonians were true believers or just using the town's many churches for their own ends, for slaves, these houses of worship were also educational centers. Given Protestantism's emphasis on the ability to access scripture, teaching reading was central to knowing God. Yet, for the many black faces in Boston's pews, reading meant more than the Bible.[10]

Knowing how to read (and possibly write) opened a world of possibilities to enslaved Bostonians. Even if they could not personally read, most knew someone who could. They had access to books, pamphlets, and newspapers and this access gave slaves leverage and the ability to resist their masters. In Boston's newspapers, for example, slave-for-sale advertisements rarely contained the names of masters or slaves and usually only offered vague physical descriptions. Since so many slaves could read, it would be relatively easy for them to tip each other off about potential sales and being ripped away from family and friends.[11] Likewise, combined with their informal oral networks and enslaved sailors bringing news from abroad, enslaved men and women in Boston would have had a good sense of what was happening around the world.

Like their use of religion to gain literacy, enslaved Bostonians also used the legal system to their own advantage. Unlike today, eighteenth-century law was not as professionalized and legal knowledge was readily available to most members of society. Books on legal methods, practice, and theory proliferated across the Atlantic and were easily accessible. In addition to this general access – facilitated by literacy – many enslaved Bostonians had experience with the law. Considering the many different statutes targeting them, it should not be surprising that blacks often ran afoul of the law and appeared in court. Through reading, discussions, and experience, slaves learned how to use the law. They learned which justice of the peace would give them the fairest hearing or listen if they were being abused. Likewise, slaves learned how to file petitions or found white allies who could help. The petition was the primary tool for initiating any legal action in Anglo-American courts and multiple

9. The classic work on cultural appropriation is James Sidbury, *Ploughshares into Swords: Race, Rebellion, and Identity in Gabriel's Virginia, 1730–1810* (New York, 1997).

10. For more on the use of religion by enslaved people in Boston, see Jared Hardesty, "An Angry God in the Hands of Sinners: Enslaved Africans and the Uses of Protestant Christianity in Colonial Boston", *Slavery & Abolition*, 35 (2014), pp. 66–83.

11. Robert E. Desrochers, Jr, "Slave-For-Sale Advertisements and Slavery in Massachusetts, 1704–1781" *William and Mary Quarterly*, 59 (2002), pp. 634–635.

petitions from enslaved people exist in the Massachusetts records, demonstrating that enslaved Bostonians understood the law.[12]

Boston's enslaved population was skilled, mobile, and knowledgeable. During the colonial period, they used these attributes to carve out a functional independence for themselves and find creative ways to resist both their masters and colonial authorities. They had leverage in the labor market, moved around relatively freely, and understood how to use local institutions to their advantage. Such characteristics prepared enslaved Bostonians to strike for freedom when the opportunity presented itself in the era of the American Revolution.

ABOLITION AND DISPLACEMENT

Abolition in Boston coincided with the Imperial Crisis (1763–1775), the War of Independence (1775–1783), and the aftermath of the American Revolution. It was a relatively long-term process lasting from the 1760s until the early 1800s. Largely initiated by enslaved people and their free black and white allies, emancipation did not involve legislation, gradual emancipation laws, or general freedom decrees like in other places. Rather, most enslaved people found other paths to freedom and used the skills, mobility, and knowledge they had gained during their enslavement. Nevertheless, given the extended period of abolition in Boston, it is important to remember that the end of slavery did not happen at a particular moment, but was a process. Under such ambivalent conditions, abolition severely disrupted black life. Indeed, considering the end of slavery in Boston coincided with the chaos of the American Revolution and its aftermath, the process totally upended the colonial order that black Bostonians had grown to know in both positive and negative ways. In both cases, the ultimate result was to displace the town's black population. Many served in the army and settled far away from New England, while masters, seeing the writing on the wall, sold others to Canada, the Caribbean, and the American South.

The irony, however, is that the nature of slave life in Boston shaped this displacement. Highly skilled, masters knew their enslaved men and women would fetch a good price in places where slavery was not under threat. Already mobile, many enslaved people saw service in either the Continental or British armies as an opportunity to strike for freedom. Moreover, the collapse of the New England rural economy during and after the American Revolution caused a flood of poor whites into Boston looking for work, who actively sought to displace enslaved and free black people from the town's workforce and embraced an emerging scientific racism to justify that

12. For more on appropriating the law, see Hardesty, *Unfreedom*, ch. 5.

displacement. Attuned to these larger economic and ideological changes, Afro-Bostonians voted with their feet to leave entirely.

The beginning of the end of slavery in Boston was the Imperial Crisis. As white colonists began protesting their rights and freedom from the "slavery" of arbitrary government, black Bostonians took note. Most important to this process was the rise of natural rights discourse. By the early 1770s, arguments about the traditional rights of Englishmen began to be subsumed into a greater argument about the rights of humanity.[13] Ever attuned to larger intellectual developments, Boston's black population also began using natural rights language.

This appropriation of natural rights can be seen in a series of petitions that enslaved and free blacks in Boston filed with the Massachusetts government between 1773 and 1777. All told, seven of these documents survive; black Bostonians authored all of them and they provide insight into how blacks attempted to negotiate an end to slavery by appealing to human rights. Most importantly, there is an ever-stronger insistence that freedom was natural and innate. The first petition, written in January 1773 by a free black man named Felix and addressed to the Massachusetts governor and legislature, argued that slavery, their "greatest Unhappiness", was "not our Fault" and merely asked "for such Relief as is consistent with your Wisdom, justice, and Goodness".[14] When that did not work, a petition in April 1773 attempted to shame the government into action, noting that even the "Spaniards, who have not those sublime ideas of freedom that English men have, are conscious that they have no right to all the service of their fellow-men, we mean the Africans [...] therefore they [...] enable them to earn money to purchase the residue of their time".[15] Not only does this demonstrate that black Bostonians understood the Spanish concept of *coartación* (the right to self-purchase), but they could also weaponize those ideas.

Shame and pity did not work, and the government largely ignored these appeals. Later petitions were much more forceful and deployed new techniques. A third document, from May 1774, opened with a powerful decree that enslaved people "have in common with all other men a naturel right to our freedoms without Being depriv'd of them by our fellow men as we are a freeborn Pepel and have never forfeited this Blessing by aney compact or agreement whatever".[16] Even more important, this appeal was not directed at the legislature. Rather, petitioners asked the military governor of

13. The classic work concerning the language of slavery and freedom deployed by the colonists and the transition to natural rights is Bernard Bailyn, *The Ideological Origins of the American Revolution* (1965; Cambridge, MA, 1992).

14. "Slave Petition for Freedom", 6 January 1773, in Herbert Aptheker (ed.), *A Documentary History of the Negro People in the United States* (New York, 1951), vol. I, pp. 6–7.

15. "Peter Bestes and Other Slaves Petition for Freedom", 20 April 1773, in *Ibid.*, vol. I, pp. 7–8.

16. "Petition of a Grate Number of Blackes", 25 May 1774, in *Ibid.*, vol. I, pp. 8–9.

Massachusetts, Thomas Gage – sent to quell rebellious Bostonians following the Boston Tea Party in December 1773 – for relief. This move was politically calculated. By appealing to Gage, the petitioners sent the message that although they sought an end to slavery, they were also still loyal British subjects and could possibly be called upon to confront rebellious white colonists. It is unclear how Gage regarded the petition, and, as with the previous ones, there was no movement on the issue.

The final petition, from 1777 and addressed to the revolutionary government in Massachusetts, deployed the same natural rights language as the 1774 document, arguing the petitioners were "detained in a state of Slavery in the Bowels of a free and Christian Country". It also reflected the exasperation of petitioning six previous times to no avail, noting black Bostonians "have long and patiently waited the event of Petition after Petition by them presented to the legislative Body of this State, and can not but with grief reflect that their success has been but too similar". Moreover, they also offered practical solutions, such as legislation that would free the children of slaves at the age of twenty-one, as part of the larger appeals to liberty.[17] Once again, however, the legislature took little action after reading the document on the floor of the assembly.

Although these petitions all failed in their stated purpose, they are still important for understanding slavery and abolition in Boston. They reveal that in an attempt to end slavery, enslaved and free black men relied on the skills and knowledge they had acquired during their time in Boston. Instead of using the petition for legal issues, they transformed it into a tool to forge freedom. Likewise, as white colonists increasingly incorporated the language of natural rights into their own appeals and arguments, black Bostonians appropriated those ideas for their own ends. They combined that knowledge with information gleaned from their own social networks and reading to appeal to local authorities.

While petitioning may have failed, increasing numbers of enslaved Bostonians gained their freedom through a variety of means. Many more enslaved people found freedom using the court system. Often referred to as "freedom suits", these occurred when enslaved men and women would sue their masters for freedom. Once again demonstrating the access slaves had to the courts and their knowledge of the law, these suits became increasingly common during the 1760s and continued until the 1790s.[18] Nevertheless, it is important to remember that these cases freed individual slaves using preexisting legal maneuvers such as claims of trespass and back wages. These cases, besides establishing a precedent that enslaved people could sue their masters

17. "Petition of a Great Number of Negroes", 13 January 1777, in *Ibid.*, vol. I, pp. 9–10.
18. Margot Minardi notes there were twenty freedom suits in Massachusetts between 1760 and 1779, but they increase following the ratification of the Massachusetts Constitution of 1780 (see below). Minardi, *Making Slavery History*, p. 17.

and win freedom, were relatively ineffective at helping end slavery as an institution. Moreover, there are no records of freedom suits in Boston from that period because the British occupation forces took the Suffolk County (where Boston is located) civil and criminal court records from the 1760s and early 1770s with them when they evacuated in March 1776.

We can, however, examine a case close to Boston. In 1769, James, an enslaved man belonging to Richard Lechmere, a merchant in Cambridge, Massachusetts, sued his master in the Middlesex County Court of Common Pleas (civil court). James found a white lawyer, Francis Dana, to represent him and in his suit accused Lechmere of trespass, claiming the merchant "assaulted [...] him took & imprisoned & restrained him of his Liberty & hold him in Servitude". Instead of demanding his freedom outright, however, James wanted to be paid £100 in damages and back wages. That sum was much higher than James's market value and put Lechmere in something of a bind. He could always allow the case to work its way through the courts and possibly win, but if he lost, he would have to pay his already recalcitrant bondsman an exceptional amount of money. In short, freedom would be cheaper than paying back wages. In this case, Lechmere pleaded not guilty in the lower court and won, namely because the court upheld Lechmere's right to hold James as property. When James and Dana appealed, however, the merchant gave up, freeing his bondsman and giving him £2 in return for James dropping the suit.[19]

Perhaps the most important aid to enslaved Bostonians finding freedom was the Massachusetts Constitution of 1780. When promulgated, the document laid the groundwork for the end of slavery. Indeed, the very first part of the constitution, Article I, Part 1, declared "All men are born free and equal, and have certain natural, essential, and unalienable rights". Since the ratification of the constitution, historians have largely agreed that the drafter of the document, future American president John Adams, himself a lifelong opponent of black bondage, meant to undermine the institution of slavery in the Bay State. The first historian of slavery in Massachusetts, Jeremy Belknap, made the explicit connection, noting in a published letter to St. George Tucker of Virginia that Article I, Part 1, was meant to "establish the liberation of the negroes on a general principle, and so it was understood by the people at large".[20]

19. For more information on the case, see "Court Document, 1769", in Slavery and Abolition in the Longfellow Archives. Available at: https://www.nps.gov/long/learn/historyculture/slavery-related-objects-at-longfellow-nhs.htm; last accessed 9 September 2019. This website contains a digitized copy of the summons and information about the case.

20. Jeremy Belknap, "Queries Respecting the Slavery and Emancipation of Negroes in Massachusetts, Proposed by the Hon. Judge Tucker of Virginia, and Answered by the Rev. Dr. Belknap", in *Collections of the Massachusetts Historical Society*, 1st ser., vol. IV (1795), p. 203.

Regardless of whether or not the "people at large" interpreted the constitution of 1780 in that way, it did not really matter to enslaved people who saw an opportunity. There was a sharp uptick in the number of freedom suits and important court decisions, most importantly *Commonwealth v. Jennison* (1783) where Massachusetts Chief Justice William Cushing, in his instructions to the jury, declared slavery was "wholly incompatible and repugnant" to the Massachusetts Constitution.[21] While the case was not as widely publicized or important as historians once thought, it nonetheless gets us in the minds of leading Massachusetts jurists, who by the mid-1780s believed that the law did not protect the rights of slaveholders.[22] This transformation opened the door to any enslaved person who could bring a suit to find their freedom. Yet, many slaves did not even bother going to court. In a letter to Jeremy Belknap, Samuel Dexter, a political leader during the revolutionary era, explained that after hearing about the constitution of 1780, "one negro after another deserted from the service of those who had been their owners, till a considerable number had revolted". A few "were seized and remanded to their former servitude", Dexter continued, but would then sue and win their freedom. Dexter bluntly explained the consequence of these actions: "Thus ended slavery in Massachusetts".[23] Empowered by the constitution of 1780 and using the mobility and legal knowledge they learned as slaves, the 1780s were a moment of self-emancipation.

Yet, this abolition was not without consequences. Most tellingly, the end of slavery in Boston, both because of the effects of the American Revolution and changing attitudes towards race and bondage, seriously disrupted black life in the town and ultimately displaced many of the formerly enslaved. Many found freedom by simply absconding, joining the Patriot army or navy with or without the permission of their masters, or running away to the British and exchanging service to the Crown for freedom. But it was not all positive. The chaos of occupation and war destroyed black families; freedom struggles caused many masters to sell them away to extract one last bit of wealth and changing labor and race relations meant that many enslaved people could not practice artisanal trades and looked elsewhere for work.

One of the leading causes of disruption and displacement of Boston's black population was the British Army's occupation of Boston following the 1773 Boston Tea Party. Between the occupation itself and, after April 1775, the Continental army's siege of the town, large numbers of Bostonians left. Many took their slaves with them, undermining the communities and families

21. Quoted in Minardi, *Making Slavery History*, pp. 17–18.

22. For more on this point, see Emily Blanck, "Seventeen Eighty-Three: The Turning Point in the Law of Slavery and Freedom in Massachusetts", *The New England Quarterly*, 75 (2002).

23. Samuel Dexter to Jeremy Belknap, 23 February 1795, in Jeremy Belknap, "Queries Relating to Slavery in Massachusetts", *Massachusetts Historical Society Collections*, 3rd ser., vol. III (1877), p. 386.

created by the black population. A good example of this can be seen in the letters of Josiah Quincy, a merchant and politician from Braintree, Massachusetts. Quincy spent considerable time in Boston and had an enslaved woman, whose name is never revealed, who married a slave, Sharper, belonging to Enoch Brown. Under normal circumstances, Sharper and Quincy's enslaved woman would have had plenty of time to interact and spend time together when Quincy was in Boston. But these were not ordinary times. Writing to James Bowdoin, the leader of the Patriot Massachusetts Provincial Congress that coordinated the Siege of Boston, in December 1775, Quincy, in a "grateful sense of the faithfull service of my black female servant", enquired after Sharper. According to the politician, the woman had not heard from her husband in over two months, despite "diligent enquiry". Even worse, despite belonging to Enoch Brown, Sharper was not residing with his master-in-exile, but rather with Colonel Ebenezer Sproat of the Continental army. Bowdoin, in his reply, noted he had met with Colonel Sproat and that Sharper had been for a "considerable time on a trading journey" to southeastern Massachusetts and had returned to the army's camp in Cambridge.[24]

The exchange between Quincy and Bowdoin is important for understanding the effect of war and occupation on black life in Boston. On the one hand, we see the sundering of a black family and an already difficult situation given most enslaved husbands and wives lived apart in Boston – where spouses lost all communication with one another. Moreover, Sharper presents an interesting example. He was very similar to other enslaved Bostonians in that he was highly mobile, seemed to work on his own, and lived away from his master. Yet, his home under occupation, Sharper traveled further than normal, all around eastern Massachusetts to a variety of different towns and army encampments. Nobody found this situation unusual, most likely because it was an extension of the slavery that already existed in Boston. Within this continuity, however, came change. The military shaped Sharper's post-occupation life, providing him a place to live and his trading mission was most likely to procure supplies for the soldiers besieging Boston. It removed the enslaved man further and further from his family and the life he knew before the Revolution. While we do not know the fate of Sharper (or his wife), his association with the military was quite common and would shape black life in the years to come.

As Sharper's story suggests, many enslaved men from Boston served in the military, providing ample opportunity to leave home. While figures for Boston and Massachusetts are not available, in neighboring Connecticut, twenty per

24. The exchange can be found in Josiah Quincy to James Bowdoin, 11 December 1775, and James Bowdoin to Josiah Quincy, 16 December 1775, in "The Bowdoin and Temple Papers", in *Collections of the Massachusetts Historical Society* (Boston, MA, 1897), 6th ser., vol. IX, pp. 391–393.

cent of the black heads of household listed in the 1790 United States census served in American army.[25] Again an outgrowth of the mobility they experienced as slaves, the relatively widespread acts of joining a campaign or serving on board a ship brought massive changes to black lives. While many were loyal soldiers, in some cases, service was a way to escape. In January 1778, American Commodore Samuel Tucker wrote to the lieutenant of the Boston-based frigate *Boston* demanding the officer look for and "Apprehend [...] Two Negro Men who belong to the Ship" that absconded, most likely seeing the navy as their chance to run away from servitude.[26] Whether through loyal service or escape, the military presented slaves an opportunity to throw off the yoke of bondage.

Like the black Bostonians who served in the Continental army, many also served the British in their attempt to quell their rebellious colonists. Historians have intensively studied these Black Loyalists in recent years.[27] Most of them escaped to British lines where they pledged support to the Crown in exchange for liberty. Thousands evacuated with British forces, mostly from New York City, following the war and settled in Nova Scotia, London, and further afield. Unlike American forces, the British accepted – often reluctantly – most people who appeared, meaning women, children, and the elderly in addition to able-bodied men who found freedom with the British. Records, including the *Book of Negroes*, a register of African Americans who evacuated with the British, demonstrate that many black Bostonians found their way to New York City and pledged their support. Most interesting was Pompey Fleet, a skilled printer. A "Short & Stout" twenty-six-year-old, Fleet escaped his master, Patriot printer Thomas Fleet Jr, or as the clerk euphemistically stated, "left him", during the "Evacuation of Boston" in March 1776.[28] Fleet's case indicates that black Bostonians saw

25. Douglas R. Egerton, *Death or Liberty: African Americans and Revolutionary America* (New York, 2009), p. 95.

26. Samuel Tucker to Mr Barron, dated Boston, 17 January 1778, Commodore Tucker Papers, vol. I, Houghton Library, Harvard University, Cambridge, MA.

27. Recent works include Alan Gilbert, *Black Loyalists and Patriots: Fighting for Emancipation in the War of Independence* (Chicago, IL, 2012); Alexander X. Byrd, *Captives and Voyagers: Black Migrants Across the Eighteenth-Century British Atlantic World* (Baton Rouge, LA, 2010); Maya Jasanoff, *Liberty's Exiles: American Loyalists in the Revolutionary World* (New York, 2011); Simon Schama, *Rough Crossings: The Slaves, the British, and the American Revolution* (New York, 2007); and Cassandra Pybus, *Epic Journeys of Freedom: Runaway Slaves of the American Revolution and Their Global Quest for Liberty* (Boston, MA, 2007).

28. This reference to Fleet can be found in the *Book of Negroes*, which the Nova Scotia Archives has digitized at http://novascotia.ca/archives/Africanns/archives.asp?ID=26; last accessed 28 December 2016. There is a bit of an age discrepancy for Fleet between the *Book of Negroes* and what we can extrapolate from his father's will and the writings of Isaiah Thomas. In the book, Fleet claims to be twenty-six, but based on other documentation, he would have been around thirty-five. One possibility is that he reported his age when he escaped rather than his actual age. He could have also lied, hoping to receive a larger concession as a younger man.

the British as offering the opportunity for freedom denied them by American authorities.

Although service in the American or British armies caused many black Bostonians to leave the town altogether, it was largely voluntary, and slaves would have understood the consequences of their service. Other forms of displacement were more insidious. Coinciding with the Imperial Crisis, many masters in Boston began to sell their enslaved men and women out of the colony. This trend continued all the way through the 1780s and early 1790s. Part of it was economic. First the recession following the Seven Years' War and then the chaos of the Revolution disrupted Boston's economy, slowing manufacturing, driving down wages, and disrupting overseas trade.[29] Yet, ideological factors also have to be considered. By the mid-1760s, African slavery had come under assault across the British empire, but particularly in Boston, the center of resistance to the post-1763 imperial reforms.[30] Famed orators such as James Otis made slavery a special target in speeches, while newspapers ran opinion pieces condemning slavery, sometimes by enslaved and free black people.[31] Such agitation possibly served to shame masters. One way of absolving that guilt was through sale, which would get rid of the problem entirely. For the more unscrupulous, black activism, such as freedom suits and petition campaigns, strongly signaled that slavery was coming to an end. Instead of risking their valuable property in a court case, which by the 1780s masters were guaranteed to lose, many took the initiative to sell their enslaved men and women. Either through shame or greed, the result was the same: a nearly three-decade sell-off that decimated black Boston.

Evidence for selling out is largely circumstantial, but there are a few clues to how it happened and its effect. Bills of sale from merchants provide some clues as to how masters sold their slaves. Some transactions were straightforward, such as when Boston tobacconist Simon Elliot sold his enslaved woman Peggy to Archimedes George of Jamaica in 1769.[32] Given that many Boston masters were tradesmen or not part of slaving networks, however, merchants with overseas connections seem to have served as intermediaries and facilitated the commerce. We can see this in a 1772 letter of Virginia merchant and planter Benjamin Harrison to Boston merchant William Palfrey. Harrison served as Palfrey's agent in the Old Dominion and the men had long been business

29. For Boston's economy during the 1760s and 1770s, see Nash, *The Urban Crucible*, ch. 12.

30. This antislavery moment in the British empire is the focus of Gerald Horne, *The Counter-Revolution of 1776: Slave Resistance and the Origins of the United States of America* (New York, 2014).

31. Otis attacked slavery in a number of tracts, most famously in James Otis, *The Rights of the British Colonies Asserted and Proved* (Boston, MA, 1764). For an example of black op-ed writers, see Caesar Sarter's front-page editorial in *The Essex Journal and Merrimack Packet*, 17 August 1774.

32. Bill of Sale, 11 September 1769, Ezekiel Price Notarial Records, vol. V, Boston Athenæum.

partners. As part of their commerce, Harrison agreed to sell a slave belonging to a Mr Crequi of Boston.[33]

Often sent by merchants to Canada, the Caribbean, or the American South, selling out had serious social consequences. Again, solid numbers are hard to find, but qualitative evidence offers some clues. In 1787, Massachusetts minister Peter Thacher told abolitionist Moses Brown that there were "many instances of the negroes being kidnapped & privately conveyed away to Canada where they were sold for slaves". Neighboring Connecticut, which passed a gradual emancipation law in 1784, faced similar sales. Jonathan Edwards Jr, son of the famous revivalist, remembered after the passage of the act, he knew a man "employed in purchasing Negroes for exportation". Likewise, Rhode Island banned selling slaves out of the state in 1779, suggesting it was a problem there as well.[34]

These sales had a chilling effect on black life. Evidence of the uneasiness comes from notary books. In 1789, a free black man named Charleston approached Boston notary Ezekiel Price and had the notary record his manumission certificate. Interestingly, however, Charleston was not manumitted in 1789, but rather twelve years earlier in May 1777.[35] The gap between manumission and recording suggests that Charleston feared being sold away and wanted a copy of his manumission certificate on file, which would also provide Charleston more evidence in case he ever had to engage in the habeas corpus suits used by free blacks to protect themselves from being sold.

Economics and ideology provided plenty of impetus for masters to sell their slaves away, but the very nature of slavery made this practice feasible and facilitated the sale of enslaved Bostonians. As historian Trevor Burnard reminds us, slavery was economically advantageous for three reasons. Not only did enslaved people provide labor free of charge, but they were an investment that generally appreciated in value over time and, in a world of labor shortages, slaves could always be readily sold for cash.[36] Given the relatively early date of Boston's abolition, there were still plenty of labor-starved economies across the Atlantic looking for enslaved workers. Moreover, many of the skills acquired by enslaved Bostonians proved appealing to potential buyers. These skills are why the records are replete with references to slaves and free blacks being illegally sold to Canada. Mostly sent to Nova Scotia and New Brunswick, many black Bostonians would have been employed in the emer-

33. Benjamin Harrison to William Palfrey, dated Berkeley, 9 December 1772, Folder 86, MS Am 1704.3 Part II, Palfrey Family Papers, Houghton Library, Harvard University.

34. Quotes and information are from John Wood Sweet, *Bodies Politic: Negotiating Race in the American North, 1730–1830* (Philadelphia, PA, 2006), pp. 260–261.

35. Manumission, 25 February 1789, Ezekiel Price Notarial Records, vol. VII, Boston Athenæum.

36. Trevor Burnard, *Mastery, Tyranny, and Desire: Thomas Thistlewood and His Slaves in the Anglo-Jamaican World* (Chapel Hill, NC, 2004), 55–58.

ging port cities of Annapolis, Halifax, and Saint John. Settled by tens of thousands of Loyalists, both black and white, during and after the War of Independence, these ports were bustling centers of economic and military activity by the mid-1780s. Townspeople, in desperate need of skilled labor, turned to many different sources of slaves, but particularly to New England given that many of the settlers in Atlantic Canada had ties to the region and understood its system of enslavement.[37] In short, the same skills that helped generate autonomy under slavery helped to create misery and dislocation during emancipation.

For those not relocated by war or sold away, the changing nature of Boston and New England's economy after the American Revolution further decimated the town's black population. The same skills that aided enslaved people in resisting slavery made them a target for changing notions of race and class. Much of this economic change can be linked to the collapse of New England's rural economy (Figure 2). By the 1750s and 1760s, in long-settled parts of the region such as eastern Massachusetts, the land began to give out, but the population continued to grow. Too little good land and too many people ultimately caused the agrarian economy to suffer as crop yields declined and the farmers who remained turned their land over to livestock on tiny plots that often did not provide for their subsistence. Young farmers faced two options. First, they could head to the frontier, both north and west, to build new farms on fresh land. Others began moving to larger towns and cities, especially Boston, looking for employment.[38] This mass movement into urban areas created, for the first time in American history, a surplus of unskilled white working people, or in other words, solved the labor shortages that drove the expansion of slavery in Boston.[39]

As poor whites flooded into Boston during the last quarter of the eighteenth century, they began to lay claim to the skilled and semiskilled jobs that had been performed by slaves. Indeed, they demanded them as a sort of right and were willing to use political pressure and threats of violence to achieve their ends. In a letter about the end of slavery in Massachusetts, then Vice

37. See Harvey Amani Whitfield, *North to Bondage: Loyalist Slavery in the Maritimes* (Vancouver, 2016), esp. ch. 2.

38. This phenomenon has often been studied at the local level. See, for example, Robert Gross, *The Minutemen and Their World* (New York, 1976) for Concord, and Daniel Vickers, *Farmers and Fishermen: Two Centuries of Work in Essex County, Massachusetts, 1630–1850* (Chapel Hill, NC, 1992), esp. chs 5 and 6, for the region north of Boston.

39. Historians have studied the social consequences of this transiency. See Douglas Lamar Jones, "The Strolling Poor: Transiency in Eighteenth-Century Massachusetts" *Journal of Social History*, 8:3 (1975), pp. 28–54, and *Idem*, *Village and Seaport: Migration and Society in Eighteenth-Century New England* (Hanover, NH, 1981); Ruth Wallis Herndon, *Unwelcome Americans: Living on the Margins in Early New England* (Philadelphia, PA, 2001); Cornelia H. Dayton and Sharon V. Salinger, *Robert Love's Warning: Searching for Strangers in Colonial Boston* (Philadelphia, PA, 2014).

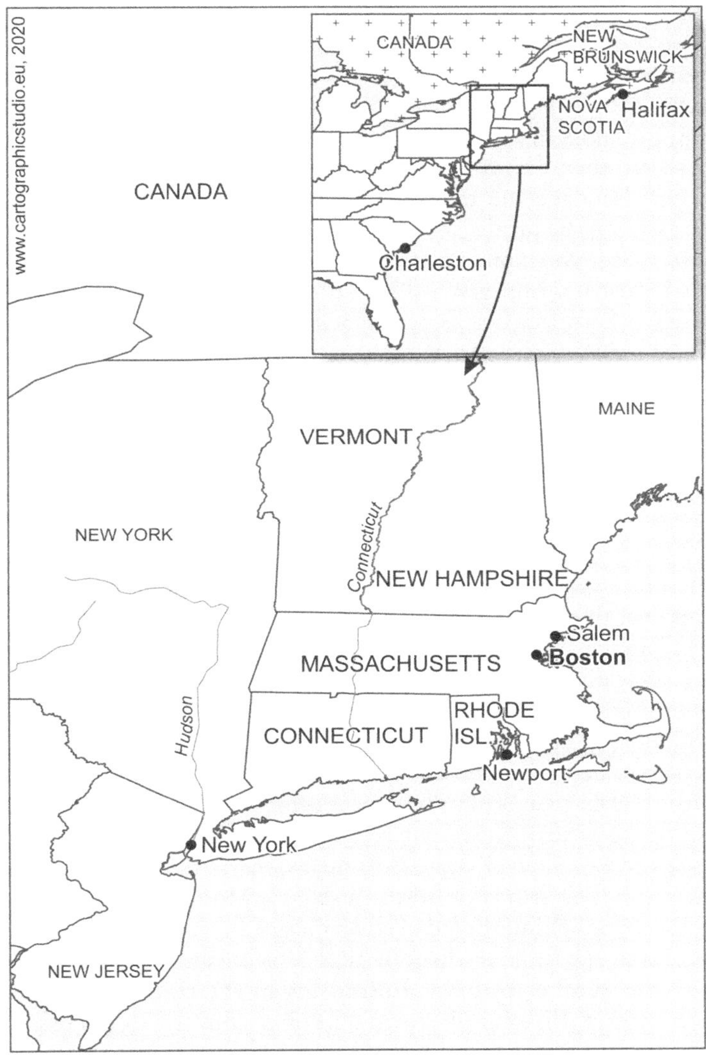

Figure 2. Map of Southern New England, ca. 1777.

President John Adams, rarely one to discuss class issues, described his take on emancipation. Adams blamed the end of slavery on the "multiplication of labouring white people" who believed that they should not have to compete with slaves for work. "Common people", Adams continued, "would not suffer the labour, by which alone they could obtain a subsistence, to be done by slaves". Had the labor market not changed to favor them, Adams predicted "the common white people would have put the negroes to death, and their masters, too, perhaps".[40]

Coinciding with the rise of a politicized and racialized white working class, racial attitudes towards enslaved Africans and free blacks, especially regarding their labor, began to change. If slavery made people of African descent "natural" workers, then freedom rendered them worthless and "unnatural". Without legal bondage and the disciplinary violence of their masters, blacks could not expect to be productive and were thought to be lazy, idle, and shiftless. By the 1780s, you could still find Boston's few remaining slaves working in various industries, but, given these attitudes and the violent competition from white workers, free blacks performed the most menial of tasks and usually under coercive conditions. Moreover, outside of a few activist judges, neither the town of Boston nor the state of Massachusetts offered much protection from these attitudes as they capitulated to the white working class and many of those in power believed these ideas themselves.[41]

LEGACIES

Ultimately, the legacy of abolition in Boston was the disappearance of black Bostonians over the course of a generation. Between the chaos of war, kidnapping, and changing labor markets, freed people disappeared from the town altogether. This disappearing act raises two important questions that will be the focus of this section. First, what happened to Afro-Bostonians? An analysis of both demographic data and the experiences of the town's former black residents help to better address this question. Second, how do we reconcile this legacy with the fact that Boston became a center of the American abolitionist movement in the 1820s? As we will see, these two factors went hand-in-hand as the black exodus allowed white Bostonians, many the descendants of slave owners, to wash their hands of Boston's slavery. Most importantly, much like abolition, the town's unique brand of slavery shaped the legacies of emancipation in Boston and the post-slavery lives of black Bostonians.

Tracking the number of black Bostonians in the colonial period is near impossible. In 1752, for example, town selectmen counted 1,541 enslaved people, but just two years later, the colony of Massachusetts's "slave census" enumerated only 989 slaves.[42] Later colonial censuses and assessments are

40. John Adams to Jeremy Belknap, 21 March 1795, "Letters and Documents Relating to Slavery in Massachusetts", in *Collections of the Massachusetts Historical Society*, vol. III (Boston, MA, 1877), p. 402.

41. The discussion of "natural" and "unnatural" and changing conceptions of race can be found in Melish, *Disowning Slavery*, pp. 108–109.

42. These numbers can be found in Lorenzo Johnston Greene, *The Negro in Colonial New England, 1620–1776* (New York: Columbia University Press, 1942), p. 84, and Appendix C.

even worse, with one from 1764 noting there were only 811 slaves in Boston and another from 1771 listing only 325.[43] These numbers are not accurate. The purpose of the censuses of 1754 and 1764 and the assessment of 1771 was to figure out tax rates for households in Massachusetts. Since slaves were taxable property, masters hid them from census takers or lied about the number that lived in their households. Nevertheless, a general downward trend in the black population is apparent by the 1770s, although not as dramatic, as shown by these census returns.

Post-independence demography also shows the downward spiral and the beginnings of recovery. The two most important figures are in 1781 and 1800. In the former, town records indicate that 848 blacks lived in Boston, nearly half the number that lived there during the 1750s. By 1800, the black population had grown by twenty-eight per cent or 326 people to 1174. Yet, this figure is deceptive for two reasons. First, much like poor whites, in the 1790s and 1800s, there were many free blacks wandering around looking for work. Census takers in 1800, then, captured a static picture of a large-scale population movement through the town. Confirming this fact is that between 1800 and 1850, Boston's black population grew at a slower pace (nine per cent per decade rather than fourteen per cent) from 1,174 to 1,999. Second, the black population grew at a much slower rate than the white. In 1781, Boston's total population was roughly 16,000, but it grew to nearly 25,000 by 1800, a fifty-six percent increase compared with thirty-eight per cent for the black population. Indeed, although the black population grew between 1781 and 1800, its percentage of the population fell from about six per cent to four per cent (see Tables 1 and 2).[44]

Colony/statewide and regional data also show an interesting trend. During the middle decades of the eighteenth century, Massachusetts's black population almost doubled, from 2,150 in 1720 to 4,075 in 1750. Yet, over the next three decades, the population only grew from 4,075 to 4,822 in 1780. Although there was a net increase in the black population of Boston, the anemic growth – only increasing by sixty-eight people between 1770 and 1780 – suggests disruption.[45] Indeed, birth rates among blacks remained relatively high and there were few epidemics during this period. Likewise,

43. For 1764, see United States Bureau of the Census, *A Century of Population Growth from the First Federal Census of the United States to the Twelfth, 1790–1900* (Washington, DC, 1909), p. 158. The 1771 Tax Assessment can be found online at http://sites.fas.harvard.edu/~hsb41/masstax/masstax.cgi; last accessed 30 December 2016.

44. For these population figures and statistics, see Jaqueline Barbara Carr, *After the Siege: A Social History of Boston, 1775–1800* (Boston, MA, 2005), p. 257, n. 114.

45. United States Bureau of the Census, *Historical Statistics of the United States, Colonial Times to 1970*, Part II, (Washington, DC, 1976), ser. Z, pp. 1–19.

Table 1. *Black population of Boston based on official census and tax records, 1752–1800.*

Year	Alleged Black Population
1752	1,541
1754	989
1764	811
1771	325
1781	848
1800	1,174

Sources: see notes 42, 43, and 44.

New England as a whole witnessed similarly low increases in the black population. Connecticut's black population only grew at 0.6 per cent between 1790 and 1850.[46]

Perhaps the most telling population figures come from nearly two generations after the abolition of slavery in 1850. The 1850 federal census was the first to collect information on every member of households and enumerate birthplace. For that reason, we can glean the decline of Boston's black population during the era of abolition. In 1850, there were 1,999 blacks living in the town, only 458 greater than its colonial population zenith in the 1750s. Moreover, according to the census, only 44.8 per cent were from Massachusetts.[47] Unfortunately, the census did not break down origins by locality, but even if we accept that all those listed as being born in Massachusetts were from Boston, only 896 would have been native to the city. While the majority of the colonial black population was also foreign and not native-born, this number still suggests the demographic devastation wrought by abolition. In the aftermath of emancipation, the black population in Boston was so small that even after two generations of reproduction and immigration, it was only slightly larger than during the colonial era and numbered less than 2,000 souls. All these figures suggest is that between 1760 and 1800, Boston's black population declined between fifty and seventy-five per cent, only to very slowly recover over the next five decades.

While population figures give us a better idea of the total effect of abolition on black Bostonians, individual stories of post-emancipation life provide more concrete details about what happened to them after they left Boston. We can also see that even after leaving Boston, the experience of slavery in the town shaped post-emancipation lives. Pension and other records detailing service in the American army speak to this. Jamaica James, a slave from Boston

46. See Edgar J. McManus, *Black Bondage in the North* (Syracuse, NY, 1973), pp. 182–183.

47. These figures come from James Oliver Horton and Lois E. Horton, *Black Bostonians: Family Life and Community Struggle in the Antebellum North* (New York, [1979] 1999), Table 1 and Table 6.

Table 2. *Black population growth vs. total population growth in Boston, 1781–1800.*

	1781	1800	Percent Increase (Rounded to Nearest Percent)	Percent Growth (Rounded to Nearest Percent)
Black Population	848	1,174	28%	38%
Total Population	~16,000	24,937	36%	56%

Sources: see notes 42, 43, and 44.

who found his freedom serving in the 10th Massachusetts Regiment during the Revolutionary War, fought for nearly the entire duration of the conflict. Wounded at Bunker Hill in 1775, he then reenlisted in 1777 and stayed with the Continental army until George Washington disbanded it at Newburgh, New York, in 1783. Yet, James did not return home. Rather, he stayed in Orange County, where Newburgh is located, and lived there until he died. It is unclear what he did for the rest of his life, but when James applied for a pension in 1819, there were frequent references to his poverty and that he was unable to support himself in his old age, which was either sixty-two or seventy-seven depending on who testified. Combined with the men who testified on his behalf, many of whom were merchants engaged in commerce on the Hudson River, James's poverty suggests that he worked as a longshoreman on the riverfront until his body could no longer support physical labor. James, then, would have most likely pursued the same type of waterfront work he would have in Boston.[48] Despite deep differences of experience and the dislike that poor whites had of men like James, he, like the growing mass of rural landless men and women in New England, left the region and settled on the western frontiers of the growing nation.

As Jamaica James settled in the west, a slower process, one with roots dating back two generations, was playing out in the background. Ever since the 1740s, black men from Boston and surrounding towns had been marrying into local Indian communities. Not that demographics was destiny, but black Bostonians and local native groups seemed a perfect match for one another. More than sixty per cent of enslaved Bostonians were men, leaving many in search of mates. Allowed to marry by law, but only other people of color, they turned to Indian communities in eastern Massachusetts. These communities were disproportionally female as many of the men, obligated to serve the colony in its wars and also employed as fishermen and whalers, died during the eighteenth century. It was not foreordained, however.

48. James, Jamaica, Record # S.44.984, Massachusetts, Revolutionary War Pension Records, National Archives and Records Administration, Washington, DC.

Already mobile, many black men sought out native brides for a variety of reasons. Most importantly, it was a calculation on behalf of the men. Certainly, love played a part in these matches, but for an enslaved man to marry an Indian woman meant his children would be born free with a claim to tribal land. Intermarriage accelerated in the post-Revolutionary years as many black Bostonians left the city for good.[49] Indeed, by the 1790s, many Indian communities in eastern Massachusetts were thoroughly mixed, leaving Reverend Stephen Badger of Natick, a town founded for Christian Indians in the seventeenth century and still containing a number of native inhabitants, to say that Indians "intermarried with *blacks*, and some with whites; and the various shades between these, and those that are descended from them". This made it near impossible to distinguish who was black and who was Indian, causing consternation for white authorities seeking to quantify and delineate the races, which is exactly what blacks wanted.[50] For black Bostonians, Indian communities offered access to land, protection from slave traders, and, given native nations tended to welcome them, some semblance of stability. In short, escaping to Indian country offered them a chance to resist the degradation of post-emancipation life and should be seen as an extension of the appropriation of local institutions that occurred under slavery.

Whether they settled in Indian communities, led uprooted lives, settled on the frontier, or left the United States altogether, the result was ultimately the same: Boston's black population precipitously declined. Importantly, this disappearance influenced the budding antislavery movement in Boston. Effectively, it gave politicians and antislavery activists a blank slate on which to write their own history of slavery – and freedom – to better suit their ideological needs. Two legislative actions, less than forty years apart, help to illustrate this change. In 1788, as slavery was ending in Massachusetts, the legislature passed a ban on free black immigration into the state, fearing that large numbers of southern and West Indian freed people, looking for "free soil", would settle in a place already dealing with growing poverty. By 1822, these attitudes had changed. In that year and in response to the Missouri Crisis, the Massachusetts assembly appointed Theodore Lyman, a legislator from Boston, to head a committee to examine the condition of free blacks in the state. In issuing his report, Lyman rewrote history, suggesting, unlike in 1788, just how removed he and other policymakers were from the experience of slavery. Lyman argued that since its founding in the seventeenth century, Massachusetts had been against slavery. As one historian describes it, Lyman believed antislavery was "endemic" to the people of

49. For more on this phenomenon, see Daniel R. Mandell, "Shifting Boundaries of Race and Ethnicity: Indian-Black Intermarriage in Southern New England, 1760–1880", *The Journal of American History*, 85 (1998), pp. 466–501.

50. Quoted in Daniel R. Mandell, *Beyond the Frontier: Indians in Eighteenth-Century Eastern Massachusetts* (Lincoln, NE, 1996), p. 185.

Massachusetts. The existence of slavery there was more of a historical accident that the Revolution quickly rectified, making Massachusetts the "cradle of liberty". Arguing in favor of a long tradition of liberty, the Lyman report overturned the legislation of 1788 and opened the door to large-scale free black immigration into Massachusetts, where they would be treated as equals (at least according to Lyman).[51]

Central to sanitizing the history of slavery in Boston and Massachusetts was the nature of slavery itself. If the people of the Commonwealth had long favored liberty, then the slavery they had enacted could not have been that bad or that important. These tropes were especially common in the popular local histories of the early nineteenth century where antiquarians, digging around in their towns' records, found much evidence of slavery. Rather than coming to terms with the fact that their forebears owned human beings, it was often written off as being a mild and benevolent bondage. Indeed, these histories depicted enslaved people as dutifully working beside their masters, performing skilled jobs in workshops, moving around town, and even going to church, i.e. the unique characteristics of slavery in Boston.[52] Antiquarians also sought to downplay the actual numbers of enslaved people, often noting that slavery was incompatible with the economy of the colony. In one history of Boston, for example, the author dismissed an account of the town's relatively large slave population, explaining its author had "written with but a shadow of regard for the truth".[53] While it is easy to dismiss these local histories, they mattered for shaping how white people in Boston and Massachusetts perceived themselves and society. Unlike those in the South, Massachusetts had long been a place of freedom and against slavery. And the few slaves they did hold were treated well and even allowed to go to church. Never on firm footing, slavery died during the American Revolution. Such histories and the disappearance of black Bostonians allowed whites to paint themselves as the "good guys" in the struggle against the evil of slavery. In short, while enslaved people had to live with the experiences and legacies of slavery, whites were able to absolve themselves of the activities of their ancestors.

As the antislavery attitudes in early-nineteenth-century Massachusetts suggest, the legacy of slavery in Boston was a tragic one. Uprooted by war, racism, and a lack of work, many freed Bostonians left altogether. Available demographic data tell us that this caused a precipitous decline in the black population, while anecdotal evidence suggests just how severe and complete this disappearing act was. Deliberate or not, whites in Boston used this disappearance to rewrite history, promoting Massachusetts as a place of eternal liberty and dismissing slavery as little more than a blip in a long history of freedom.

51. For more on this contrasting legislation, see Minardi, *Making Slavery History*, pp. 29–33.
52. Minardi, *Making Slavery History*, pp. 36–37.
53. Samuel G. Drake, *The History and Antiquities of Boston. From Its Settlement in 1630, to the Year 1770* (Boston, MA, 1856), p. 729.

From the misremembrance to the post-Revolutionary labor markets that drove so many blacks out of the region, Boston's slavery influenced all of these processes. Envious of skilled black labor, many whites forced blacks into menial work or forced them to find work elsewhere. Already mobile, leaving for the frontier or roaming the countryside was an easy path forward. Finally, as settling in Indian communities suggests, freed blacks continued to appropriate local institutions to resist the degradation that came with their race.

The nature of slavery profoundly shaped abolition and its legacy in Boston. In this urban context, slaves were highly skilled in trades, mobile, and had knowledge of local institutions, namely the law and religion, which they appropriated. Such a system of enslavement allowed slaves to carve out a space for themselves and find autonomy from the master class. It also equipped enslaved Bostonians to forge their freedom during the era of the American Revolution. Slaves petitioned the government, sued their masters, or simply absconded. Yet, this freedom came at a price. It decimated Boston's black population by displacing them. Intricately linked with the War of Independence, many slaves and free blacks joined the Continental army or the British never to return home. Masters saw the writing on the wall and sold their slaves away, while the rise of racism and a changing labor market devalued black labor and drove many from Boston in search of employment. All told, at least half of Boston's pre-Revolutionary black population disappeared, scattered to the far corners of the new United States and Atlantic world. Ironically, the skills, mobility, and knowledge of the pre-Revolutionary slave population laid the groundwork for the post-Revolutionary diaspora. At the same time that Boston's black population reached its nadir in the 1790s, whites began crafting an image of an eternally free Boston, the cradle of American liberty. Making slavery an insignificant part of Boston's history, by the 1820s they transformed the town into a center of American abolition and welcomed a new generation of runaway slaves and freed blacks from the South and West Indies.

While Boston's slave population was relatively small compared with the centers of plantation agriculture in the Americas, this post-emancipation disappearing act is important for understanding abolition across the Atlantic world. Even in a place where enslaved people were skilled laborers and, for premodern people, well-educated, they still faced racial animus following their freedom. Black Bostonians, as in so many other places, were only valuable when their labor and productivity was the property of another. It was only when they voted with their feet and disappeared, removing the reminders of chattel bondage, that whites could envision a place of liberty and equality for all.

IRSH 65 (2020), pp. 169–195 doi:10.1017/S0020859020000115

Runaway Slaves in Antebellum Baltimore: An Urban Form of Marronage?*

Viola Franziska Müller

Department of History and Civilization
European University Institute
Villa Paola, Via dei Roccettini 9
50014 San Domenico di Fiesole, FI, Italy

E-mail: viola.muller@eui.eu

Abstract: The starting point of this article is the observation that thousands of enslaved people escaped bondage and managed to find refuge in the city of Baltimore between 1800 and 1860. There, they integrated into a large free black community. Given the use of the term "urban marronage" to categorize slave flight to cities in some historical literature, this chapter discusses the concept of marronage and its applicability to the urban context of antebellum Baltimore. It examines individual escapees from slavery, the communities they joined, and the broader slaveholding society to emphasize that the interplay and mutual relations of all three should be considered when assessing the applicability of this concept. Discussing the historiography around marronage and the arguments that speak both in favour of and against applying the concept of urban maroons to Baltimore's runaway slaves, this article ultimately dismisses its suitability for this case. In the process, this examination reveals the core of the concept, which, above all, concerns the aspect of resistance. In this context, it will be argued that resistance in the sense of rejecting the control of the dominant society should be included in the general definition of marronage.

INTRODUCTION

On Saturday evening, 21 June 1851, near Cockeysville, Maryland, an enslaved man named Ralph Thompson, "aged about 33 years, a bright mulatto, about 5 feet 10 inches in height", decided to take matters into his own hands and claim his liberty, fleeing his legal owner Samuel Moore. One month later, on Monday 21 July, after Thompson "was seen entering Baltimore on

* The author would like to extend her gratitude to Mariana Dantas for commenting on an earlier version of this article, as well as to Jorge Díaz Ceballos, Ian Hathaway, and Gašper Jakovac for helping improve the final version. Thanks also to Seth Rockman, who contributed to the original idea. This article is based on research that has received funding from the Netherlands Organisation for Scientific Research (NWO).

Thursday or Friday afternoon last", Moore placed an advertisement in the local newspaper, *The Baltimore Sun*. "He has an impediment in his speech", and was "wearing blue pantaloons and a white felt ha[t]". Moore described him in a few words and offered the rather low reward of $3 "for his recovery and return".[1] Though sparse, this information is sufficient to conclude that Ralph Thompson was a runaway slave who sought refuge within an urban setting. Some historians have used the term "urban maroon" to categorize people like him – but how appropriate is the term maroon?

Latin Americanists feature most prominently among those who have described slave flight to urban areas as a form of "urban marronage". Historians have labelled runaway slaves hiding in cities *cimarrones urbanos* (urban maroons), and cities like Havana and Buenos Aires an immense *palenque urbano* (urban maroon settlement).[2] In Francophone settings, runaway slaves in cities are likewise claimed to be performing *marronnage urbain*.[3] North Americanists and Anglophone scholars have also increasingly applied the term marronage, including in very recent publications.[4] Simultaneously, there are a number of works that focus on runaway slaves in urban settings, yet do *not* use the terms maroons and marronage.[5]

Noting these different approaches in scholarship, it is worthwhile taking a close look at the concept of marronage. While this discussion of its definition no doubt contains a great deal of controversy, it should be clear that while all marronage entails the dimension of escape from slavery, not all escapes from slavery should be seen as marronage. So, what are the features that turn some escapees from slavery into maroons and others not? To contribute to a more nuanced understanding, this article examines individual escapees

1. *The Baltimore Sun*, 21 July 1851.

2. Pedro Deschamps Chapeaux, "Cimarrones urbanos", *Revista de la Biblioteca Nacional de Cuba José Martí*, 2 (2015), pp. 147, 162, originally published as *Los cimarrones urbanos* (La Habana, 1983); Eduardo R. Saguier, "La crisis social. La fuga esclava como resistencia rutinaria y cotidiana", *Revista de humanidades y ciencias sociales*, 1:2 (1995), p. 125.

3. Jean-Germain Gros, *State Failure, Underdevelopment, and Foreign Intervention in Haiti* (New York, 2012), p. 72; Aline Helg, *Plus jamais esclaves! De l'insoumission à la révolte, le grand récit d'une émancipation (1492–1838)* (Paris, 2016), p. 64; Anne Pérotin-Dumon, *La ville aux îles, la ville dans l'île. Basse-Terre et Pointe-à-Pitre Guadeloupe, 1650–1820* (Paris, 2000), p. 665.

4. Shauna J. Sweeney, "Market Marronage: Fugitive Women and the Internal Marketing System in Jamaica, 1781–1834", *William & Mary Quarterly*, 76:2 (2019), pp. 197–222; Mary Niall Mitchell, "Lurking but Working: City Maroons in Antebellum New Orleans", in Marcus Rediker, Titas Chakraborty, and Matthias van Rossum (eds), *A Global History of Runaways: Workers, Mobility, and Capitalism, 1600–1850* (Oakland, CA, 2019), pp. 199–215.

5. José Maia Bezerra Neto, "Histórias urbanas de liberdade. Escravos em fuga na cidade de Belém, 1860–1888", *Afro-Asia*, 28 (2002), pp. 221–250; Damian Alan Pargas, "Freedom in the Midst of Slavery", in Damian Alan Pargas (ed.), *Fugitive Slaves and Spaces of Freedom in North America, 1775–1860* (Gainesville, FL, 2018), pp. 116–136; Viola F. Müller, "Illegal but Tolerated: Slave Refugees in Richmond, Virginia, 1800–1860", in *idem*, pp. 137–167.

from slavery, the communities they joined, and the broader slaveholding society to emphasize that the interplay and mutual relations of all three should be taken into consideration.

Historian Steven Hahn has carried out a similar examination, discussing whether some African American communities in the US northern states during the antebellum period (c.1800–1860) showed features of a maroon society. While, ultimately, he does not come to an explicit conclusion, he recognizes the value of the concept because it reveals insights into the political consciousness of enslaved and free African Americans.[6] This article agrees with Hahn, in that marronage is a concept that promises a great many insights into the lives of people of whom we have few first-hand accounts in the historical archives. In cases of very limited self-documentation, we must shift the analysis to group behaviour to draw conclusions about identity and modes of thinking. The concept of marronage can deliver many such insights, but we should have a conversation about how to use it.

Given that publications on slave flight are numerous, and that they increasingly include urban areas as destinations as well, a city will also be the *locale* of this analysis. Baltimore presents an ideal case for establishing whether runaway slaves and their receiving societies were maroons because, in the antebellum period, it hosted a substantial and growing free black population and continuously attracted runaway slaves. This article will therefore discuss the applicability of the concept of marronage to runaway slaves and their receiving society in the urban context of Baltimore. The first section analyses the historiography of marronage in the Americas. The second introduces the historical context of the city of Baltimore and documents the presence of runaway slaves in the city. The third and fourth sections respectively discuss the arguments that speak in favour of and against marronage in Baltimore. Ultimately, this article dismisses the suitability of the concept of marronage for describing slave flight to Baltimore. However, this examination will reveal the core of the concept. This concerns, above all, the aspect of resistance. In this context, it will be argued that resistance in the sense of rejecting the control of the dominant society should be included in the general definition of marronage.

HISTORIOGRAPHICAL CHALLENGES

The idea of urban maroons derives from the concept of "conventional" maroons. Historical literature usually defines them as legally enslaved men and

6. Steven Hahn, *The Political Worlds of Slavery and Freedom* (Cambridge [etc.], 2009), pp. 43–44. Hahn has followed up on Ira Berlin's thought experiment of whether the entire black population of the antebellum northern states of the United States was a maroon community. Ira Berlin, "North of Slavery: Black People in a Slaveholding Republic", *Yale, New Haven and American Slavery Conference* (26–27 September 2002). Available at: http://www.virginia.edu/woodson/courses/aas-hius366a/berlin.pdf; last accessed 16 June 2017.

women in the Americas who escaped slavery by fleeing to remote wilderness areas and securing their freedom. They either formed a settlement with others or joined an existing community. The best-known maroon communities of the Americas were to be found in Jamaica, Brazil, and Suriname, because they posed a threat to colonial authority and, consequently, left a variety of archival traces. This holds particularly true for maroon communities that engaged in warfare or other violent confrontations with the authorities.[7] Besides, there were also maroons whose existence was less known, but who also enjoyed autonomy and organized themselves separately from dominant white society. For example, Sylviane Diouf explores several US-American maroons in her book *Slavery's Exiles*. These were slaves who escaped their bonded condition, inhabited wilderness areas on the peripheries or in the general vicinity of plantations and formed groups of different sizes.[8] These people tried to avoid open confrontation with authorities at all costs.

A number of Latin and North American revisionists have lately started to challenge the emphasis on physical isolation and independence from slaveholding society. These scholars recognize that many maroons did in fact remain in contact with white society (including their fellow bondspeople).[9] Diouf and Ted Maris-Wolf have shown, in the US-American context, that the grade of isolation experienced by wilderness maroons was not as high as has been hitherto assumed. Especially in the nineteenth century, some wilderness maroons moved into closer contact with the dominant society and were even employed by white people.[10] For Brazil, historians already claimed in the 1990s that there had always been interaction and even cooperation between maroons and slaveholding society.[11]

In order to keep the concept broad, João José Reis and Flávio dos Santos Gomes have suggested that marronage is "flight that led to the formation of

7. This is the conventional concept that prevails within Latin American and Caribbean slavery studies. See Richard Price (ed.), *Maroon Societies: Rebel Slave Communities in the Americas* (Baltimore, MD [etc.], 1979); Alvin O. Thompson, *Flight to Freedom: African Runaways and Maroons in the Americas* (Kingston, 2006); Glenn Alan Cheney, *Quilombo dos Palmares: Brazil's Lost Nation of Fugitive Slaves* (Hanover, CT, 2014).

8. Diouf consciously distinguishes runaways and maroons in her study. Sylviane A. Diouf, *Slavery's Exiles: The Story of the American Maroons* (New York [etc.], 2014), p. 81.

9. This revision allowed Diouf in the first place to identify many of the protagonists of her study as maroons.

10. Diouf, *Slavery's Exiles*, pp. 213–214; Ted Maris-Wolf, "Hidden in Plain Sight: Maroon Life and Labor in Virginia's Dismal Swamp", *Slavery & Abolition*, 34:3 (2013), pp. 446–464. Without explicitly challenging the territorial claim of the prevailing concept of marronage, Gwendolyn Midlo Hall, in the early 1990s, pointed to maroons working as lumberjacks and supplying white-owned sawmills. Gwendolyn Midlo Hall, *Africans in Colonial Louisiana: The Development of Afro-Creole Culture in the Eighteenth Century* (Baton Rouge, LA, 1992).

11. For very contradictory insights into Brazilian *quilombos* (the Portuguese term for maroon settlement) over the centuries, see João José Reis and Flávio dos Santos Gomes, *Liberdade por um fio. História dos quilombos no Brasil* (São Paulo, 1996).

groups of fugitive slaves with whom other social persons frequently associated, [and which] took place in the Americas where slavery flourished".[12] This definition shifts the focus away from geographical demarcation and pays tribute to the variety among the numerous maroon communities. It does not account for warfare, recognition of autonomy, or cultural aspects. Rather, Reis and Santos Gomes emphasize flight, community, and the continual arrival of newcomers. This approach is helpful because it makes the concept of marronage applicable to different contexts throughout the Americas. However, it runs the risk of inflating the concept by simply equating marronage with slave flight.

These broader definitions have an important linguistic dimension. In Hispanic and Francophone contexts, all runaway slaves are usually called *cimarrones* or *marrons* (maroons), respectively. The use of these terms is often based on archival material. In Spanish, for example, the equivalents of runaway slave depots (where runaways were jailed) were *depósitos de cimarrones*, with the word "maroon" used as a substitute for runaway slave.[13] In Anglophone settings, however, the application of the concept is not justified by historical sources. Within the United States, Louisiana presents a special case where jail ledgers, up until the mid-nineteenth century, were kept partly in French and in which the terms "runaway slave" and "*marron*" were used interchangeably.[14] The issue is that historians often do not sufficiently explain their use of the terms they find in archival sources. Transfers from primary sources as well as translations of scholarship into English often lack a sufficient level of reflection.[15]

This linguistic aspect also has another historiographical consequence. Until this day, many historians refer to *petit* and *grand marronage* to mark the distinction between runaway slaves who absconded for a short period of time and

12. Translation by the author of "A fuga que levava à formação de grupos de escravos fugidos aos quais freqüentemente se associavam outras personagens sociais, acounteceu nas Américas onde vicejou a escravidão". João José Reis and Flávio dos Santos Gomes, "Introdução. Uma História da Liberdade", in *Liberdade por um fio*, p. 10. Equally broad, Alvin O. Thompson claimed that marronage "involved both flight from slavery and the establishment of free communities". Thompson, *Flight to Freedom*, p. 1.

13. For example, D. Joaquin Rodriguez San Pedro (ed.), *Legislacion Ultramarina*, vol. 3 (Madrid, 1865), p. 413.

14. Police Jail Daily Reports, 1820–1840, New Orleans (LA) Police Jail/Parish Prison, New Orleans Public Library. Moreover, New Orleans authorities faced the phenomenon of both urban runaways within the city and "conventional" marrons in its surroundings. See newspaper coverage, e.g. *The Picayune*, 19 July 1837.

15. Michel S. Laguerre, *Voodoo and Politics in Haiti* (New York, 1989), p. 72; Sweeney, "Market Marronage"; N.A.T. Hall, "Maritime Maroons: *Grand Marronage* from the Danish West Indies", *William & Mary Quarterly*, 42:4 (1985), pp. 476–498; Linda M. Rupert, "Marronage, Manumission and Maritime Trade in the Early Modern Caribbean", *Slavery & Abolition*, 30:3 (2009), pp. 361–382; and the English translation of Helg's *Plus jamais esclaves*: Aline Helg, *Slave No More: Self-Liberation before Abolitionism in the Americas* (Chapel Hill, NC, 2019).

those who did so on a long-term or permanent basis.[16] Although this terminology is likewise rooted in historical documents, namely the writings of the French colonial authorities of the nineteenth century,[17] its adoption is deeply problematic because it connects a duration to the impact of the action. The implications are manifold. It obscures the original intentions of the people fleeing, shifts the focus away from what happened after they absconded, and ranks the outcome of slave flight as resistance.[18]

Coming back to the urban context, Dennis Cowles has noted the difficulty of including urban runaways into the category of marronage but mistakenly implied that the reason was that urban fugitives did not escape slavery definitively.[19] His assumption is understandable since historians have only recently begun to engage in depth with long-term and permanent slave flight to urban areas.[20] Earlier contributions usually approached runaway slaves in cities, located within slaveholding territory, as temporary absconders because it is difficult to find explicit evidence about the length of their presence in the cities.[21] The argument here is not that urban maroons did not exist, nor that

16. Flávio Gomes, "Africans and *Petit Marronage* in Rio de Janeiro, ca. 1800–1840", *Luso-Brazilian Review*, 47:2 (2010), pp. 74–99; Mitchell, "Lurking but Working", p. 203; Marcus P. Nevius, "Lurking about the Neighbourhood: Slave Economy and Petit Marronage in Virginia and North Carolina, 1730 to 1860" (Ph.D., Ohio State University, 2016). See also the contribution by political scientist Neil Roberts, *Freedom as Marronage* (Chicago, IL, 2015), pp. 98–99. The introduction of this concept into history writing is attributed to Gabriel Debien, "Les origines des esclaves des Antilles", *Bulletin de l'IFAN*, 27:3–4 (1965), pp. 5–29.

17. *Bulletin officiel de l'île Bourbon*, vol. 2 (Saint-Denis, 1819; available in the Rare Books section of the Bibliothèque nationale de France), in Jean-Pierre Le Glaunec, "Résister à l'esclavage dans l'Atlantique français. Aperçu historiographique, hypothèses et pistes de recherché", *Revue d'histoire de l'Amérique française*, 71:1–2 (2017), p. 7. Available at: https://id.erudit.org/iderudit/1042785ar; last accessed 10 October 2019.

18. For a critique of the concept of *petit* and *grand marronage*, see Le Glaunec, "Résister à l'esclavage", pp. 6–11.

19. Dennis Cowles, "Maroons", in David Head (ed.), *Encyclopedia of the Atlantic World, 1400–1900: Europe, Africa, and the Americas in an Age of Exploration, Trade, and Empires* (Santa Barbara, CA, 2018), p. 393.

20. Bezerra Neto, "Histórias urbanas"; Gomes, "Africans and *Petit Marronage*;" Pargas, "Freedom in the Midst of Slavery;" Müller, "Illegal but Tolerated;" Mitchell, "Lurking but Working." In the United States, several scholars have earlier noted the phenomenon of permanent urban fugitive slaves but never engaged with it in depth. For example, Peter Kolchin, *American Slavery 1619–1877* (New York [etc.], 1995), p. 158; William A. Link, *Roots of Secession: Slavery and Politics in Antebellum Virginia* (Chapel Hill, NC, 2003), p. 106; Leonard Curry, *The Free Black in Urban America, 1800–1850: The Shadow of the Dream* (Chicago, IL, 1981), p. 4. Michael Zeuske has identified *huida urbana* (urban flight) in the black neighbourhoods of large Atlantic cities like Havana, Matanzas, New Orleans, and Santiago. Michael Zeuske, *Sklavereien, Emanzipationen und atlantische Weltgeschichte. Essays über Mikrogeschichten, Sklaven, Globalisierungen und Rassismus* (Leipzig, 2002), p. 146.

21. The main work of reference is John Hope Franklin and Loren Schweninger, *Runaway Slaves: Rebels on the Plantation* (Oxford [etc.], 1999), ch. 6: "They Seek a City".

maroons never went to the cities,[22] but rather that we need to thoroughly reflect on what marronage means before we can apply it to the urban context – or not.

These reflections lead us to Leslie Manigat's widely cited definition of marronage. She has claimed that the aspiration of a maroon was "to live, actually free, but as an outlaw, in areas (generally in the woods or in the mountains) where he [or she] could escape the control of the colonial power and the plantocratic establishment".[23] The aspects of being outlaws and escaping the control of the authorities have often been disregarded in other, broader, definitions, but this is precisely where the strength of the concept lies. Hence this article will take these two points as deserving of closer attention.

The following parts will scan runaway slaves in Baltimore through the lens of marronage, thereby applying Manigat's definition of outlawing and avoidance of control, and the revisionists' call not to focus on geographical location and territorial integrity. It is particularly important to keep in mind that looking at the individuals fleeing does not suffice. Standing alone, slave flight does not tell us enough about the escapee's relation with slaveholding society.[24] Because marronage has a dimension of identity within the broader community, we must include those who absorb the runaways into the analysis.[25] The next part, however, will first provide evidence of the presence of runaway slaves in Baltimore.

RUNAWAY SLAVES IN BALTIMORE

Ralph Thompson, the enslaved man named in the opening paragraph, escaped slavery by running away, joining an existing free black community in Baltimore, and trying to live as de facto free within slaveholding territory.

22. Louisiana maroons, for example, went to the city of New Orleans to sell wood. Diouf, *Slavery's Exiles*, p. 122. Brazilian historians might have a point approaching some urban communities as maroons. See Maria Helena Pereira Toledo Machado, "From Slave Rebels to Strikebreakers: The Quilombo of Jabaquara and the Problem of Citizenship in Late-Nineteenth-Century Brazil", *Hispanic American Historical Review*, 86:2 (2006), pp. 247–274. In Brazil, historical research is further incentivized by urban communities who keep a maroon identity upright until this day. See Márcia L. A. Souza and Neusa M. M. Gusmão, "Identidade Quilombola e processos educativos presentes num Quilombo urbano. O caso do Quilombo Brotas", *Educação & linguagem*, 14:23/24 (2011), pp. 75–93.

23. Leslie F. Manigat, "The Relationship between Marronage and Slave Revolts and Revolution in St. Domingue-Haiti", *Annals of the New York Academy of Sciences*, 292 (1977), pp. 421–422.

24. On marronage and identity, see Jorge Díaz Ceballos, "Cimarronaje, jurisdicción y lealtades híbridas en la Monarquía Hispánica", in Tomás Mantecón (ed.), *Dimensiones del conflico. Resistencias, violencia y policía en el mundo urbano* (Santander, forthcoming). On marronage as a counter-ideology, see Carlos Aguirre, "Cimarronaje, bandolerismo y desintegración esclavista. Lima, 1821–1854", in Carlos Aguirre and Charles Walker (eds), *Bandoleros, abigeos y Montoneros. Criminalidad y violencia en el Perú, siglos XVIII–XX* (Lima, 1990), pp. 137–182.

25. In this context, it is important to recall that maroons could both establish new, independent communities or join existing ones.

Thompson is not an isolated case. Already during the eighteenth century, but much more markedly during the nineteenth century, runaway slaves gravitated to the growing cities of the southern states in increasing numbers. As is well known, enslaved people also fled to the northern states and places outside the US, where slavery was abolished and freedom could be obtained in official ways.[26] But their endeavours in southern cities are especially remarkable, because, by staying within the slaveholding South, the freedom these escapees could obtain was of an *illegal* nature. It had no basis in law but nevertheless allowed them to live as if they were free – just like conventional maroons who went "underground".[27]

Jail statistics and newspaper announcements show that in the early 1830s, the Baltimore City Jail locked up one suspected runaway slave on average every one and a half days. Over the entire course of the antebellum era, newspapers were full of advertisements for runaway slaves believed to be hiding in the city.[28] Due to its expansion and rapid growth, this article estimates that Baltimore received dozens of them annually in the early nineteenth century and hundreds in the decades before the Civil War. The new and confusing environment of burgeoning cities added to the chances of successful concealment. And for the whole South, historian Richard Wade has claimed that "[t]hose living in illegality in the city must have been several times as numerous as those who were discovered".[29] Although the numbers remained small in comparison to the overall numbers of black residents, and even more so to the total population, the runaway community and their offspring must have amounted to thousands of undocumented city dwellers over the course of the period under analysis.

Baltimore was a thriving commercial city situated on the northern border of the southern states (see Figure 1). It grew to be the second largest American city until around 1850 and became the fourth largest by 1860. Among its 212,000 inhabitants, 25,700 were free men, women, and children of African descent. This part of the population had grown extensively from 2,700 in 1800 (see Table 1). Part of the growth was the result of immigration of refugees from Saint-Domingue following the Haitian Revolution.[30] The number of free

26. A very brief selection of contributions includes Leon Litwack, *North of Slavery: The Negro in the Free States, 1790–1860* (Chicago, IL, 1961); Daniel G. Hill, *Freedom Seekers: Blacks in Early Canada* (Toronto, 1992); Eric Foner, *Gateway to Freedom: The Hidden History of the Underground Railroad* (New York [etc.]: W.W. Norton, 2015); Sean Kelley, "Mexico in His Head: Slavery and the Texas-Mexican Border, 1810–1860", *Journal of Social History*, 37:3 (2004), pp. 709–723.

27. Compare with Manigat, "Relationship between Marronage", pp. 421–422.

28. Baltimore City Jail (Runaway Docket), 1836–1850, Maryland State Archives (hereafter MSA); for runaway slave ads, see *The Baltimore Sun*.

29. Richard Wade, *Slavery in the Cities: The South 1820–1860* (New York [etc.], 1964), p. 219.

30. *Gens de couleur* and their slaves might have added thirty per cent to the existing black population of Baltimore. Sherry H. Olson, *Baltimore: The Building of an American City* (Baltimore, MD [etc.], [1980] 1997), p. 30.

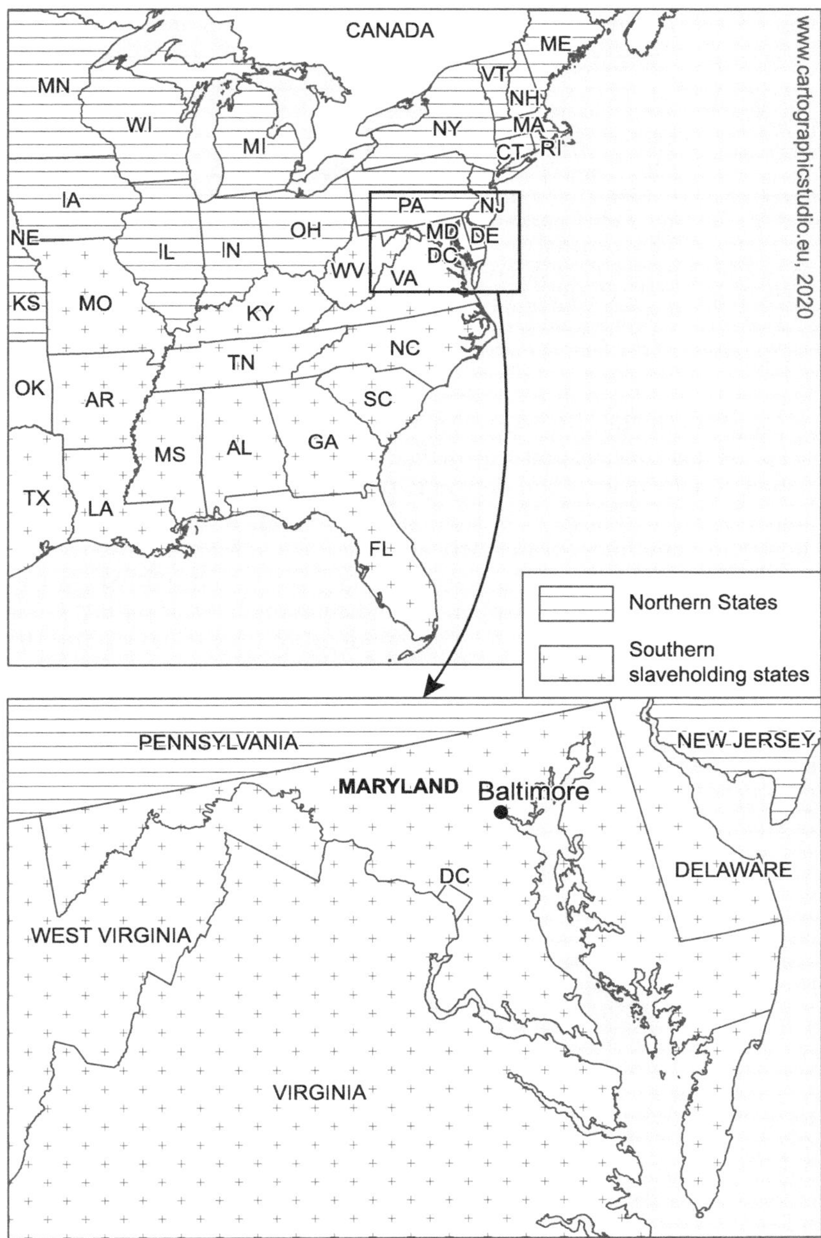

Figure 1. Map of the eastern part of the United States, circa 1860.

Table 1. *Free African American, enslaved, and total population of Baltimore.*

	1800	*1810*	*1820*	*1830*	*1840*	*1850*	*1860*
Free black	2,700	5,700	10,300	14,800	18,000	25,400	25,700
Enslaved	2,800	4,700	4,400	4,100	3,200	2,900	2,200
Total	26,500	46,600	62,700	80,600	102,300	169,100	212,400

Sources: US Bureau of the Census, *Population of the 100 Largest Cities and Other Urban Places in The United States: 1790 to 1990*, available at: https://www.census.gov/library/working-papers/1998/demo/POP-twps0027.html; last accessed 8 January 2019; US Bureau of the Census, *Aggregate Number of Persons within the United States in the Year 1810* (Washington, DC, 1811); DeBow, *Seventh Census*; US 8th Census, 1860, *Population of the United States.*

black people in the state of Maryland increased from 8,000 in 1790 to 84,000 by 1860. At that time, a similar growth and the relative predominance of free black people were to be found only in Latin America and the Caribbean.[31] By the mid-century, these people were almost exclusively born in the state.[32] The rapid growth in numbers of free African Americans in Maryland was a legacy of the ideological changes of the revolutionary era, which produced more liberal manumission laws in the Upper South than in the Lower South.[33] Giving in to the pressures of their slaves, it led hundreds of slaveholders to free their bondspeople, up until approximately 1810, and spurred the autonomous growth of the free black population in the years afterwards.[34] These were the same developments that led to formal abolitions in the US northern states and throughout the Americas.

Baltimore's location is important, as enslaved African Americans heading to the city from the surrounding counties or further south could also have chosen

31. J.D.B. DeBow (ed.), *The Seventh Census of the United States: 1850; Embracing a Statistical View of Each of the States and Territories, Arranged by Counties, Towns, etc., Under the Following Divisions…* (Washington, DC, 1853), p. 221; US 8th Census, 1860, *Population of the United States in 1860; Compiled from the Original Returns of the Eighth Census* (Washington, DC, 1864), p. 214. See also J.D.B. DeBow, *Industrial Resources, Etc. of the Southern and Western States*, vol. 1 (New Orleans, LA, 1852), p. 102, cited in Barbara Fields, *Slavery and Freedom on the Middle Ground: Maryland during the Nineteenth Century* (New Haven, CT [etc.], 1985), pp. 1–2, 62.

32. Leonard P. Curry, "Free Blacks in the Urban South, 1800–1850", *Southern Quarterly*, 43 (2006), p. 36.

33. Anita Aidt Guy, "The Maryland Abolition Society and the Promotion of the Ideals of the New Nation", *Maryland Historical Magazine*, 84:4 (1989), p. 342; Ira Berlin, *Many Thousands Gone: The First Two Centuries of Slavery in North America* (Cambridge [etc.], 1998), pp. 219–224. Additional note: The Upper South encompasses Maryland, Delaware, Virginia, North Carolina, Kentucky, Tennessee, and Missouri. The Lower South encompasses South Carolina, Georgia, Florida, Alabama, Mississippi, Arkansas, Louisiana, and Texas.

34. 1810 was also the year with the highest percentage of black city dwellers in Baltimore. James M. Wright, *The Free Negro in Maryland 1634–1860* (New York and [etc.], 1921), p. 83.

the free soil of the North where slavery had been abolished.[35] Ralph Thompson, for instance, escaped from Cockeysville. From there, the distance to the Pennsylvanian border was almost the same as to Baltimore. A number of reasons, though, encouraged Thompson and others like him to make the choices they made. Employment prospects for black men were better in the southern than in the northern states (in fact, they became better the farther south one went, as demonstrated by Leonard Curry[36]), families and friends provided an incentive to stay, and the lack of networks in the North acted as a discouragement.

For example, nineteen-year-old runaway James Harris, with a "very large mouth [and] thick African lips", as his owner described him in an advertisement, could have used his private and work-related network to conceal himself in Fell's Point, a waterfront area in Baltimore. He had lived there prior to his sale and his new owner therefore believed him to be "lurking about that part of the city" in 1842.[37] Moreover, the information on the timespan of flight that some slaveholders included in the announcements clearly indicates that it was not only temporary absconders who gravitated to Baltimore. To give two examples out of many, a slaveowner knew in 1832 that his bondsman Ben Anderson had "been secreting himself about this city [Baltimore] for three months, passing as a free man" but he was unable to find him.[38] In 1853, Henry Kemp had already been gone for five months, when his Baltimore master advertised that "[h]e is an excellent waiter, and is supposed to be at some large Hotel acting in that capacity".[39]

Historian T. Stephen Whitman has noticed that, from the slaveholders' point of view, the threat of losing a runaway slave to the growing ranks of Baltimore's free black population became more pronounced over time. Maryland slaveowners therefore systematically employed delayed manumissions as a strategy to keep their slaves under control. The idea was that bondspeople, who saw the prospect of becoming *legally* free in the future, would more willingly surrender to their fate in the present. Control and the impetus to high performance were, hence, important incentives for manumission. In Baltimore, many slaveholders who manumitted slaves out of this logic bought others in the aftermath. This is why the number of manumissions in Maryland was relatively high. Between 1790 and 1860, 45,000 enslaved people gained

35. This observation contradicts Mary Niall Mitchell who largely dismisses Upper South cities by claiming that it was mostly cities in the Deep South that functioned as places of refuge for runaways. Mitchell, "Lurking but Working", p. 202.
36. Curry, *Free Black in Urban America*, ch. 2: "The Most Laborious and Least Profitable Employments: Urban Free Black Occupational Patterns".
37. *The Baltimore Sun*, 18 January 1842.
38. *Daily National Intelligencer*, 21 February 1832.
39. *The Baltimore Sun*, 24 November 1853.

their freedom by manumission.[40] These dynamics led to the highest absolute numbers of free black persons of all the American states and dramatically changed the social worlds of black and white Marylanders. Hundreds of runaways joined the free black population and contributed to its growth.

Despite the higher odds of being legally set free, enslaved men, women, and children from Maryland and other regions in the Upper South were the most severely affected by sale and forced migration. In the nineteenth century, a massive domestic slave trade trafficked bondspeople to the southern and western territories of the expanding republic. Between 1790 and 1860, approximately one million enslaved people were moved from the Upper to the Lower South. An additional two million were displaced within the same states.[41] As historians have calculated, between 1830 and 1860, approximately 18,500 enslaved men, women, and children were sold out of Maryland. In Baltimore, every third first marriage was broken up, ten to fifteen per cent of enslaved young adults were sold out of state, and one in three children under fifteen years old were separated from at least one parent.[42]

Separating families and uprooting them through forced migrations, the internal slave trade of the nineteenth century was a factor that both aggravated the lives of enslaved people and triggered escapes. Slaveholders were eager to excuse this common practice, which contradicted their claims of being benevolent masters, by blaming the slaves for their own sales. Recounting the story of a free black man in Baltimore whose family was about to be sold to New Orleans, *The Baltimore Sun* wrote in 1850 that "these slaves would have been permitted to have remained here undisturbed for years if all sense of security had not been destroyed by the temptation held out to run away. Every man who owns this kind of property now thinks of hurrying it off further south".[43] With this opinion, the editor claimed it was the slaves' own fault if they were sold – and he expressed how much of an issue slave flight was.

According to Whitman, many more owners suspected that runaways remained in the city after 1790. During the 1810s, fugitive slaves were thought to be in that city three to four times more often than in other places. If taking locations close to the city into consideration as well, the share grows even

40. T. Stephen Whitman, "Manumission and Apprenticeship in Maryland, 1770–1870", *Maryland Historical Magazine*, 101:1 (2006), p. 56, in Jessica Millward, "'That All Her Increase Shall Be Free': Enslaved Women's Bodies and the Maryland 1809 Law of Manumission", *Women's History Review*, 21:3 (2012), p. 365; T. Stephen Whitman, *The Price of Freedom: Slavery and Manumission in Baltimore and Early National Maryland* (Lexington, KY, 1997), pp. 4, 92–94.

41. Kolchin, *American Slavery*, p. 96; Damian Alan Pargas, *Slavery and Forced Migration in the Antebellum South* (New York, 2015), p. 2.

42. Fields, *Middle Ground*, pp. 8, 17, 33; Michael Tadman, *Speculators and Slaves: Masters, Traders, and Slaves in the Old South* (Madison, WI, 1989), pp. 5–7, 169–173.

43. *The Baltimore Sun*, 12 August 1850.

more.[44] Runaway slaves to Baltimore did not usually migrate long distances. As jail records reveal, most were from counties in proximity to the city. Some came from the city itself or from northern Virginia counties. A small number of runaways were caught attempting to return home after being sold further south in the direction of the internal slave trade.[45] Additionally, some runaways to Baltimore viewed Baltimore as a transit zone, from which to migrate to the free states, even though, as historian Barbara Fields has noted, it was a better place of refuge than a departure point for other safe harbours.[46]

Like other southern cities, Baltimore received two types of runaways: urban (from Baltimore or other cities and towns) and rural. In addition to the challenges all escaped slaves faced, rural runaways had to adapt to an urban economy and become urban workers. Slaves who had experienced greater mobility, for example by having worked as (self-)hired slaves, or who had lived apart from their masters, had clear advantages. Many were used to an autonomous life and the requirements of work in the city. The same mobility described by Jared Hardesty and Marion Pluskota in this issue for eighteenth-century Boston and for the French Caribbean, respectively, also allowed urban bondspeople in the nineteenth-century US South to leave their owners. This was increasingly the case for enslaved people in the southern cities, where the self-hire system came to be an integral part of urban slavery. It holds true even for Baltimore, where slavery had never been strong (see Table 1).[47]

To be sure, those who dared to flee enslavement were determined and courageous persons who risked a lot to set themselves free. Runaways who went to Baltimore escaped for very similar reasons as those who became maroons in the classic sense: fear of sale; separation from loved ones; mistreatment; overwork; or the simple conviction that they no longer wanted to be slaves.[48] As already stated, to determine whether they can be understood as maroons, we

44. T. Stephen Whitman, "Slavery, Manumission, and Free Black Workers in Early National Baltimore" (Ph.D., Johns Hopkins University, 1993), pp. 220–221.

45. See "Baltimore City and County Jail Runaway and Accommodations Dockets, 1831–1864", in Jerry M. Hynson (ed.), *Absconders, Runaways and Other Fugitives in the Baltimore City and County Jail* (Westminster, MD, 2004); and "Committed" ads in various newspapers.

46. Fields, *Middle Ground*, p. 34.

47. Historians have shown that slave hiring had existed during colonial times, too, but the dimensions it assumed in the decades before the Civil War in towns and cities were striking. In the antebellum period, between five and fifteen per cent of the enslaved population were on hire, with an increase closer to the Civil War. In later decades, one third to one half of enslaved people were hired at some point in their lives, at least in parts of the Upper South. John J. Zaborney, *Slaves for Hire: Renting Enslaved Laborers in Antebellum Virginia* (Baton Rouge, LA, 2012), pp. 11–14; Thomas D. Morris, *Southern Slavery and the Law, 1619–1860* (Chapel Hill, NC, 1996), p. 132; Calvin Schermerhorn, *Money over Mastery, Family over Freedom: Slavery in the Antebellum Upper South* (Baltimore, MD, 2011), p. 136.

48. On reasons for becoming a maroon, see Wieke Vink, *Creole Jews: Negotiating Community in Colonial Suriname* (Leiden, 2010), p. 114; Christian Delgado Escobar, "Esclavitud, cimarrones y

must expand the view to include the community they chose to join. As the next two sections will show, arguments exist both for and against applying the concept of marronage to Baltimore's black population.

RESEMBLANCES OF BLACK BALTIMOREANS TO A MAROON COMMUNITY

Before turning to the points that repudiate the concept of marronage for Baltimore, this section engages with aspects that might lead us to consider black Baltimoreans as maroons in the first place. These include the recruitment of newcomers, solidarity among black people, legal attacks by slaveholding society, and criminalization.[49]

Family networks were an important reason for the significant increase in slave flight to Baltimore in the nineteenth century – despite abolition in the North. People who fled slavery were motivated to stay close to their loved ones. Because manumitted slaves often moved to Baltimore, an increasing number of bondspeople had free family members in the city. In general, their personal networks were broad. Calvin Schermerhorn has laid out that many enslaved families were rooted in this region of the country for several generations. The Chesapeake Bay, home to the city of Baltimore on its northwestern shores, had been one of the pilot projects of African American slavery. Two hundred years after the first enslaved Africans put their feet on soil that would later become the United States, family networks were firm and extended over rural and urban areas. In later times, Schermerhorn stresses, as enslaved families were increasingly broken up and a significant number of slaves experienced greater mobility and more varied employment, these kin networks expanded geographically.[50]

It was not only the desire of enslaved people to break free and join their loved ones in Baltimore, the latter also had an incentive in actively supporting slave flight. Through this constant reception of newcomers, the free black community responded to a topic that was a common feature of maroon societies.[51] Free black people had always been suspected of aiding runaways, but the harbouring of relatives and acquaintances must have worked increasingly well over time. As the nineteenth century progressed, a growing number of enslaved people had friends and relatives who lived in Baltimore, as evidenced by runaway slave advertisements in newspapers. Whereas in the late eighteenth

palenques", *Anacrónica. Revista de los estudiantes de história*, 4 (2006). Available at: http://anacronica.univalle.edu.co/esclavitud,_cimarrones_y_palenques.htm; last accessed 9 November 2017.

49. Berlin, "North of Slavery".

50. Schermerhorn, *Money over Mastery*, pp. 10, 23, 32.

51. See Diouf, *Slavery's Exiles*, p. 267; Michael Craton, *Testing the Chains: Resistance to Slavery in the British West Indies* (Ithaca, NY [etc.], 1982), p. 78.

century, a few of these mentioned the family relations of the runaways,[52] masters later increasingly gave information about the relatives of the absconder and also, in numerous cases, about presumed employment.

Charles A. Pye, the legal owner of the twenty-year-old, "rather handsome", Watt, who left him around 1 March 1816, announced a reward of $100. "He has some relations at Mr. Foxall's, in Georgetown, and a free brother in Baltimore, where he will probably endeavour to reach. It is likely he will have a pass, as some of his relations read and write", Pye claimed.[53] Likewise, enslaved Ellick, eighteen years old, who called himself Alexander Brown, absconded from Jefferson County, (now West) Virginia. His mother lived near Baltimore and his sister in the city. Therefore, his owner believed that he had gone there in 1840.[54] These and other comparable sources reveal important information about the personal networks of African Americans. As early as the 1830s, free black inhabitants outnumbered the city's enslaved residents by over 10,000, meaning they had more possibilities to shelter and aid runaways.[55] (For an impression of the size of Baltimore, see Figure 2) These practical aspects combined with the broad social networks increased the willingness to aid runaways from slavery.

Also outside of family structures, black people of different legal statuses showed a remarkable solidarity with each other. For instance, newspapers frequently published advertisements by free black residents claiming to have lost their freedom papers.[56] Many must have passed them on to slaves who, in turn, could use them to travel to Baltimore and to pass themselves off as free people. Others forged passes for runaways, harboured them, or provided them with contacts to find work. Autobiographer John Thompson, for instance, gave the example of an enslaved man writing passes for other slaves.[57] Runaway Tom was believed to use the papers of the dead James Lucas to pass himself off as the deceased.[58] The African American community must not be viewed only as a passive receiving society, but also as an active recruiter of enslaved sisters, husbands, friends, and co-workers.

This loyalty in the black community originated in their shared lived realities but was also affected by material conditions and influenced by broader

52. Robert L. Hall, "Slave Resistance in Baltimore City and County, 1747–1790", *Maryland Historical Magazine*, 84:4 (1989), p. 306.
53. *Baltimore Patriot*, 12 September 1816.
54. *The Baltimore Sun*, 6 August 1840.
55. Christopher Phillips, *Freedom's Port: The African American Community of Baltimore, 1790–1860* (Urbana, IL, 1997), p. 58.
56. For example, "Lost – On Friday last, my FREE PAPERS, (they were in a tin box,) somewhere near the old Fair Grounds. [...] Jas. Brown, A free man of color." *Richmond Dispatch*, 16 January 1861.
57. John Thompson, *The Life of John Thompson, a Fugitive Slave: Containing His History of 25 Years in Bondage, and His Providential Escape. Written by Himself* (Worcester, MA, 1856), p. 86.
58. Unknown newspaper, February 1840.

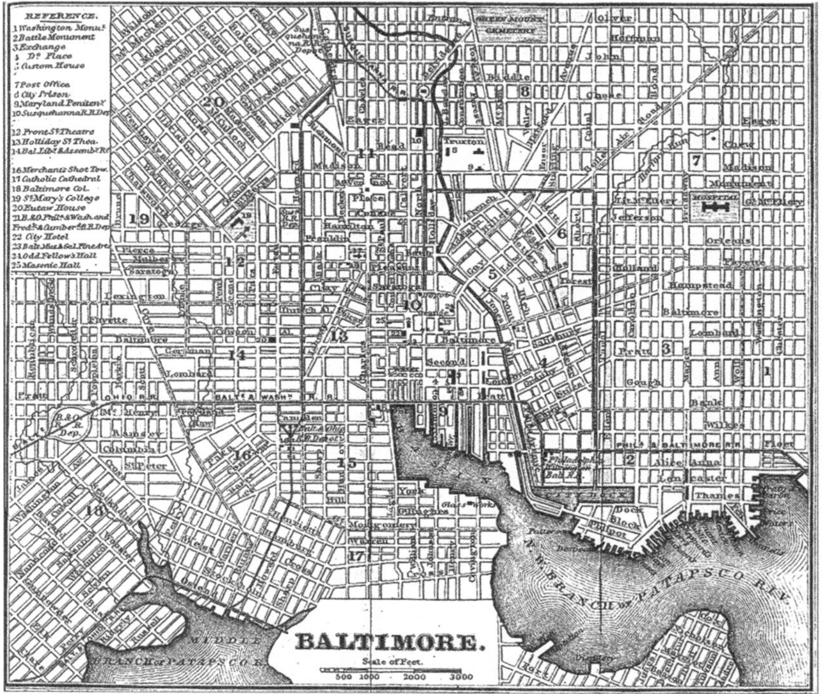

Figure 2. Map of Baltimore, Maryland, 1848.
Source info: Edward H. Hall, Appleton's Hand-Book of American Travel *(New York, 1869), pp. 298–299. Courtesy of the University of Texas Libraries, University of Texas at Austin.*

society.[59] Solidarity was especially strong in Baltimore, compared to other American places. One of the reasons for this was that, in the Upper South, upward social mobility was almost unachievable for any person of visible African descent, which led to the strengthening of horizontal solidarities and a degree of "racial unity".[60] This unity extended over slavery and freedom because both free and enslaved African Americans came to be treated very

59. Walter Johnson, "Agency: A Ghost Story", in Richard Follett, Eric Foner, and Walter Johnson (eds), *Slavery's Ghost: The Problem of Freedom in the Age of Emancipation* (Baltimore, MD, 2011), pp. 28–29.

60. Conversely, Sidney Chalhoub has claimed that slavery in nineteenth-century Brazil allowed for some degrees of social advancement through competition, which had negative effects on the horizontal solidarity amongst the enslaved. Sidney Chalhoub, "The Precariousness of Freedom in a Slave Society (Brazil in the Nineteenth Century)", *International Review of Social History*, 56:3 (2011), p. 409. Ira Berlin speaks of racial unity of the black society of the Upper South in comparison to the Lower South. Ira Berlin, *Generations of Captivity: A History of African American Slaves* (Cambridge, MA, 2003) p. 140. Christopher Phillips notes that there was of course a social

much alike. Slavery was not only a labour relation and a legal status, it was also a racial order that affected people who stood outside of this institution.

Part of this racial control was that black Baltimoreans were criminalized for actions that did not qualify as offences for white people. For example, black people who did not work in the service of white economic interests could be apprehended and forced to work and their children could be bound out as apprentices.[61] Since 1831, any free black person who moved into Maryland or returned from a trip outside the state could legally be enslaved. Furthermore, free black Marylanders could be sold into slavery for crimes for which whites were punished significantly less harshly.[62] This befell Thomas Phelps in 1838, "a mulatto" who "was arraigned for stealing sundry bead bags and a quantity of ribbons and lace" of a value of fifteen dollars. "He was found guilty, and, this being his second offence, he was sentenced to be sold out of the State."[63] Conventional maroons also faced the constant danger of (re-)enslavement.[64] This threat of enslavement for free African Americans moved them closer to those already (or still) enslaved. And this proximity was further reinforced by legislation that aimed to define the status and the behaviour of all black people. From 1832 onwards, Baltimore's free blacks started to receive the same punishments for offences as legally enslaved people. The focus on race, rather than legal status, further blurred the distinction between free and enslaved.[65]

Paired with a process of criminalization went a process of systematic illegalization. If black Baltimoreans purchased firearms, liquor, or dogs without a licence, they were criminalized. The same applied to almost everything sold by African Americans without a written permit. When they did it nonetheless, it was seen as illegal. Other institutions, such as black schools and benevolent societies, had to operate clandestinely and were frequently shut down. Significantly, after 1831, black people were prohibited from assembling and were required to follow a 10 o'clock curfew.[66] Since black people still had to

stratification within Baltimore's black community, but they were less divided than in other cities and also less divided than Baltimore's white society. Phillips, *Freedom's Port*, pp. 145–146.

61. Compare this to the vagrancy laws Marion Pluskota discusses in this issue to force free black people to work.

62. MSA, Archives of Maryland Online, vol. 141, Laws of Maryland 1831, ch. 323, p. 1068; Fields, *Middle Ground*, p. 79. All materials from Archives of Maryland Online cited in this article can be accessed via http://aomol.msa.maryland.gov/html/index.html. Fields, *Middle Ground*, p. 79.

63. *The Baltimore Sun*, 10 February 1838.

64. Berlin, "North of Slavery", pp. 7–8.

65. Baltimore Ordinances, in Wade, *Slavery in the Cities*, p. 249, 266.

66. MSA, Archives of Maryland Online, vol. 141, Laws of Maryland 1831, ch. 323, p. 1068, cited in Hynson, *Absconders*, p. 61. See also Fields, *Middle Ground*, p. 35; Ira Berlin, *Slaves Without Masters: The Free Negro in the Antebellum South* (New York: Pantheon Books, 1974), p. 76. Brazilian scholars have extended this thread to today, comparing favelas to *quilombos* because of their being "criminalized spaces". Andrelino Campos, *Do quilombo à favela. A produção do "espaço criminalizado" no Rio de Janeiro* (Lisbon, 2005); Hugo Albuquerque, "Rocinha. O

survive, they were driven into semi-clandestine or illegal economic and social activities, which meant being driven underground.

Baltimore's free black population also became partly illegalized in itself; this corresponded to the outlawing of maroons.[67] Although not all maroons lived in illegality, most moved outside the reach of the law and jurisdiction.[68] The illegalization occurred on various levels. Already in 1805, Maryland's General Assembly warned that "great mischiefs have arisen from slaves coming into possession of certificates of free Negroes, by running away and passing as free under the faith of such certificates". Consequently, free black Marylanders were asked to prove their freedom and to acquire corresponding documentation.[69] From 1824 onwards, manumitted slaves were required to pay a one-dollar fee to receive a certificate of freedom from the clerk of the court.[70] Those who could not afford the dollar, had a problem and could not prove their freedom without major efforts. In 1832, another law was enacted requiring slaves manumitted from that year onwards to leave Maryland. This was a response to the violently suppressed Nat Turner rebellion of 1831 in Virginia, which heightened white fears of black people. Legislators knew that the law would not work, because it was a copy of a similar, Virginia law of 1806, which ordered manumitted slaves out of the state within twelve months of becoming free.[71] It was nevertheless enacted, first

Quilombo e a Favela", *O Descurvo* (2011). Available at: http://descurvo.blogspot.nl/2011/11/rocinha-o-quilombo-e-favela.html; last accessed 9 November 2017.

67. See Manigat, "Relationship between Marronage", pp. 421–422; Monica Schuler, "Maroons (Cimarrones)", in *Encyclopedia of Latin American History and Culture* (2008). Available at: http://www.encyclopedia.com/humanities/encyclopedias-almanacs-transcripts-and-maps/maroons-cimarrones; last accessed 7 November 2017.

68. Whether the freedom of maroons was illegal or not depended on many factors and could vary over time, for example through truces. For one, the maroons of the Great Dismal Swamp were illegal throughout their existence. The Windward Maroons of Jamaica and the Saramaka from Suriname, by contrast, were granted legal autonomy in exchange for certain concessions. Diouf, *Slavery's Exiles*; Kenneth M. Bilby, *True-Born Maroons* (Gainesville, FL, 2008), p. xi; Richard Price, *Rainforest Warriors: Human Rights on Trial* (Philadelphia, PA [etc.], 2011), p. 80.

69. Laws of Maryland, 1805, Ch. 66, in Certificates of Freedom, Guide to Government Records, MSA, 'Descriptions of African American Records'. Available at: http://guide.msa.maryland.gov/pages/viewer.aspx?page=afridesc; last accessed 14 December 2019.

70. Archives of Maryland, Laws of Maryland, 1824, ch. 85, vol. 141, p. 807, cited in Hynson, *Absconders*, p. 59.

71. General Assembly, "An ACT to amend the several laws concerning slaves" (1806), transcribed from Samuel Shepherd (ed.), *The Statutes at Large of Virginia, from October Session 1792, to December Session 1806* (Richmond, VA, 1836), p. 252, Encyclopedia Virginia (last modified 31 July 2012). Available at: https://www.encyclopediavirginia.org/_An_ACT_to_amend_the_several_laws_concerning_slaves_1806; last accessed 26 October 2016. In Maryland, it exempted those who were able to convince a "respectable" white person to testify each year that they deserved to remain. MSA, Archives of Maryland Online, vol. 141, Laws of Maryland 1831, ch. 281, pp. 1035–1041, extract cited in Fields, *Middle Ground*, pp. 36–37.

as a desperate move to convince free African Americans to migrate to Liberia (which eventually proved unsuccessful), and second, because it had the side effect of creating a large population of undocumented people who were stripped of any legal grounds to become politically active. Although there is no evidence of an organized round-up of illegal residents, as happened in Richmond, Virginia,[72] the law of 1832 attached an illegal status to hundreds of newly freed black people who were not willing to abandon their families and homes.[73]

Like illegalized free black Baltimoreans, runaway slaves depended on anonymity and invisibility before the authorities. This was the nature of the illegal freedom that they could achieve in regions where slavery officially existed. And in Baltimore, they joined a population that faced criminalization and illegalization itself. This does, admittedly, bring the experiences of the city's black community very close to those of maroons, whose freedom was most of the time insecure and fragile. However, there are more factors of marronage to consider. Thus far, it has been shown that Baltimore's black community was discriminated against and excluded. The next section will argue that this exclusion did not stem from the desire of black Baltimoreans and that they, quite contrarily, aspired to inclusion in the dominant society. Hence they were not maroons.

ARGUMENTS AGAINST SEEING BLACK BALTIMOREANS AS A MAROON COMMUNITY

Slaveholding society usually sees marronage as a threat to the social order.[74] The measures taken against this threat are often visible in legislative sources. In Maryland, by contrast, the legislative framework developed over time in a way that made it *less* difficult for runaway slaves to pass as free people, and for their helpers at least not more difficult to shelter or employ them. In the early nineteenth century, in Maryland, as in most other states of the American South, people of African descent were generally supposed to be slaves.[75] This was problematic when they were taken up as alleged runaway

72. See Carey H. Latimore IV, "A Step Closer to Slavery? Free African Americans, Industrialization, Social Control and Residency in Richmond City, 1850–1860", *Slavery & Abolition*, 33:1 (2012), pp. 124–125.

73. For more on the process of illegalization of African Americans, see Viola F. Müller, "Early Undocumented Workers: Runaway Slaves and African Americans in the Urban South, c.1830–1860", *Labor History* (2019). Available at: https://doi.org/10.1080/0023656X.2019.1649377; last accessed 14 December 2019.

74. Manigat, "Relationship between Marronage", 425. Sylviane Diouf has stressed white people's fear of maroons. Diouf, *Slavery's Exiles*, 17.

75. This remained the case in all southern states except Maryland and Delaware. Berlin, *Slaves Without Masters*, 158.

slaves. If they could not prove their freedom, they ran the risk of being sold into slavery. From 1817 onwards, however – although discriminating greatly against the *free* black population (see the previous section) – legislative adjustments made it easier for runaways to succeed in their endeavours – *within* the state of Maryland, nota bene.[76]

As legal documents show, in 1817, due to the large numbers of free black inhabitants, the state of Maryland relieved black people of the burden of proof to verify their legal freedom and instead assumed all of them to be free unless proven otherwise.[77] If a black person jailed as a suspected runaway in Maryland was believed to be free, she or he was to be released and the expenses were levied on the county. In 1824, the General Assembly complained "that Baltimore county is subjected to great annual expense on account of negroes being committed to the jail of that county, on suspicion of being runaway slaves".[78] The act, however, remained unchanged until the Civil War. In 1831, a new law prohibited the hire, employment, or harbouring of illegal free black immigrants to the state, but no mention was made of runaway slaves from Maryland. And although a reward of $6 for persons apprehending runaway slaves was made mandatory in 1806, and increased to $30 in 1832, by 1860 the reward was retracted if the runaways did not remove themselves to a sufficient distance: "[N]o reward shall be paid under this section for taking up any slave in the county in which said slave is hired, or in which his owner resides".[79]

Additionally, from 1860 on, the commitment of an assumed runaway slave to jail was to be only announced in the Baltimore city papers. Earlier, it was also to be made public in the surrounding areas and in Washington, DC.[80] Slave flight from Baltimore City or County did not entail a mandatory bounty that would have encouraged uninvolved persons to be on the lookout for the absconder. This is remarkable, especially because it seemed that by the early 1850s, a growing number of runaways taken up in Baltimore were from the city itself.[81] In 1849, slaveholders from Maryland's Eastern Shore publicly

76. The following explanations of the relaxation of the legislature against individual runaways within Maryland stood in sharp contrast to the tightening laws regarding white and especially black persons who supported slave flight by enticing away or "stealing" slaves. This corresponded to the major concern about losing slaves beyond state lines.

77. MSA, Archives of Maryland Online, vol. 141, Laws of Maryland 1817, ch. 112, pp. 658ff.

78. Chapter 171, Laws of 1824, in Runaway Docket, Baltimore City and County, Guide to Government Records, MSA, "Descriptions of African American Records". Available at: http://guide.msa.maryland.gov/pages/viewer.aspx?page=afridesc; last accessed 14 December 2019.

79. MSA, Archives of Maryland Online: vol. 192, Session Laws, Nov 1806–Jan 1807, p. 693; vol. 141, Laws of Maryland 1831, ch. 323, p. 1068, Laws of Maryland 1833, ch. 11L, p. 1115; vol. 145, Maryland Code 1860, art. 66, pp. 450–453.

80. Laws of Maryland, 1860, Art. 66, Vol. 145, pp. 450–453.

81. Baltimore City Jail (Runaway Docket), 1836–1850, MSA. This observation is in line with Barbara Field's report of Maryland slaveholders who saw a growth in slave flight in the 1850s. Fields, *Middle Ground*, pp. 66–67.

reproached their bondspeople for fleeing in large numbers: "If something is not done, and that speedily too, there will be but few slaves remaining on the Eastern Shore of Maryland in a few years. They are running off almost daily", lamented a local master.[82] Sixty slaves allegedly absconded in 1856 alone, and another rash of escapes took place in 1858.[83] In this context, the calculations by John Hope Franklin and Loren Schweninger are important, as they do not account for an increase in flight to the northern states.[84] Thus, a large share of fleeing enslaved people must have found themselves in Baltimore. These developments, which spread over the course of the antebellum era, stood in contrast to the common attitudes of legislators towards maroons, who usually tried to implement harsher codes to hamper slave flight.[85] Legislative relaxation is an indication that legislators did not see runaway slaves within Maryland as a particular threat to the social order.

This observation is also important when it comes to the receiving society in Baltimore. Slavery had many facets and implications, but it was primarily an institution to make some people work for the benefit of other people. In the United States, many white people held the belief that black people were there to serve them.[86] However, slavery in Baltimore and other cities dramatically decreased. By 1860, the census counted 2,200 enslaved Baltimoreans, who constituted a mere one per cent of the city's total population.[87] Most slaveholders in the city owned but a single slave.[88] Quaker Joseph Gurney, who visited Baltimore in the late 1830s, claimed that "the influence of the system [of slavery] on society in general is much limited by the small proportion of slaves".[89] Yet, institutionalized slavery had another "influence on society" in that it cast a shadow on those who were affected by the same racial order as slaves. Slavery was much more powerful than Gurney assumed.

Early in the century, the abolition of slavery was openly discussed in the Maryland press, in religious congregations, and even by the General Assembly – but the state never brought itself to formally end it. Despite the

82. *The Baltimore Sun*, 16 October 1849.
83. This according to James L. Bowers (1810–1882), who published two articles discussing slavery in *The Cecil Whig* on 24 July 1858. See Accomplice to slave flight, Kent County, Maryland, 1858, MSA SC 5496-8991. Available at: https://msa.maryland.gov/megafile/msa/speccol/sc5400/sc5496/008900/008991/html/008991sources.html; last accessed 14 December 2019.
84. Franklin and Schweninger, *Runaway Slaves*, p. 279.
85. See, for example, Edward B. Rugemer, *Slave Law and the Politics of Resistance in the Early Atlantic World* (Cambridge [etc.], 2018), p. 127; Thompson, *Flight to Freedom*, p. 112.
86. For instance, Mia Bay, *The White Image in the Black Mind: African-American Ideas about White People, 1830–1925* (New York [etc.], 2000), pp. 13–14.
87. US 8th Census, 1860, *Population of the United States*.
88. Fields, *Middle Ground*, p. 47. This furthermore shows that urban slavery evolved to a largely domestic labour force for those who could afford it. Edward L. Ayers *et al.*, *American Passages: A History of the United States*, 4th edn (Boston, MA, 2010), p. 148; Whitman, *Price of Freedom*.
89. Joseph John Gurney, *A Journey in North America, Described in Familiar Letters to Amelia Opie* (Norwich, 1841, reprinted in Carlisle, 2007), p. 87.

subordinate position of slavery in Maryland, however, the new constitution of Maryland of 1851, finally, included a prohibition of abolition.[90] The reasons were not of an economic nature, although slavery was still widespread in rural Maryland, especially in wheat agriculture.[91] The argument for the prohibition of abolition is, rather, that the racialized system kept people of African descent in their assigned places.

The fact that the social order white society envisioned was also working well without holding large numbers of black people in legal slavery can be retraced with the statements of anti-black institutions, which changed in tone over time. For example, in 1817, the Maryland Colonization Society voiced that free black people had a clear "vicious and mischievous" potential and strongly advocated their removal from the entire country.[92] Around the same time, the widely read *Niles' Weekly Register* warned that "free blacks among us are less honest and correct, less industrious and not so much to be depended upon" than slaves.[93] Free black people in Maryland were seen explicitly as a problem, including being a danger. By the later antebellum period, however, the voices were no longer that strong, and some came to opposite opinions. In 1858, the governor of Maryland, Thomas H. Hicks, made it clear that where black people "can find employment, chiefly as domestics and laborers, as in her populous city [Baltimore], and in the more thickly settled portions of the State, [...] there is but little of the evil of their vagrancy and idleness felt, not much complaint of its existence".[94]

A year later, the Convention of Maryland Slaveholders likewise showed no interest in removing free African Americans from the state: "[T]he committee came to the conclusion", it reported, "that it was highly inexpedient to undertake any measure for the general removal of our free black population from the State. [...] Their removal from the State would deduct nearly 50 per cent from the household and agricultural labor furnished by people of this color [...]". Instead of enslaving the entire free black population or expelling them from

90. Fields, *Middle Ground*, pp. 20–21. Looking at the entire nation, the number of enslaved people rose from 700,000 in 1790 to four million in 1860. *Return of the Whole Number of Persons within the Several Districts of the United States, According to "An Act Providing for the Enumeration of the Inhabitants of the United States"* (Philadelphia, PA, 1791), p. 3; US 8th Census, 1860, *Population of the United States.*

91. The economic orientation towards the North became clear at the latest on the eve of the Civil War when Maryland (together with Missouri, Delaware, and Kentucky) decided that their clinging to slavery was less important than other factors and stayed in the Union.

92. A Letter from Gen. Harper, of Maryland, to Elias B. Caldwell, Esq., Secretary of the American Society for Colonizing the Free People of Colour, in the United States, with Their Own Consent, 20 August 1817 (Baltimore, 1818), Maryland State Colonization Society Papers, 1827–1871, Maryland Historical Society, in Whitman, "Slavery and Manumission", p. 379.

93. *Niles' Weekly Register*, 22 May 1819.

94. The Inaugural Address of Thomas H. Hicks, Governor of Maryland, delivered in the Senate Chamber, at Annapolis, Wednesday 13 January 1858, MSA.

the country, it would be better to "make these people orderly, industrious and productive", the slaveholders agreed.[95]

Whereas contradictory opinions of white people regarding free black people had always existed, the ones in favour of expelling them were markedly less unanimous in the later years of the antebellum period.[96] The labour aspect, as mentioned by Hicks and the Maryland slaveholders, was very important. Compliance with their own labour exploitation and the subordination free black people displayed were precisely what white society expected from them. Black men and women undertook the most menial work requiring the least skills. Over time, their already precarious socio-economic situation noticeably worsened, and poverty aggravated racial discrimination.[97] Baltimore was the southern city where black people owned the least property. In 1850, free black inhabitants who owned property constituted a mere 0.06 per cent of the city's inhabitants.[98] Remarkably, this was still too much for some white Marylanders. In 1860, the spokesman of the Baltimore convention asked to legally bar black people from purchasing houses or leasing them for more than a year.[99] Due to racist legislation, free black people had very few resources to resist. Although they were considered persons by law, not property like slaves, their societal, political, and economic opportunities were dramatically limited. In most states, persons of colour were not allowed to vote, to testify in court, or to sit on juries. They were not allowed to freely travel or assemble, nor could they marry whites. Legislative restrictions emphasized political and judicial exclusion.[100]

Steven Hahn has also taken the dimension of exclusion into account. His considerations are of special interest in this last section on points that further reject the application of the concept of marronage to Baltimore. Hahn has examined black communities in the US northern states along demographics, migration patterns, residency, and social and political organization. He points to their internal coherence, social experiences, autonomous institutions, and

95. *The Baltimore Sun*, 10 June 1859. The same Convention of Maryland Slaveholders had just a decade and a half earlier recommended a number of propositions "for the consideration of the legislature", including a "responsible security" free blacks should give to ensure "his or her good behavior". If they absconded from service, they should be sold out of state. *The Baltimore Sun*, 18 January 1842.

96. Seth Rockman has even claimed that in Baltimore, there was less racist coverage in the media than elsewhere because black people were too pivotal in the labour market. Seth Rockman, *Scraping By: Wage Labor, Slavery, and Survival in Early Baltimore* (Baltimore, MD, 2009), p. 13.

97. On black occupations, see *Matchett's Baltimore Director, Corrected up to June 1831. Containing (With, or Without) A Plan of the City; With Reference to the Public Buildings* (Baltimore, MD, 1831), MSA; Curry, *Free Black in Urban America*, p. 26; Olson, *Baltimore*.

98. Phillips, *Freedom's Port*, pp. 98–100, 155.

99. *Planter's Advocate*, 22 February 1860, in Fields, *Middle Ground*, p. 79.

100. A. Leon Higginbotham, Jr, *In the Matter of Color: Race and the American Legal Process; The Colonial Period* (New York [etc.]: Oxford University Press, 1978), p. 206; Kolchin, *American Slavery*, pp. 17, 82–84.

legal background as factors that might qualify them for marronage.[101] Hahn's view corresponds to the revisionists' call for a reassessment of the physical isolation of maroons. They agree that it is more fruitful to put weight on their social outsider status instead of territorial integrity.[102] The issue is that while Hahn expressly stresses societal exclusion and autonomous organization as a prominent feature of marronage, he fails to see that this exclusion emanated from white society alone.[103]

African Americans organized themselves independently of white society, through ideology, religion, schools, benevolent societies, and social spaces. In fact, Baltimore's black community established their own religious institutions quite early on. Although severely restricted in many aspects of their lives, free black Baltimoreans had their own official places of worship since the early nineteenth century. The African Methodist Bethel Society was founded in 1815, and by 1860 there were sixteen black churches and missions in Baltimore with at least 6,400 registered members who worshipped in their own fashion. This relative autonomy allowed preachers the liberty to interpret the Bible in a way that did more justice to black people's experiences. Moreover, through churches, black communities in different places interacted with each other. The African Methodist Episcopal Church of Baltimore, established in 1816, was connected to those in Philadelphia, Charleston, and New Orleans.[104]

This social exclusion and independent organization, however, did not stem from a desire for demarcation from white society. Rather, it was the second-best choice black people had *after being rejected*. There is a considerable amount of literature dedicated to the fight of African Americans to be recognized as equal elements of American society.[105] Hahn has rightly observed

101. Hahn, *Political Worlds*, pp. 29, 32.
102. Maris-Wolf, "Hidden in Plain Sight", p. 457.
103. Hahn, *Political Worlds*, p. 34. Independent organization of black life indeed corresponds to the day-to-day experiences of maroons. Kevin Olson, *Imagined Sovereignties: The Power of the People and Other Myths of the Modern Age* (New York, 2016), p. 127; Marjolein Kars, "Maroons and Marronage", *Oxford Bibliographies* (30 August 2016). Available at: http://doi.org/10.1093/obo/9780199730414-0229; last accessed 15 June 2017.
104. Phillips, *Freedom's Port*, pp. 133, 140–142; Kami Fletcher, "The History of African American Undertakers", *Black Perspectives*. Available at: http://www.aaihs.org/the-history-of-african-american-undertakers-in-baltimore/; last accessed 11 July 2017; Albert J. Raboteau, *Slave Religion: The "Invisible Institution" in the Antebellum South* (Oxford [etc.], 2004), p. 204. Independent organization, however, did not mean that black Baltimoreans were left in peace. Churches operated autonomously, but whites viewed their religious services with suspicion.
105. David Waldstreicher, *In the Midst of Perpetual Fetes: The Making of American Nationalism, 1776–1820* (Williamsburg, VA, 1997), 317; Mariana L. R. Dantas, *Black Townsmen: Urban Slavery and Freedom in the Eighteenth-Century Americas* (New York, 2008); Patrick Rael, *Black Identity and Black Protest in the Antebellum North* (Chapel Hill, NC, 2002), p. 282; Martha S. Jones, *Birthright Citizens: A History of Race and Rights in Antebellum America* (New York [etc.], 2018).

that exclusion created spaces to construct new black politics,[106] yet the fight for citizenship ultimately always dominated black struggle.[107] Moreover, historian Martha Jones has recently shown for Baltimore that independent black organizations also followed the rules of white society. The very incorporation of the church, the symbolic and literal centre of most black communities, occurred according to official law. Land had to be formally purchased, the church officially registered, an enslaved minister perhaps manumitted. In this process, they became involved with white attorneys, justices of the peace, and clerks.[108] It is not that black Baltimoreans did not fight to change the system, but they did it from *within*.

All these are points where Baltimore's free black community palpably diverges from the concept of a maroon society. While many maroon communities had economic ties to slaveholding society as well, they did not integrate as thoroughly into the economic place assigned to them by white society as the majority of black people in Baltimore did. Although they lived in severe poverty, they did not elude the legal reach of society, which drastically discriminated against them. On the one hand, it was a clear improvement for escapees from slavery as they were not under the control of a master. On the other, the loss of individual control gave way to the collective control of the whole African American population. Whereas, as Frederick Law Olmsted, a journalist from the US North, wrote in 1860 that in the countryside, "the security of the whites" depended "upon the constant, habitual, and instinctive surveillance and authority of all white people over all black",[109] in the urban context, the authorities took on the matter of social control.[110] Apparently, control by society at large and the restrictions of severe, discriminatory laws was something African Americans could collectively handle, especially in the anonymity of a city.

The compliance with their own subordination was exactly what black activist David Walker criticized in his *Appeal to the Coloured Citizens* in 1829.[111] As historian Stephen Kantrowitz has claimed, rather than challenging the political system and the nation itself, Walker demanded a place in it.[112] Maroons, by contrast, would not strive for citizenship in a slaveholding republic. They

106. Hahn, *Political Worlds*, p. 43.
107. Jim Cullen, *American Dream: A Short History of an Idea that Shaped a Nation* (Oxford [etc.], 2003), pp. 64, 82.
108. Jones, *Birthright Citizens*, p. 18.
109. Frederick Law Olmsted, *Our Slave States*, vol. III: *A Journey in the Back Country* (New York, 1860), p. 444.
110. Wade, *Slavery in the Cities*, p. 40.
111. David Walker, *Walker's Appeal, in Four Articles; Together with a Preamble, to the Coloured Citizens of the World, but in Particular, and Very Expressly, to Those of the United States of America, Written in Boston, State of Massachusetts, September 28, 1829* (Boston, MA, 1830).
112. Stephen Kantrowitz, *More than Freedom: Fighting for Black Citizenship in a White Republic, 1829–1889* (New York, 2012), pp. 28–29.

would not vote and not subordinate themselves to the rules and laws of the very people that upheld the slavery they or their co-maroons had escaped from. Sylviane Diouf has neatly summarized that maroons were distinct from runaways in that the latter "refused enslavement but not the larger society, which they wanted to be part of even if they knew it could only be at its periphery". Instead of rejecting its hegemony, they "continued to live under the discriminatory laws of white society, still subservient and controlled".[113] Persons who fled slavery sought physical liberation from bondage and forced labour. For them, freedom meant acknowledgement and acceptance, and the power to decide freely about their private and public lives.[114] Joining or establishing a maroon community would have provided these privileges. These people, however, abandoned the hopes of being fully accepted into American society.

CONCLUSION

This article has discussed a number of aspects that speak in favour of and against understanding runaway slaves in Baltimore as maroons and their receiving society as a maroon community. Based on some of the findings, African Americans in Baltimore could well have been a maroon community. They were de facto free people surrounded by slavery, and the community existed at the (not physical) margins of white society. The reception of runaways, a freedom in danger, criminalization of their activities, and illegalization of (parts of) its members were realities conventional maroons also experienced. What contradicts marronage is the view of them by white society and the collective attitude of Baltimore's black population towards their own condition. Those in power came to see them not as a threat, and black Baltimoreans condoned the forms of control and surveillance white society imposed on them. Most important was their desire to be included in the larger society. Because these counterarguments are integral features of the concept of marronage and cannot be disregarded, this article concludes that marronage is not an adequate concept to understand their experiences.

Applying this concept to runaway slaves in Baltimore, however, has provided some insights. By following the footsteps of people fleeing slavery and seeking refuge in the city, it has become apparent that the nature of resistance changed in this process. Individuals absconding from their – legally righteous – enslaved condition were rebels in the truest meaning of the word. Yet, by integrating into Baltimore's black community, runaway slaves turned into assimilated residents who attempted to elevate their status by following the very rules that kept the members of this community at the lowest

113. Diouf, *Slavery's Exiles*, p. 2.
114. Kantrowitz, *More than Freedom*, p. 85.

social and economic levels.[115] This course is different from the resistance displayed by maroons. In this light, this article hopes to contribute to the way historians use the term marronage. Far from claiming that urban maroons did not exist, it has argued that running away alone is not a sufficient indication to qualify for marronage; we always have to consider the community as a whole. Particularly, the dimension of resistance should also be an (perhaps the most) important measurement to be included in the concept. Maroons made conscious choices to reject the control and hegemony of the larger society over their lives. This element should be part of the generic definition of marronage.

115. This article claims to speak only for urban runaway slaves in Baltimore. It is, however, an invitation for scholars working on other periods and regions to more thoroughly investigate the relationship of runaway slaves and their receiving communities with the dominant society.

IRSH 65 (2020), pp. 197–223 doi:10.1017/S0020859020000188

Remembering Slavery in Urban Cape Town: Emancipation or Continuity?

Samuel North

20C Queen Street, Chesterfield
Derbyshire, S40 4SF United Kingdom

E-mail: samuelisnorthofhere@gmail.com

Abstract: This article examines how slavery has been remembered in the urban space of Cape Town over time. It explores how individuals and groups have commemorated the history of slavery from the late nineteenth century onwards. It outlines how memory of slavery faded as the number of people with direct experience of enslavement decreased, with burgeoning racial segregation influencing the way that the past was viewed. It then examines how post-1994 democracy in South Africa has once again changed approaches to history. Colonial-era abuses such as slavery have not always been readily remembered in an urban space where their legacies are visible, and this article examines the interplay of politics and identity at the heart of public memorialization of these contested pasts.

INTRODUCTION

In his seminal study of public memory and urban politics, Andreas Huyssen writes of Berlin as a "palimpsest", describing how the contemporary city incorporates and reworks numerous elements of a disparate and often troubled past.[1] Huyssen's engagement with Berlin on such terms is a fitting point of departure for considering many modern cities. Situated at the southern tip of Africa, the built environment of Cape Town in South Africa is a multi-layered tapestry of societies past and present. Cape Town functions as the provincial capital of Western Cape Province and serves as a prime tourist destination for international visitors. Depictions of the city in tourist publications as an inclusive world of adventuring, beaches, mountain backdrops, fine dining, and warm weather sometimes sit at odds with the uncomfortable history of colonialism, enslavement, and formal racial segregation that have shaped Cape Town's built features.[2] In spite of the Western Cape being the former epicentre

1. Andreas Huyssen, *Present Pasts: Urban Palimpsests and The Politics of Memory* (Stanford, CA [etc], 2003), p. 81.
2. Useful overviews of how Cape Town and wider South Africa have been marketed to tourists over time can be found in Vivian Bickford-Smith, "Creating a City of the Tourist Imagination:

of the slave trade to Southern Africa, efforts to confront this history in the city remain fitful and highly contested. These contestations are heavily interlinked with the socio-economic and urban spatial legacies of the white-minority National Party's apartheid system of racial segregation, which was used to govern South Africa between 1948 and 1994.

This article examines remembrance in Cape Town over time, exploring how different actors and groups have commemorated the history of slavery in this urban space. Beginning in the late nineteenth century, it highlights how awareness of slavery amongst direct descendants of enslaved people often figured in efforts to resist increasing racial segregation. The upheaval created by forced removals under apartheid obliterated much of this engagement with the slave past, contributing to a situation in post-1994 South Africa where the urban spaces previously inhabited by the enslaved had fallen silent. More recent representations of slavery by museums, private enterprises, and heritage bodies in the post-apartheid era have sometimes been at odds with the interpretation of slavery held by people identifying as slave descendants who may live with the legacies of apartheid-era forced removals and segregation. The article reveals both the post-slavery experiences of communities who descend from the enslaved and offers insights into how slavery has been remembered in Cape Town over time. The city will be posited as a contested space in terms of discourses surrounding its extensive history of enslavement and colonialism. In doing this, the paper reinforces the idea that the afterlives of slavery in urban areas correspond with the evolving subjectivities of the groups and individuals who perform acts of remembrance.[3]

SLAVERY AT THE CAPE

Slavery at the Cape differed in style from most other systems of enslavement involving Europeans and Africans. Rather than serving as a source of African labour, the Cape was the recipient of enslaved people from Dutch Batavia – in modern-day South East Asia – as well as from elsewhere in Africa, predominantly Madagascar and Mozambique. The desire to import

The Case of Cape Town, 'The Fairest Cape of Them All'", *Urban Studies*, 46:9 (2009), pp. 1763–1785; Leslie Witz, Ciraj Rassool, and Gary Minkley, "Repackaging the Past for South African Tourism", in Gerard Corsane (ed.), *Heritage, Museums and Galleries: An Introductory Reader* (London [etc.], 2005), pp. 308–320.

3. Ana Lucia Araujo, "Introduction", in *Idem* (ed.), *Politics of Memory: Making Slavery Visible in the Public Space* (London [etc.], 2010), pp. 1–13 discusses these ideas. Slavery has variously been denied, celebrated as a foundation history, or celebrated in terms of abolitionist triumph. Jared Hardesty, "Disappearing from Abolitionism's Heartland: The Legacy of Slavery and Emancipation in Boston", in this Special Issue, discusses the way in which histories of Boston depicted slavery as mild and something inimical to the interests of this freedom-driven urban space in order to suit the needs of activists and politicians.

human beings to service colonial society arose from the Dutch East India Company's refusal to permit the enslavement of indigenous Khoi people, although such people were widely used as contract labourers.[4] Roughly 60,000 enslaved people were either imported to or were born at the Cape between 1658 and 1834, and at various times their number marginally outnumbered that of the colonists.[5] These people did not work on plantations, but provided heavy labour in the rural wine farming regions, domestic service in settler households, general labour for the government in urban areas, and artisanal work catching fish or manufacturing furniture. The Dutch administration's Slave Lodge in Cape Town was by far the largest single holding of enslaved people, with a population numbering around 1,000 by 1770.[6] Throughout much of the colony, a pattern of small-scale households enslaving a handful of people was maintained.[7]

The second British occupation of 1806 coincided with waves of domestic abolitionism, and one year later the country outlawed its slave trade. Slavery remained legal at the Cape until emancipation on 1 December 1834, however the value of the freedom achieved by the formerly enslaved was questionable. Facing the prospect of drifting into urban poverty or homelessness, the safest option for a sizeable percentage of the newly liberated was to remain as waged labourers for their former masters by providing a definition of "servant" and circumscribing the rights of such people. The master–slave relationship was effectively perpetuated, aided by measures such as the 1841 Masters & Servants Ordinance, which solidified the balance of power with the former. For Nigel Worden and Clifton Crais, this legislation formed part of a "connective historical tissue" that linked the economic subordination associated with enslavement with attempts at controlling cheap black labour through the colonial, industrial, and apartheid eras.[8] Additionally, a source of exploitative labour for colonists in the immediate post-slavery period was supplied by several thousand "liberated Africans" who arrived at the Cape off condemned slave ships. These people were indentured for periods of up to fourteen years from the 1810s onwards, with the migration stream ebbing and flowing until the 1860s.[9]

4. Nigel Worden, *Slavery in Dutch South Africa* (Cambridge [etc.], 1985), p. 7.

5. Robert Shell, *Children of Bondage: A Social History of the Slave Society at the Cape of Good Hope, 1652–1838*, reprint (Johannesburg, 1997), p. 155.

6. *Ibid.*, p. xxxi.

7. Worden, *Slavery in Dutch South Africa*, pp. 85–95.

8. Nigel Worden and Clifton Crais, "Introduction", in Nigel Worden and Clifton Crais (eds), *Breaking the Chains: Slavery and its Legacy in the Nineteenth Century Cape Colony* (Johannesburg, 1994), pp. 5–6.

9. Christopher Saunders, "Liberated Africans in Cape Colony in the First Half of the Nineteenth Century", *The International Journal of African Historical Studies*, 18.2 (1985), pp. 223–239; Patrick Harries, "Negotiating Abolition: Cape Town and the Trans-Atlantic Slave Trade", *Slavery & Abolition: A Journal of Slave and Post-Slave Studies*, 34:4 (2013), pp. 579–597.

Society at the Cape became more stratified along racial lines as the Victorian period matured.[10] In Cape Town, burgeoning racial segregation was particularly targeted at inner-city working-class neighbourhoods in response to public health fears.[11] Many of the formerly enslaved and their descendants lived in these racially mixed areas. They formed a constituent part of a "race" increasingly labelled "coloured" by the state.[12] This was effectively an all-encompassing label applied to anyone who was neither designated white, nor native black African. In contemporary South Africa it is a contested term, though it remains common language, used both to self-identify and in official documents such as census records.[13] Though racial segregation was initially targeted at so-called natives, many slave descendants were effectively confined to unskilled, low-paid work in the late nineteenth and early twentieth centuries, lacking the economic means to access skilled training and meet necessary licencing terms.[14] Segregationist policies were increasingly introduced as the twentieth century progressed, culminating with the introduction of the Afrikaner nationalist system of apartheid in the then postcolonial South Africa in 1948. This resulted in the forced displacement of hundreds of thousands of black and coloured people across the country into racially segregated townships under the auspices of the Group Areas Act, first introduced in 1950. It was shortly followed by the formal disenfranchisement for coloured people.

URBAN CULTURE AND MEMORY OF SLAVERY

Evidence that explicitly recalls the existence of enslaved people at the Cape has never been available in any great volume. The kind of memory objects such as shackles and yokes that have helped to define memory of transatlantic slavery are almost entirely lacking in relation to Cape slavery. Enslaved people are instead recalled through customs such as eastern-influenced cuisine, naming patterns among the city's population, and urban built spaces such as Cape Town's Greenmarket Square where a busy market that continues to function today saw the enslaved purchase produce for their masters. As will be

10. Vivian Bickford-Smith, Elizabeth Van Heyningen, and Nigel Worden, *Cape Town: The Making of a City* (Cape Town, 1998), pp. 211–220.
11. Vivian Bickford-Smith, "Mapping Cape Town: From Slavery to Apartheid", in Sean Field (ed.), *Lost Communities, Living Memories: Remembering Forced Removals in Cape Town* (Cape Town, 2001), pp. 16–18.
12. For discussion of the origins of the term "coloured", see Mohamed Adhikari, "The Sons of Ham: Slavery and the Making of Coloured Identity", *South African Historical Journal*, 27 (1992), pp. 95–112.
13. See, for example, Statistics South Africa, "Census 2011: Census in Brief" (2011).
14. Vivian Bickford-Smith, "Meanings of Freedom: Social Position and Identity Among Ex-Slaves and Their Descendants in Cape Town, 1875–1910", in Worden and Crais (eds), *Breaking the Chains*, pp. 291–293.

discussed, activists over time have contended that socio-economic dislocation experienced by coloured people is an additional tangible legacy of slavery. Although records documenting the first-person perspectives of enslaved people and their immediate descendants in Cape Town are scarce in number, academics have attempted to probe the social environment of the inner-city melting pot in the late nineteenth and early twentieth centuries. Existing scholarship enables an understanding of how enslaved people and their descendants negotiated the post-emancipation city and interacted with its diverse inhabitants. The work of Andrew Bank suggests that there existed not so much a culture forged by slavery among urbanized coloured people in the century between emancipation and apartheid, but a working-class culture that transcended racial lines and was bound by the everyday experience of work and survival.[15] Bank posits the experience of enslavement as an important element of this creolized urban culture given that it grew out of an eastern-influenced slave society that existed in the public meeting spaces and kitchens of Cape Town between the seventeenth and nineteenth centuries.[16] Additionally, Vivian Bickford-Smith has identified how the most visible part of this culture that directly recalled slavery was the annual Emancipation Day celebrations on 1 December, which commemorated the coming of freedom in 1834.[17] These events included picnics, midnight celebrations, and excursions to the countryside.[18]

A second distinctive element of this culture that demonstrated an awareness of slave roots were the political organizations that emerged among predominantly coloured people during the late nineteenth century to contest burgeoning racial segregation.[19] These political claims were frequently voiced at events marking Emancipation Day at the turn of the century. During the early 1900s, coloured educationist John Tobin began a regular series of meetings in the District Six area of Cape Town. Based around contesting the idea of white hegemony, black consciousness formed a core component of these group meetings that soon incorporated commemorating Emancipation Day as part of their activist agenda.[20] At this point, it is perhaps useful to recall Paul Gilroy's idea of political culture as a form of slave memory in his seminal work on the black Atlantic. Gilroy suggested that slavery in North America nurtured a dissonant political culture that has been maintained over time among black people in the transatlantic world and is mobilized in order to

15. Andrew Bank, *The Decline of Urban Slavery at the Cape, 1806 to 1843* (Cape Town, 1991), pp. 99–102.
16. *Ibid.*, p. 100.
17. Bickford-Smith, "Meanings of Freedom", p. 304.
18. Kerry Ward and Nigel Worden, "Commemorating, Suppressing, and Invoking Cape Slavery", in Sarah Nuttall and Carli Coetzee (eds), *Negotiating the Past: The Making of Memory in South Africa* (Oxford [etc.], 1997), p. 203.
19. Bickford-Smith, "Meanings of Freedom", p. 309.
20. Farieda Khan, "The Elim Slave Route Pilot Project: Report on a Project Executed on Behalf of the Department of Environmental Affairs and Tourism", (February 1999), p. 17.

question power structures.[21] Although Pumla Gqola has critiqued the way in which she claims Gilroy homogenizes the pre-slavery experience and argues that this reduces the utility of his work in terms of understanding the creolization that occurred as a product of slavery in South Africa, his thoughts on post-slavery are arguably still relevant.[22] They are suggestive of a sense of overcoming slavery and of using this to stake claims in the contemporary world and safeguard against returning to a slave-like state. These links are worthy of attention in the South African context, much as they have been commonly associated with African American people.

The validity of these links was demonstrated in events marking the centenary of abolition in 1934 and the centenary of the ending of the apprenticeship period in 1938. Here, political comment infused the celebrations with greater contemporary utility. A 1938 Emancipation Day mass meeting on the Grand Parade saw various trade union and workers' representatives link slavery with the growing racist agenda of the time.[23] While this was not the only platform available for such figures, it demonstrates how memory and perceptions of the slave past held utility as a means of mobilizing against an increasingly segregationist state. Although commemorations led by the state and the moderate reformist African People's Organization took a predominantly religious character with homage paid to Christian European abolitionists, the Grand Parade event hints at how some people of slave descent perceived their post-emancipation fortunes in less positive terms.[24] Racial segregation and apartheid were not direct continuations of slavery, but similarities were evident. Although Cape slavery was not strictly biracial, the balance of power under both systems was such that it benefited the white minority population in material and social terms.

This tendency to evoke the iconography of slavery as a means of contesting political voice in the urban space of Cape Town did, however, faded as the onset of apartheid loomed. The far-left, non-racialist organization, the Non-European Unity Movement – founded in 1943 – continued to associate slavery with all forms of colonial conquest, capitalism, and racial segregation into the 1950s.[25] From the early 1960s, however, anti-apartheid organizations including the Unity Movement increasingly espoused ideals of black consciousness. Presenting a united front, activists rejected the separatist idea of coloured and

21. Paul Gilroy, *The Black Atlantic: Modernity and Double Consciousness* (London, 1993), p. 39.
22. Pumla Dineo Gqola, *What Is Slavery to Me?: Postcolonial/Slave Memory in Post-Apartheid South Africa* (Johannesburg, 2010), pp. 205–209.
23. Khan, "Elim Slave Route", p. 22.
24. Ward and Worden, "Commemorating, Suppressing, and Invoking Cape Slavery", pp. 205–207.
25. *Ibid.*, p. 207.

black imposed by state racial categorization.[26] Accordingly, this prompted the end of using slavery as a metaphor and rallying point for coloured opponents of racial segregation.[27] Rather than looking to lineages such as slavery as a source of inspiration for contesting the segregationist present, a united front against racial persecution was presented by the victims of National Party legislation.

The white minority state, for its part, was also disinterested in histories such as slavery. Mirroring state-led commemorations of the centenary of abolition during the 1930s, National Party recognition of the past tended to obscure the history of slavery in order to buttress representations of settler hegemony. The state-led Cape Town celebrations of the 1952 tercentenary of Jan van Riebeeck's arrival at the Cape incorporated the experiences of coloured people through the lens of the exoticized "Malay" stereotype constructed by the commissioner for coloured affairs, I.D. du Plessis.[28] The term "Malay" had become synonymous for "Muslim" by the 1850s, referring primarily to the Muslim population living in Cape Town and the wider area, which could trace its origins variously to slaves and princely Indonesian political prisoners.[29] Owing perhaps to the way in which Islam was forbidden until the early nineteenth century and practised in secret, the Muslim community was somewhat distinct from the urban working-class settlements in which many slave descendants lived in the century following emancipation.[30] "Malay", however, was the extent of the apartheid regime's engagement with slavery, and du Plessis's attempts to construct a Malay identity downplayed the topic as an ancestral lineage to focus instead on princely origins, exotic cookery, dance rituals, and delicate physical features.[31] Official commemoration of the past in Cape Town's public spaces under apartheid was consequently directed away from recognizing the contributions made by enslaved people to forging the contemporary city.

26. Mohamed Adhikari, "From Narratives of Miscegenation to Post-Modernist Reimagining: Toward a Historiography of Coloured Identity in South Africa", *African Historical Review*, 40:1 (2008), pp. 79–80.

27. Gqola, *What Is Slavery To Me?*, pp. 41–42.

28. Leslie Witz, *Apartheid's Festival: Contesting South Africa's National Pasts* (Bloomington, IN, 2003), pp. 131–147.

29. Bickford-Smith, "Meanings of Freedom", pp. 298–299; Abdulkader Tayob, *Islam in South Africa: Mosques, Imams, and Sermons* (Gainesville, FL, 1999), pp. 21–25.

30. Bickford-Smith, "Meanings of Freedom", pp. 298–299; Bank, *Decline of Urban Slavery*, pp. 111–112.

31. Shamil Jeppie, "Reclassifications: Coloured, Malay, Muslim", in Zimitri Erasmus (ed.), *Coloured by History, Shaped by Place: New Perspectives on Coloured Identities in Cape Town* (Cape Town, 2001), pp. 84–94. More conservative Muslims were willing to work with du Plessis; however, active participants in the anti-apartheid movement were more inclined to reject the Malay construct.

The combined influences of state-imposed racial categories and opposition to these policies in the form of black consciousness resulted in a move away from earlier forms of remembering slavery among slave descendants in Cape Town. Indeed, it is only thanks to revisionist scholarship led by academics such as Mohamed Adhikari in the post-apartheid period that the idea of self-defined coloured identity under apartheid has become apparent.[32] Within this body of work, it has been suggested that the forging of a pan-African oppositional front to apartheid between coloured and black activists was an act limited to small numbers of coloured community leaders, with the majority of people continuing to live their lives defined by race.[33] Commenting on oral history work, Henry Trotter has suggested that apartheid and the trauma of forced displacement led to the creation of an alternative coloured metanarrative that emphasized the harmony of pre-Group Areas Act life. Through reminiscences, this rewriting of history offered people a means of coping with the often dangerous and dispiriting conditions in racially segregated townships on the Cape Flats where gang violence and drug abuse remain a feature of life today.[34] While this narrative offers evidence that coloured people developed their own identities under apartheid, this new self-generated version of the past ignored ancestral origins such as slavery much as did du Plessis's Malay identity construct. This process of memory displacement was not necessarily limited to people who suffered forced removals and also occurred in rural areas of the Western Cape where unequal access to resources has maintained a strict labour hierarchy over the centuries.[35]

AN INCLUSIVE CITY? REIMAGINING THE SLAVE PAST IN POST-APARTHEID CAPE TOWN

Present-day Cape Town is a city of great contrasts; a place where decades of formal racial segregation continue to influence where people live, work, and how they interact with the city space. Rudimentary shack housing in certain townships, informal settlements, and widespread homelessness stand in stark difference to the sleek towers of the central business district. Put bluntly,

32. This scholarship is associated chiefly with Adhikari but see also Erasmus, *Coloured by History*.

33. Shannon Jackson, "Coloureds don't Toyi-Toyi: Gesture, Constraint and Identity in Cape Town", in Steven L. Robins (ed.), *Limits to Liberation after Apartheid: Citizenship, Governance and Culture* (Oxford [etc.], 2005), p. 211.

34. Henry Trotter, "Trauma and Memory: The Impact of Apartheid-Era Forced Removals on Coloured Identity in Cape Town", in Mohamed Adhikari (ed.), *Burdened by Race: Coloured Identities in Southern Africa* (Cape Town, 2009), pp. 49–50.

35. Kerry Ward, *The Road to Mamre: Migration, Memory, and the Meaning of Community c.1900–1992* (MA thesis, University of Cape Town, 1992), pp. 152–154; Khan, "Elim Slave Route", pp. 30–33.

there is a far greater chance of being poor if you or your descendants were classified as black or coloured under apartheid than there is of occupying the same status if from a white family. The legacies of Group Areas forced removals are still evident in townships, which largely remain de facto racially segregated, and many black or coloured people experience the city as part of a daily process of commuting in the morning from non-central locations into the city to perform low-wage jobs before reversing the process in the evening. The centre of Cape Town and its immediate residential areas can be accurately described as exclusive spaces, where home ownership is restricted to all but the most affluent clients (Figure 1). The City of Cape Town municipality has actively sought to attract international investment to the central City Bowl, and has supported pledges of capital by implementing a number of City Improvement Districts that "tidy" areas using money raised in taxes levied against businesses. Courting this global investment has been cited as one of the main drivers of gentrification in contemporary Cape Town.[36] As much as Cape Town is now posited as an inclusive city, the resettlement of poorer residents from social housing to make way for developments has been portrayed as a perpetuation of apartheid-era forced removals by campaigners.[37]

The way in which private enterprise has often approached Cape Town's uncomfortable history of slavery has been frequently problematic, too. As Hall and Bombardella have explained, Cape Town redevelopment projects including the GrandWest Casino and Entertainment World, and Century City shopping centre are interested in the past only for the extent to which it can complement commercial activities. Elements of the past such as Cape Dutch architecture are selectively integrated into these developments in an attempt to evoke nostalgia and little else among customers.[38] Nigel Worden's work on the V&A Waterfront and its historical interpretation panels too demonstrates how the interests of business often work to obscure an open discussion of the past in Cape Town. For Worden, the Waterfront downplays the historical role of the harbour area as a site of enslavement, imprisonment,

36. Gustav Visser and Nico Kotze, "The State and New-build Gentrification in Central Cape Town, South Africa", *Urban Studies*, 45:12 (2008), pp. 2565–2593. Using the veneer of regeneration, state-led urban redevelopment projects are increasingly fuelling gentrification in South Africa. This follows an Anglo-American model of attempting to insert a city into a globalized world by courting investment from international parties.

37. "Reclaim the City". Available at: https://www.facebook.com/ReclaimCT/?fref=ts; last accessed 10 March 2017. Reclaim the City is a movement, popularized through social media, that aims to draw attention to the ongoing plight of Cape Town's poorer residents in its campaign to retain tenancy of social housing located in areas earmarked for redevelopment by the municipality.

38. Martin Hall and Pia Bombardella, "Paths of Nostalgia and Desire through Heritage Destinations at the Cape of Good Hope", in Noeleen Murray, Nick Shepherd, and Martin Hall (eds), *Desire Lines: Space, Memory and Identity in the Post-Apartheid City* (London [etc.], 2007), pp. 246–252.

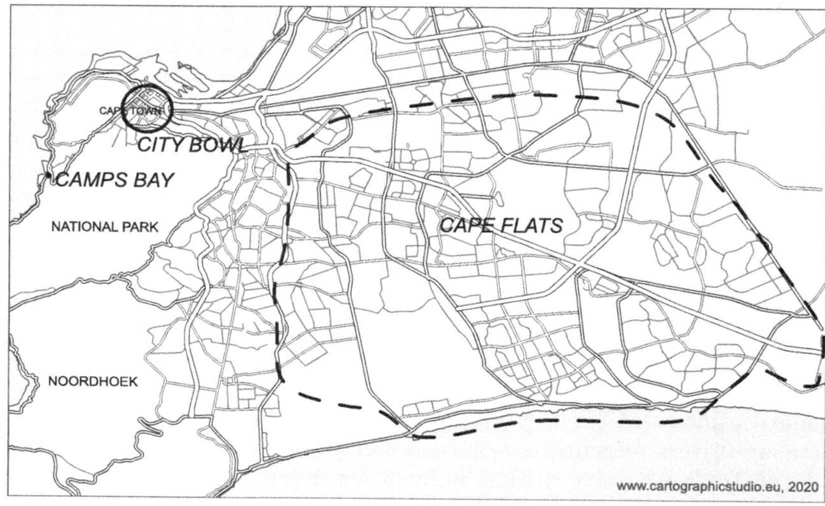

Figure 1. Map showing Cape Town including Cape Flats, City Bowl, and Camps Bay.

and working-class labour to portray a city at one with its dock area and thus posit its current role as a shopping and entertainment centre as an extension of this harmony to the present.[39] There seems to be little space for integrating difficult histories into commercially orientated redevelopments of the supposedly inclusive city that is Cape Town.

Although the egalitarianism of the immediate post-1994 period has faded in part through protests over service delivery, allegations of state-level corruption, and, arguably, a society that neoliberal economics have increasingly stratified along class lines, the democratic era has nonetheless provided fresh opportunities to explore identities among city dwellers. These questions are particularly pertinent for people – including slave descendants – who were classified as coloured under apartheid and the less formal segregation that preceded it. This was a category defined as being between two extremes, a catch-all term for people who were deemed neither white nor black. As a classification, it was premised upon the idea of being forged by racial mixture rather than an easily identifiable source of ancestry; on the idea of not adhering to binaries. The question of coloured identity has been a source of self-exploration for some in the post-apartheid era, although there has been

39. Nigel Worden, "Unwrapping History at the Cape Town Waterfront", *The Public Historian*, 16:2 (1994), pp. 38–45. Although Worden was writing over twenty years ago, his criticisms can still be applied to the contemporary Waterfront as subsequent revisions to historical interpretation at the complex have done little to offer a more balanced interpretation of the past.

something of a reluctance among coloured people to engage with the ideas of the African National Congress (ANC) state. There has typically been a fear among working-class coloured people that the "new" dispensation is more concerned with furthering the interests of people classified as black under apartheid than with coloured people, and that affirmative action policies are consequently more likely to benefit the former group.[40] These fears culminated in a vote for the National Party – the party that instituted apartheid – in the 1994 democratic elections among the Western Cape coloured electorate. Literary scholar Zoe Wicomb has argued that this defensive separatism arises from a sense of shame that has dominated the coloured outlook. For Wicomb, shame has been conditioned by the way in which coloured people were subjugated under slavery and consequently told they were inferior to white people by colonial and apartheid regimes.[41] This shame has manifested itself in various ways, from attempting to claim European lineage under apartheid to engineering distance from black people.

State policy in post-1994 South Africa has stressed the need to transform all areas of the country influenced by the legacies of apartheid-era racial segregation. This ranges from service distribution and residential patterns to employment practices and access to education. The idea of a shared national past has been an important component of attempts to create national cohesion, and has formed the centrepiece of the ANC's arts, culture, and heritage policies from 1994 onwards.[42] In spite of this agenda, sections of the post-apartheid ANC state have themselves not always been enthusiastic about what are perceived as coloured histories. Slavery has been one of these, and was viewed as a separatist threat to attempts to promote a shared national history that would buttress reconciliation attempts by some officials involved in meetings to open a Cape chapter of United Nations Educational, Scientific and Cultural Organization's global Slave Routes Project during the late 1990s.[43] Although then deputy president and future president Thabo Mbeki's 1996 "I Am an African" speech offered a broad definition of what it meant to belong to not only South Africa but to the wider continent, the interpretation of history often promoted by the ANC has tended to occupy a more narrow terrain. Opposition to apartheid, and particularly male-dominated political agitation, has been promoted as a unitary, shared history, with the new

40. Michael Besten, "'We Are the Original Inhabitants of This Land': Khoe-San Identity in Post-Apartheid South Africa", in Adhikari, *Burdened by Race*, p. 149.

41. Zoe Wicomb, "Shame and Identity: The Case of the Coloured in South Africa", in Derek Attridge and Rosemary Jolly (eds), *Writing South Africa: Literature, Apartheid, and Democracy, 1970–1995* (Cambridge [etc.], 1998), p. 100.

42. Republic of South Africa Department of Arts, Culture, Science and Technology, *White Paper on Arts, Culture and Heritage* (Pretoria, June 1996).

43. Nigel Worden, "The Changing Politics of Slave Heritage in the Western Cape, South Africa", *The Journal of African History*, 50:1 (March 2009), p. 29. See also Ward and Worden, p. 216.

South Africa forged as a nation that overcame oppression. Earlier human rights violations such as slavery and others conducted under colonialism have been relatively marginalized. The way in which the former prison complex on Robben Island was reopened as a museum in the late 1990s is emblematic of these tendencies. Posited as a site depicting the "triumph of the human spirit over suffering and hardship", the interpretation of the past offered on the site is a relatively narrow glimpse into the island's post-1960 use as a political prison.[44] Both the neglect of a centuries-old history of use as a site of exile and imprisonment, and a tendency to privilege ANC opposition to apartheid at the expense of other groups, have been noted as criticisms.[45] The sense that this can bypass coloured ancestral histories such as slavery builds upon claims in some quarters that the ANC is not interested in coloured people.

The work of small numbers of dedicated activists and museologists, as well as the idea that national reconciliation has lost currency as time has passed, has ensured that slavery is at least discussed by heritage spaces in Cape Town's urban centre. Wicomb's thoughts on shame effectively amounted to a call to embrace coloured identity as distinctive but simultaneously part of a wider black politics. Operating within the theoretical egalitarianism encouraged by the post-apartheid state, other coloured intellectuals have also called for people to redefine the meaning of "coloured", liberating it from its origins as a white supremacist imposition.[46] Independent of these debates, there has been a renewed focus in public discourse on the impact of colonialism on South Africa in recent years. In 2015, a student protest movement titled #RhodesMustFall identified the statue of the arch-imperialist Cecil Rhodes at the University of Cape Town's Upper Campus as representative of prevailing white privilege and a number of other inequalities in contemporary South African society. Taking Rhodes as an example of an individual who introduced lasting patterns of violence and trauma to South Africa, the students successfully campaigned for the removal of the statue. This protest movement precluded debates regarding decolonization that, though chiefly originating with the South African student population and targeted at the university sector, have extended to critiques of wider society. By design, such a discourse focuses on the salience of colonialism and how its influences continue to shape society today. There is a sense from these debates that the post-apartheid ANC state has not openly discussed these issues, with the landmark Truth and Reconciliation Commission primarily orientated towards enabling people to come to terms with lived human rights abuses. While community leaders are redefining identities in relation to racial categories imposed under

44. Annie Coombes, *History after Apartheid: Visual Culture and Public Memory in a Democratic South Africa* (Durham, NC [etc.], 2003), p. 58.
45. *Ibid.*, pp. 59–63, 77.
46. Ebrahim Rasool, "Unveiling the Heart of Fear", in Wilmot James, Daria Caliguire, Kerry Cullinan, Janet Levy, and Shauna Wescott (eds), *Now That We are Free: Coloured Communities in a Democratic South Africa* (Cape Town, 1996), p. 56.

colonialism and apartheid, there is a definite sense that broader society is gaining awareness of the more distant past.

Quite what resonance discourses surrounding identity and the colonial past have with working-class people is questionable; however, it would be fair to suggest that community leaders are very much part of the debates.[47] Identification as Khoisan has become relatively popular, enabling not only an alternative identity to coloured, but also allowing actors to contest first-nation people status previously limited to Bantu-speaking Africans.[48] Though less widely recognized, acknowledgement of slave ancestry has also become increasingly evident.[49] For some people, this involves identifying with ancestors who fought against slavocratic hegemony as a source of pride and guidance.[50] Accordingly, Adhikari has defined the present as a "third paradigm" in coloured identity politics; an era of "social constructivism" in which coloured identity is recognized as self-defined and reworked as such.[51]

Where slavery has been recalled by post-apartheid museological projects in Cape Town (Figure 2) it has not always been on harmonious terms with how coloured slave descendants view their ancestral histories. While enslavement has different meanings on a global scale, it is also understood differently on a much more local level, and contestations have frequently occurred in Cape Town over the representation of this past. The case of the Slave Lodge, a distinctive feature of Cape Town's built environment, demonstrates this point. Dating from 1679, the Slave Lodge is the second oldest building in Cape Town after the Castle of Good Hope, making it one of the oldest in South Africa. After the Cape became a British colony, use of the Lodge as slave quarters was gradually scaled back, and passed through various uses including as government offices, as a post office, and perhaps most famously as the Supreme Court building.[52] It entered its current phase in 1966 when it opened as the South Africa Cultural History Museum (SACHM), a satellite site of the South African Museum and its natural history exhibitions.[53] Typical of

47. Michele Ruiters, "Collaboration, Assimilation and Contestation: Emerging Constructions of Coloured Identity in Post-Apartheid South Africa", in Adhikari, *Burdened by Race*, p. 125.

48. Besten, "'We Are the Original Inhabitants of this Land'", pp. 134–156. "Khoisan" refers to the pastoral Khoi tribes and hunter-gatherer San or Bushmen. Following persecution under colonialism, descendants were absorbed into the coloured population.

49. This can be attributed to a climate in which self-exploration has been encouraged, as well as to more explicit attempts around the turn of the century by academics based at the University of Cape Town and University of the Western Cape to encourage coloured people to investigate their potential slave routes using archival material.

50. Patric Tariq Mellet (heritage activist and writer), in discussion with the author, Cape Town, 12 April 2016.

51. Adhikari, "From Narratives of Miscegenation", p. 91.

52. Helene Vollgraaff, *The Dutch East India Company's Slave Lodge at the Cape* (Cape Town, 1997), p. 7.

53. *Ibid.*

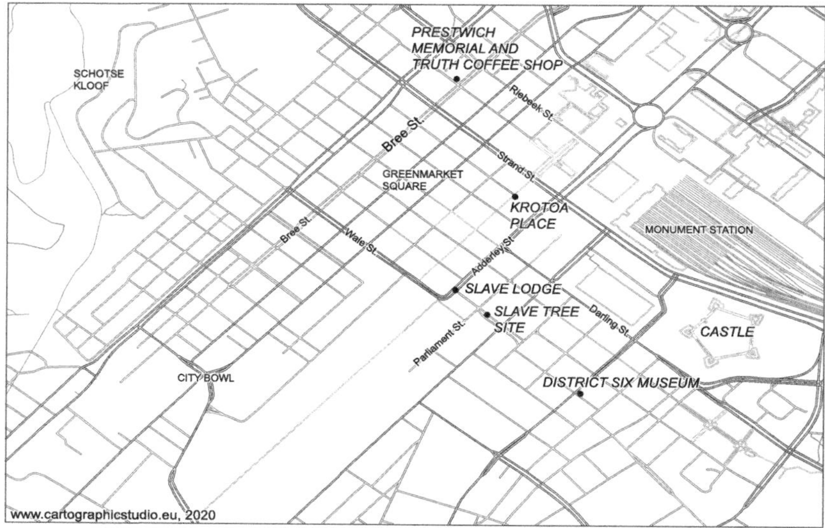

Figure 2. Map showing sites of slave memory in Cape Town's City Bowl.

apartheid-era museum displays, little reference was made to the lives of marginalized people in a museum that instead exhibited collections of Greek vases, Roman archaeology, Tibetan weaponry, and South African stamps.[54] Reflecting moves towards more inclusive representations of the past, the museum was renamed Slave Lodge in 1998, and thus theoretically was reconnected with its historical role as a site of confinement (Figure 3). It was shortly afterwards one of a number of state-funded museums grouped under the new southern state "flagship" museum management organization, Iziko Museums.[55]

This symbolic name change did not immediately herald any revisions to displays, and the museum's displays remain a visible legacy of apartheid, even today. While the ground floor has been redeveloped to host a permanent slavery exhibition and various temporary exhibitions with a human rights focus, much of the building's first floor continues to display apartheid-era SACHM exhibitions. In this sense, the Slave Lodge is almost a "meta-museum"; defining a space that tells us as much about the museological practices of the apartheid era as it does about Cape slavery. Current staff are well aware of these issues, although it has been suggested that its present form

54. Hans Fransen, *Guide to the Museums of Southern Africa* (Cape Town, 1978), pp. 23–25. See also Carohn Cornell, "Whatever Became of Slavery in Western Cape Museums?", *Kronos*, 25 (1998), pp. 259–279.

55. Iziko currently manages eleven sites in the Cape Town area.

Figure 3. The exterior of the Slave Lodge, 2015.

offers a useful case study of post-apartheid transformation and its limitations.[56] Various reasons including a prevailing institutional preoccupation with artefacts and funding deficiencies have been cited as factors that have stymied change.[57] Identity politics may have played a longer-term role, as some perceived the state to view the history of slavery as divisive during the late 1990s and early 2000s, a time when reconciliation was on the national agenda.[58] Consequently, governmental investment in new exhibitions at the Slave Lodge was not readily forthcoming.

Eventually, South Africa's first museum exhibition dedicated purely to Cape slavery opened in 2006 in the southern ground floor wing of the Slave Lodge. The *Remembering Slavery* exhibition offers a contextual background that makes clear to the visitor the context of Cape slavery in the Indian Ocean trading world, the origins of the people enslaved at the Cape, and the history of the Slave Lodge. Although one feature titled "Column of Light" (Figure 4) displays the names of some of the people who were forcibly confined in the

56. Paul Tichmann (Director Social History at Iziko Museums), in discussion with the author, Cape Town, 26 May 2016.
57. *Ibid.*
58. Anne Eichmann, "Representing Slavery in South Africa", in Robert Shell (ed.), *From Diaspora to Diorama: The Old Slave Lodge in Cape Town*, vol. 3 (Cape Town, 2013), pp. 3220–3240; Worden, "The Changing Politics of Slave Heritage", pp. 28–32. Promoting reconciliation was outlined as a responsibility of state-funded heritage sites in 1996 by Republic of South Africa, *White Paper on Arts, Culture and Heritage*.

Figure 4. The "Column of Light", 2015.

Slave Lodge, content exploring individual stories and human agency are relatively scarce. Part of this owes to the absence in South Africa of the kind of first-person narratives that characterize the retelling of transatlantic slavery. Simultaneously, the curatorial decision to depict the rebellion leaders on the VOC slave ship *Meermin* as "mutineers" raises questions as to whose perspective the *Remembering Slavery* exhibition advocates.[59] There is also a general lack of artefacts in the exhibition, reflecting how any relevant objects were not viewed as a priority for preservation by successive white supremacist regimes. As such, recreations take centre stage, including a mock-up slave ship hold and a simulation of life in the historic Slave Lodge.

Perhaps reflecting the perception held by some at the turn of the century that slavery was a divisive history, issues pertaining to coloured identity are almost entirely negated by the *Remembering Slavery* exhibition. Instead, Cape slavery is packaged within a reconciliatory discourse that posits it as a lesson both for South Africans and humanity. In this sense, *Remembering Slavery* shares many characteristics with what Paul Williams has identified as the "memorial museum". Williams explains a tendency for sites that commemorate notable atrocities to posit "their" atrocity as a lesson for humanity, along the lines of inviting visitors to pledge "never again".[60] He problematizes the way he claims that this universalizing narrative can in fact obscure the gravity of the event that the museum primarily is intended to commemorate.[61] At

59. VOC is an abbreviation for Vereenigde Oost-Indische Compagnie (Dutch East India Company).

60. Paul Williams, *Memorial Museums: The Global Rush to Commemorate Atrocities* (Oxford, 2007), pp. 153–155.

61. *Ibid.*, pp. 147–148.

the Slave Lodge, the evocation of this human rights discourse borrows both from global patterns of thought and from national efforts to posit common histories as a means of supporting post-apartheid reconciliation work. The opening of *Remembering Slavery* saw the Slave Lodge rebranded as a space with the motif, "human wrongs to human rights". The foyer area of the Slave Lodge informs the visitor that slavery "continues to exist in different forms" before offering statistics showing the number of people enslaved globally today (Figure 5). Other sections of the building that have been redeveloped host temporary exhibitions focusing on various elements of the anti-apartheid campaign. This is suggestive of a space that aims to portray a range of South African human rights abuses, and depict a nation that has overcome a challenging past.[62] In this sense, the discourse of national reconciliation that characterized the ANC's initial post-apartheid arts and culture policies is an evident influence in the exhibition.

In presenting a critical examination of the narrative on display at Elmina Castle in Ghana, Ana Lucia Araujo suggests that evoking a generalized human rights discourse in a slavery museum can marginalize the often fraught post-slavery experience of many slave descendants.[63] In the case of Elmina, compared with international visitors to the site, the local population lives in relative poverty, which can be partially attributed to the legacies of slavery and is visible to anyone visiting the castle.[64] Similar comments could be aimed at the Slave Lodge. Although – galvanized by the discovery of the wreck of the slaver *São José* off Camps Bay in 2015 – work is now underway to engage with communities who descend from enslaved people in Cape Town, the permanent displays at the Slave Lodge have typically been silent on issues of identity and legacy in the city. In contrast to Elmina, slavery's legacies are perhaps not quite so visible in Cape Town. The majority of the city's poorer residents continue to live in apartheid-era townships away from the city centre. These residential areas remain largely racially exclusive and are blighted by social problems, particularly gangsterism and substance abuse. Though connecting modern social problems with slavery is a fraught process, it would be fair to suggest that the descendants of people who were enslaved later experienced racial segregation and forced removal and currently form the backbone of Cape Town's labour force. Slavery's legacies arguably manifest in labour organization and access to socio-economic resources today. The visibility of these effects may have been removed from the city centre, but they continue to shape the city itself. A narrative that posits a glorious present in the way reconciliation discourse in South Africa has done marginalizes the

62. The potential impact of such a narrative is arguably stymied at present in the Slave Lodge by the number of displays that are remnants of the SACHM and have yet to be removed.
63. Ana Lucia Araujo, *Shadows of the Slave Past: Memory, Heritage, and Slavery* (Florence, 2014), p. 53.
64. *Ibid.*

Figure 5. Displays in the foyer area of the Slave Lodge, 2015.

ongoing dislocation experienced by many South Africans. In this sense, people are potentially further alienated, rather than brought together in commonality as intended. Numerous conclusions can be drawn from this point. First, the weaknesses of national metanarratives in terms of facilitating discussion of the past are revealed. The possibility of slavery ever functioning as part of such a narrative is highlighted, as are the problems inherent in trying to provide closure on the past when its legacies still figure in the lives of the people effected.

This tension between Cape Town's slave past, the everyday lives of slave descendants, and differing approaches to slavery as an identity issue was revealed in visceral terms by debates raised by excavations in the Prestwich Street area in the 2000s. In 2003 developer Ari Estathiou of Styleprops Ltd stumbled across human remains while laying the foundations for an exclusive apartment development in the Green Point area of Cape Town. The presence of similar unmarked gravesites for Cape Town's marginalized classes dating from the Dutch and British colonial eras is well known to academics.[65] This was quite literally a case of the dead and their memories resurfacing in a society that had largely forgotten them. Following protocol, the developer notified the South African Heritage Resources Agency (SAHRA), construction was halted, and a public consultation process launched. Two sides of the debate immediately crystalized. On the one hand, a predominantly coloured group of people organizing as the Hands-Off Prestwich Street Ad Hoc Committee objected to both the development and potential exhumation of the human remains, having identified them as belonging to their enslaved

65. Nick Shepherd and Christian Ernsten, "The World Below: Post-Apartheid Urban Imaginaries and the Bones of the Prestwich Street Dead", in Murray *et al.*, *Desire Lines*, pp. 215–216.

ancestors. Opposing these activists were a group comprised of academics – including archaeologists and human biologists – who, tacitly supported by SAHRA, supported the exhumation of the bones on the grounds of the unprecedented opportunities the discovery presented for furthering knowledge of a period of time largely understood through the colonial documentary archive.[66] Following an emotive and charged campaign, the development was permitted to proceed and the bones exhumed, although biological testing has been forbidden and access restricted via an application process including a panel comprising campaigners from both sides of the argument.[67] At the time of writing, no research applications have been accepted.

As Shepherd and Ernsten argue, the exhumation debate reflected who does and does not have access to power and voice in post-apartheid South Africa.[68] While the issue of exhumation was being contested, there was a sense of an emotive connection with assumed ancestors colliding with the regulations and management speak of the new elite. Running throughout was a sense that local government officials and coloured identity activists did not share the same interpretation of the slave past, with the former misunderstanding its importance to small, vocal groups of people. These themes again moved to the forefront with the opening of coffee shop Truth on the grounds of the Prestwich Memorial, and their recurrence is probably the result of ignorance towards slavery and the way in which it has been disremembered over time. Although members of the PPPC had been involved in the constructive dialogical process behind the original opening of the memorial, the City of Cape Town municipality failed to consult with them before accepting Donde's proposal.[69] They had approved plans originally circulated prior to the memorial's opening for some form of small-scale tea kiosk, but argued that the scale of the Truth cafe surpassed this.[70] It is difficult to disagree with this point. The presence of Truth gives the memorial building a coffee shop ambience, with the rattle of cutlery, scraping of chair legs across the floor, and filling of coffee cups dominating the soundscape. Menus for the coffee shop have even been placed among the interpretive

66. *Ibid.*, pp. 217–223.

67. For detailed accounts of the consultation process from perspectives sympathetic to the arguments proposed by anti-exhumation campaigners, see Shepherd and Ernsten, "The World Below", pp. 215–233; Nick Shepherd, "Archaeology Dreaming: Post-Apartheid Urban Imaginaries and the Bones of the Prestwich Street Dead", *Journal of Social Archaeology*, 7:1 (2007), pp. 3–28; Heidi Grunebaum, *Memorializing the Past: Everyday Life in South Africa after the Truth and Reconciliation Commission* (New Brunswick, NJ, 2011), p. 130. For the viewpoint of some of the academics who supported exhumation, see Antonia Malan and Nigel Worden, "Constructing and Contesting Histories of Slavery at the Cape, South Africa", in Paul J. Lane and Kevin C. MacDonald (eds), *Slavery in Africa: Archaeology and Memory* (Oxford [etc.], 2011), pp. 409–411.

68. Shepherd and Ernsten, "The World Below", pp. 222–223.

69. "Coffee Shop 'Out of Place' at Memorial", *The Cape Towner*, 22 April 2010.

70. *Ibid.*

Figure 6. The exterior of the Prestwich Memorial, 2015.

panels, and there is a sense that the visitor must request permission to proceed to the memorial area from Truth staff.

The way in which Truth conceives its connection to the Prestwich Memorial (Figures 6 and 7) serves to reinforce perceptions of exclusivity and restricted voice. Though now replaced with a revised design that makes no reference to the memorial, Truth's website at one stage included astoundingly crass claims to how "a growing number of Cape Town locals, tourists and coffee aficionados have unwittingly been lured to this undercover burial ground. And been given a taste [of] how good slavery can be [...] (To artisan coffee of course, in this case!)".[71] It referred not to a complex and contested history, but carelessly described the human remains interred in the same building as "skeletons in our closet". This light-hearted and disrespectful attitude to the past serves to appropriate what is for some a personal and emotive history for commercial gain. It is useful here to note M. Christine Boyer's incisive analysis of city planning. Boyer argues that, in redeveloping urban areas, middle-class professionals subscribe to the concept of a universal "community", eschewing the possibility that not every resident of the city holds the means to access and participate in what often becomes a process of gentrification.[72]

71. The current edition of Truth's website (https://truth.coffee/; last accessed 16 December 2019) omits this text.

72. M. Christine Boyer, *The City of Collective Memory: Its Historical Imagery and Architectural Entertainments* (Cambridge [etc.], 1996), p. 9.

Figure 7. The interior of the Prestwich Memorial, ossuary area behind the black gate, 2015.

This process played out at Prestwich. Largely removed from city centre residence by apartheid-era racial segregation and excluded from returning by high property prices in prime locations, slave descendants have been refused a stake in the memorialization process by the same forces of gentrification and an assumption that everyone has equal access to resources in post-apartheid South Africa. Much like representations of slavery at the Slave Lodge, this approach to the past posits slavery as a universal history. The terms by which it does it, however, are different. They originate not from a fundamental subscription – however justifiable in reality – to using the past to encourage positive change, but from a sense that history is malleable for commercial gain, with its specificities expendable on the grounds that the past is a distant place with scant resonance among contemporary Capetonians. The remnants of slavery in the form of its unnamed dead become linked with its legacies in the continued marginalization of slave descendants in Cape Town's public sphere today. Working-class Capetonians are excluded from gentrified spaces on economic grounds, and there is a sense that their concerns are not taken on board by municipality bureaucrats. As with the *Remembering Slavery* exhibition at the Slave Lodge, the possibility of slavery functioning in the tapestry of identities that form modern Cape Town is marginalized, as is the significance of this history to groups of activists.

Evidence drawn from the contestations surrounding Prestwich and recent developments at the Slave Lodge do however point towards the possibility of slavery being embraced as an ancestral identity in Cape Town. The rediscovery of the remains of the Portuguese slaver *São José* off the coast of Camps Bay in 2015 by a team led by members of Iziko's maritime archaeology unit has heralded new possibilities for the museum's future.[73] Although a number of the artefacts recovered have been loaned to the Smithsonian's National Museum of African American History and Culture, which part-funded the project, a portion were retained in Cape Town for an exhibition that opened in December 2018. The artefacts include copper fastenings and ballast items and represent not only rare examples of items preserved from a slave ship, but also the kind of tangible links with the slave past that are widely absent from Cape Town. Iziko organized a number of public events – beginning with a June 2015 symposium titled "Bringing the *São José* into Memory" – with the aim of reaching a consensus as to how to display the artefacts and communicate their significance. At an event in April 2016, community representatives and staff discussed ancestral links with Mozambique.[74] This highlights how the *São José* rediscovery has not only galvanized a more outward-facing approach at Iziko, but has also encouraged people to consider where slavery fits in to their lineage.

This change of approach at Iziko and more open discussion of slavery and its legacies sit within a broader context of an increased focus on the more distant past. In successfully campaigning for the removal of the Rhodes statue, the student activists who formed #RhodesMustFall in 2015 suggested that colonial-era injustices require discussion to enable South Africa to come to terms with its role in establishing patterns of socio-economic inequality that persist in the present. In a nation that used the Truth and Reconciliation Commission to come to terms with apartheid, longer-term systemic issues have perhaps been marginalized. The way historical slavery has been viewed by various branches of government and museum professionals is a strong example of this. Not only was it frequently ignored, but the way that the Prestwich consultation was carried out and the narrative voice adopted in *Remembering Slavery* seemed to deny its relevance to questions of identity. While the example of the Truth coffee shop suggests that there is still distance to be travelled before this significance is universally understood, the open approach Iziko has taken to the *São José* artefacts points towards an interpretation of slavery that reconnects urban Capetonians with its impact on the contemporary city and its inhabitants. Developing these themes, a temporary exhibition titled *My Naam is Februarie: Identities Rooted in Slavery* opened at the Slave Lodge in October 2016. Based on the idea of a calendar designed

73. The vessel foundered in 1794 while crossing the Atlantic with an estimated 212 out of a human cargo of around 500 perishing. "South Africans Honour Slaves Drowned in 1794 Shipwreck", *Mail & Guardian*, 2 June 2015.

74. This event formed part of the international Slave Wrecks Project, a collaboration between a number of museums including Iziko and the Smithsonian. As well as enslaved Mozbiekers, twentieth-century workers in South African mines who originated in Mozambique were also discussed, as was the existence of families with distinctive Mozambique heritage in pre-Group Areas Act District Six.

by the marketing company Geometry Global whose creative director approached Iziko with the belief that the Cape's slave heritage warranted greater discussion, the exhibition matched each month of the year with the surname of a participant. John January represented January, Felix February for February, and so forth, with obvious links to slave naming patterns at the Cape. An accompanying video featured participants reflecting on this heritage, with several commenting how in the past these links were simply not discussed at family or any other level. Speaking about these previously unspeakable, long-term legacies is a role that a Slave Lodge mindful of the way in which history impacts contemporary residents of Cape Town can play. The previously unspoken legacies of slavery encoded in the city's contemporary population begin to become visible, and slavery gains greater recognition as an ancestry.

The debates generated by Prestwich, and interest in recent museological milestones in the *São José* rediscovery and the *My Naam is Februarie* exhibition point towards the sense that identification with slavery is being embraced by descendants of the enslaved in Cape Town. Increasingly, the same activists who object to developments such as Prestwich and question the interpretation of slavery visible at the Slave Lodge are offering their own interpretations of Cape slavery to the public. These representations offer alternative meanings of slavery, identifying the institution as an ancestral history, rather than as a universal lesson for humanity. Although the number of people openly claiming slave ancestry and espousing an identity based around recognition of these roots remains relatively small, these claims have nonetheless increased in volume and acceptance in the 2010s. This perhaps owes itself to efforts by historians of Cape slavery to veritably "reconnect" people with their history by encouraging genealogical enquiries, increased visibility of slavery through public exhibitions such as *Remembering Slavery*, and people gradually acknowledging calls by coloured community leaders to revaluate how they define themselves. Although *Remembering Slavery* should be accorded with influence in terms of raising awareness of the history of Cape slavery, it has frequently attracted criticism from people claiming slave ancestry for the way it represents this past. As the Prestwich case highlights, there is frequently a disconnect between how Cape Town's slave past is imagined by people identifying as slave descendants and representations of this past by state-funded heritage projects.

Lucy Campbell is one person who has used the public space created by the heritage industry to contest representations of what she perceives as a personal history. As a coloured woman born under apartheid, Campbell intertwines numerous traumatic histories into the forthright narrative offered on historical walking tours of Cape Town. The name of her company, Transcending History Tours, is indicative of the way she questions the "official" narrative, and urges alternative interpretations of the past that resonate with everyday Capetonians. Her tours seek to illuminate the imprints made by the forgotten history of slavery on the urban landscape and offer a reminder of the disadvantages suffered by many slave descendants today. She is critical of the Slave Lodge, claiming that the *Remembering Slavery* exhibition fails to speak to communities by negating to engage with the more violent aspects of Cape slavery.[75] In this sense, the concept of slavery as a traumatic foundational experience that ancestors overcame is similar to the way in which transatlantic slavery has often been remembered by African American people.[76]

Identifying with a broad Khoisan and slave ancestry, Campbell claims to have become enthralled with this past while working in customer service for Iziko at Groot Constantia.[77] Reading about the lives of people enslaved on the estate gave her a sense of place previously lacking, and motivated her to embark upon what she describes as a therapeutic journey of self-discovery.[78] It is this therapy-through-history she now aims to facilitate through her walking tours. These tours exist in a competitive heritage market in Cape Town, with numerous other operators offering what are frequently sanitized narratives of reconciliation and post-apartheid prosperity as the logical outcome of a troubled history to international visitors. Although Campbell concedes that the majority of Cape Town's working-class residents are too preoccupied with the daily struggles of life to engage with subversive interpretations of a past that they may not even acknowledge exists, she is still able to act as a willing spokesperson for this group to the non-governmental organizations and academics who provide the bulk of her customers.[79]

A tour in September 2015 involving a mixed-age community group from Tafelsig on the Cape Flats was perhaps an exceptional case. On this occasion, Campbell was able to play the role of facilitator in reconnecting people with a forgotten past. Starting at the Castle of Good Hope – the oldest colonial building in Cape Town – she urged the group to embrace their history as far back as colonial times. This, she explained, would initiate a therapeutic process as it would enable them to better understand the social problems facing their communities today. Throughout the tour, Campbell highlighted various objects of historical interest and reminded the group of the contributions their ancestors made towards constructing modern Cape Town. The way in which this contribution had largely been written out of the cityscape by the selective memorialization of colonial notables figured prominently, and the group appeared to embrace this narrative. At the Castle, for example, one member of the group

75. Lucy Campbell, in discussion with the author, Cape Town, 29 June 2015.
76. Christine Mullen Kreamer, "Shared Heritage, Contested Terrain: Cultural Negotiation and Ghana's Cape Coast Castle Museum Exhibition 'Crossroads of People, Crossroads of Trade'", in Ivan Karp, Corrine A. Kratz, Lynn Szwaja, and Tomas Ybarra-Frausto, with Gustavo Buntinx, Barbara Kirshenblatt-Gimblett, and Ciraj Rassool, (eds), *Museum Frictions: Public Cultures/Global Transformations* (Durham, NC [etc.], 2006), pp. 443–454.
77. Campbell, discussion.
78. *Ibid.*
79. *Ibid.*

attempted to claim free entry on the grounds that they descended from the people whose labour constructed the building. The VOC emblems fixed to the pavement of the renamed Krotoa Place were symbolically stamped upon. A mock slave auction was conducted at the former site of the slave tree on Spin Street, with participants asked to visualize what their ancestors suffered in their status as the property of strangers. By the end, the group were chanting "We are slaves! We are San! We are Khoi!" and had pledged to establish their own community history museum in Tafelsig to contest some of the narratives on offer in central Cape Town.

This particular tour evidences how working-class people can take note of calls from community leaders in terms of reconsidering the self. This is one of the primary means by which awareness of slave ancestry is spreading in Cape Town. For the community group, Campbell was not only a tour guide offering an alternative historical narrative but a relatable voice who understood the social problems facing poorer areas of Cape Town having experienced them first-hand herself. This understanding and associated advocacy reveals an additional dimension to how slave memory is resurfacing in post-apartheid South Africa, recalling the claims of political activists during the first half of the nineteenth century. Identifying slavery as an institution that caused suffering for their ancestors, activists such as Campbell compare this experience with the socio-economic lot of Cape Town's poorer communities – and particularly likely slave descendants – today. Understanding this history also enables people to make claims for increased recognition in the present on the grounds of their ancestors' contribution to shaping history, thus highlighting a parallel with the Khoisan movement and a sense of how claiming a slave ancestry may gain broader traction.[80] This forms the basis of critiques of post-apartheid society, making it possible to highlight how working-class people remain marginalized in spite of liberations from slavery in 1834 and from apartheid in 1994. While with the group from Tafelsig, Campbell identified the psychological remnants of enslavement among Cape Town's coloured population as manifesting in substance abuse and employment practices.

It is in this sense that memory of slavery in Cape Town can increasingly be thought of as the "living intellectual resource" Gilroy wrote of in the transatlantic sense.[81] A reimagined narrative of slavery in which ancestors form the basis of a proud and emotive connection with the past is mobilized to critique the present. Criticisms do not only cover socio-economic inequalities, but, as the case of the PPPC demonstrated, can also be applied to the way in which

80. The aforementioned attempt to gain free entry to the Castle exemplified this tendency. Press articles such as "Slaves: South Africa's First Freedom Fighters", *Mail & Guardian*, 4 December 2015, demonstrate how there is an increasing awareness of the contribution enslaved people made to shaping South Africa.
81. Gilroy, *Black Atlantic*, p. 39.

Figure 8. Participants in the 2015 1 December commemorations gathered at the Castle, Cape Town.

activists perceive the post-1994 state to have marginalized "their" history. Renewed efforts to commemorate 1 December as Emancipation Day over the past decade have frequently adopted this rhetoric. Led primarily by the acclaimed independent District Six Museum, a midnight march on 30 November is currently held on the streets of Cape Town each year, recalling the commemorations led by slave descendants during the nineteenth and early twentieth centuries. This event draws in an increasingly large audience, many of whom come from poorer communities on the Cape Flats. The 2015 event culminated with entertainment in the form of music and dance at the Castle (Figure 8). The Castle's CEO, Calvyn Gilfellan, who has been instrumental in inviting heritage activists to use what was previously considered a colonial space since being appointed in 2013, delivered a short address to the gathered crowd. "Our communities are still enslaved", he reminded them, with "enslavement" in this sense referring to sexual violence, the debilitating influence of AIDS on poorer communities, and prevailing substance abuse in townships. "Enslavement" here acts as a proxy for the ways in which the past has dictated troubles in present-day South Africa. The communities Gilfellan was addressing were enslaved by the Dutch, enslaved by the racial segregation of the British and apartheid eras, and remain enslaved by injustice now. In evoking this memory, community leaders are actively reconnecting people with history in a way that was popularized by predecessors opposing racial segregation in the early twentieth century.

CONCLUSION

Slavery is resurfacing in post-apartheid Cape Town in a number of different ways. Over time, this urban space has been built on slavery, remembered slavery selectively, forgotten it entirely, and now hosts contested claims to its meaning today. Political activists during the early twentieth century frequently used the imagery of slavery as a means of analysing progress towards political freedoms; however, the memorial practices and everyday suffering unleashed by formal racial segregation necessitated the disremembering of this past. The post-apartheid state has focused on coming to terms with the more recent past, often marginalizing the influence of more distant colonial history in the process. It is only in recent years that this past has gained greater public exposure through the efforts of identity activists, museologists, and political activists calling for decolonization. The often highly personalized identification with the slave past evoked by community historians is frequently at odds with the way in which state-funded museums such as the Slave Lodge interpret slavery in more universal terms. Here, the city's past is the basis for a lesson in human rights, with deference both to national discourses of reconciliation and international human rights exhibitions in museums. Elsewhere, Cape Town's history of slavery has clashed with urban redevelopment programmes. In the case of the rediscovered bones in Prestwich and their subsequent memorial, the interests of the municipality, private business, and people who identify as slave descendants were not harmonious. There was a sense here of intergenerational exclusion, from enslavement in the colonial era, racial segregation under apartheid, and exclusion from the post-apartheid order for coloured people. Arguably, the concerns raised by activists claiming slave ancestry require greater attention from all parties concerned if Cape Town is to truly eschew the legacies of enslavement in the post-apartheid era.

IRSH 65 (2020), pp. 225–236 doi:10.1017/S0020859020000164

Afterword: Ghosts of Slavery

Ana Lucia Araujo

Department of History, Howard University
Washington DC, 20059, United States

E-mail: aaraujo@howard.edu

Abstract: This afterword engages with the theme of this Special Issue by discussing the significance of urban slavery in slave societies and societies where chattel slavery existed in Europe, Africa, and the Americas. It discusses how, despite the omnipresence of slavery in cities such as Rio de Janeiro, Salvador, New York, and Charleston, the tangible traces of the inhuman institution were gradually erased from the public space. It also emphasizes that, despite this annihilation, over the last three decades, black social actors have made significant interventions to make the slavery past of Atlantic cities visible again.

With the emergence of the Atlantic slave trade, plantation slavery shaped the development of slave societies in the Americas. Yet, as all the articles in this Special Issue have demonstrated, slavery was also present in many urban settings of societies where bondage was central or existed in the three continents involved in the inhuman commerce. Especially during the so-called age of abolition, a period covering more than one century (c.1770s–c.1880s), urban slavery continued to be prominent. Cities were spaces where enslaved and freed people joined rebellions, formed fugitive communities, and petitioned the courts to obtain their freedom. In the age of abolition, enslaved, freed, and free black urban populations also participated in campaigns to pass legislation to end slavery. However, in 1888, when slavery was eventually abolished in all societies of the Americas, cities continued to be the site of racial and social inequalities. Although offering opportunities of social mobility for the descendants of enslaved men and women, cities remained the privileged space where black social actors persisted in fighting against racism.

As early as in the sixteenth century, European artists painted people of African descent performing all kinds of activities near the Chafariz-del-Rey in Lisbon (Figure 1). Many contemporary observers, including European travelers, extensively commented on the strong presence of enslaved, freed, and free black men and women in the cities of Latin America and the Caribbean. Several of these travelers, like the French artists Jean-Baptiste Debret (1768–1848),

Figure 1. *Chafariz d'el Rei*, c.1560–1580, anonymous Flemish painting, oil on wood, 93 × 163 cm, Berardo Collection, Lisbon, Portugal.
Source info: © Wikimedia Commons.

Édouard Manet (1848–1883), and later François-Auguste Biard (1799–1882), who visited Brazil in the second half of the nineteenth century, were often surprised that when walking the streets of Rio de Janeiro and Salvador they rarely saw any white individuals, but could only identify black women, especially street vendors (Figure 2).[1] Despite the racist views of their authors, European travelogues provide a wealth of information on urban slavery in the Americas. Through texts and images, these travelers described how slavery shaped the urban landscapes, with its places of physical violence and suffering such as whipping posts and slave markets and its refuge spaces such as the churches housing Catholic black brotherhoods.

As historian Rashauna Johnson explains, in port cities like New Orleans, enslaved persons "were commodities in the flesh trade, laborers who produced addictive staple crops, consumers who purchased local and imported goods, vendors who peddled products to multilingual customers, and modes of transport to buyer and sellers".[2] In port and inland cities such as Rio de Janeiro, Sabará, Baltimore, Bridgetown, New York City, Lima, Puebla, Cartagena, Quito, as well as Lisbon, Seville, Luanda, and Benguela, enslaved men had a

1. Ana Lucia Araujo, *Brazil Through French Eyes: A Nineteenth-Century Artist in the Tropics* (Albuquerque, NM, 2015), pp. 76–78.
2. Rashauna Johnson, *Slavery's Metropolis: Unfree Labor in New Orleans during the Age of Revolutions* (New York, 2016), p. 56.

Figure 2. "Les rafraîchissements de l'après dîner sur la place du palais" [After-dinner refreshments in the Palace Square]. Jean-Baptiste Debret, *Voyage pittoresque et historique au Brésil* (Paris, 1834–1839), plate 9.
Source info: The Miriam and Ira D. Wallach Division of Art, Prints and Photographs: Print Collection, The New York Public Library. New York Public Library Digital Collections. Available at: http://digitalcollections.nypl.org/items/510d47df-7978-a3d9-e040-e00a18064a99; last accessed: 29 December 2019.

variety of professions: they were coachmen; porters; barbers; gardeners; shoemakers; surgeons; healers; carpenters; tailors; craftsmen; blacksmiths; hatters; and silversmiths, whereas enslaved women could work in convents and shops and were also street vendors, prostitutes, nannies, wet nurses, cooks, washerwomen, and domestic servants.[3]

3. There is an abundant literature on slavery in each of these cities; see among many others: Mary Karasch, *Slave Life in Rio de Janeiro, 1808–1850* (Princeton, NJ, 1987); Mariana Dantas, *Black Townsmen: Urban Slavery and Freedom in the Eighteenth-Century Americas* (New York, 2008); Marisa J. Fuentes, *Dispossessed Lives: Enslaved Women, Violence and the Archive* (Philadelphia, PA, 2016); Leslie M. Harris, *In the Shadow of Slavery: African Americans in New York City, 1626–1863* (Chicago, IL, 2003); Michelle A. McKinley, *Fractional Freedoms: Slavery, Intimacy, and Legal Mobilization in Colonial Lima, 1600–1700* (New York, 2016); Pablo Miguel Sierra Silva, *Urban Slavery in Colonial Mexico: Puebla de los Ángeles, 1531–1706* (New York, 2019); Sherwin K. Bryant, *Rivers of Gold, Lives of Bondage: Governing Through Slavery in Colonial Quito* (Chapel Hill, NC, 2014); Arlindo Manuel Caldeira, *Escravos em Portugal. Das origens ao século XIX* (Lisbon, 2017); Alessandro Stella, *Histoire d'esclaves dans*

Urban areas were places of struggle and resistance, where bondsmen and bondswomen wandered, gossiped, and hid. Along the network of dark and stinking streets, in several cities of the American continent bondspeople plotted conspiracies and rebellions. Led and supported by enslaved, freed, and freeborn black individuals, the Denmark Vesey's conspiracy in 1822 and the Malê rebellion in 1835, respectively, emerged in the urban settings of Charleston, South Carolina and Salvador, Bahia. The streets of Philadelphia and Baltimore also offered enslaved people the ideal context to run away from bondage.[4] Yet, during the decades that preceded the beginning of the Civil War, cities also provided opportunities to professional gangs of kidnappers to abduct free black men, women, and children and sell them into slavery in the United States South.[5] Still, cities were sites where enslaved people preserved, adapted, and recreated African cultures, by preparing food and prescribing remedies whose recipes they had brought from the African continent. For enslaved people and their descendants, the urban fabric was also the stage for drumming, dancing, singing, reveling, and participating in religious and pagan festivals. Afro-Brazilian martial arts, dance, and music such as capoeira and samba emerged during slavery in Brazilian cities like Salvador and Rio de Janeiro. Bondspeople also paraded in religious processions and celebrated carnivals in the streets of Havana, New Orleans, Nassau, and Kingston.

The rise of gradual abolition in the late eighteenth and early nineteenth century progressively provoked the disappearance of tangible traits of urban bondage. The streets and buildings where slavery bloomed were transformed by several layers of works intended to sanitize and modernize the cities. Black populations were not welcome in this process. Still, many towns of the Atlantic world preserved entertainments, music festivals, and dance traditions that emerged with the development of slavery and the growth of black populations in urban areas. Over the twentieth century and during the two first decades of the twenty-first century, black men, women, and children who have been historically identified as descendants of enslaved people have continued

la péninsule ibérique (Paris, 2000); Roquinaldo Ferreira, *Cross-Cultural Exchange in the Atlantic World: Angola and Brazil During the Era of the Slave Trade* (New York, 2012); Mariana P. Candido, *An African Slaving Port and the Atlantic World: Benguela and Its Hinterland* (New York, 2013); and Jorge Cañizares-Esguerra, Matt D. Childs, and James Sidbury (eds), *The Black Urban Atlantic in the Age of the Slave Trade* (Philadelphia, PA, 2013).

4. See the case of Ona Judge, an enslaved woman owned by George Washington, who escaped from bondage while in Philadelphia; Erica Dunbar, *Never Caught: The Washington's Relentless Pursuit of Their Runaway Slave, Ona Judge* (New York, 2017).

5. Historian Richard Bell explores the history of one of these gangs who kidnapped five black boys in Philadelphia in 1825; see Richard Bell, *Stolen: Five Free Boys Kidnapped into Slavery and Their Astonishing Odyssey Home* (New York, 2019). Likewise, Henrietta Wood, a freedwoman, was kidnapped and sold into slavery in Cincinnati in 1853; see W. Caleb McDaniel, *Sweet Taste of Liberty: A True Story of Slavery and Restitution in America* (New York, 2019).

to struggle to occupy the public spaces of cities built with slave labor. Maintaining this presence has always been a difficult challenge. The state and its institutions, such as the courts of justice and the police, have criminalized black people's participation in carnivals, samba parties, capoeira circles, and African-based religious ceremonies. Many decades after its end, the violence of slavery still marks many cities in the Americas. In 2019, attending a funk ball in one of Rio de Janeiro's favelas can be the equivalent of a death sentence. Likewise, in the United States, because they were black, men and women have been profiled, targeted, and killed by police officers in Charleston, Ferguson, New York City, Cleveland, Baltimore, and many other cities.

The ghosts of slavery continue to haunt former slave ports and cities where slavery once existed. Slave wharfs, cemeteries, and markets were among the central tangible sites associated with slavery and the Atlantic slave trade. Although their traces have survived, in many cities of the Atlantic world they also remain unnoticed in the public space. The slave markets of Salvador and Rio de Janeiro attracted the attention of European travelers who visited Brazil. Amédée François Frézier, a Savoyard military man who had traveled to Chile, Peru, and Brazil between 1712 and 1714, describes Salvador's slave market in his travelogue: "There are shops full of these poor unfortunates that are exposed all naked, and they bought them like animals and acquire upon them the same power, so that on minor discontent, they can kill them almost with impunity, or at least mistreat them as cruelly as they want".[6] Likewise, British traveler Thomas Lindley, who sojourned in Bahia in 1802, also provides a description of a slave market in Salvador: "The streets and squares of the city are thronged with groups of human beings, exposed for sale at the doors of the different merchants to whom they belong; five slave ships having arrived within the last three days".[7] British traveler Maria Graham who visited the port area of Salvador's Lower City described it as being the place where the slave market was located: "passing the arsenal gate, we went along the low street, and found it widen considerably at three quarters of a mile beyond: there are the markets, which seem to be admirably supplied, especially with fish. There also is the slave market, a sight I have not yet learned to see without shame and indignation".[8] But despite these accounts, to this day no markers indicate where these sites were located. This absence has led city residents to develop accounts according to which

6. Amédée François Frézier, *Relation du voyage de la mer du Sud aux côtes du Chili et du Pérou fait pendant les années 1712, 1713, et 1714* (Paris, 1716), vol. 2, p. 533.

7. Thomas Lindley, *Narrative of a Voyage to Brazil: Terminating in the Seizure of a British Vessel; with General Sketches of the Country, its Natural Productions, Colonial Inhabitants* (London, 1805), p. 176.

8. Maria Graham, *Journal of a Voyage to Brazil and Residence There, During Part of the Years 1821, 1822, and 1823* (London, 1824), p. 137.

the basement of the present-day central market, known as Mercado Modelo, was a former slave market.[9] Residents report that they can hear the laments of enslaved persons who were held in the basement during the night. Stories of ghosts of enslaved men and women are also widespread in cities such as New Orleans, where ghost tours disseminate similar narratives.[10] These stories, expressing how the collective and public memory of slavery has been repressed in former slave societies, show how social actors continuously respond to the lack of initiatives publicly recognizing sites of slavery. By relying on existing images and recollections, narratives of slave ghosts allow black citizens to imagine where slave markets were located and what the experience of confinement was like for enslaved individuals in these slave depots.

Despite the long-lasting invisibility of slavery in the public space of former slave societies and societies where slavery existed, there are signs that this context is changing. After creating a Slave Trail Commission in 1998, the city of Richmond, capital of Virginia, in the United States, conceived a self-guided walking trail highlighting the city's sites associated with slavery and the Atlantic slave trade. In 2011, Richmond eventually unveiled seventeen markers along the trail. Likewise, the Williams Research Center (The Historic New Orleans Collection) inaugurated the exhibition *Purchased Lives: The American Slave Trade from 1808 to 1865* in 2015. The traveling exhibition portrays the importance of New Orleans as the largest market for the domestic slave trade in the United States. In 2018, the New Orleans Committee to Erect Markers on the Slave Trade dedicated a plaque at the intersection of Esplanade Avenue and Charles Street marking the site where "the New Orleans offices, showrooms, and slave pens of over a dozen of slave trading firms" were located. In 2015, New York City also unveiled a modest plaque marking the New York's Municipal Slave Market situated where Wall Street meets the East River.

For more than three decades, a variety of black social actors have put pressure on municipal authorities and politicians to make slavery visible in urban spaces. Activists and other citizens have also protested the presence of monuments honoring slave traders and pro-slavery individuals. In European cities such as Liverpool and Bordeaux, activists of African descent demanded the municipalities rename the streets named after individuals involved in the Atlantic slave trade. As recently as in 2018, a monument honoring the slave

9. The actual slave market was housed in another building close to the current central market. In 1969, the building where the slave market was once located was destroyed by a fire. In 1971, the central market moved to the present-day three-story building. In 1984, following a huge fire, the current building of Mercado Modelo was renovated, and the basement was discovered, rehabilitated, and opened to the public.

10. See Tiya Miles, *Tales from the Haunted South: Dark Tourism and Memories of Slavery from the Civil War Era* (Chapel Hill, NC, 2015).

trader Antonio Lopez y Lopez was removed from downtown Barcelona.[11] Every December, concerned citizens continue to organize demonstrations in various cities of the Netherlands to protest the notorious Black Pete, a racist depiction of a black helper of Saint Nicholas or Sinterklaas (Santa Claus) associated with the country's long history of involvement in the Atlantic slave trade and colonialism. Similarly, in numerous cities of the United States, citizens have protested the presence of Confederate monuments and flags and demanded their removal, especially after June 2015, when a white domestic terrorist killed nine African American parishioners in Charleston.

In addition to these intentional actions, sometimes the history of slavery and the Atlantic slave trade literally emerges from the ground. In the last twenty-five years, cities in Europe and the Americas have uncovered various burial grounds where enslaved people were interred. In 1991, hundreds of human remains were discovered during an excavation to construct a new federal building at 290 Broadway, in New York City. A team of scholars concluded that the site was a former burial ground containing the remains of about 15,000 enslaved and free black individuals (African or of African descent) buried during the seventeenth and eighteenth centuries. The site became known as the New York African Burial Ground, to this day the largest of its kind in the United States. The uncovering of the burial ground emphasized the importance of slavery in New York City and led to the dedication of a memorial in October 2007.[12]

Unlike New York City, whose past associated with slavery has been a forgotten chapter in the history of the United States, slavery was a central element in Rio de Janeiro's daily life until the end of the nineteenth century. Between 1758 and 1831, nearly one million enslaved Africans came ashore in the Valongo Wharf. But the site was gradually erased from the urban space after the international slave trade was banned in 1831 and during the chaotic processes of modernization and urbanization in the early twentieth century. During this period, the old port zone in Rio de Janeiro's downtown area remained nearly abandoned.[13] The city administration failed to preserve the heritage sites and buildings located in the region, and also neglected its underprivileged black residents.[14] But like what occurred in New York City in 1991,

11. Richard Drayton, "Rhodes Must Not Fall? Statues, Postcolonial 'Heritage' and Temporality", *Third Text*, 4 (2019), pp. 651–666.

12. Cyril Josh Barker, "Respect Due: African Burial Ground Memorial Opened", in *New York Amsterdam News*, 11 October 2007, p. 1.

13. See Jaime Rodrigues, *De Costa a Costa. Escravos, marinheiros e intermediários do tráfico negreiro de Angola ao Rio de Janeiro (1780–1860)* (São Paulo, 2005), p. 298.

14. See André Cicalo, *Memories on the Edge of Oblivion*, documentary film (2010). Available at: http://vimeo.com/41609298; last accessed 15 January 2020. See also André Cicalo, "From Public Amnesia to Public Memory: Re-Discovering Slavery Heritage in Rio de Janeiro", in Ana Lucia Araujo (ed.), *African Heritage and Memory of Slavery in Brazil and the South Atlantic World* (Amherst, NY, 2015), pp. 179–212.

Figure 3. Valongo Wharf, Rio de Janeiro, Brazil.
Photograph: Ana Lucia Araujo, 2018.

in 1996 an archaeological excavation on a private property at 36 Pedro Ernesto Street (formerly Cemitério Street) in the Gamboa neighborhood recovered a burial ground containing bone fragments of dozens of enslaved African men, women, and children. The site was identified as being the Cemitério dos Pretos Novos (Cemetery of New Blacks), a common grave where recently arrived Africans who died before being sold in the Valongo market were buried. Without official and public support, the private site remained in the hands of the Guimarães family who owned the house where the bones were uncovered and who gradually transformed the building into a non-governmental organization. But in 2011, as Rio de Janeiro prepared to host the 2014 FIFA World Cup and 2016 Olympic Games, drainage works eventually revealed the old ruins of Valongo Wharf. The excavations also recovered numerous African artifacts, therefore giving a new visibility to the slave burial ground. Although the lack of public support persists, both the Valongo Wharf (Figure 3) and the Cemetery of New Blacks (Figure 4) have been gradually incorporated into Rio de Janeiro's urban landscape that now recognizes the importance of the Atlantic slave trade and Brazil's crucial role in it. In 2012, the site of the Cemetery of New Blacks was transformed into a memorial and its main exhibition was reshaped. In 2017, UNESCO added the Valongo Wharf to its World Heritage List. The local community slowly appropriated the Valongo area, organizing black heritage tours, public religious

Figure 4. Façade of the Cemetery of New Blacks, Rio de Janeiro, Brazil.
Photograph: Ana Lucia Araujo, 2018.

ceremonies, and spectacles of capoeira.[15] Despite these developments, the Valongo area remains negligible compared with most other Rio de Janeiro's tourist sites, and many locals are not aware of its historical importance. Yet, its presence is a permanent reminder of the role of slavery in Rio de Janeiro, which will be hardly erased again from public view.

On the other shore of the Atlantic Ocean, despite the enduring traces of the Atlantic slave trade in its urban areas, Portugal was one of the last European countries to respond to the demands to memorialize slavery and the Atlantic slave trade. In 2009, during work to construct the Anel Verde Parking Lot in the Gafaria Valley in Lagos (a former slave port situated nearly 300 kilometers south of Lisbon), the skeletons of 158 enslaved Africans were uncovered from an urban waste dump that functioned as a "blacks' pit", dating back to the period between the fifteenth and seventeenth centuries.[16] The analysis of the remains revealed corpses of men, women, and children disposed in

15. Simone Candida, "Achados arqueológicos do Cais do Valongo estão abandonados em terreno no Porto" *O Globo*, 31 January 2013. Available at: http://oglobo.globo.com/rio/achados-arqueologicos-do-cais-do-valongo-estao-abandonados-em-terreno-no-porto-7450049#ixzz2YsVw96sF; last accessed 15 January 2020.

16. Maria João Neves, Miguel Almeida, Maria Teresa Ferreira, "O caso do 'Poço dos Negros' (Lagos). Da urgência do betão ao conhecimento das práticas funerárias esclavagistas no

Figure 5. Sculptures by Karl Heinz Stock, Pro Putting Garden, Lagos, Portugal. *Photograph: Jose A., 2014, cc-by-sa-2.0, © Wikimedia Commons.*

a variety of positions, and some of them had their hands and arms tied.[17] Although the remains were extensively studied by Portuguese scholars, no memorial was established at the site. Instead, an underground parking lot now occupies the location of the waste dump, on top of which sits the Pro Putting Garden Lagos, a picturesque landscaped mini-golf course. Featuring fountains and bridges, the scenic park is decorated with colorful sculptures (Figure 5) by artist Karl Heinz Stock (who is identified as white), representing female bodies joyfully dancing over one of the oldest European sites where the remains of enslaved Africans associated with the Atlantic slave trade were discarded. But tourists are only informed about this unpleasant long chapter of Portuguese history when they visit the "slave market," a museum center created in collaboration with the UNESCO Slave Route Project in 2016. The museum, occupying a seventeenth-century building constructed in the area where the presumed first European slave market existed, comprises a modest permanent exhibition telling the story of the Atlantic slave trade and slavery in Lagos.

Portugal Moderno a partir duma escavação de Arqueologia Preventiva", *Antrope*, 2 (2015), pp. 141–160.

17. Maria João Neves, Miguel Almeida, Maria Teresa Ferreira, "Separados na vida e na morte. Retrato do tratamento mortuário dado aos escravos africanos na cidade moderna de Lagos", *Actas do 70 Encontro de Arqueologia do Algarve, Silves, 22, 23 e 24 outubro 2009*, p. 556.

Figure 6. Chafariz-del-Rey, Lisbon, Portugal.
Photograph: Ana Lucia Araujo, 2019.

Despite Portugal's continuing refusal to face its history of slavery and its central involvement in the Atlantic slave trade, over the last decade black citizens have played an important role in making Lisbon's slave past visible in the public space. In December 2017, under the leadership of the Association of Afrodescendants (an anti-racist organization) and through the city's participatory budgeting system, Lisbon residents voted for a project to create a memorial to the victims of slavery. In June 2019, the city council sanctioned the creation of the memorial along with a visitor center and initiated the selection process of its design and implementation proposal. The memorial will be constructed at Campo das Cebolas, an area associated with the presence of enslaved Africans in Lisbon, 230 meters from the Chafariz-del-Rey (Figure 6), the same portrayed in the sixteenth-century painting (Figure 1).

In the first two decades of the twenty-first century, an increasing number of scholarly works started focusing on how slavery shaped the urban areas of the three continents involved in the Atlantic slave trade. As this new interest emerges, cities where slavery existed and former slave ports have gradually attempted to come to terms with their history of bondage and trading in human beings. Despite the need of more studies focusing on the various social, economic, legal, and cultural dimensions of slavery in specific cities, comparative works can contribute to better illuminate the development of bondage in urban areas and the present-day legacies of the inhuman institution. Scholars continue to uncover a multitude of new archival documents such as parish and judicial records. Still, the use of ethnography, visual images, oral traditions, dance, music, and material culture, as well as archaeological evidence, can contribute to address the persisting lacunas and silences of written sources and capture the complex nuances of urban slavery.